W9-CNQ-279

DC ☆ SUPER FRIENDS

CALLING ALL SUPER FRIENDS

SHOLLY FISCH WRITER
J. BONE ORIGINAL SERIES COVERS

NOTHING TO FEAR 3
STEWART McKENNY / DAN DAVIS ARTISTS

STARRO AND THE PIRATES 76
STEWART McKENNY / DAN DAVIS ARTISTS

HAPPY BIRTHDAY, SUPERMAN! 22
J. BONE ARTIST

THE GREATEST SHOW ON EARTH 94
DARIO BRIZUELA ARTIST

SEASON OF LIGHT 40
DARIO BRIZUELA ARTIST

MAN'S BEST SUPER-FRIEND 112
DARIO BRIZUELA ARTIST

IMP-POSSIBLE 58
CHYNNA CLUGSTON ARTIST

BONUS SECTION! 131
GAMES - COSTUMES - PUZZLES - AND MORE!

RANDY GENTILE / TRAVIS LANHAM / SAL CIPRIANO LETTERERS
HEROIC AGE COLORS

DAN DIDIO SENIOR VP-EXECUTIVE EDITOR

RACHEL GLUCKSTERN EDITOR-ORIGINAL SERIES

BOB JOY EDITOR-COLLECTED EDITION

ROBBIN BROSTERMAN SENIOR ART DIRECTOR

PAUL LEVITZ PRESIDENT & PUBLISHER

GEORG BREWER VP-DESIGN & DC DIRECT CREATIVE

RICHARD BRUNING SENIOR VP-CREATIVE DIRECTOR

PATRICK CALDON EXECUTIVE VP-FINANCE & OPERATIONS

CHRIS CARAMALIS VP-FINANCE

JOHN CUNNINGHAM VP-MARKETING

TERRI CUNNINGHAM VP-MANAGING EDITOR

AMY GENKINS SENIOR VP-BUSINESS & LEGAL AFFAIRS

ALISON GILL VP-MANUFACTURING

DAVID HYDE VP-PUBLICITY

HANK KANALZ VP-GENERAL MANAGER, WILDSTORM

JIM LEE EDITORIAL DIRECTOR-WILDSTORM

GREGORY NOVECK SENIOR VP-CREATIVE AFFAIRS

SUE POHJA VP-BOOK TRADE SALES

STEVE ROTTERDAM SENIOR VP-SALES & MARKETING

CHERYL RUBIN SENIOR VP-BRAND MANAGEMENT

ALYSSE SOLL VP-ADVERTISING & CUSTOM PUBLISHING

JEFF TROJAN VP-BUSINESS DEVELOPMENT, DC DIRECT

BOB WAYNE VP-SALES

Cover art by J. Bone

SUPER FRIENDS: CALLING ALL SUPER FRIENDS

Published by DC Comics. Cover and compilation Copyright © 2009 DC Comics. All Rights Reserved.

Originally published in single magazine form in SUPER FRIENDS 8-14. Copyright © 2008, 2009 DC Comics. All Rights Reserved.
All characters, their distinctive likenesses and related elements featured in this publication are trademarks of DC Comics.
The stories, characters and incidents featured in this publication are entirely fictional. DC Comics does not read or accept
unsolicited submissions of ideas, stories or artwork.

DC Comics, 1700 Broadway, New York, NY 10019
A Warner Bros. Entertainment Company
Printed in Canada. First Printing.
ISBN: 978-1-4012-2289-5

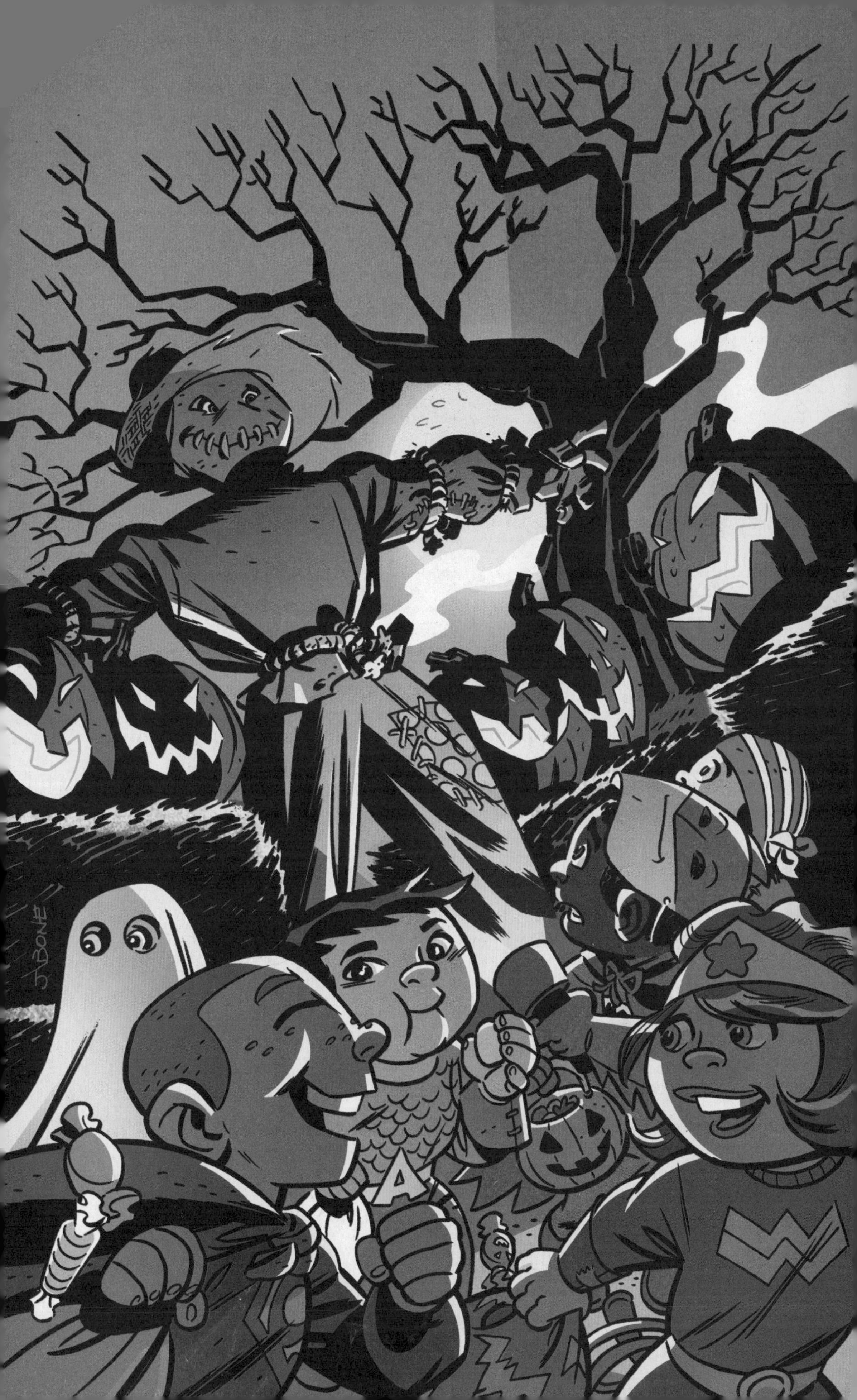
J. BONE

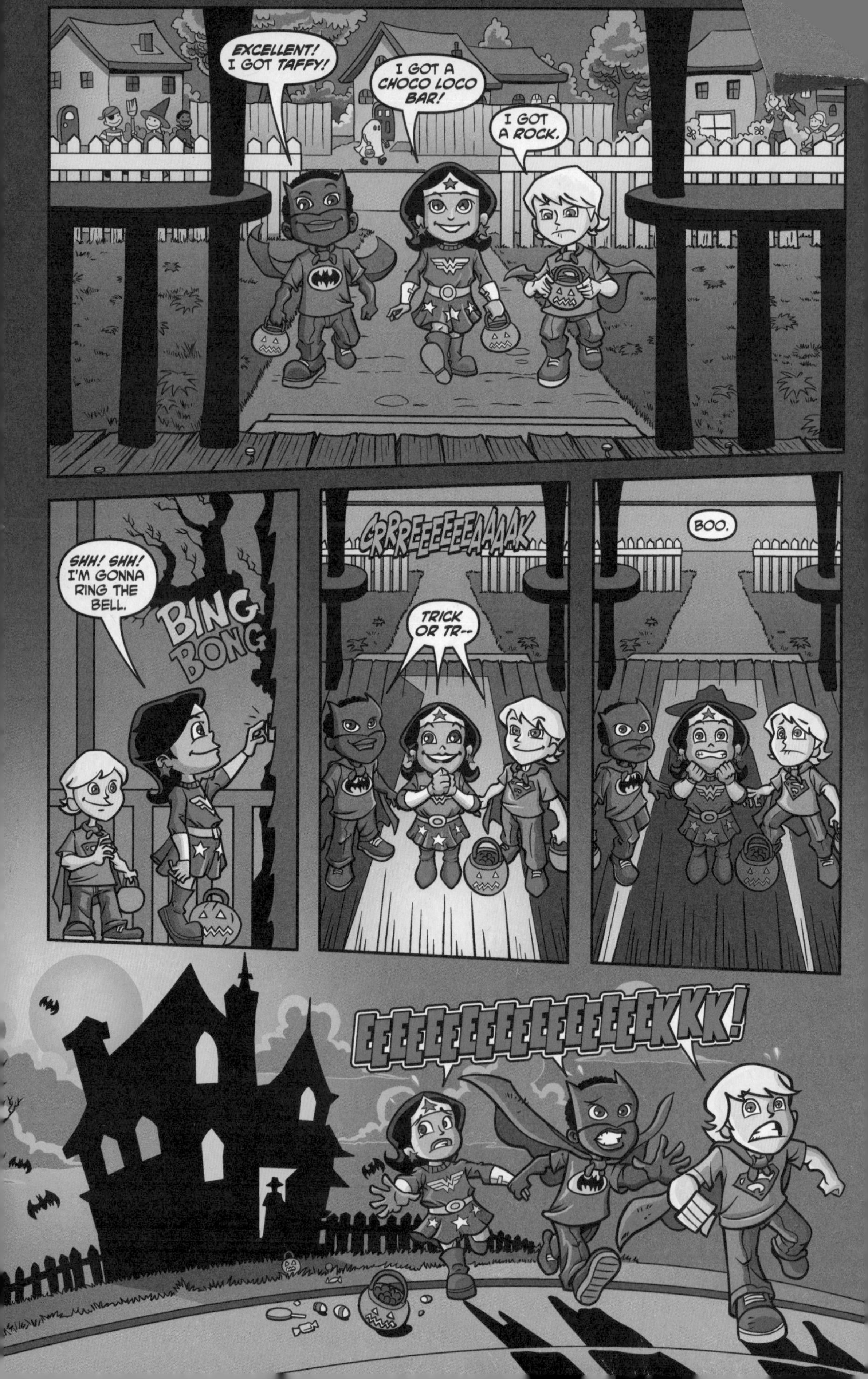
EXCELLENT! I GOT TAFFY!
I GOT A CHOCO LOCO BAR!
I GOT A ROCK.
SHH! SHH! I'M GONNA RING THE BELL.
BING BONG
CRRREEEEEEAAAAK
TRICK OR TR--
BOO.
EEEEEEEEEEEEEEEEKKK!

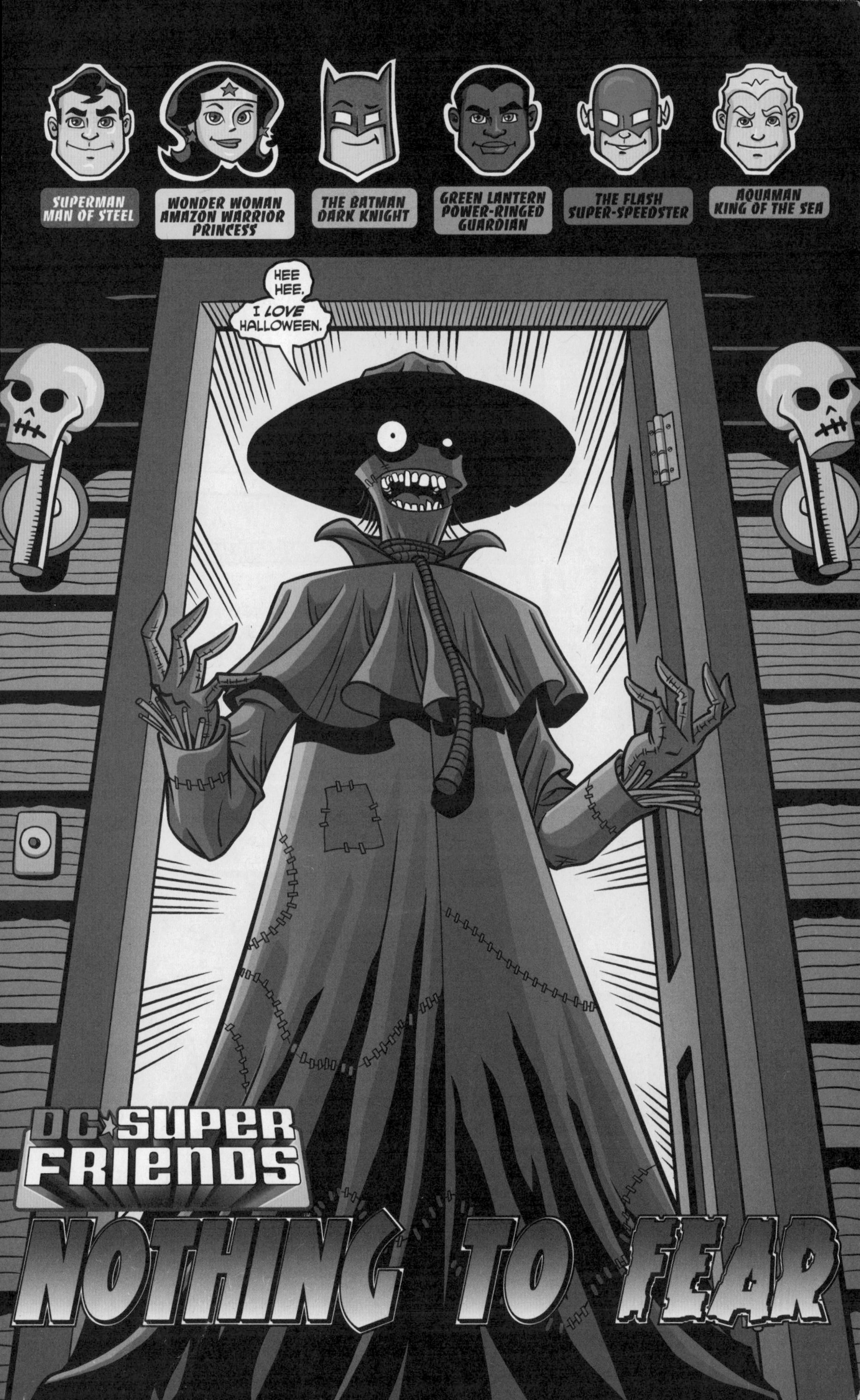
SUPERMAN
MAN OF STEEL
WONDER WOMAN
AMAZON WARRIOR
PRINCESS
THE BATMAN
DARK KNIGHT
GREEN LANTERN
POWER-RINGED
GUARDIAN
THE FLASH
SUPER-SPEEDSTER
AQUAMAN
KING OF THE SEA
HEE HEE. I LOVE HALLOWEEN.
DC SUPER FRIENDS
NOTHING TO FEAR

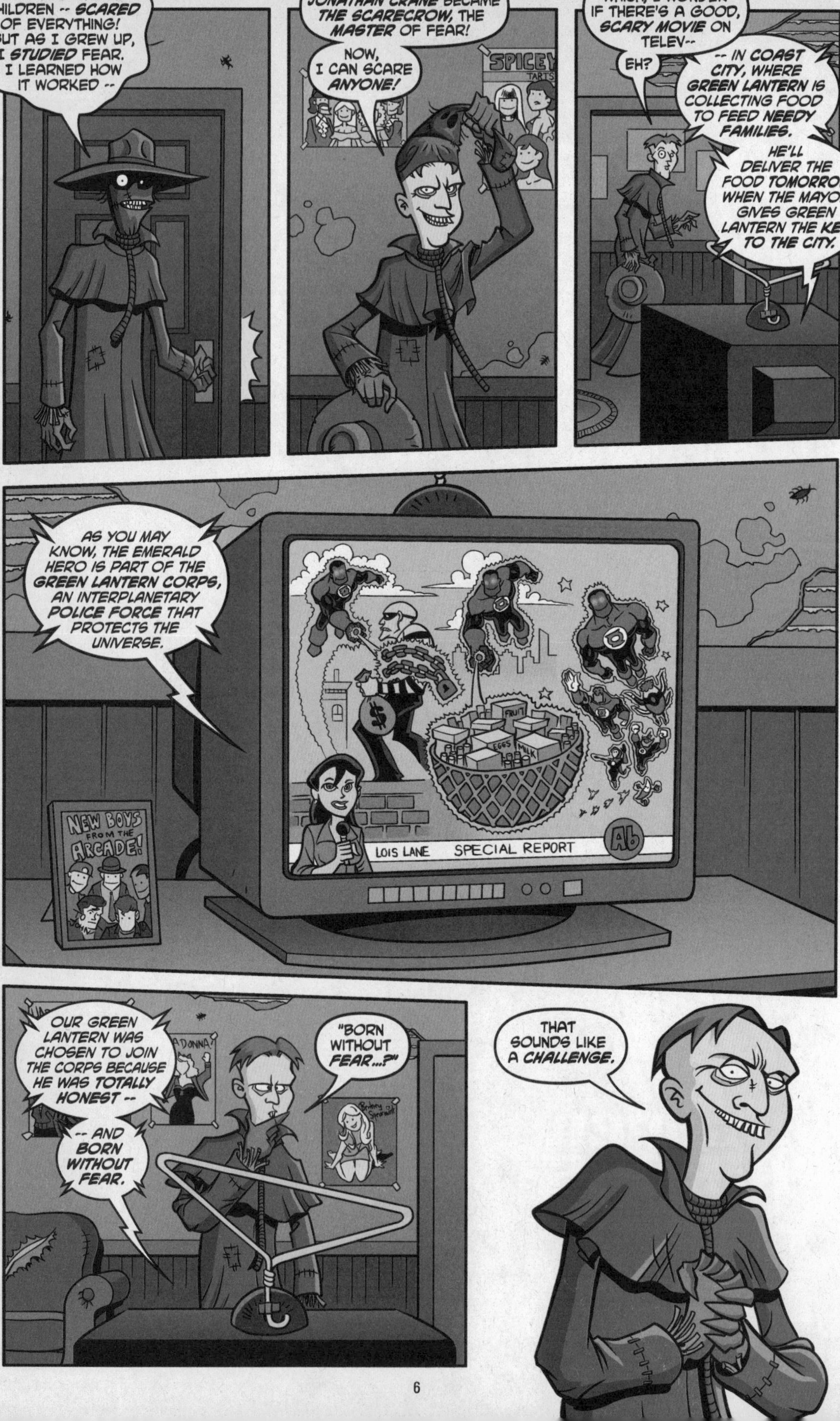
ONCE I WAS LIKE THOSE CHILDREN -- SCARED OF EVERYTHING! BUT AS I GREW UP, I STUDIED FEAR. I LEARNED HOW IT WORKED --
-- UNTIL COWARDLY JONATHAN CRANE BECAME THE SCARECROW, THE MASTER OF FEAR!
NOW, I CAN SCARE ANYONE!
SPICEY TARTS
SPEAKING OF WHICH, I WONDER IF THERE'S A GOOD, SCARY MOVIE ON TELEV--
EH?
-- IN COAST CITY, WHERE GREEN LANTERN IS COLLECTING FOOD TO FEED NEEDY FAMILIES.
HE'LL DELIVER THE FOOD TOMORROW, WHEN THE MAYOR GIVES GREEN LANTERN THE KEY TO THE CITY.
AS YOU MAY KNOW, THE EMERALD HERO IS PART OF THE GREEN LANTERN CORPS, AN INTERPLANETARY POLICE FORCE THAT PROTECTS THE UNIVERSE.
FRUIT
EGGS
MILK
LOIS LANE
SPECIAL REPORT
NEW BOYS FROM THE ARCADE!
OUR GREEN LANTERN WAS CHOSEN TO JOIN THE CORPS BECAUSE HE WAS TOTALLY HONEST --
-- AND BORN WITHOUT FEAR.
"BORN WITHOUT FEAR...?"
THAT SOUNDS LIKE A CHALLENGE.

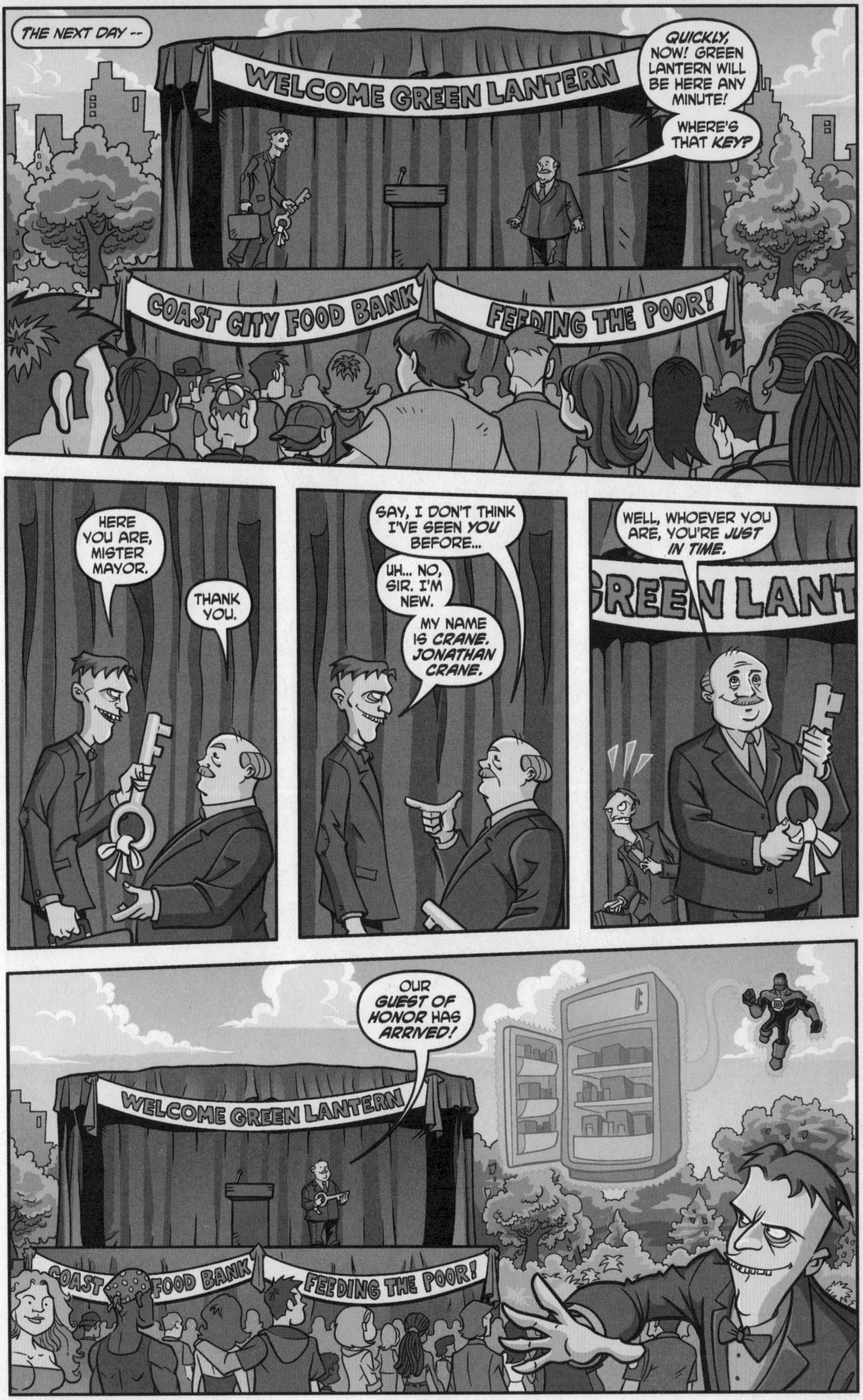
THE NEXT DAY --
WELCOME GREEN LANTERN
QUICKLY, NOW! GREEN LANTERN WILL BE HERE ANY MINUTE!
WHERE'S THAT KEY?
COAST CITY FOOD BANK
FEEDING THE POOR!
HERE YOU ARE, MISTER MAYOR.
THANK YOU.
SAY, I DON'T THINK I'VE SEEN YOU BEFORE...
UH... NO, SIR. I'M NEW.
MY NAME IS CRANE. JONATHAN CRANE.
WELL, WHOEVER YOU ARE, YOU'RE JUST IN TIME.
GREEN LANT
OUR GUEST OF HONOR HAS ARRIVED!
WELCOME GREEN LANTERN
COAST FOOD BANK
FEEDING THE POOR!

THANK YOU, GREEN LANTERN! THIS FOOD WILL FEED *HUNDREDS* OF FAMILIES WHO CAN'T AFFORD FOOD OF THEIR OWN.

GREEN LANTERN

OH, DON'T THANK ME.

THANK ALL OF THE PEOPLE WHO *DONATED* THE FOOD, SO THAT NO ONE WOULD HAVE TO GO HUNGRY.

EVEN SO, *YOU* COLLECTED IT ALL. IN RETURN, WE'D LIKE TO GIVE YOU THIS *KEY TO THE CITY!*

FWOOOSSSHHH!

THA --

!?

GREEN LANTERN? ARE YOU ALL RIGHT?

↯

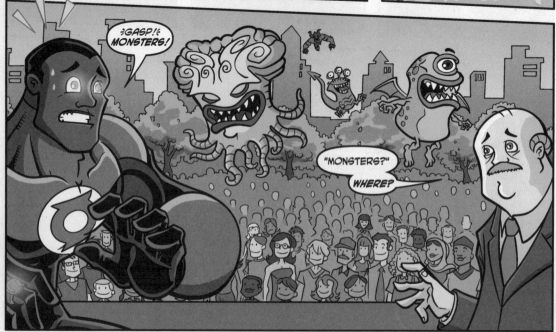

≈GASP!≈ MONSTERS!

"MONSTERS?"

WHERE?

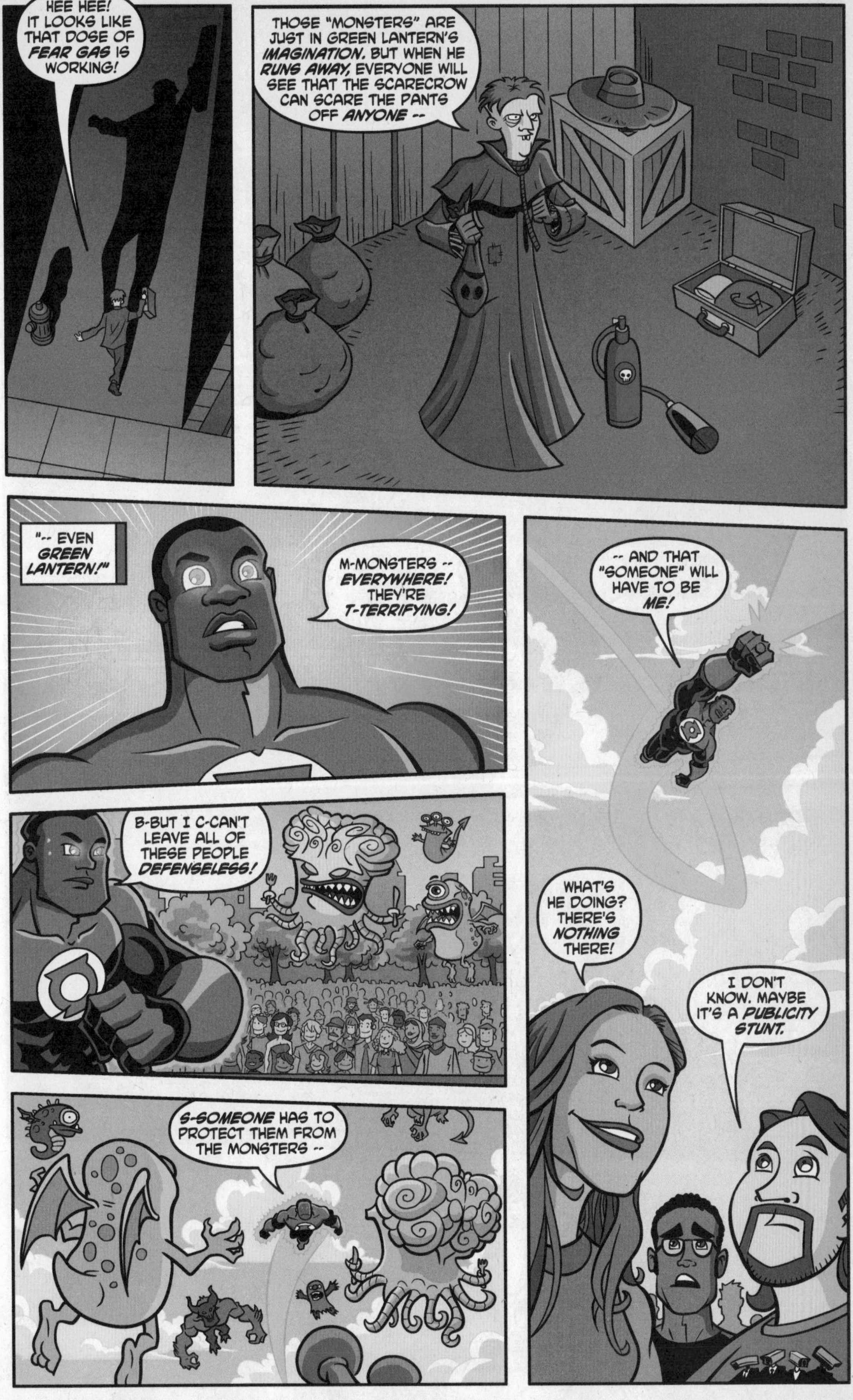
HEE HEE! IT LOOKS LIKE THAT DOSE OF *FEAR GAS* IS WORKING!
THOSE "MONSTERS" ARE JUST IN GREEN LANTERN'S *IMAGINATION.* BUT WHEN HE *RUNS AWAY,* EVERYONE WILL SEE THAT THE SCARECROW CAN SCARE THE PANTS OFF *ANYONE* --
"-- EVEN *GREEN LANTERN!*"
M-MONSTERS -- *EVERYWHERE!* THEY'RE *T-TERRIFYING!*
B-BUT I C-CAN'T LEAVE ALL OF THESE PEOPLE *DEFENSELESS!*
S-SOMEONE HAS TO PROTECT THEM FROM THE MONSTERS --
-- AND THAT "SOMEONE" WILL HAVE TO BE *ME!*
WHAT'S HE DOING? THERE'S *NOTHING* THERE!
I DON'T KNOW. MAYBE IT'S A *PUBLICITY STUNT.*

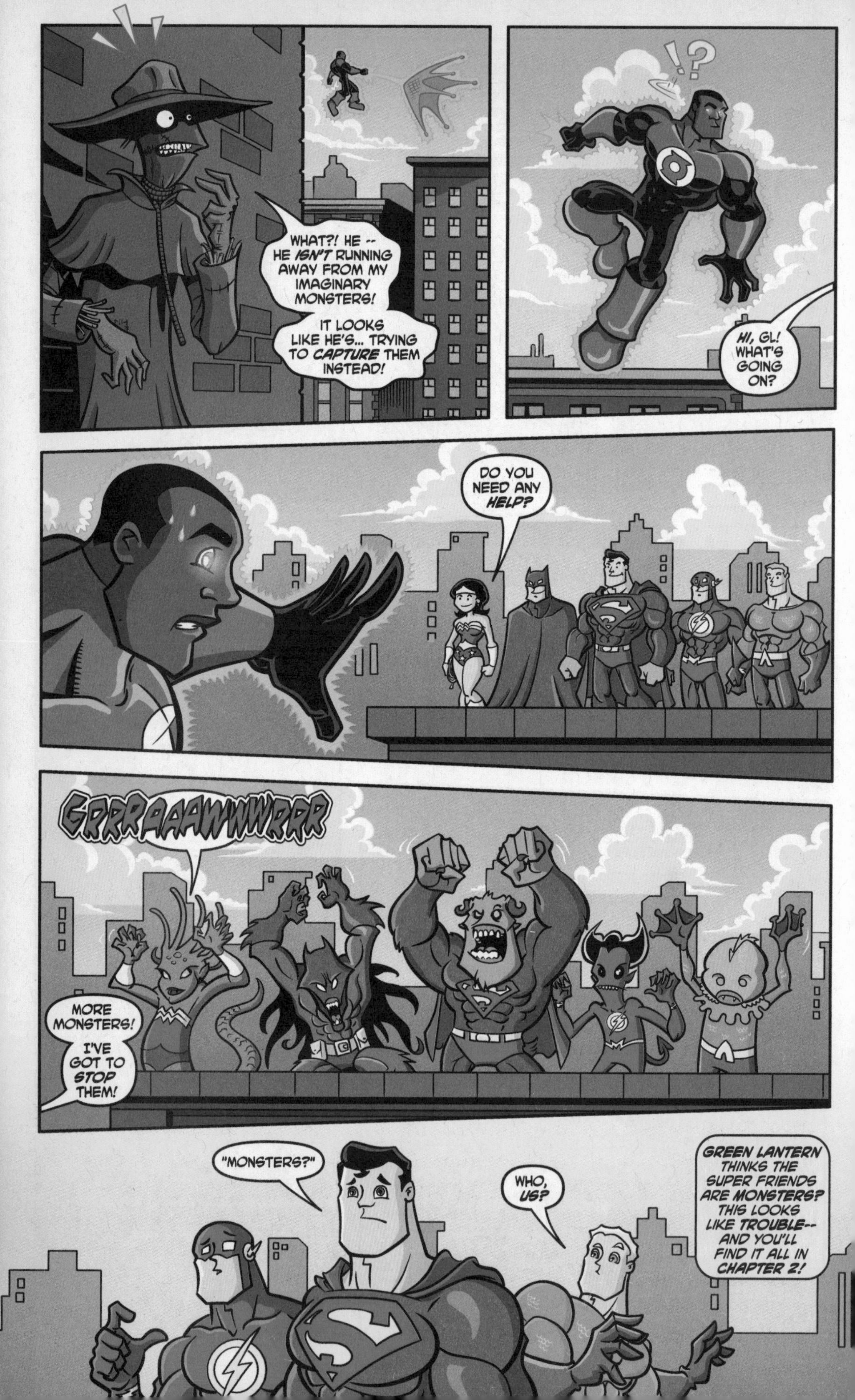
WHAT?! HE -- HE ISN'T RUNNING AWAY FROM MY IMAGINARY MONSTERS!
IT LOOKS LIKE HE'S... TRYING TO CAPTURE THEM INSTEAD!
!?
HI, GL! WHAT'S GOING ON?
DO YOU NEED ANY HELP?
GRRRAAAWWWRRR
MORE MONSTERS! I'VE GOT TO STOP THEM!
"MONSTERS?"
WHO, US?
GREEN LANTERN THINKS THE SUPER FRIENDS ARE MONSTERS? THIS LOOKS LIKE TROUBLE-- AND YOU'LL FIND IT ALL IN CHAPTER 2!

NOTHING TO FEAR -- CHAPTER 2

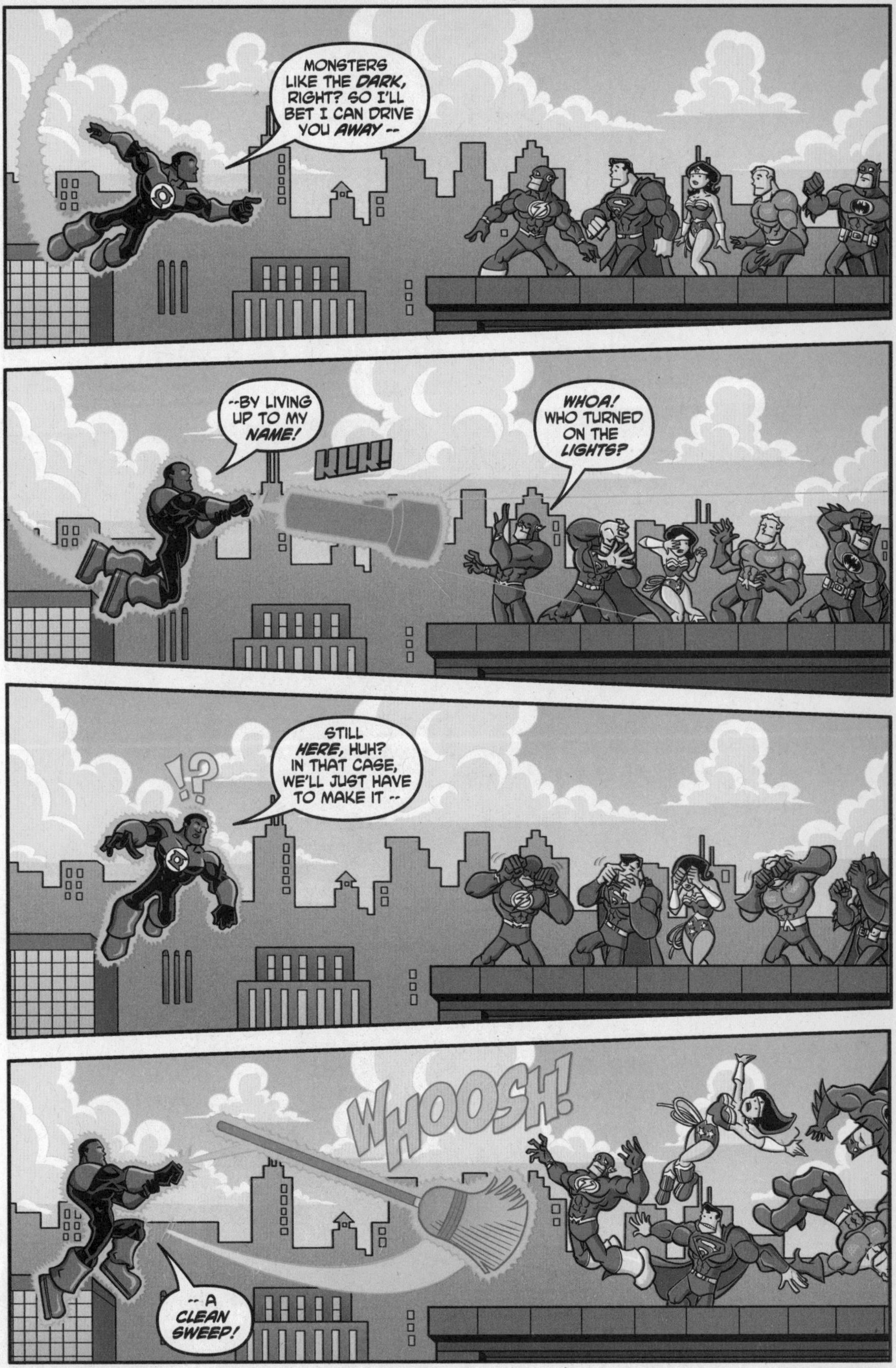

MONSTERS LIKE THE *DARK*, RIGHT? SO I'LL BET I CAN DRIVE YOU *AWAY* --
--BY LIVING UP TO MY *NAME!*
KLIK!
WHOA! WHO TURNED ON THE *LIGHTS?*
!?
STILL *HERE*, HUH? IN THAT CASE, WE'LL JUST HAVE TO MAKE IT --
WHOOSH!
-- A *CLEAN SWEEP!*

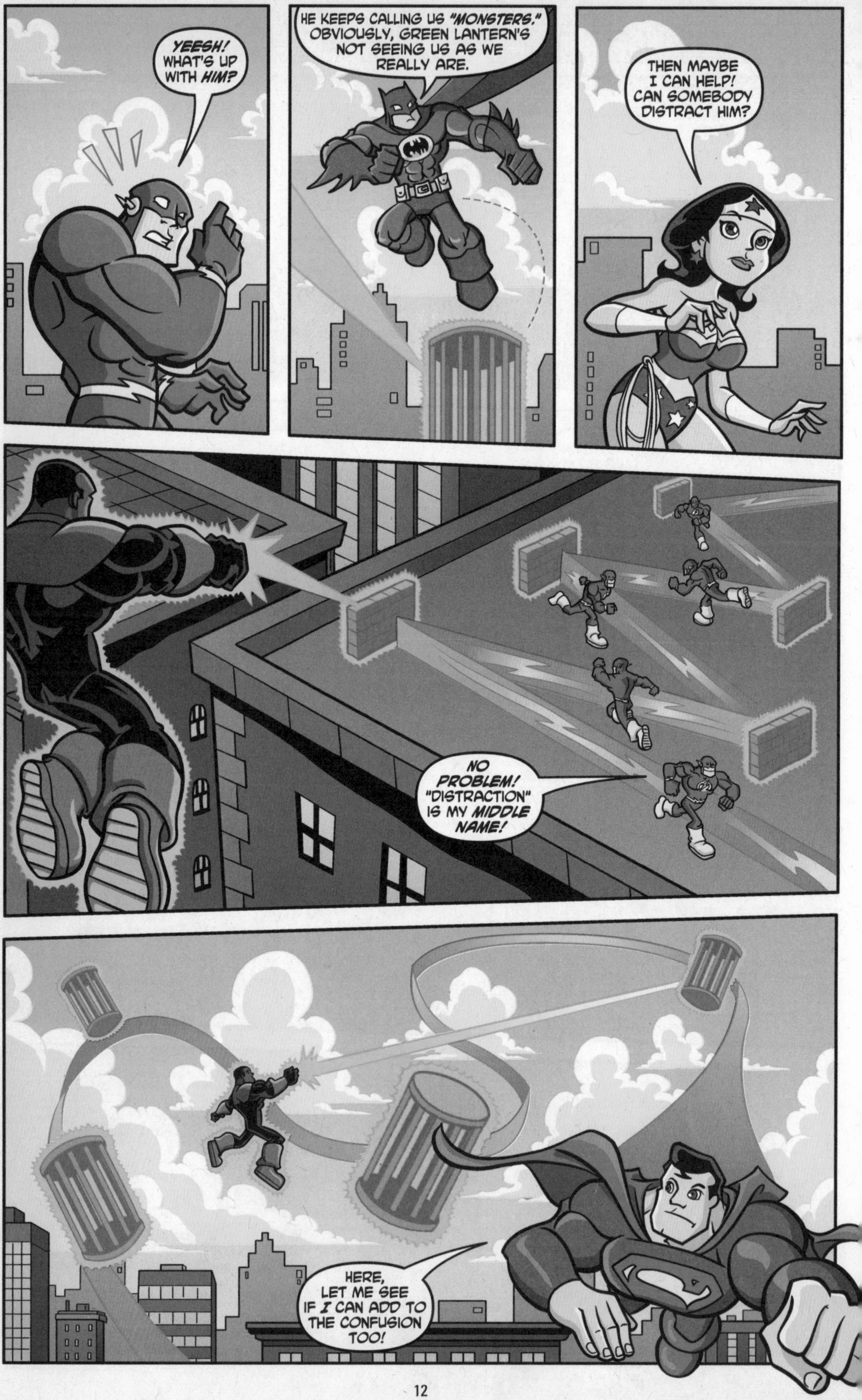

YEESH! WHAT'S UP WITH HIM?
HE KEEPS CALLING US "MONSTERS." OBVIOUSLY, GREEN LANTERN'S NOT SEEING US AS WE REALLY ARE.
THEN MAYBE I CAN HELP! CAN SOMEBODY DISTRACT HIM?
NO PROBLEM! "DISTRACTION" IS MY MIDDLE NAME!
HERE, LET ME SEE IF I CAN ADD TO THE CONFUSION TOO!

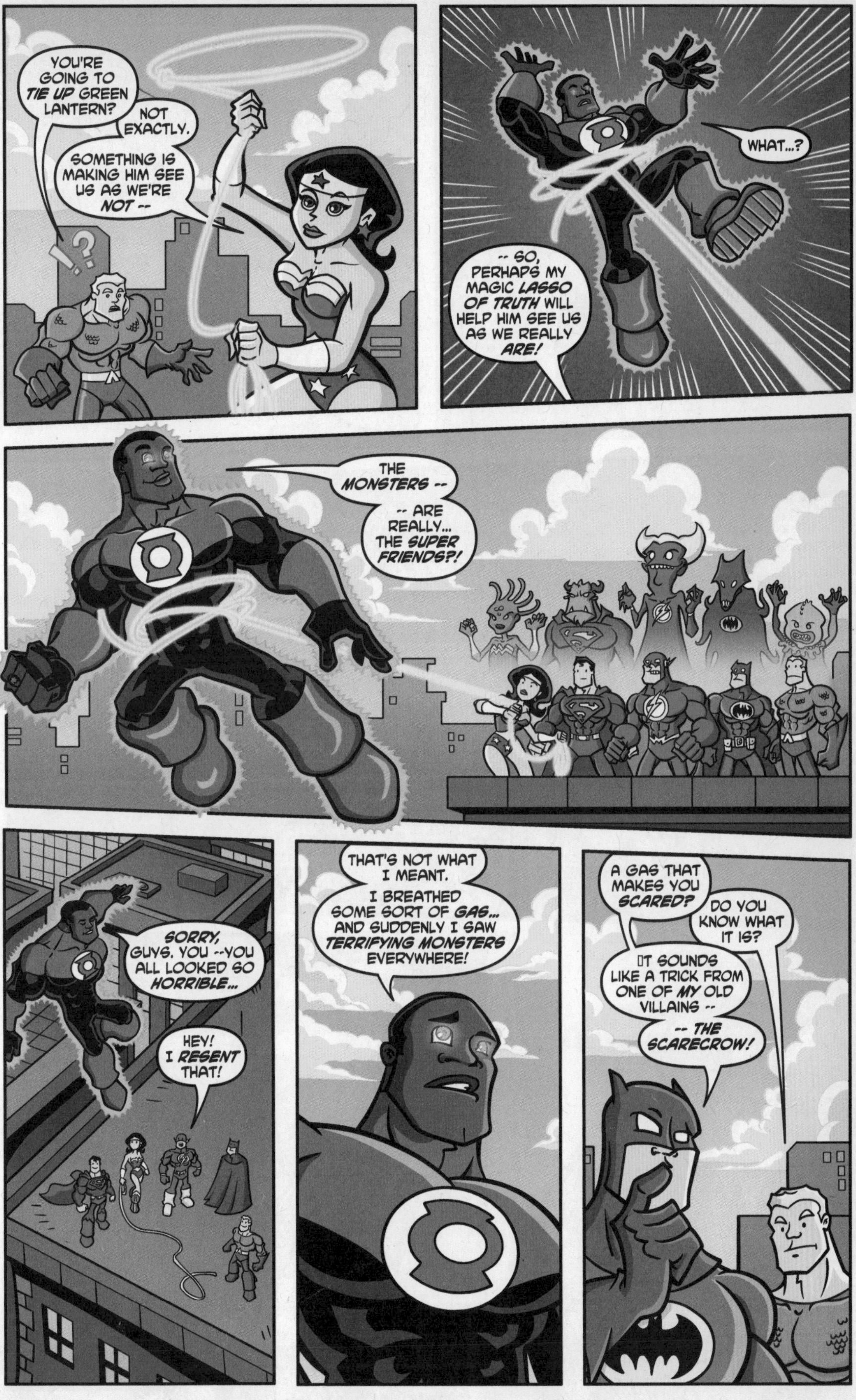
YOU'RE GOING TO TIE UP GREEN LANTERN?
NOT EXACTLY.
SOMETHING IS MAKING HIM SEE US AS WE'RE NOT --
WHAT...?
-- SO, PERHAPS MY MAGIC LASSO OF TRUTH WILL HELP HIM SEE US AS WE REALLY ARE!
THE MONSTERS --
-- ARE REALLY... THE SUPER FRIENDS?!
SORRY, GUYS. YOU --YOU ALL LOOKED SO HORRIBLE...
HEY! I RESENT THAT!
THAT'S NOT WHAT I MEANT.
I BREATHED SOME SORT OF GAS... AND SUDDENLY I SAW TERRIFYING MONSTERS EVERYWHERE!
A GAS THAT MAKES YOU SCARED?
DO YOU KNOW WHAT IT IS?
IT SOUNDS LIKE A TRICK FROM ONE OF MY OLD VILLAINS --
-- THE SCARECROW!

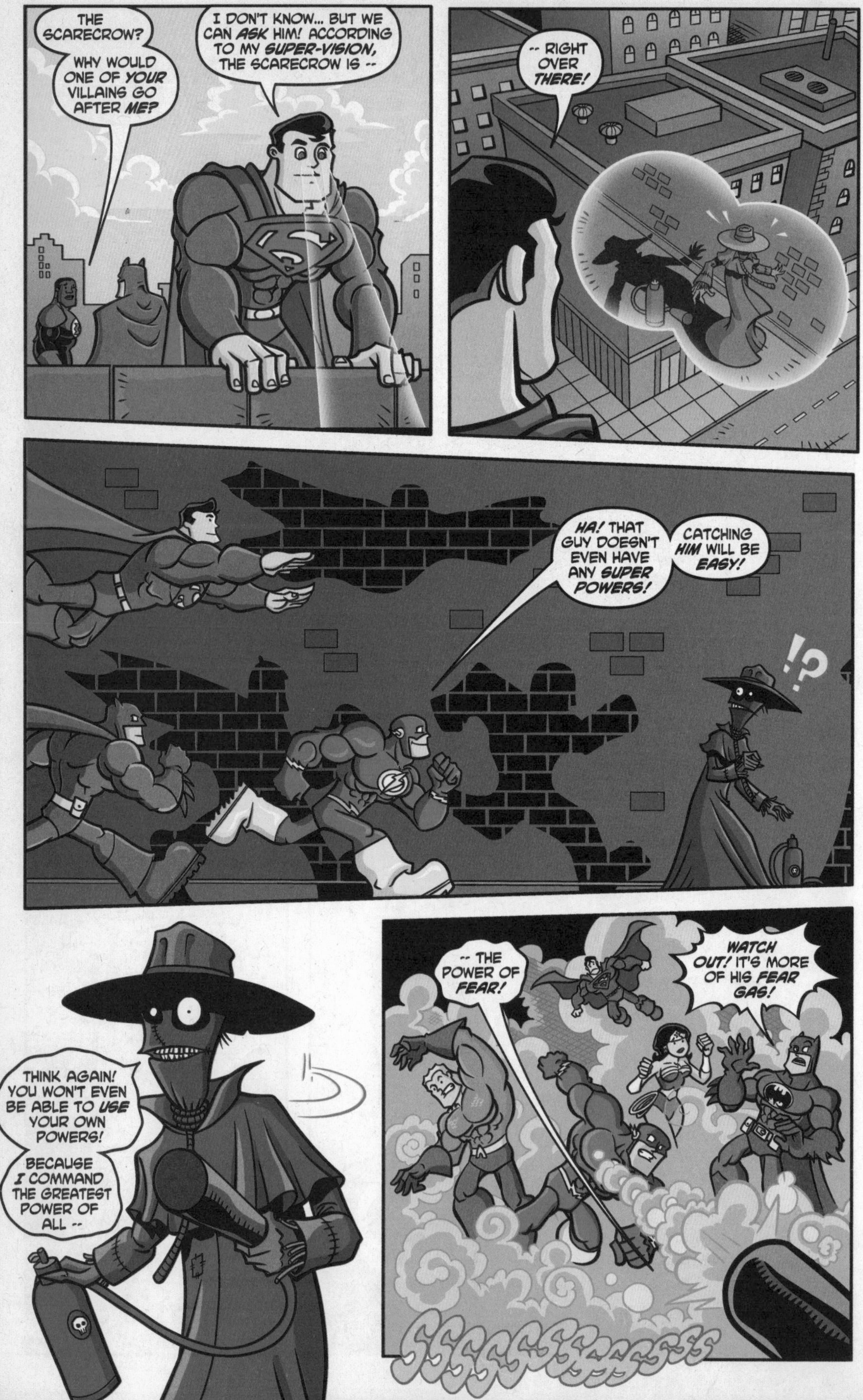
THE SCARECROW?
WHY WOULD ONE OF YOUR VILLAINS GO AFTER ME?
I DON'T KNOW... BUT WE CAN ASK HIM! ACCORDING TO MY SUPER-VISION, THE SCARECROW IS --
-- RIGHT OVER THERE!
HA! THAT GUY DOESN'T EVEN HAVE ANY SUPER POWERS!
CATCHING HIM WILL BE EASY!
!?
THINK AGAIN! YOU WON'T EVEN BE ABLE TO USE YOUR OWN POWERS!
BECAUSE I COMMAND THE GREATEST POWER OF ALL --
-- THE POWER OF FEAR!
WATCH OUT! IT'S MORE OF HIS FEAR GAS!
SSSSSSSSSSSSSSS

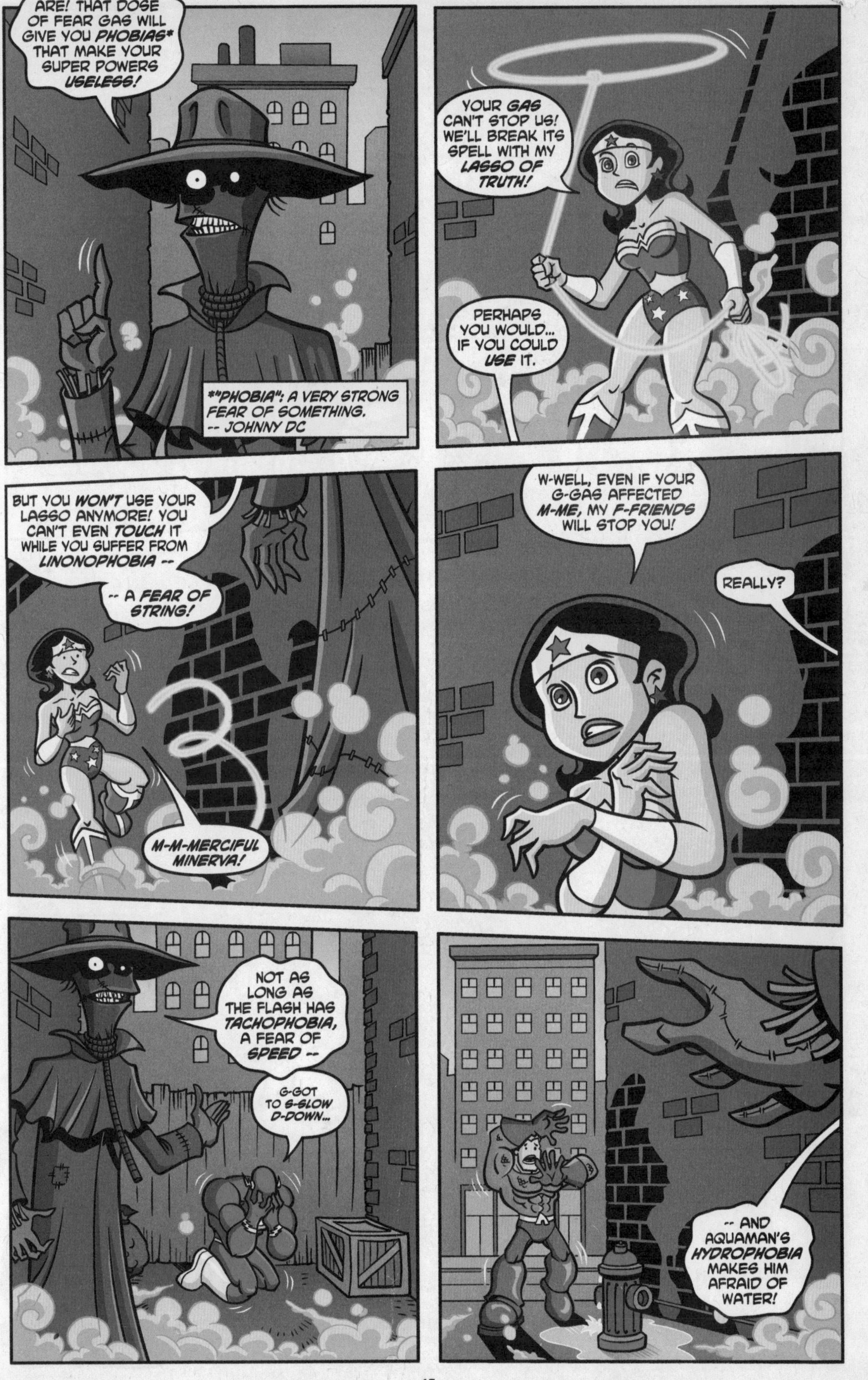
RIGHT YOU ARE! THAT DOSE OF FEAR GAS WILL GIVE YOU PHOBIAS* THAT MAKE YOUR SUPER POWERS USELESS!
*"PHOBIA": A VERY STRONG FEAR OF SOMETHING. -- JOHNNY DC
YOUR GAS CAN'T STOP US! WE'LL BREAK ITS SPELL WITH MY LASSO OF TRUTH!
PERHAPS YOU WOULD... IF YOU COULD USE IT.
BUT YOU WON'T USE YOUR LASSO ANYMORE! YOU CAN'T EVEN TOUCH IT WHILE YOU SUFFER FROM LINONOPHOBIA --
-- A FEAR OF STRING!
M-M-MERCIFUL MINERVA!
W-WELL, EVEN IF YOUR G-GAS AFFECTED M-ME, MY F-FRIENDS WILL STOP YOU!
REALLY?
NOT AS LONG AS THE FLASH HAS TACHOPHOBIA, A FEAR OF SPEED --
G-GOT TO S-SLOW D-DOWN...
-- AND AQUAMAN'S HYDROPHOBIA MAKES HIM AFRAID OF WATER!

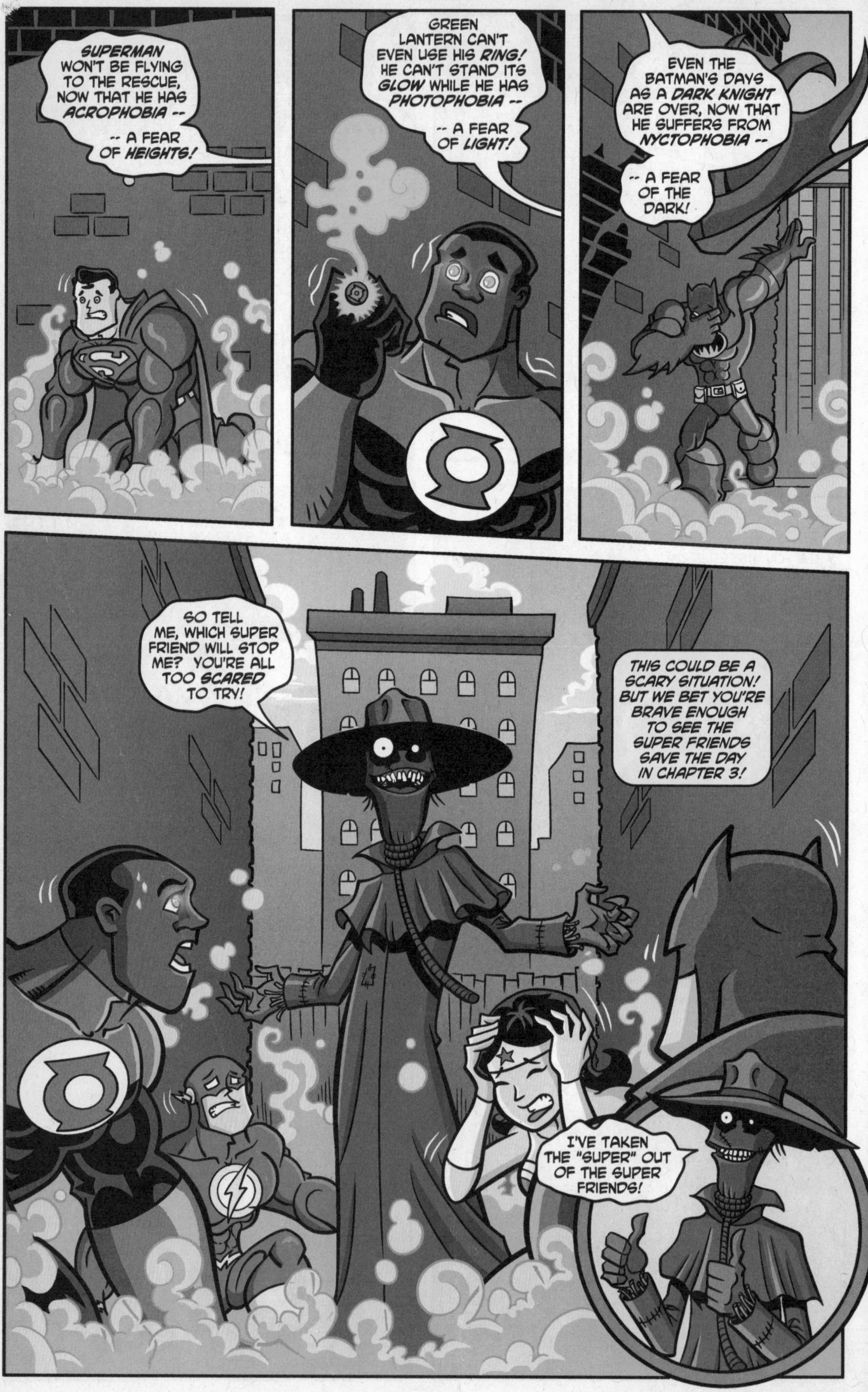
SUPERMAN WON'T BE FLYING TO THE RESCUE, NOW THAT HE HAS ACROPHOBIA --
-- A FEAR OF HEIGHTS!
GREEN LANTERN CAN'T EVEN USE HIS RING! HE CAN'T STAND ITS GLOW WHILE HE HAS PHOTOPHOBIA --
-- A FEAR OF LIGHT!
EVEN THE BATMAN'S DAYS AS A DARK KNIGHT ARE OVER, NOW THAT HE SUFFERS FROM NYCTOPHOBIA --
-- A FEAR OF THE DARK!
SO TELL ME, WHICH SUPER FRIEND WILL STOP ME? YOU'RE ALL TOO SCARED TO TRY!
THIS COULD BE A SCARY SITUATION! BUT WE BET YOU'RE BRAVE ENOUGH TO SEE THE SUPER FRIENDS SAVE THE DAY IN CHAPTER 3!
I'VE TAKEN THE "SUPER" OUT OF THE SUPER FRIENDS!

NOTHING TO FEAR -- CHAPTER 3

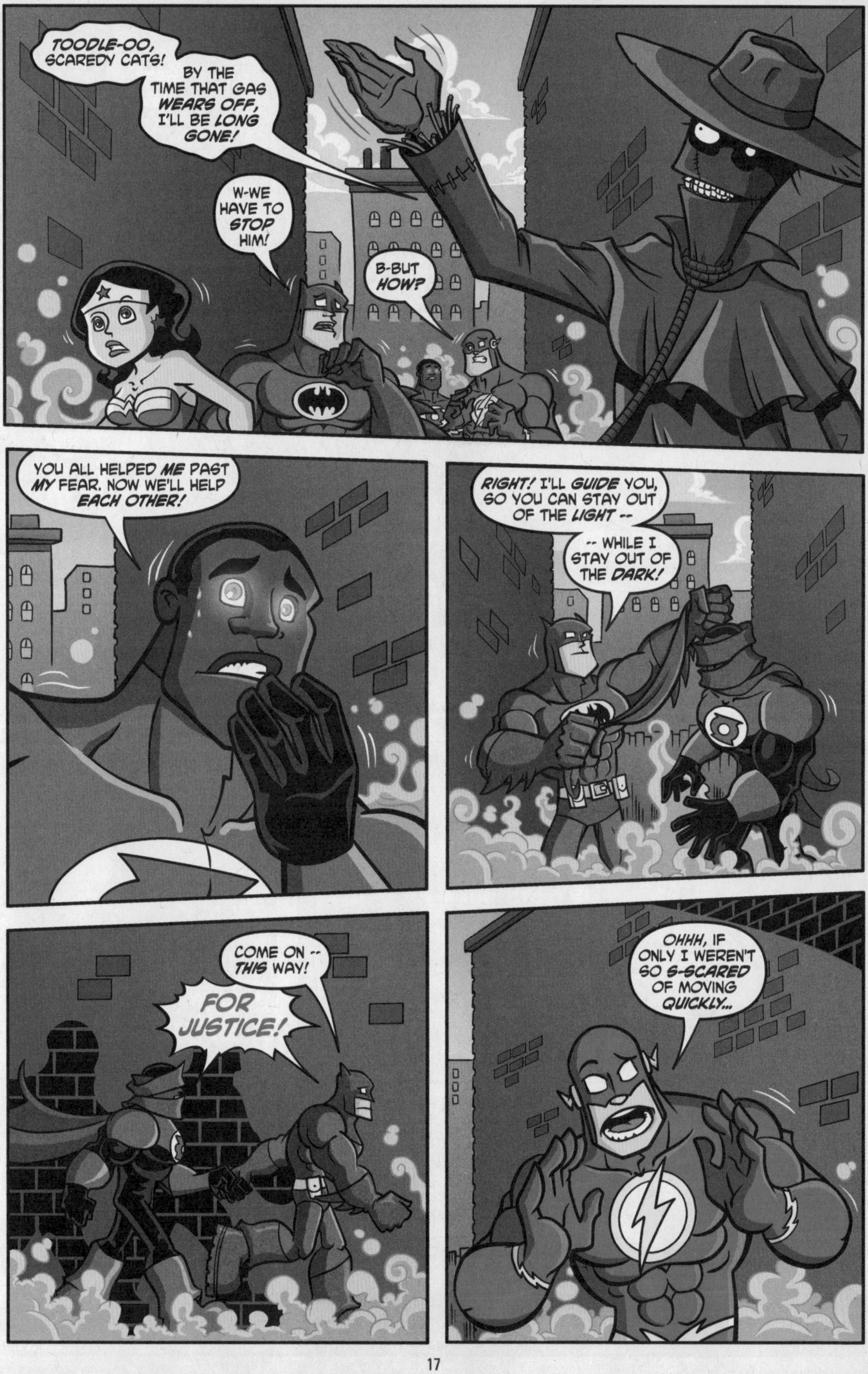
TOODLE-OO, SCAREDY CATS!
BY THE TIME THAT GAS WEARS OFF, I'LL BE LONG GONE!
W-WE HAVE TO STOP HIM!
B-BUT HOW?
YOU ALL HELPED ME PAST MY FEAR. NOW WE'LL HELP EACH OTHER!
RIGHT! I'LL GUIDE YOU, SO YOU CAN STAY OUT OF THE LIGHT --
-- WHILE I STAY OUT OF THE DARK!
COME ON -- THIS WAY!
FOR JUSTICE!
OHHH, IF ONLY I WEREN'T SO S-SCARED OF MOVING QUICKLY...

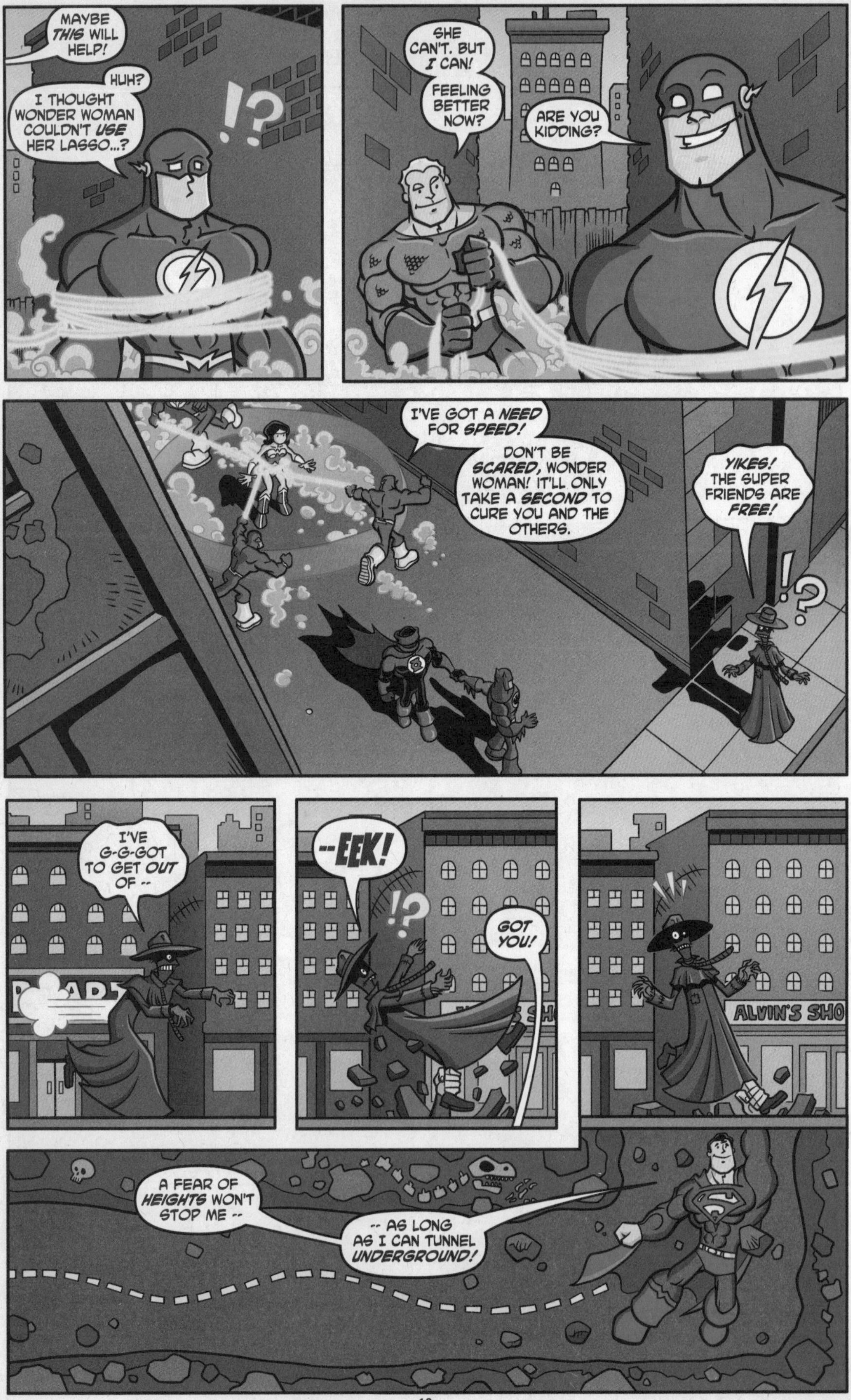
MAYBE THIS WILL HELP!
HUH?
I THOUGHT WONDER WOMAN COULDN'T USE HER LASSO...?
!?
SHE CAN'T. BUT I CAN!
FEELING BETTER NOW?
ARE YOU KIDDING?
I'VE GOT A NEED FOR SPEED!
DON'T BE SCARED, WONDER WOMAN! IT'LL ONLY TAKE A SECOND TO CURE YOU AND THE OTHERS.
YIKES! THE SUPER FRIENDS ARE FREE!
!?
I'VE G-G-GOT TO GET OUT OF --
--EEK!
!?
GOT YOU!
ALVIN'S SHO
A FEAR OF HEIGHTS WON'T STOP ME --
-- AS LONG AS I CAN TUNNEL UNDERGROUND!

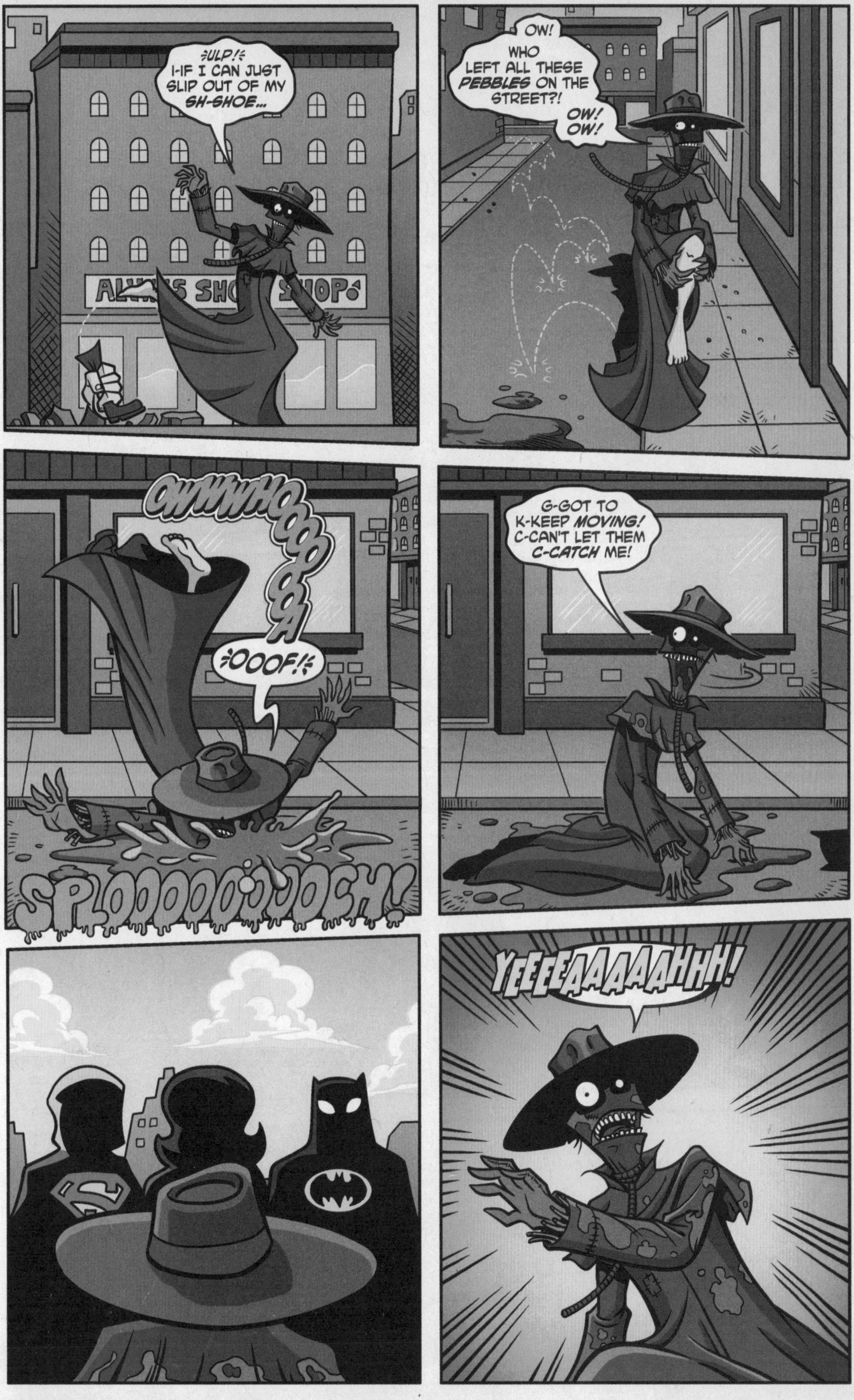
ULP!
I-IF I CAN JUST SLIP OUT OF MY SH-SHOE...
OW!
WHO LEFT ALL THESE PEBBLES ON THE STREET?!
OW! OW!
OWWWHOOOOOOOA
OOOF!
SPLOOOOOOOOCH!
G-GOT TO K-KEEP MOVING! C-CAN'T LET THEM C-CATCH ME!
YEEEEAAAAAHHH!

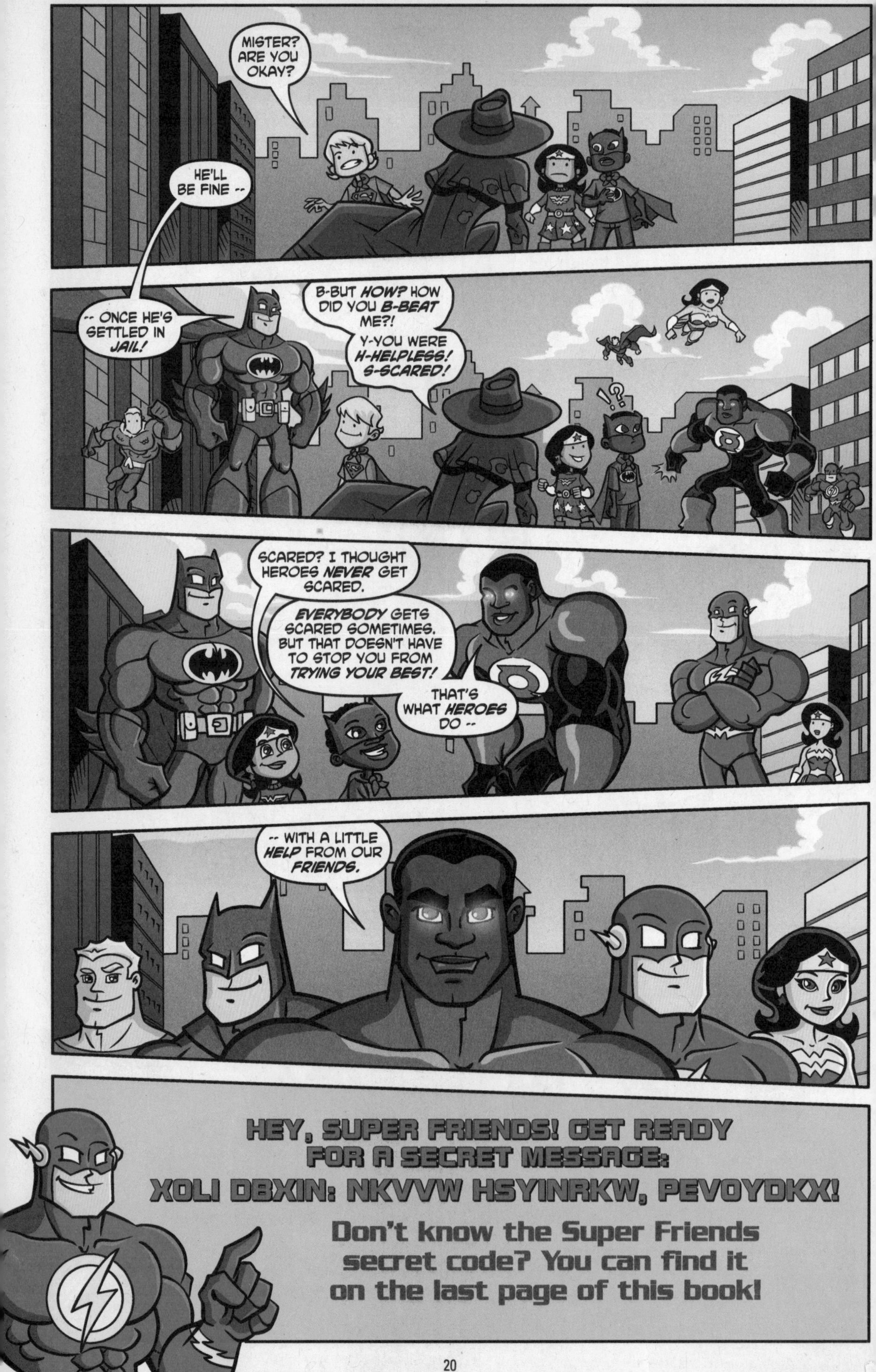
MISTER? ARE YOU OKAY?
HE'LL BE FINE --
-- ONCE HE'S SETTLED IN JAIL!
B-BUT HOW? HOW DID YOU B-BEAT ME?!
Y-YOU WERE H-HELPLESS! S-SCARED!
SCARED? I THOUGHT HEROES NEVER GET SCARED.
EVERYBODY GETS SCARED SOMETIMES. BUT THAT DOESN'T HAVE TO STOP YOU FROM TRYING YOUR BEST!
THAT'S WHAT HEROES DO --
-- WITH A LITTLE HELP FROM OUR FRIENDS.
HEY, SUPER FRIENDS! GET READY FOR A SECRET MESSAGE:
XOLI DBXIN: NKVVW HSYINRKW, PEVOYDKX!
Don't know the Super Friends secret code? You can find it on the last page of this book!

HALLOWEEN HIDE AND SEEK

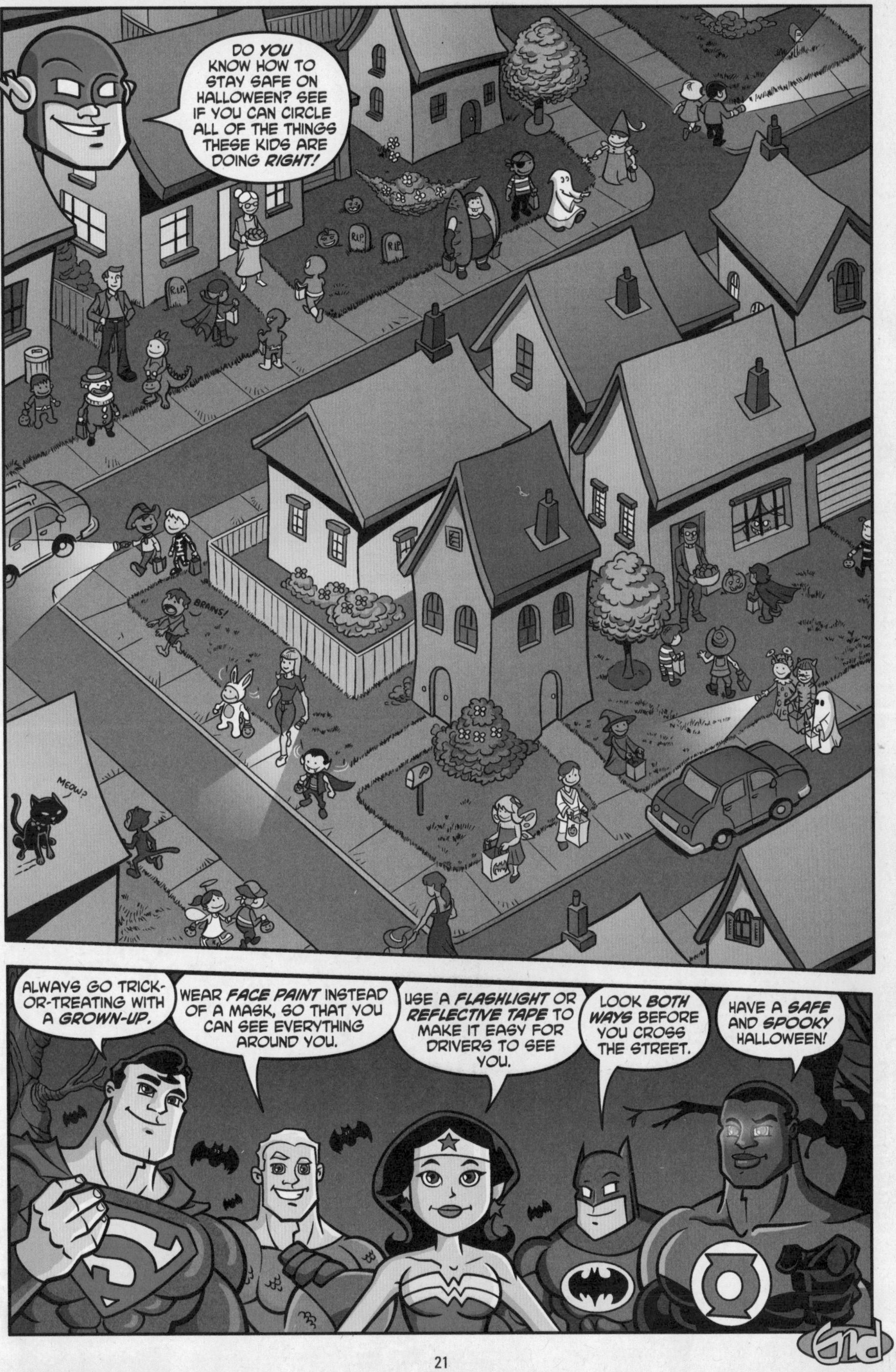
DO YOU KNOW HOW TO STAY SAFE ON HALLOWEEN? SEE IF YOU CAN CIRCLE ALL OF THE THINGS THESE KIDS ARE DOING RIGHT!
R.I.P.
R.I.P.
R.I.P.
BRAINS!
MEOW?
ALWAYS GO TRICK-OR-TREATING WITH A GROWN-UP.
WEAR FACE PAINT INSTEAD OF A MASK, SO THAT YOU CAN SEE EVERYTHING AROUND YOU.
USE A FLASHLIGHT OR REFLECTIVE TAPE TO MAKE IT EASY FOR DRIVERS TO SEE YOU.
LOOK BOTH WAYS BEFORE YOU CROSS THE STREET.
HAVE A SAFE AND SPOOKY HALLOWEEN!
End

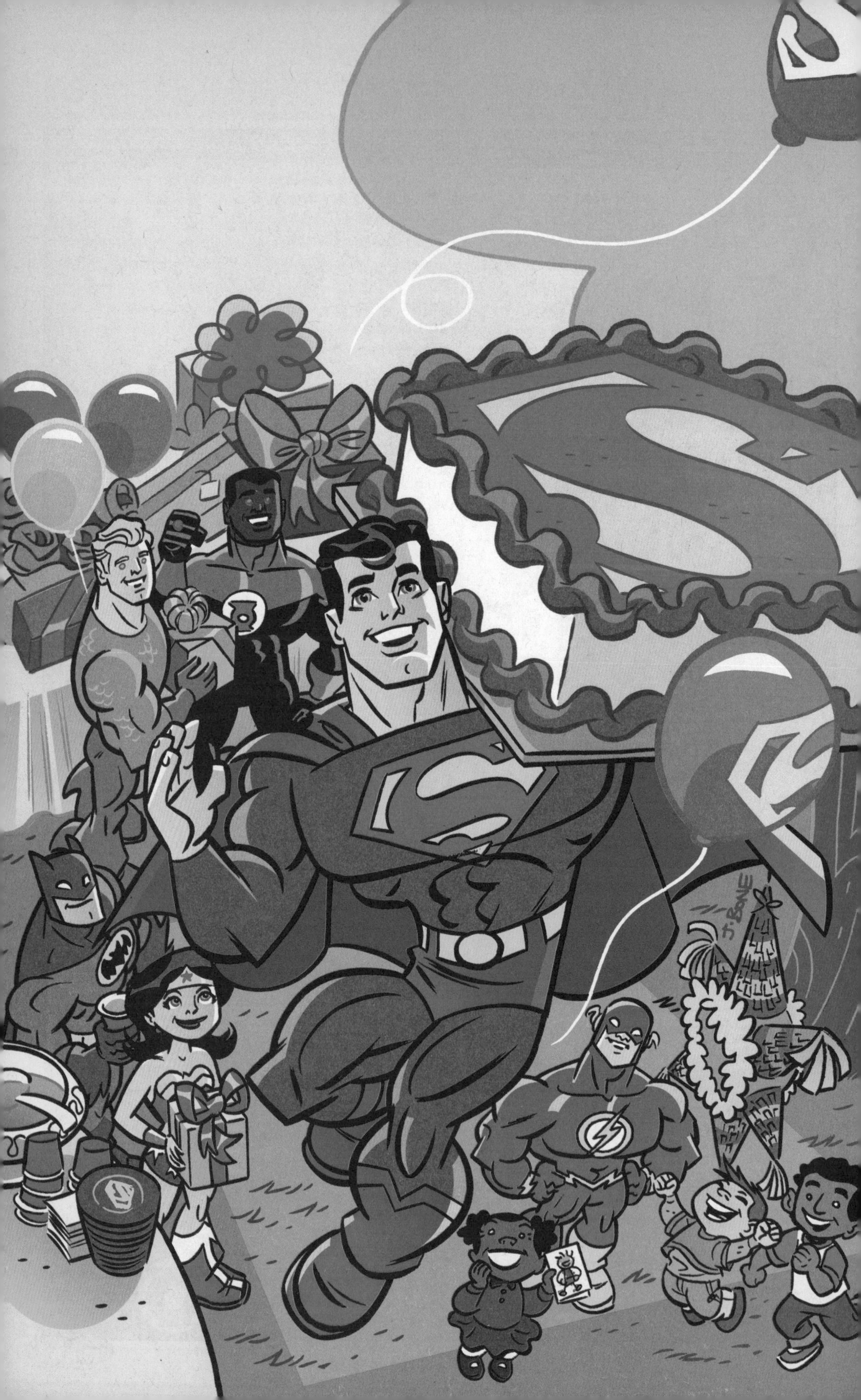
J. BONE

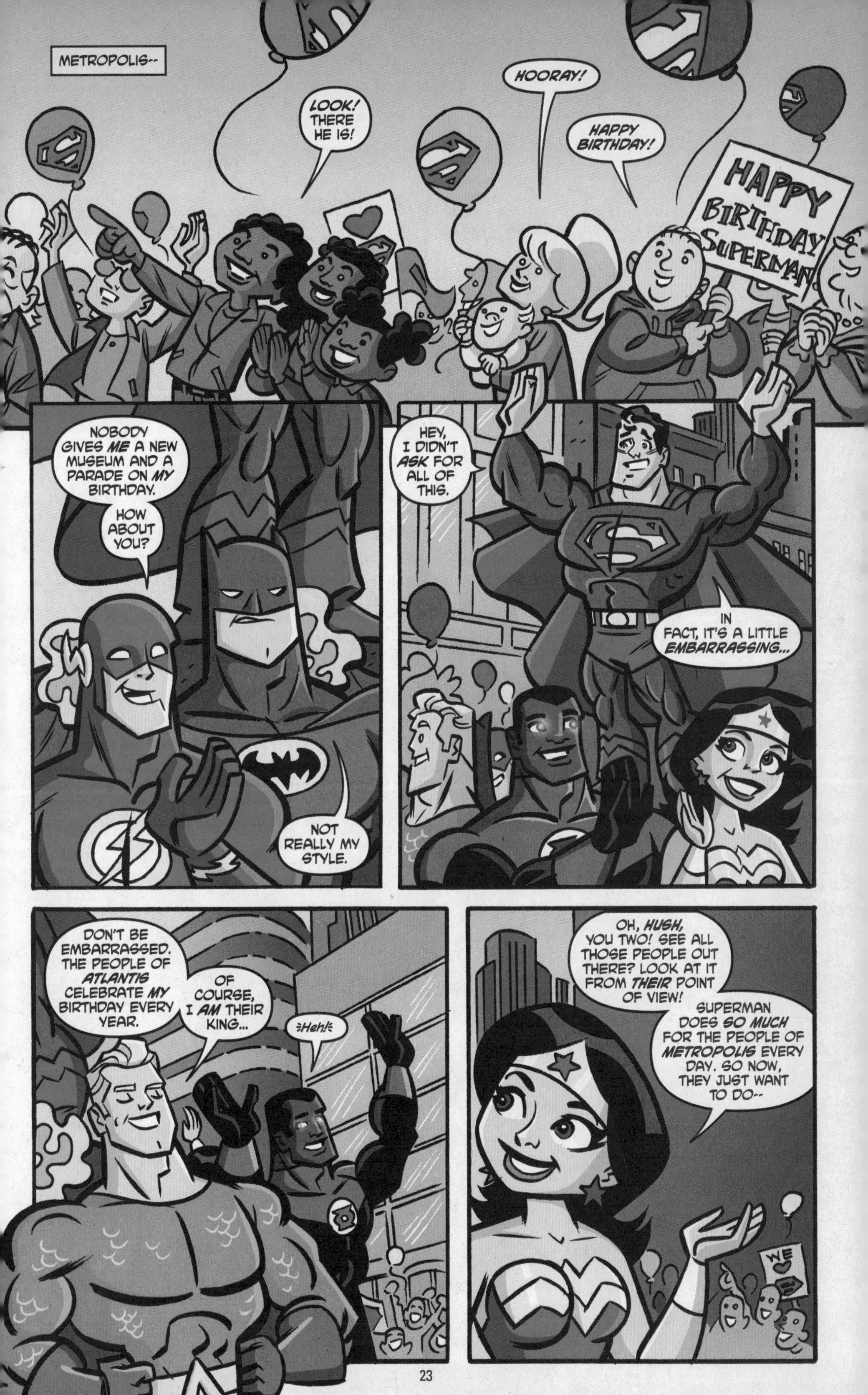
METROPOLIS--
LOOK! THERE HE IS!
HOORAY!
HAPPY BIRTHDAY!
HAPPY BIRTHDAY SUPERMAN
NOBODY GIVES ME A NEW MUSEUM AND A PARADE ON MY BIRTHDAY.
HOW ABOUT YOU?
NOT REALLY MY STYLE.
HEY, I DIDN'T ASK FOR ALL OF THIS.
IN FACT, IT'S A LITTLE EMBARRASSING...
DON'T BE EMBARRASSED. THE PEOPLE OF ATLANTIS CELEBRATE MY BIRTHDAY EVERY YEAR.
OF COURSE, I AM THEIR KING...
Heh!
OH, HUSH, YOU TWO! SEE ALL THOSE PEOPLE OUT THERE? LOOK AT IT FROM THEIR POINT OF VIEW!
SUPERMAN DOES SO MUCH FOR THE PEOPLE OF METROPOLIS EVERY DAY. SO NOW, THEY JUST WANT TO DO--

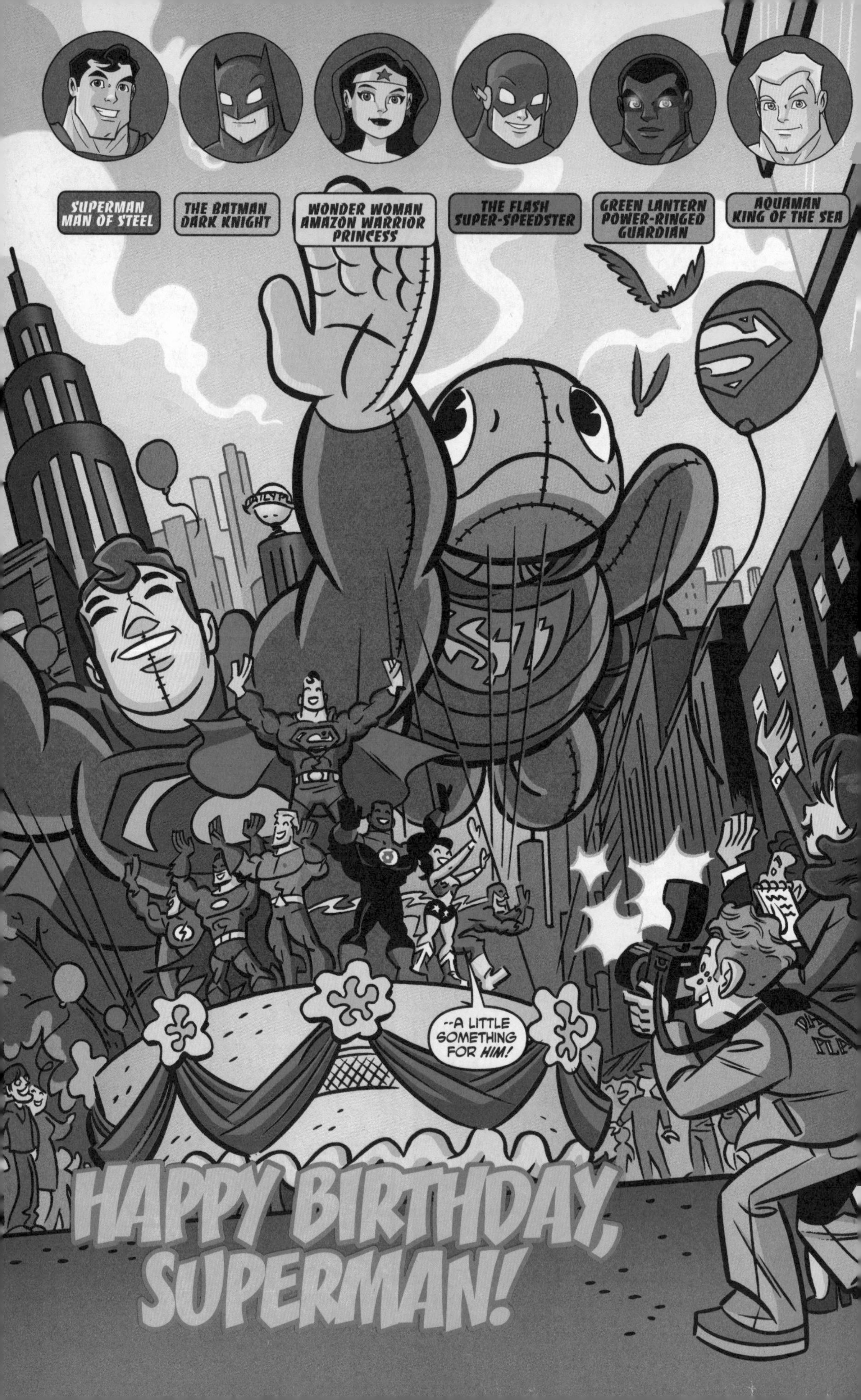
SUPERMAN
MAN OF STEEL
THE BATMAN
DARK KNIGHT
WONDER WOMAN
AMAZON WARRIOR
PRINCESS
THE FLASH
SUPER-SPEEDSTER
GREEN LANTERN
POWER-RINGED
GUARDIAN
AQUAMAN
KING OF THE SEA
--A LITTLE SOMETHING FOR HIM!
HAPPY BIRTHDAY, SUPERMAN!

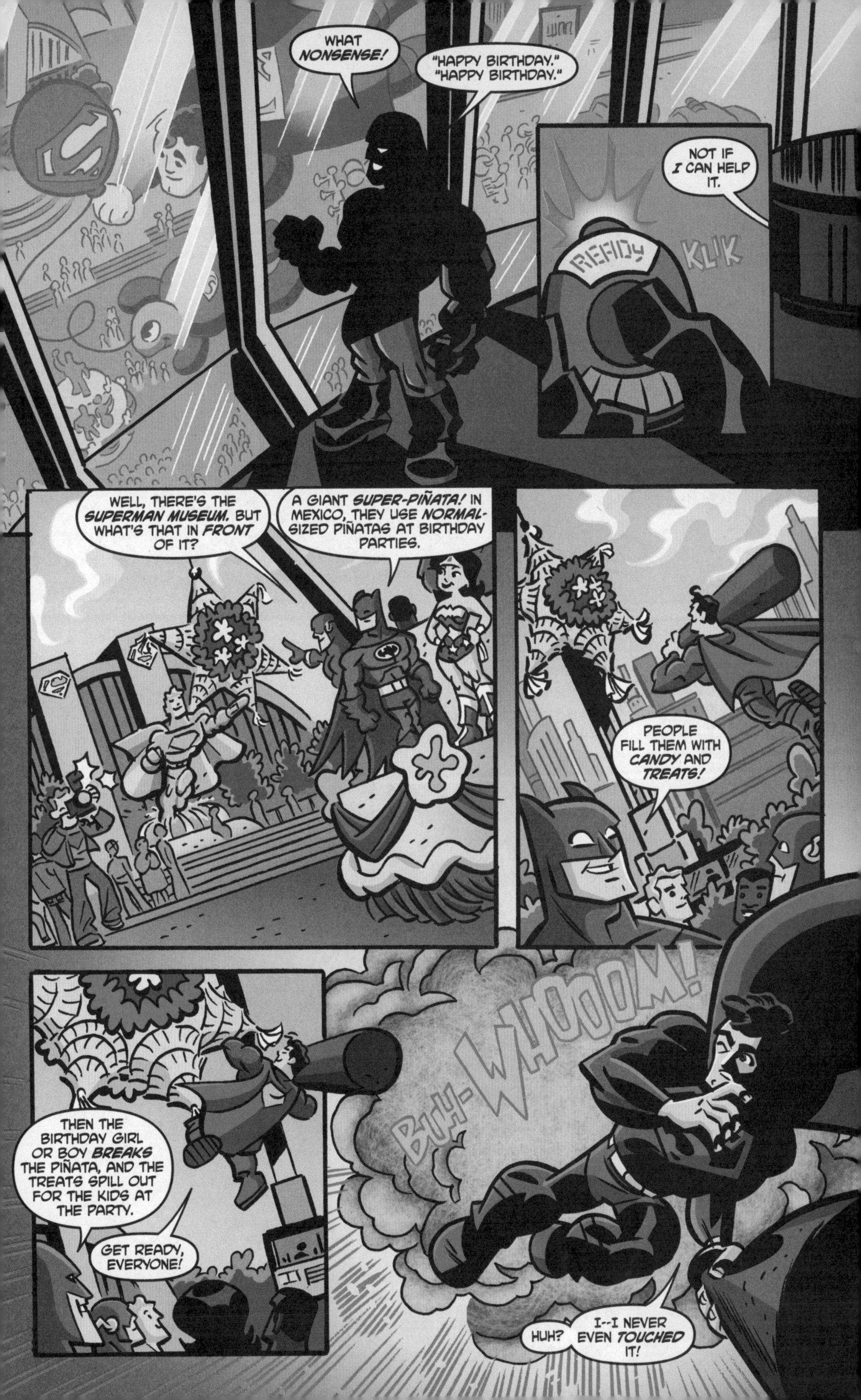
WHAT NONSENSE!
"HAPPY BIRTHDAY." "HAPPY BIRTHDAY."
NOT IF I CAN HELP IT.
READY
KLIK
WELL, THERE'S THE SUPERMAN MUSEUM. BUT WHAT'S THAT IN FRONT OF IT?
A GIANT SUPER-PIÑATA! IN MEXICO, THEY USE NORMAL-SIZED PIÑATAS AT BIRTHDAY PARTIES.
PEOPLE FILL THEM WITH CANDY AND TREATS!
THEN THE BIRTHDAY GIRL OR BOY BREAKS THE PIÑATA, AND THE TREATS SPILL OUT FOR THE KIDS AT THE PARTY.
GET READY, EVERYONE!
BUH-WHOOOM!
HUH?
I--I NEVER EVEN TOUCHED IT!

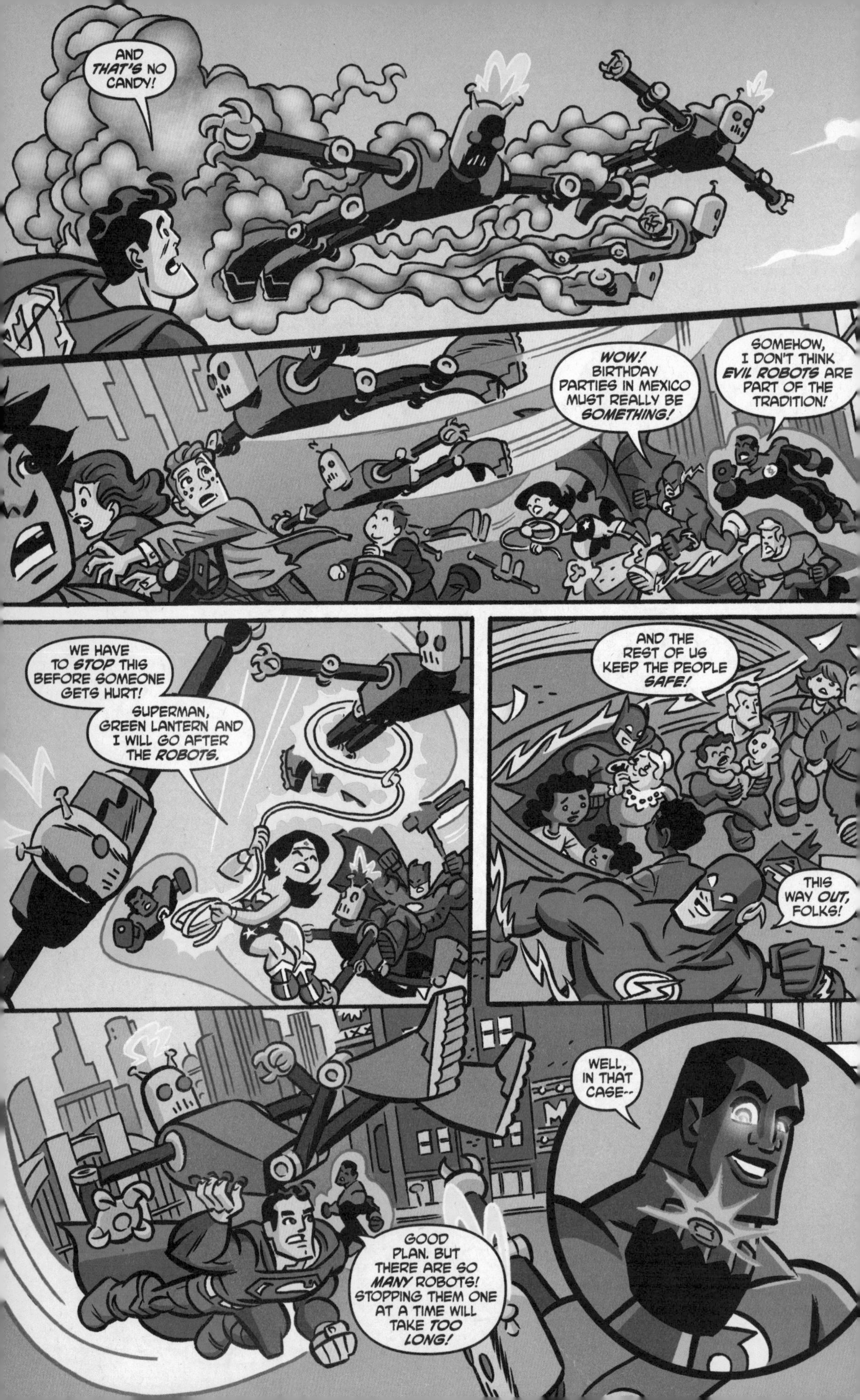
AND THAT'S NO CANDY!
WOW! BIRTHDAY PARTIES IN MEXICO MUST REALLY BE SOMETHING!
SOMEHOW, I DON'T THINK EVIL ROBOTS ARE PART OF THE TRADITION!
WE HAVE TO STOP THIS BEFORE SOMEONE GETS HURT!
SUPERMAN, GREEN LANTERN AND I WILL GO AFTER THE ROBOTS.
AND THE REST OF US KEEP THE PEOPLE SAFE!
THIS WAY OUT, FOLKS!
GOOD PLAN. BUT THERE ARE SO MANY ROBOTS! STOPPING THEM ONE AT A TIME WILL TAKE TOO LONG!
WELL, IN THAT CASE--

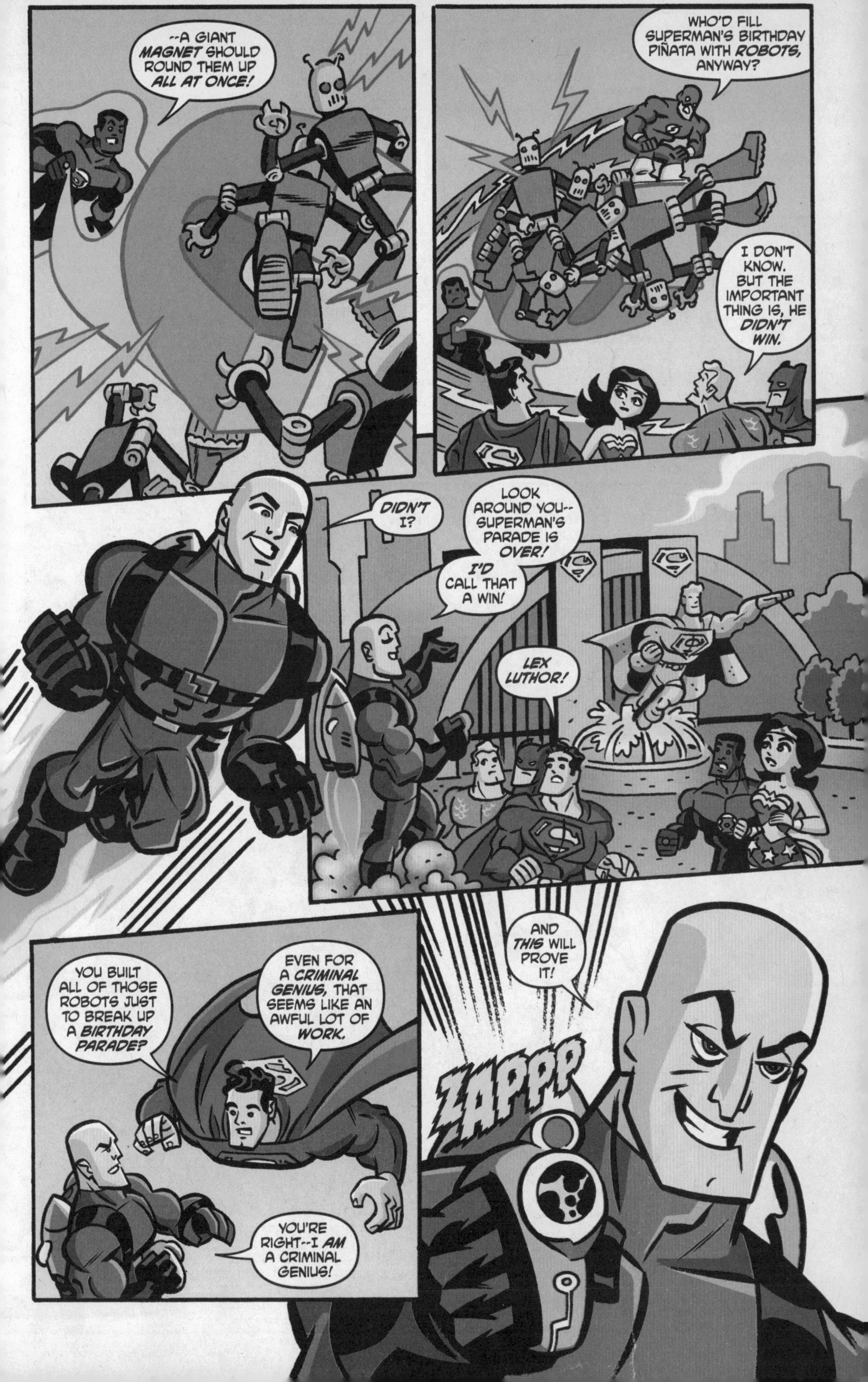

--A GIANT MAGNET SHOULD ROUND THEM UP ALL AT ONCE!
WHO'D FILL SUPERMAN'S BIRTHDAY PIÑATA WITH ROBOTS, ANYWAY?
I DON'T KNOW. BUT THE IMPORTANT THING IS, HE DIDN'T WIN.
DIDN'T I?
LOOK AROUND YOU-- SUPERMAN'S PARADE IS OVER!
I'D CALL THAT A WIN!
LEX LUTHOR!
YOU BUILT ALL OF THOSE ROBOTS JUST TO BREAK UP A BIRTHDAY PARADE?
EVEN FOR A CRIMINAL GENIUS, THAT SEEMS LIKE AN AWFUL LOT OF WORK.
YOU'RE RIGHT--I AM A CRIMINAL GENIUS!
AND THIS WILL PROVE IT!
ZAPPP

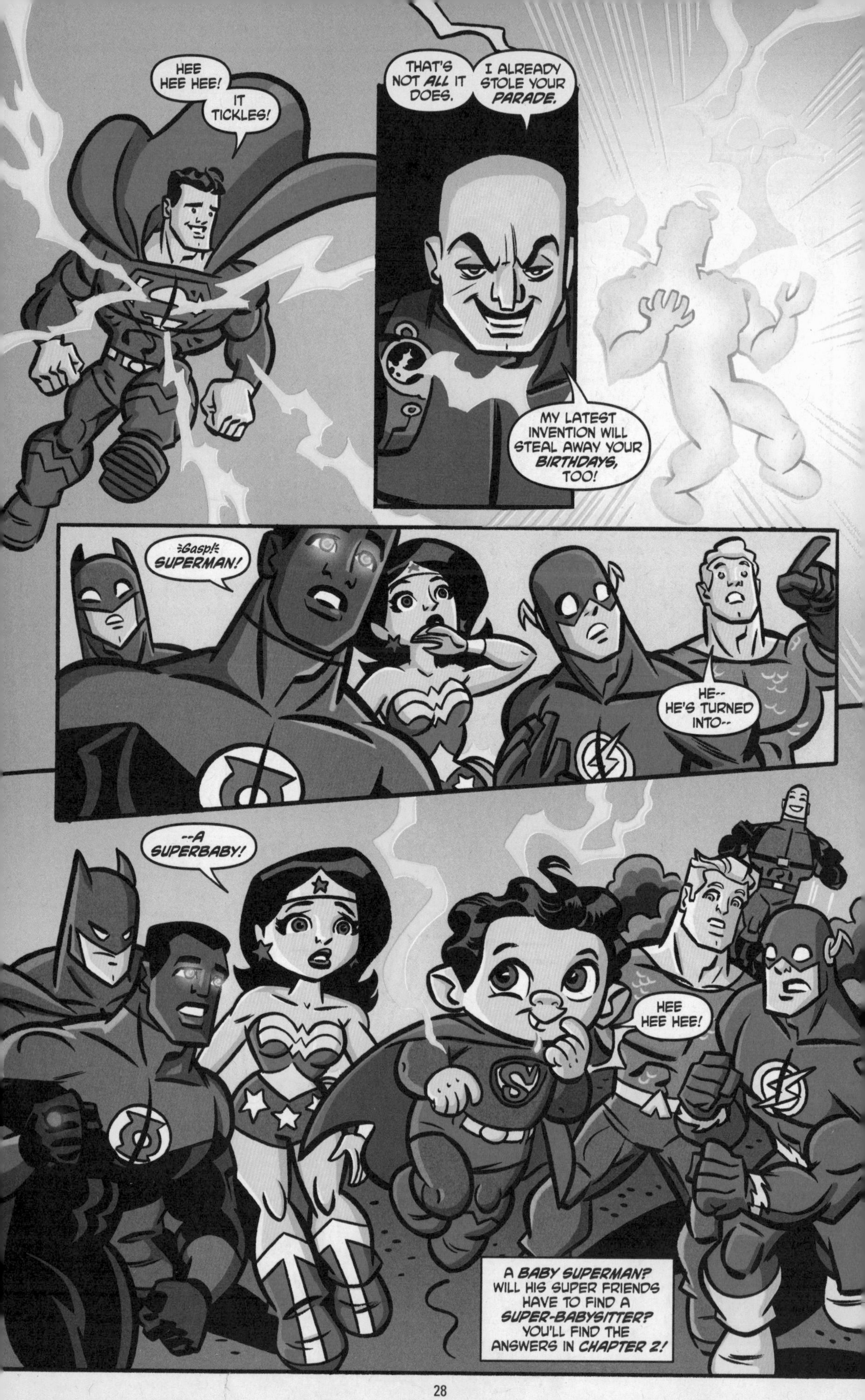
HEE HEE HEE! IT TICKLES!
THAT'S NOT ALL IT DOES.
I ALREADY STOLE YOUR PARADE.
MY LATEST INVENTION WILL STEAL AWAY YOUR BIRTHDAYS, TOO!
Gasp! SUPERMAN!
HE-- HE'S TURNED INTO--
--A SUPERBABY!
HEE HEE HEE!
A BABY SUPERMAN? WILL HIS SUPER FRIENDS HAVE TO FIND A SUPER-BABYSITTER? YOU'LL FIND THE ANSWERS IN CHAPTER 2!

HAPPY BIRTHDAY, SUPERMAN! CHAPTER 2

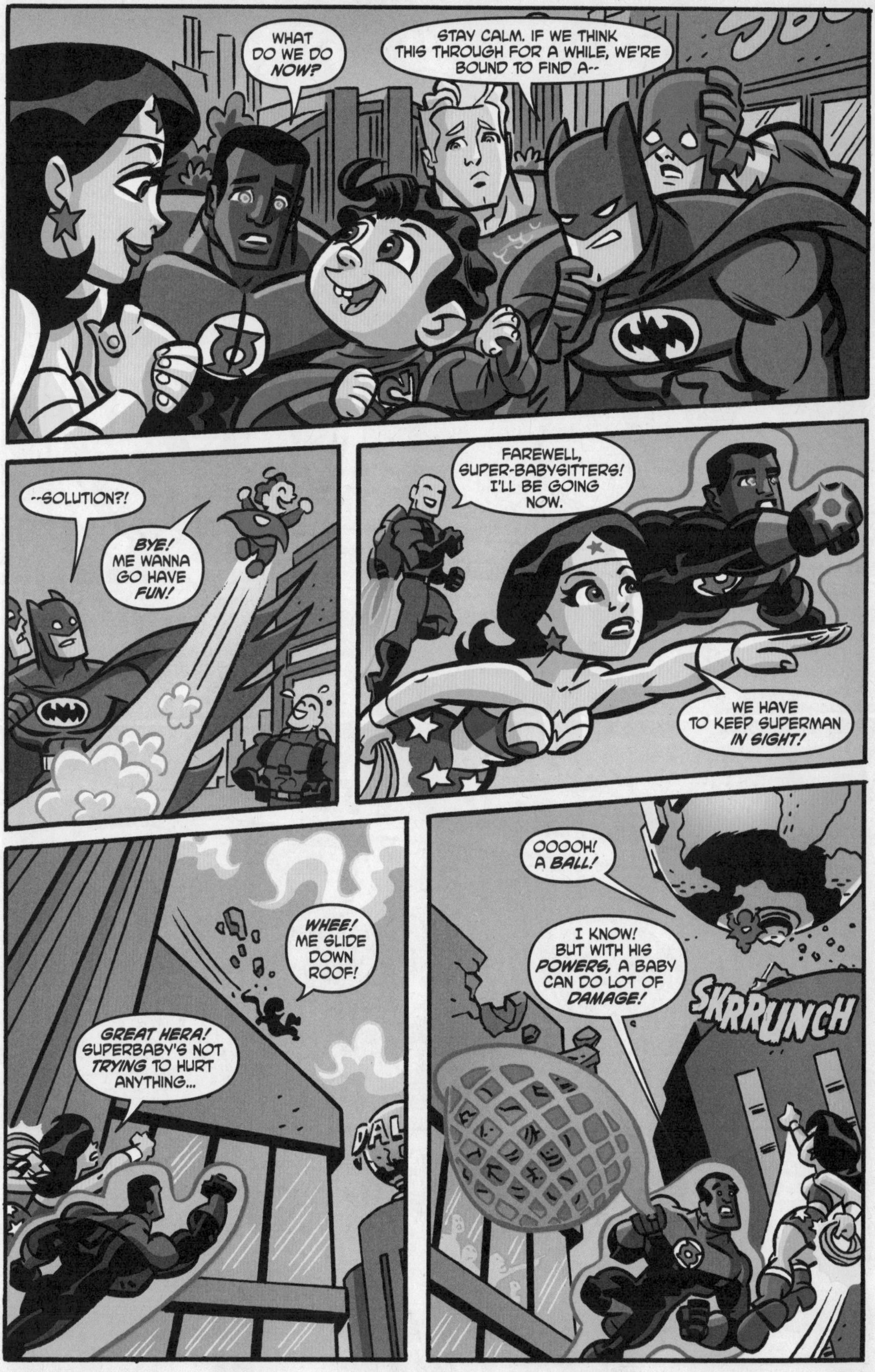

WHAT DO WE DO NOW?
STAY CALM. IF WE THINK THIS THROUGH FOR A WHILE, WE'RE BOUND TO FIND A--
--SOLUTION?!
BYE! ME WANNA GO HAVE FUN!
FAREWELL, SUPER-BABYSITTERS! I'LL BE GOING NOW.
WE HAVE TO KEEP SUPERMAN IN SIGHT!
WHEE! ME SLIDE DOWN ROOF!
GREAT HERA! SUPERBABY'S NOT TRYING TO HURT ANYTHING...
OOOOH! A BALL!
I KNOW! BUT WITH HIS POWERS, A BABY CAN DO LOT OF DAMAGE!
SKRRUNCH

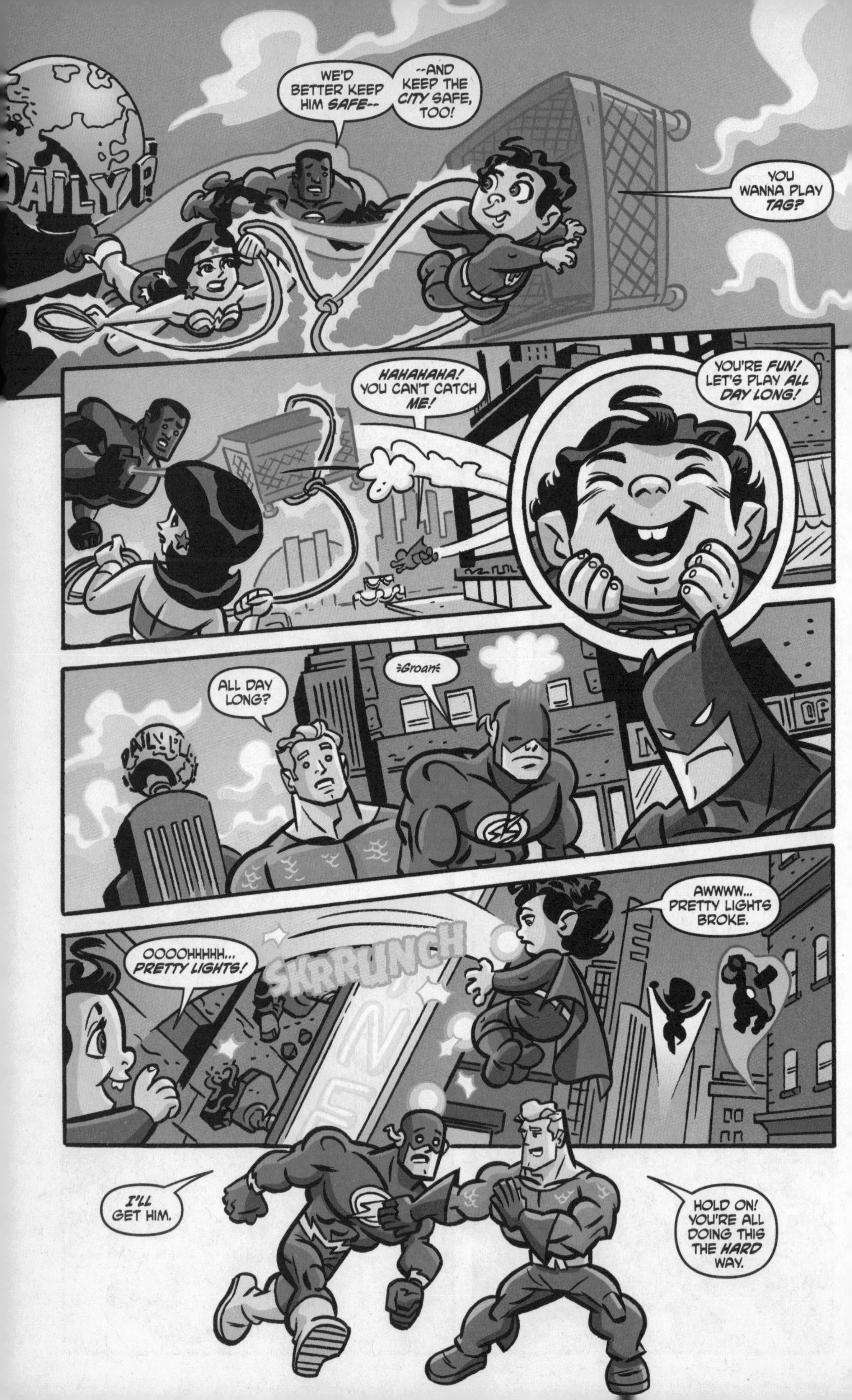
WE'D BETTER KEEP HIM SAFE--
--AND KEEP THE CITY SAFE, TOO!
YOU WANNA PLAY TAG?
HAHAHAHA! YOU CAN'T CATCH ME!
YOU'RE FUN! LET'S PLAY ALL DAY LONG!
ALL DAY LONG?
Groan
AWWWW... PRETTY LIGHTS BROKE.
OOOOHHHHH... PRETTY LIGHTS!
SKRRUNCH
I'LL GET HIM.
HOLD ON! YOU'RE ALL DOING THIS THE HARD WAY.

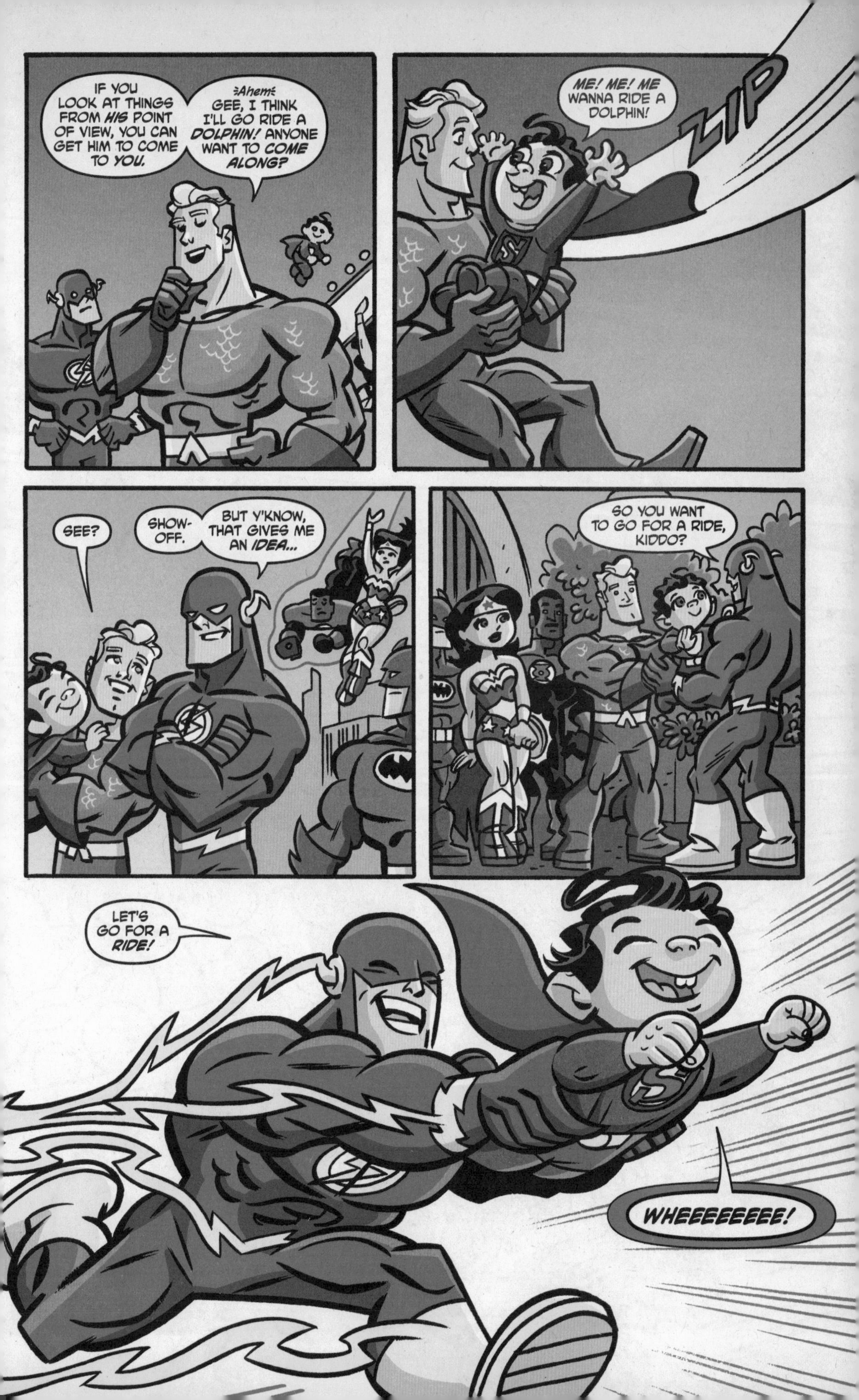
IF YOU LOOK AT THINGS FROM *HIS* POINT OF VIEW, YOU CAN GET HIM TO COME TO *YOU.*
Ahem
GEE, I THINK I'LL GO RIDE A *DOLPHIN!* ANYONE WANT TO *COME ALONG?*
ME! ME! ME WANNA RIDE A DOLPHIN!
ZIP
SEE?
SHOW-OFF.
BUT Y'KNOW, THAT GIVES ME AN *IDEA...*
SO YOU WANT TO GO FOR A RIDE, KIDDO?
LET'S GO FOR A *RIDE!*
WHEEEEEEEE!

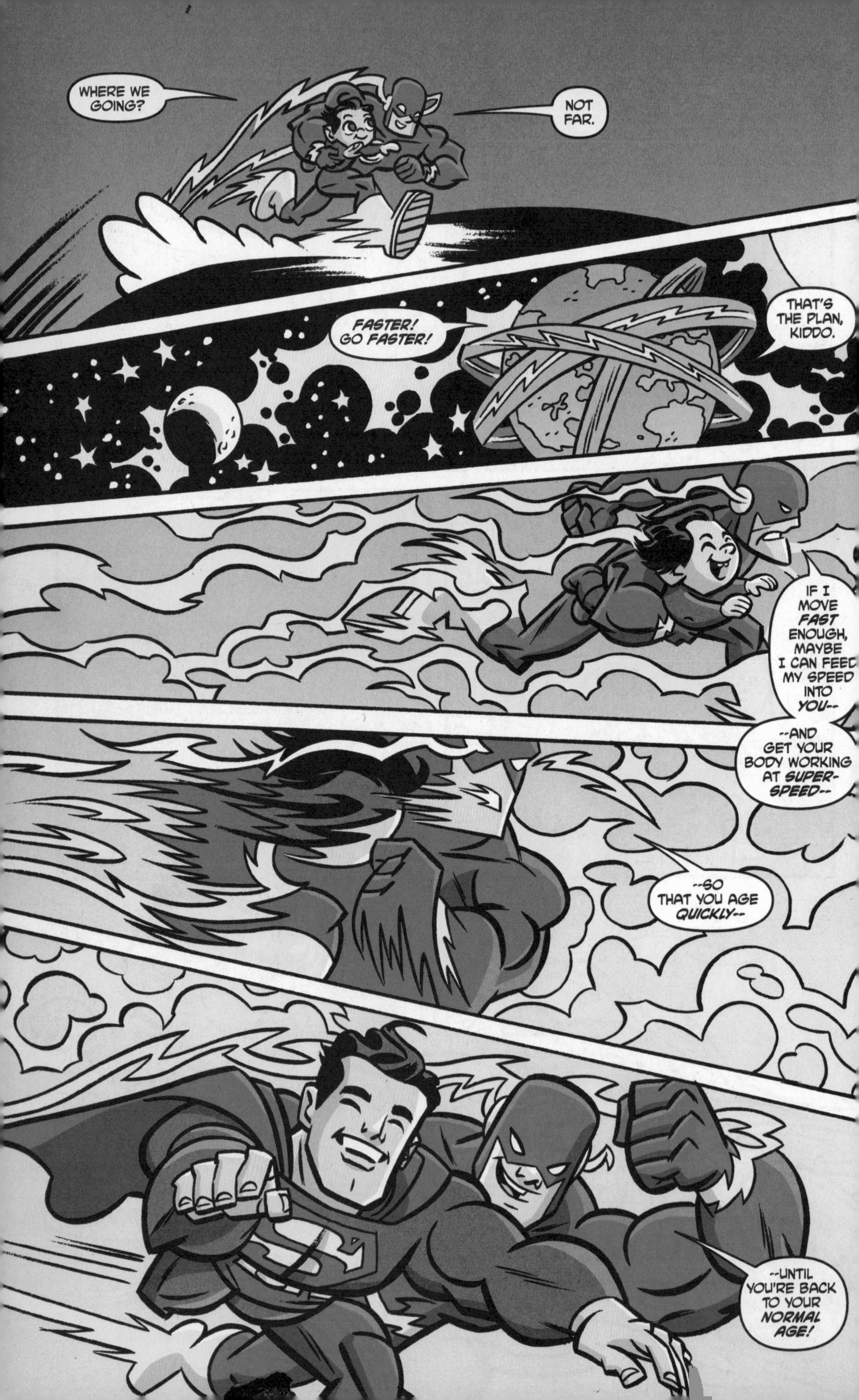

WHERE WE GOING?
NOT FAR.
FASTER! GO FASTER!
THAT'S THE PLAN, KIDDO.
IF I MOVE FAST ENOUGH, MAYBE I CAN FEED MY SPEED INTO YOU--
--AND GET YOUR BODY WORKING AT SUPER-SPEED--
--SO THAT YOU AGE QUICKLY--
--UNTIL YOU'RE BACK TO YOUR NORMAL AGE!

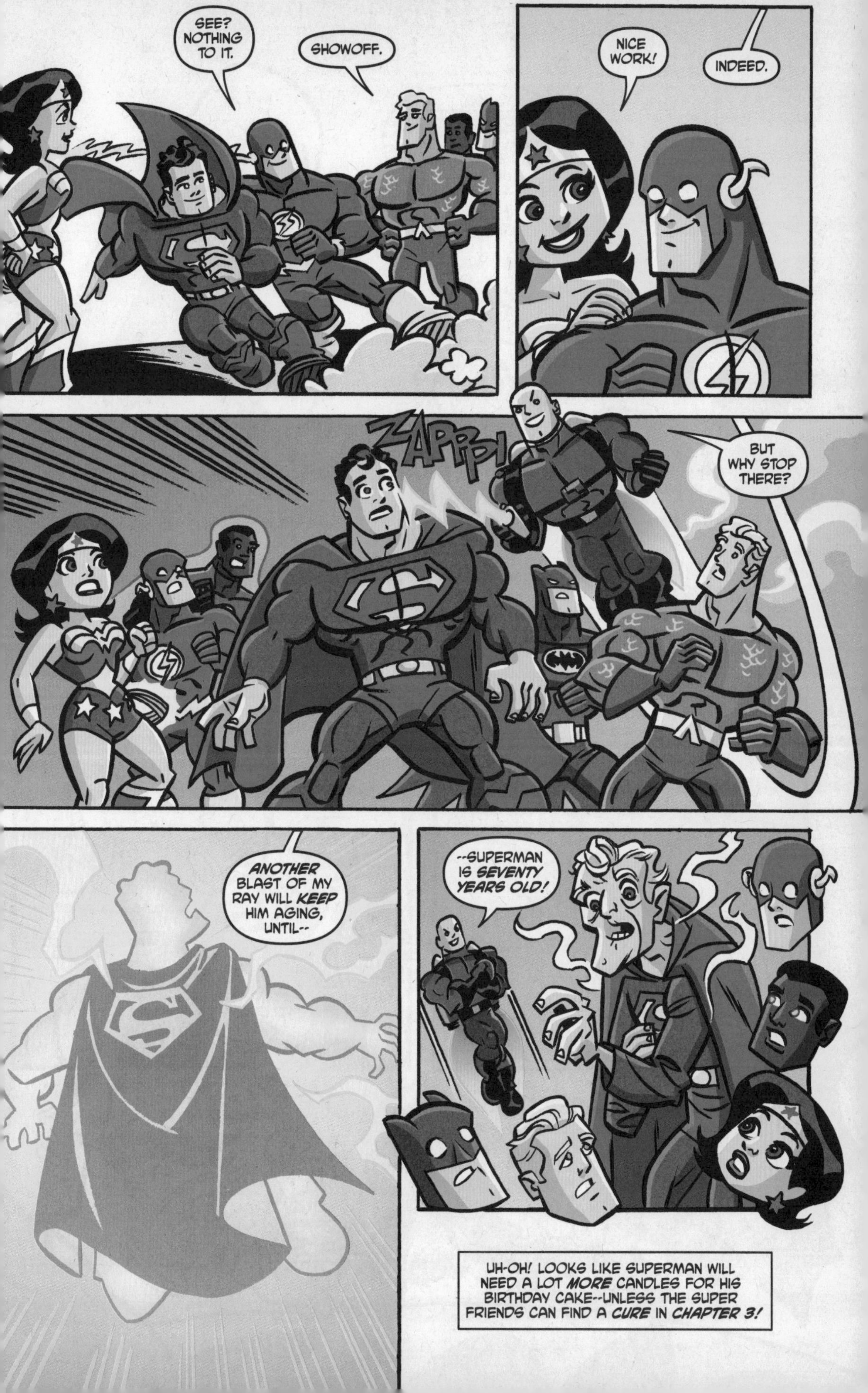
SEE? NOTHING TO IT.
SHOWOFF.
NICE WORK!
INDEED.
ZAPPP!
BUT WHY STOP THERE?
ANOTHER BLAST OF MY RAY WILL KEEP HIM AGING, UNTIL--
--SUPERMAN IS SEVENTY YEARS OLD!
UH-OH! LOOKS LIKE SUPERMAN WILL NEED A LOT MORE CANDLES FOR HIS BIRTHDAY CAKE--UNLESS THE SUPER FRIENDS CAN FIND A CURE IN CHAPTER 3!

HAPPY BIRTHDAY, SUPERMAN! CHAPTER 3

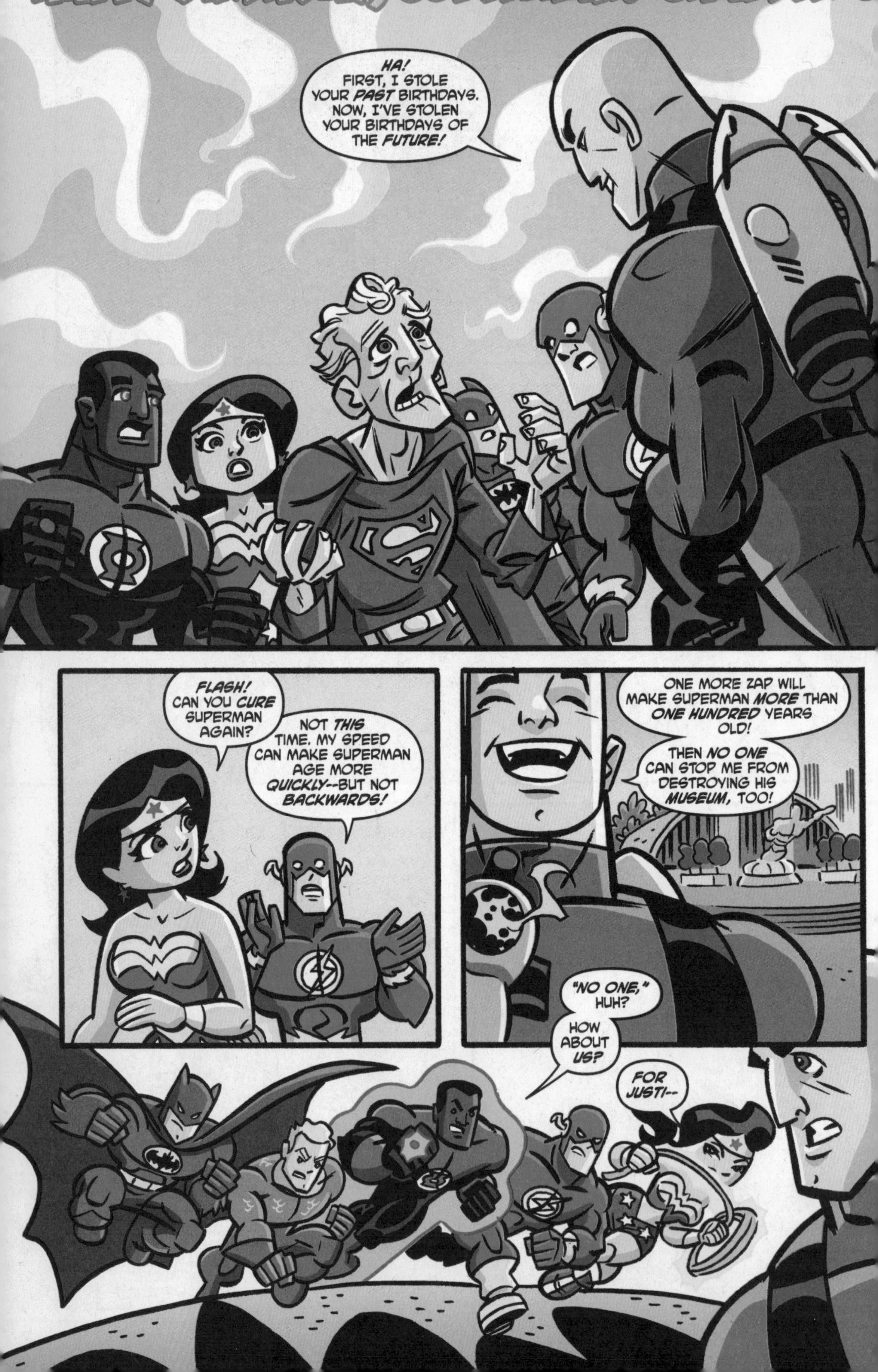
HA! FIRST, I STOLE YOUR PAST BIRTHDAYS. NOW, I'VE STOLEN YOUR BIRTHDAYS OF THE FUTURE!
FLASH! CAN YOU CURE SUPERMAN AGAIN?
NOT THIS TIME. MY SPEED CAN MAKE SUPERMAN AGE MORE QUICKLY--BUT NOT BACKWARDS!
ONE MORE ZAP WILL MAKE SUPERMAN MORE THAN ONE HUNDRED YEARS OLD!
THEN NO ONE CAN STOP ME FROM DESTROYING HIS MUSEUM, TOO!
"NO ONE," HUH?
HOW ABOUT US?
FOR JUSTI--

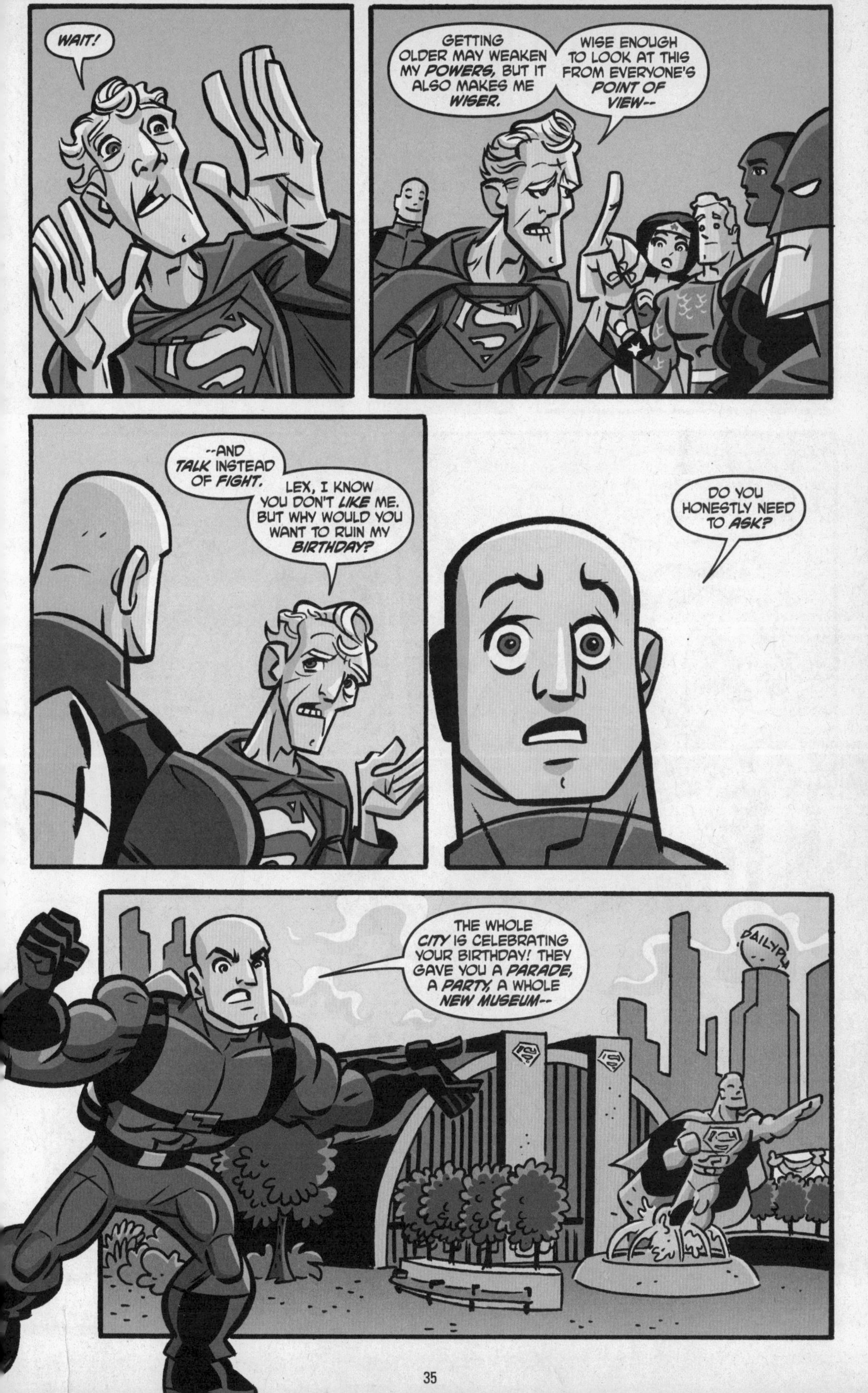
WAIT!
GETTING OLDER MAY WEAKEN MY POWERS, BUT IT ALSO MAKES ME WISER.
WISE ENOUGH TO LOOK AT THIS FROM EVERYONE'S POINT OF VIEW--
--AND TALK INSTEAD OF FIGHT.
LEX, I KNOW YOU DON'T LIKE ME. BUT WHY WOULD YOU WANT TO RUIN MY BIRTHDAY?
DO YOU HONESTLY NEED TO ASK?
THE WHOLE CITY IS CELEBRATING YOUR BIRTHDAY! THEY GAVE YOU A PARADE, A PARTY, A WHOLE NEW MUSEUM--

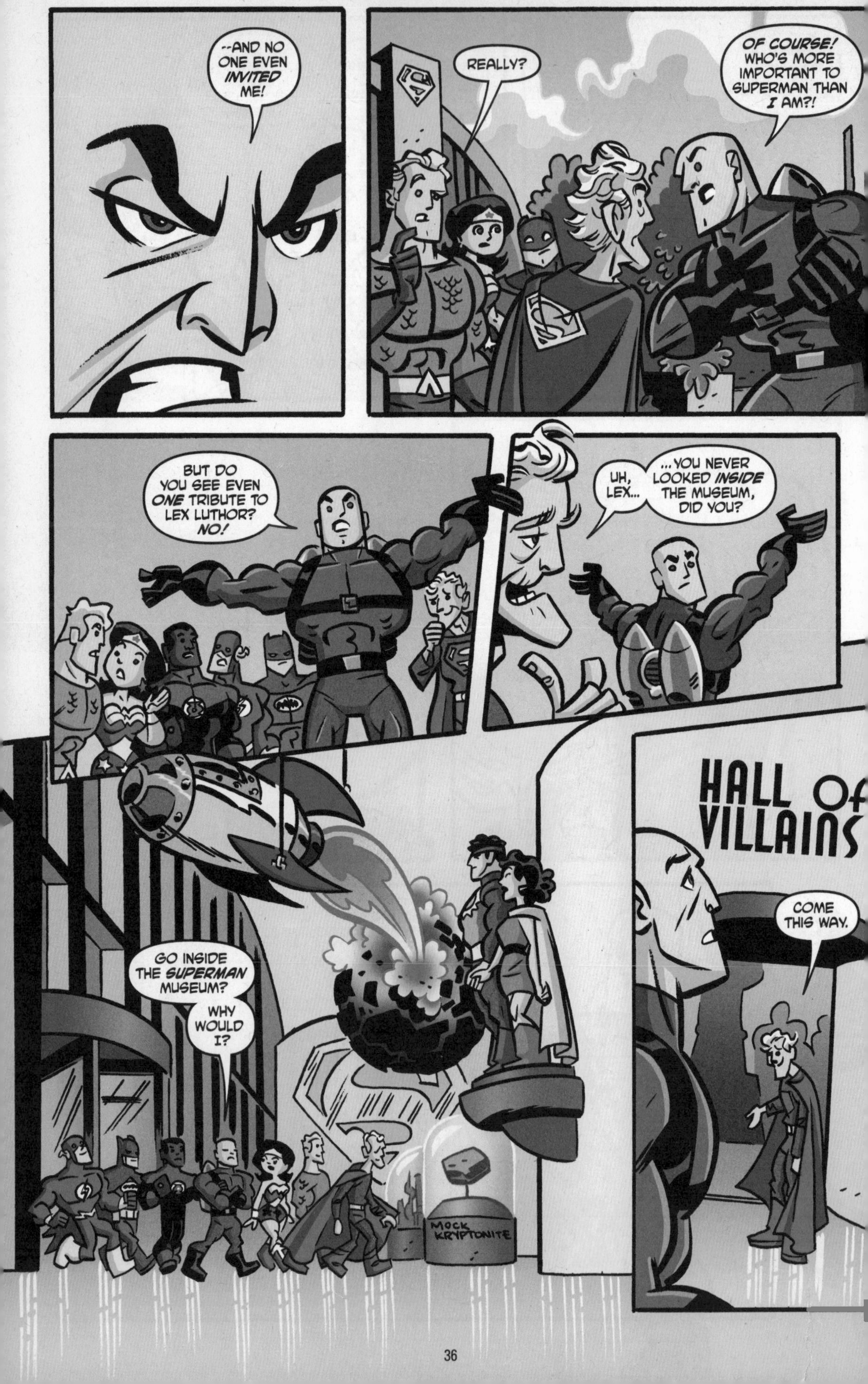
--AND NO ONE EVEN *INVITED* ME!
REALLY?
OF COURSE! WHO'S MORE IMPORTANT TO SUPERMAN THAN *I AM?!*
BUT DO YOU SEE EVEN *ONE* TRIBUTE TO LEX LUTHOR? *NO!*
UH, LEX...
...YOU NEVER LOOKED *INSIDE* THE MUSEUM, DID YOU?
GO INSIDE THE *SUPERMAN* MUSEUM?
WHY WOULD I?
MOCK KRYPTONITE
HALL OF VILLAINS
COME THIS WAY.

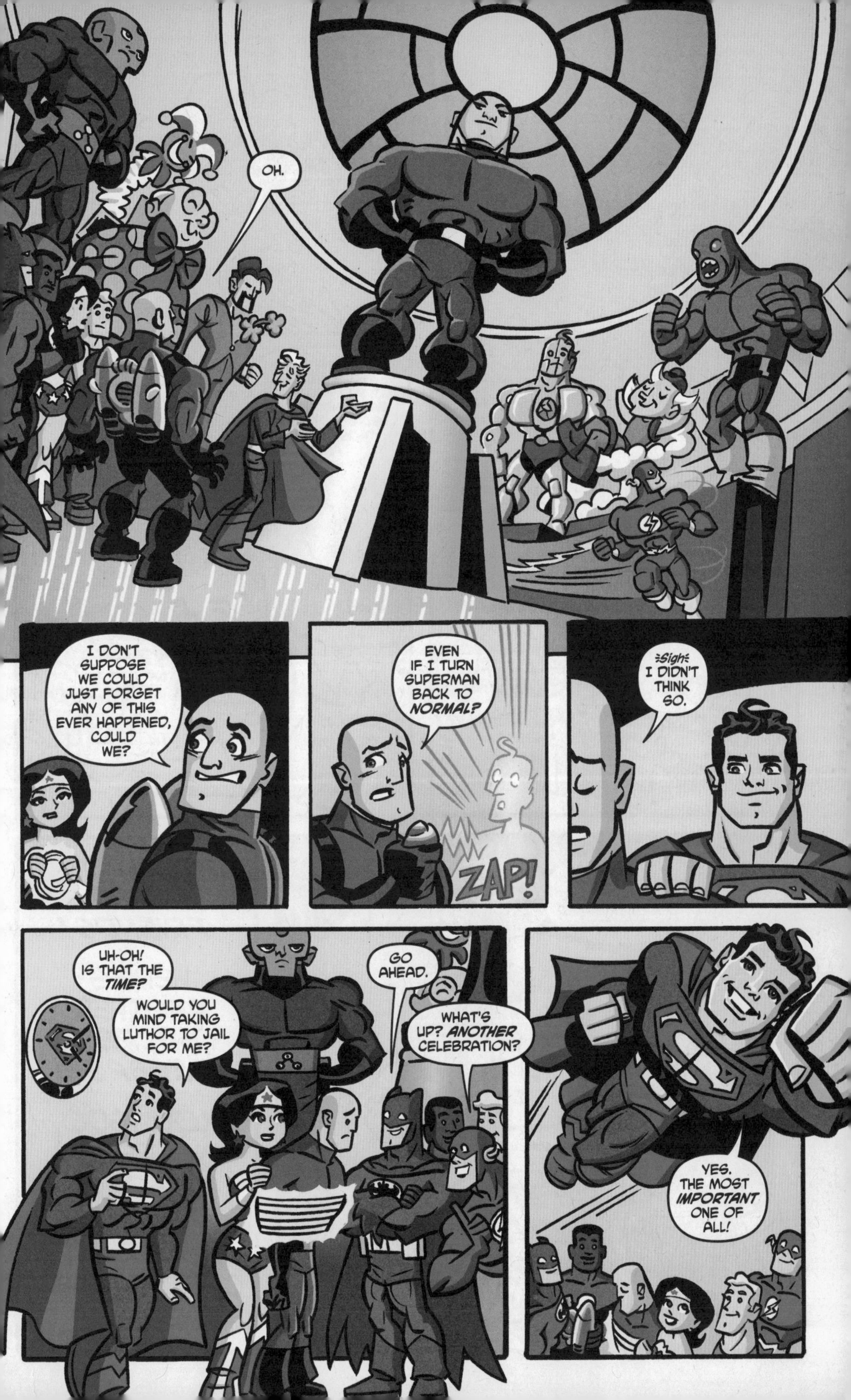
OH.
I DON'T SUPPOSE WE COULD JUST FORGET ANY OF THIS EVER HAPPENED, COULD WE?
EVEN IF I TURN SUPERMAN BACK TO NORMAL?
ZAP!
Sigh I DIDN'T THINK SO.
UH-OH! IS THAT THE TIME?
WOULD YOU MIND TAKING LUTHOR TO JAIL FOR ME?
GO AHEAD.
WHAT'S UP? ANOTHER CELEBRATION?
YES. THE MOST IMPORTANT ONE OF ALL!

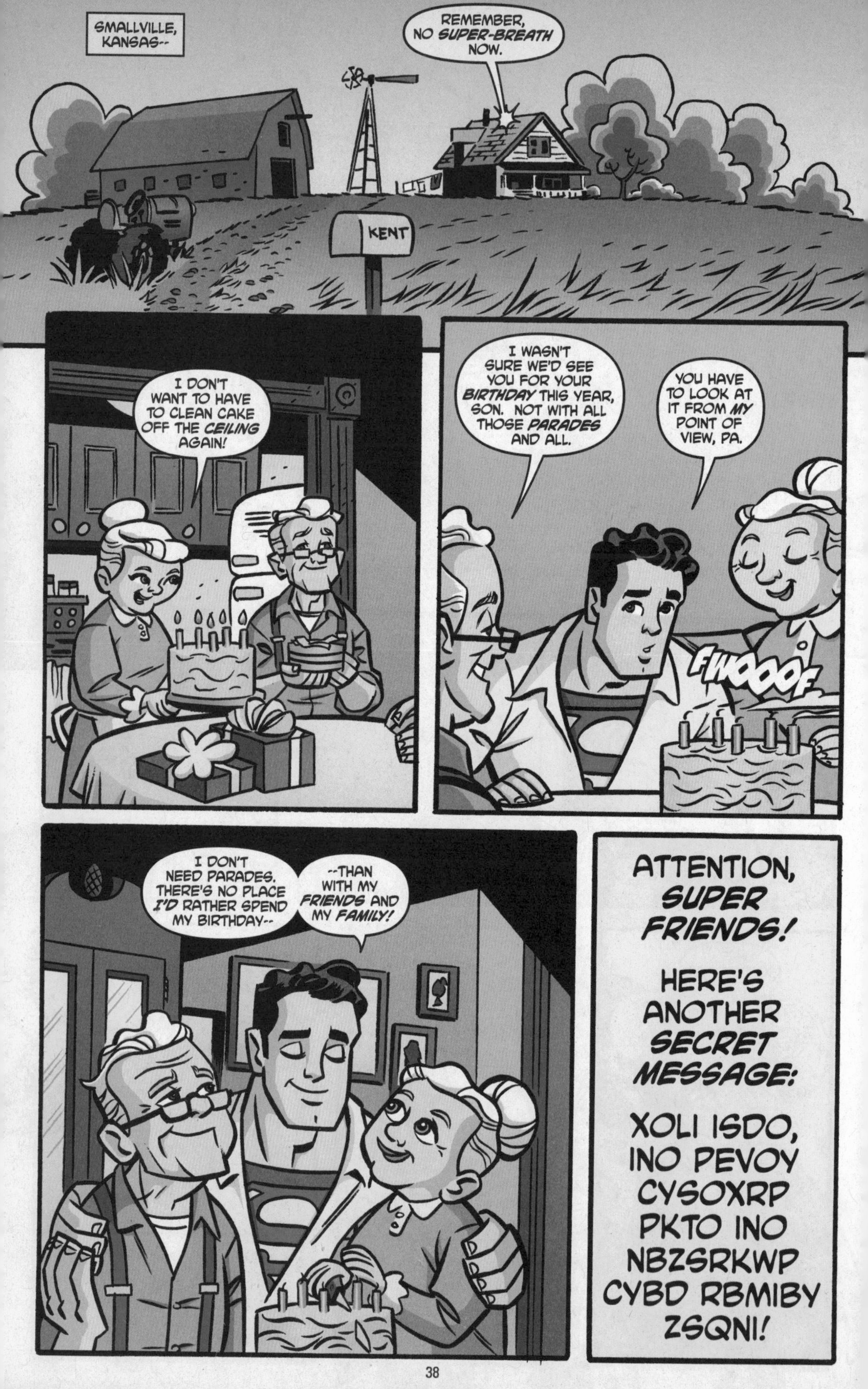

SMALLVILLE, KANSAS--
REMEMBER, NO SUPER-BREATH NOW.
KENT
I DON'T WANT TO HAVE TO CLEAN CAKE OFF THE CEILING AGAIN!
I WASN'T SURE WE'D SEE YOU FOR YOUR BIRTHDAY THIS YEAR, SON. NOT WITH ALL THOSE PARADES AND ALL.
YOU HAVE TO LOOK AT IT FROM MY POINT OF VIEW, PA.
FWOOOF
I DON'T NEED PARADES. THERE'S NO PLACE I'D RATHER SPEND MY BIRTHDAY--
--THAN WITH MY FRIENDS AND MY FAMILY!
ATTENTION, SUPER FRIENDS!
HERE'S ANOTHER SECRET MESSAGE:
XOLI ISDO, INO PEVOY CYSOXRP PKTO INO NBZSRKWP CYBD RBMIBY ZSQNI!

BIRTHDAY CARD CUT-UP

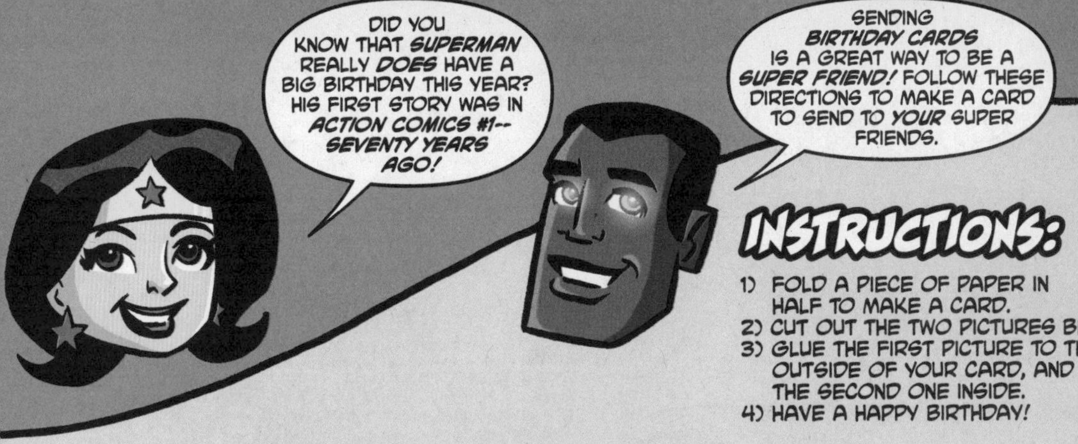
DID YOU KNOW THAT SUPERMAN REALLY DOES HAVE A BIG BIRTHDAY THIS YEAR? HIS FIRST STORY WAS IN ACTION COMICS #1-- SEVENTY YEARS AGO!
SENDING BIRTHDAY CARDS IS A GREAT WAY TO BE A SUPER FRIEND! FOLLOW THESE DIRECTIONS TO MAKE A CARD TO SEND TO YOUR SUPER FRIENDS.

INSTRUCTIONS:

1) FOLD A PIECE OF PAPER IN HALF TO MAKE A CARD.
2) CUT OUT THE TWO PICTURES BELOW.
3) GLUE THE FIRST PICTURE TO THE OUTSIDE OF YOUR CARD, AND THE SECOND ONE INSIDE.
4) HAVE A HAPPY BIRTHDAY!

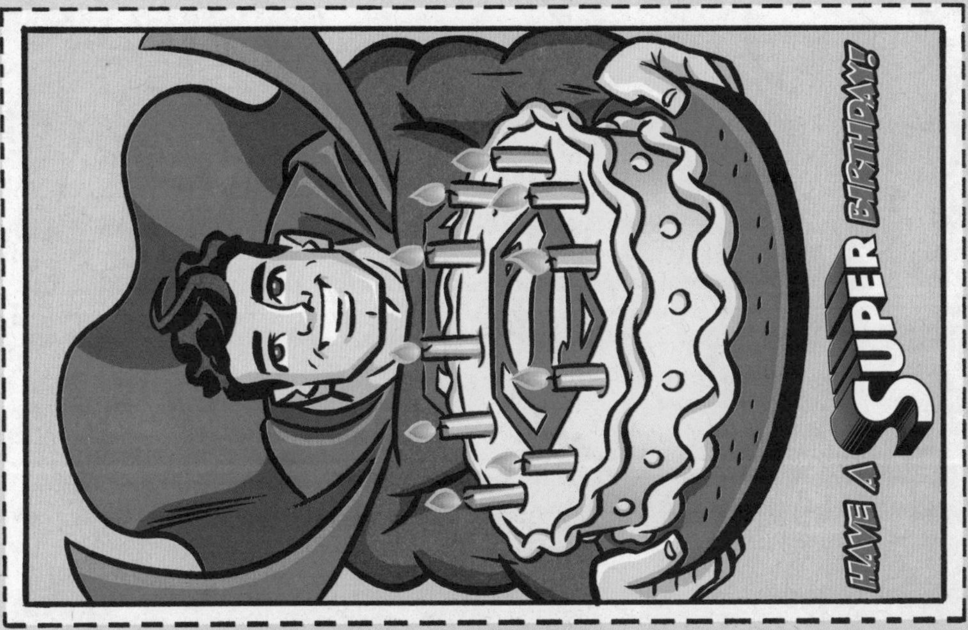
HAVE A SUPER BIRTHDAY!

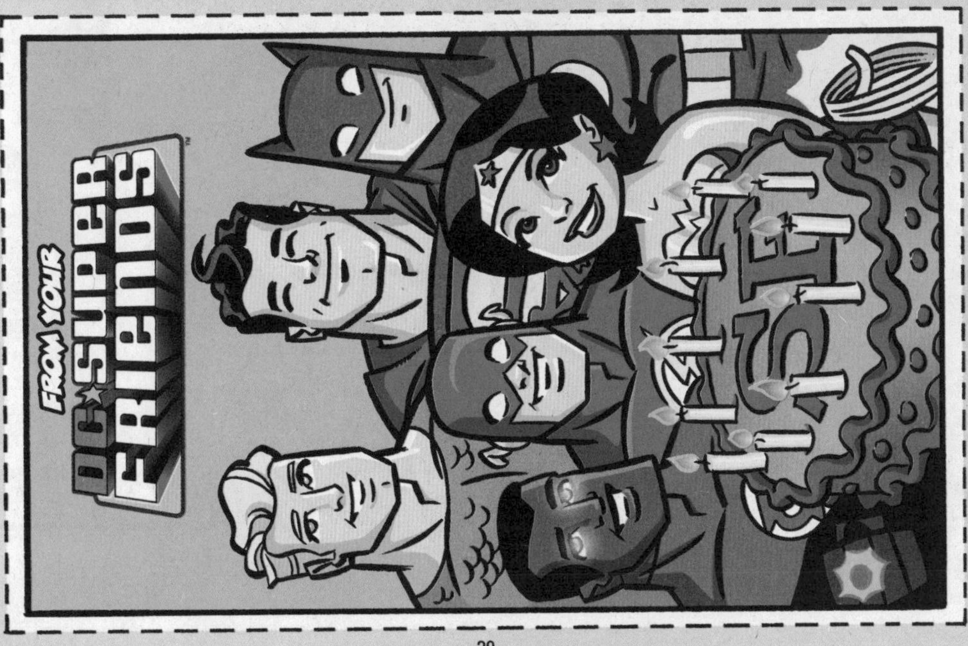
FROM YOUR
DC SUPER FRIENDS

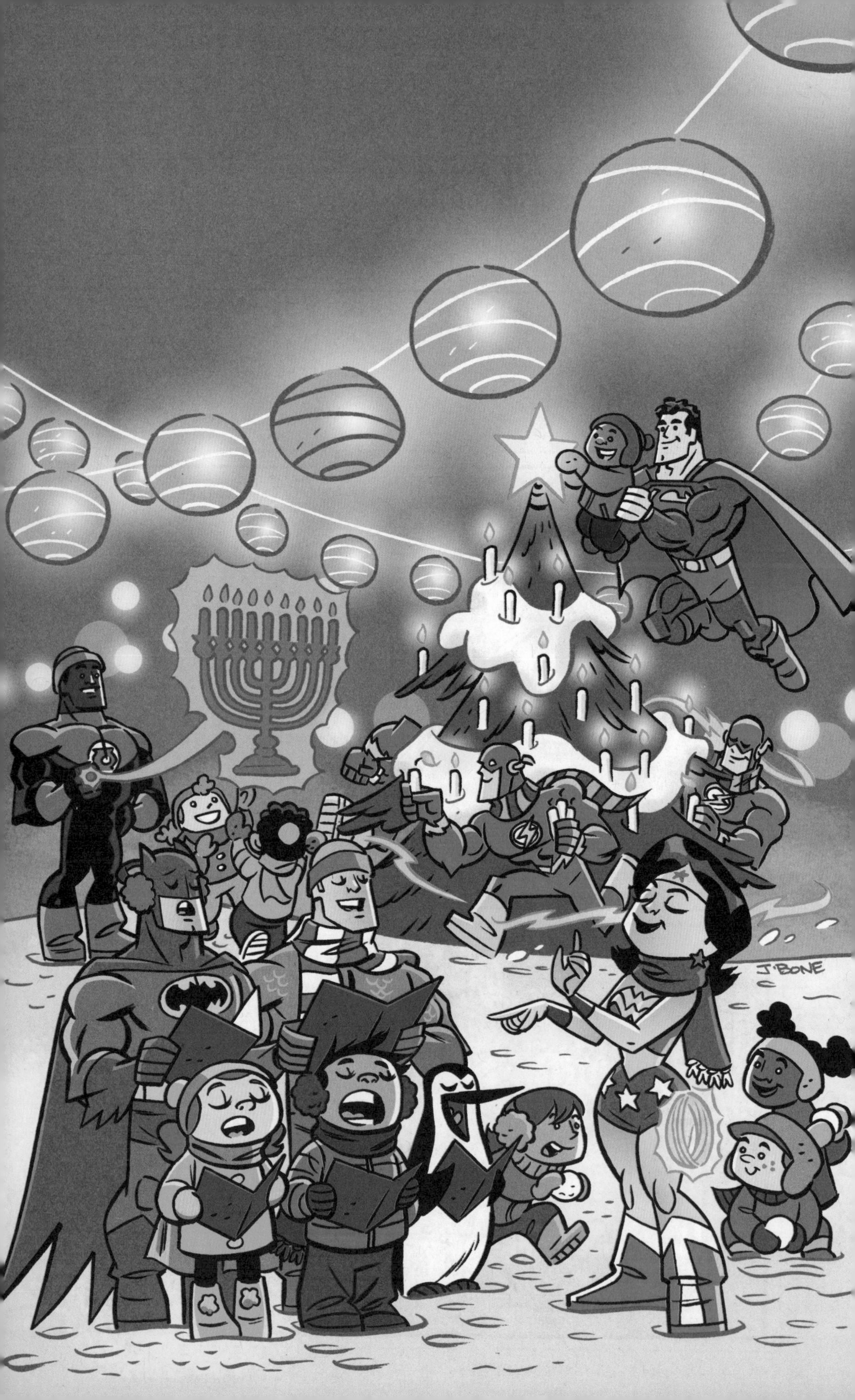
J.BONE

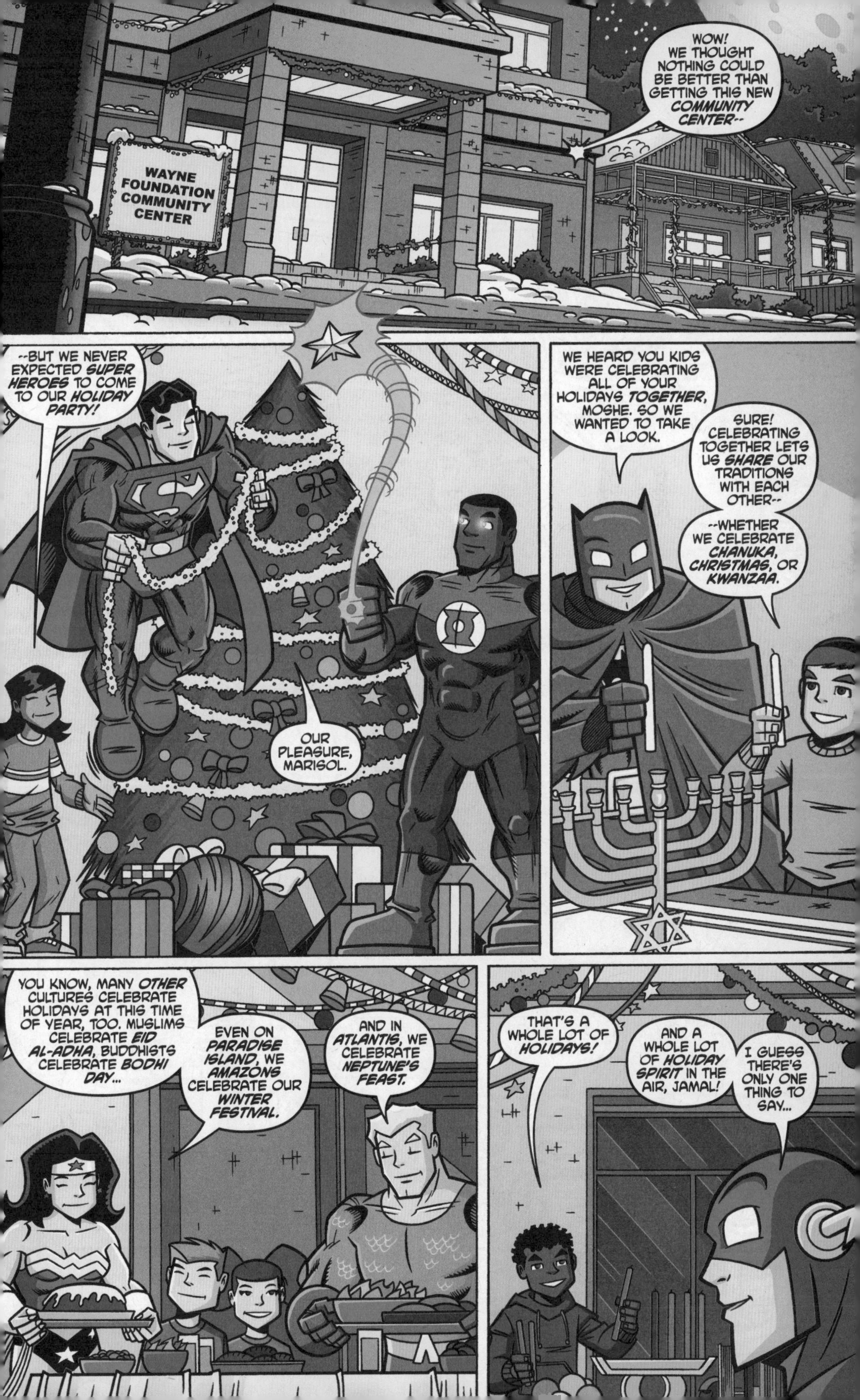
WOW! WE THOUGHT NOTHING COULD BE BETTER THAN GETTING THIS NEW COMMUNITY CENTER--
WAYNE FOUNDATION COMMUNITY CENTER
--BUT WE NEVER EXPECTED SUPER HEROES TO COME TO OUR HOLIDAY PARTY!
OUR PLEASURE, MARISOL.
WE HEARD YOU KIDS WERE CELEBRATING ALL OF YOUR HOLIDAYS TOGETHER, MOSHE. SO WE WANTED TO TAKE A LOOK.
SURE! CELEBRATING TOGETHER LETS US SHARE OUR TRADITIONS WITH EACH OTHER--
--WHETHER WE CELEBRATE CHANUKA, CHRISTMAS, OR KWANZAA.
YOU KNOW, MANY OTHER CULTURES CELEBRATE HOLIDAYS AT THIS TIME OF YEAR, TOO. MUSLIMS CELEBRATE EID AL-ADHA, BUDDHISTS CELEBRATE BODHI DAY...
EVEN ON PARADISE ISLAND, WE AMAZONS CELEBRATE OUR WINTER FESTIVAL.
AND IN ATLANTIS, WE CELEBRATE NEPTUNE'S FEAST.
THAT'S A WHOLE LOT OF HOLIDAYS!
AND A WHOLE LOT OF HOLIDAY SPIRIT IN THE AIR, JAMAL!
I GUESS THERE'S ONLY ONE THING TO SAY...

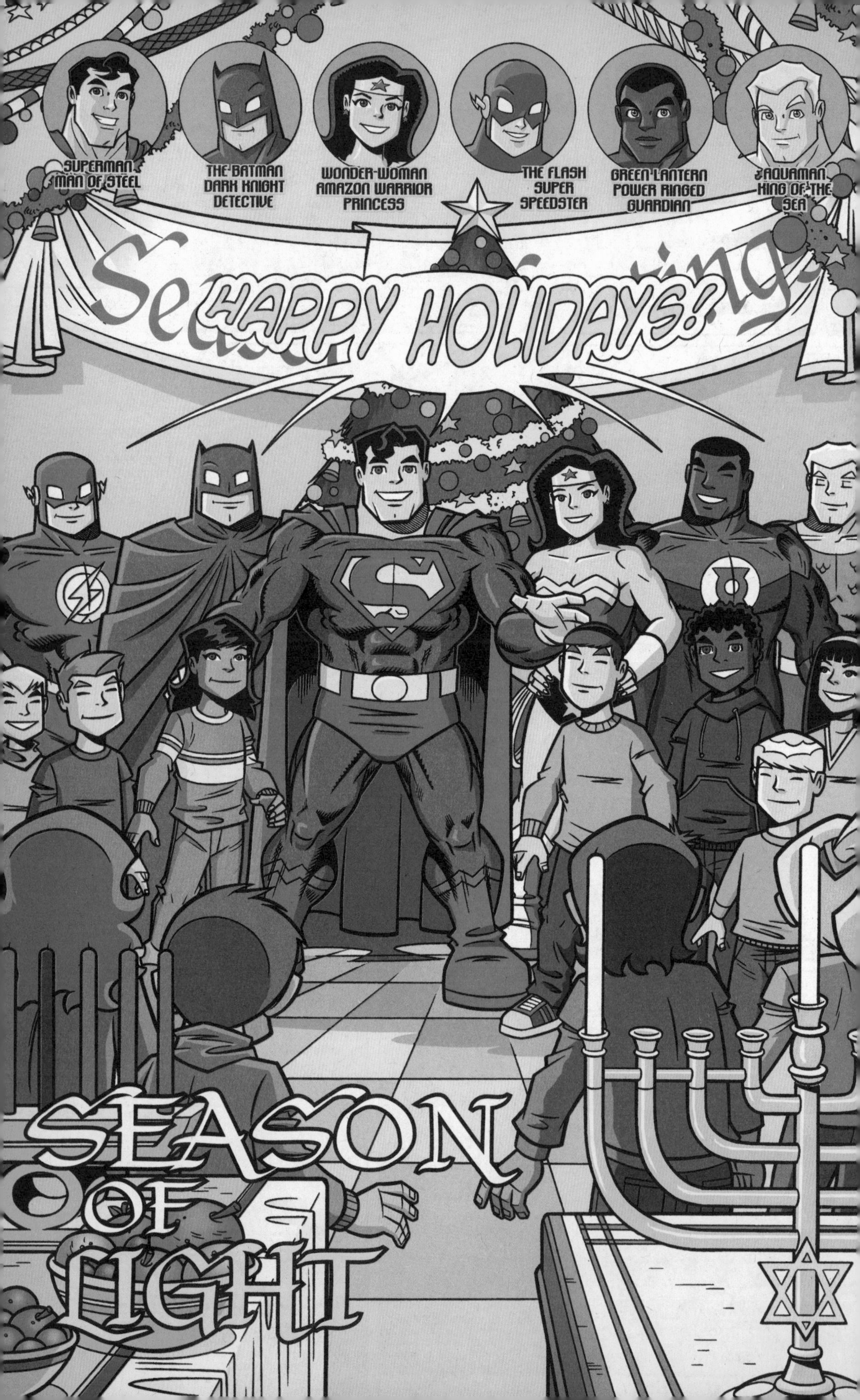
SUPERMAN MAN OF STEEL
THE BATMAN DARK KNIGHT DETECTIVE
WONDER WOMAN AMAZON WARRIOR PRINCESS
THE FLASH SUPER SPEEDSTER
GREEN LANTERN POWER RINGED GUARDIAN
AQUAMAN KING OF THE SEA
HAPPY HOLIDAYS!
SEASON OF LIGHT

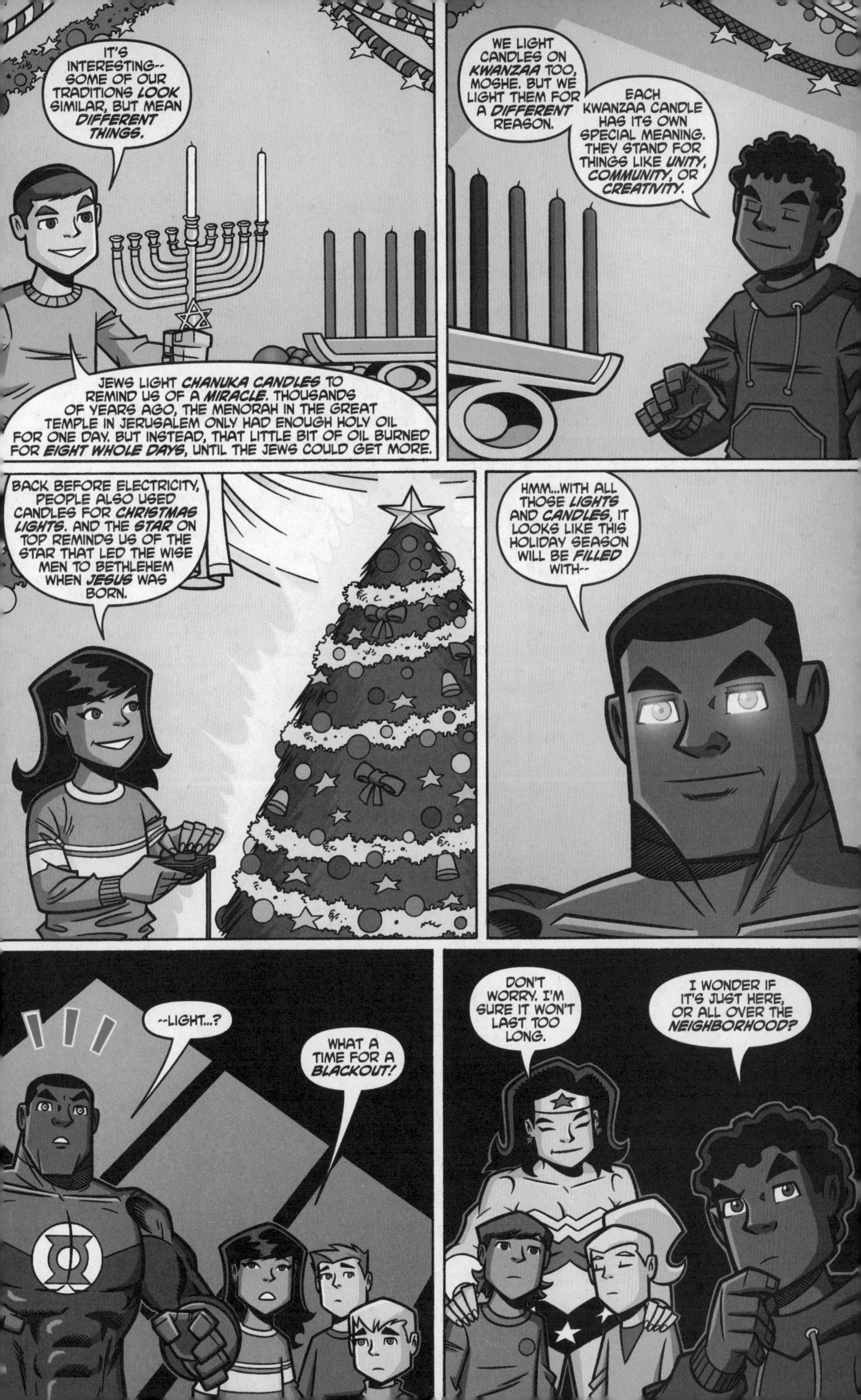
IT'S INTERESTING-- SOME OF OUR TRADITIONS LOOK SIMILAR, BUT MEAN DIFFERENT THINGS.
JEWS LIGHT CHANUKA CANDLES TO REMIND US OF A MIRACLE. THOUSANDS OF YEARS AGO, THE MENORAH IN THE GREAT TEMPLE IN JERUSALEM ONLY HAD ENOUGH HOLY OIL FOR ONE DAY. BUT INSTEAD, THAT LITTLE BIT OF OIL BURNED FOR EIGHT WHOLE DAYS, UNTIL THE JEWS COULD GET MORE.
WE LIGHT CANDLES ON KWANZAA TOO, MOSHE. BUT WE LIGHT THEM FOR A DIFFERENT REASON.
EACH KWANZAA CANDLE HAS ITS OWN SPECIAL MEANING. THEY STAND FOR THINGS LIKE UNITY, COMMUNITY, OR CREATIVITY.
BACK BEFORE ELECTRICITY, PEOPLE ALSO USED CANDLES FOR CHRISTMAS LIGHTS. AND THE STAR ON TOP REMINDS US OF THE STAR THAT LED THE WISE MEN TO BETHLEHEM WHEN JESUS WAS BORN.
HMM...WITH ALL THOSE LIGHTS AND CANDLES, IT LOOKS LIKE THIS HOLIDAY SEASON WILL BE FILLED WITH--
--LIGHT...?
WHAT A TIME FOR A BLACKOUT!
DON'T WORRY. I'M SURE IT WON'T LAST TOO LONG.
I WONDER IF IT'S JUST HERE, OR ALL OVER THE NEIGHBORHOOD?

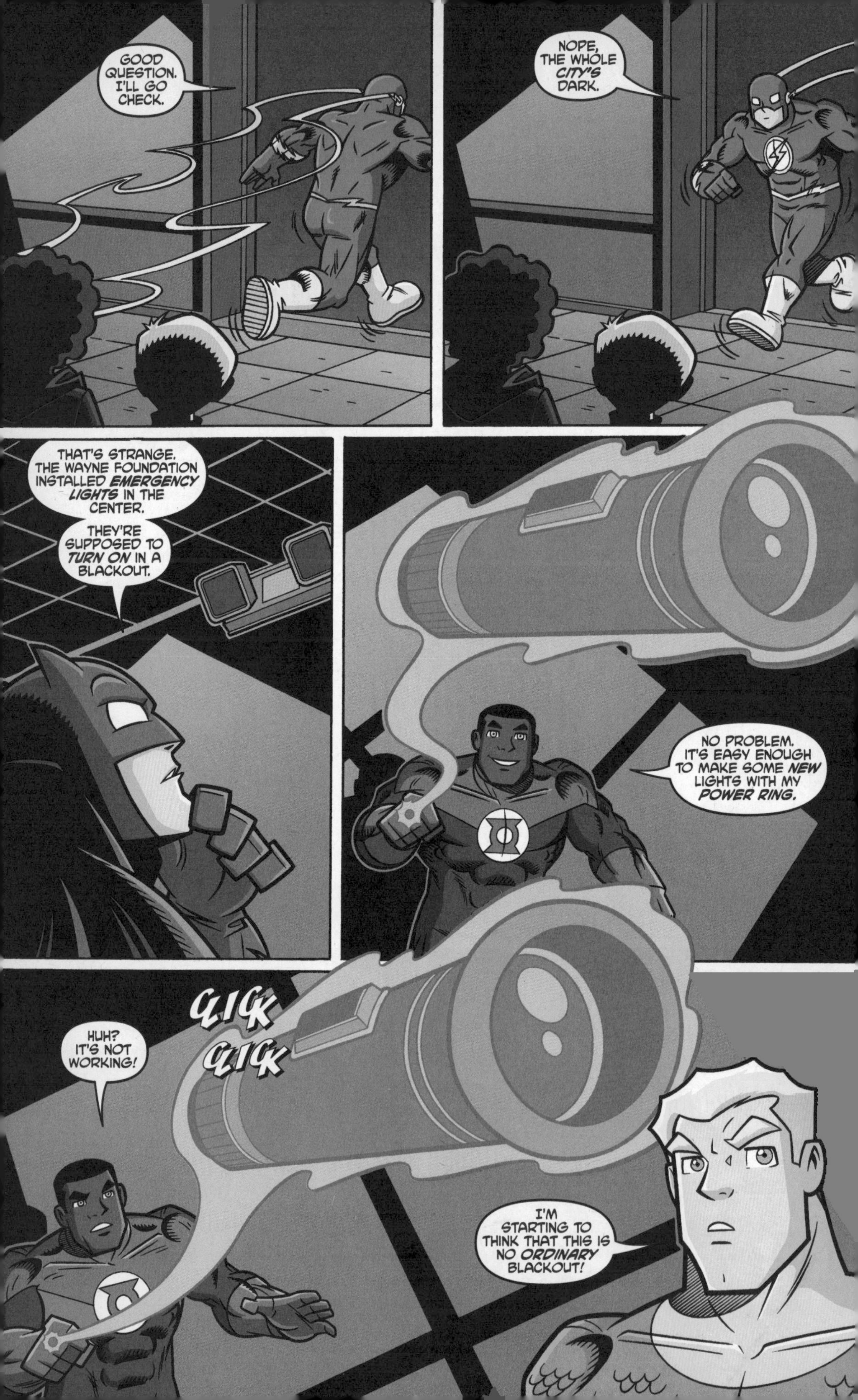

GOOD QUESTION. I'LL GO CHECK.
NOPE, THE WHOLE CITY'S DARK.
THAT'S STRANGE. THE WAYNE FOUNDATION INSTALLED EMERGENCY LIGHTS IN THE CENTER.
THEY'RE SUPPOSED TO TURN ON IN A BLACKOUT.
NO PROBLEM. IT'S EASY ENOUGH TO MAKE SOME NEW LIGHTS WITH MY POWER RING.
CLICK
CLICK
HUH? IT'S NOT WORKING!
I'M STARTING TO THINK THAT THIS IS NO ORDINARY BLACKOUT!

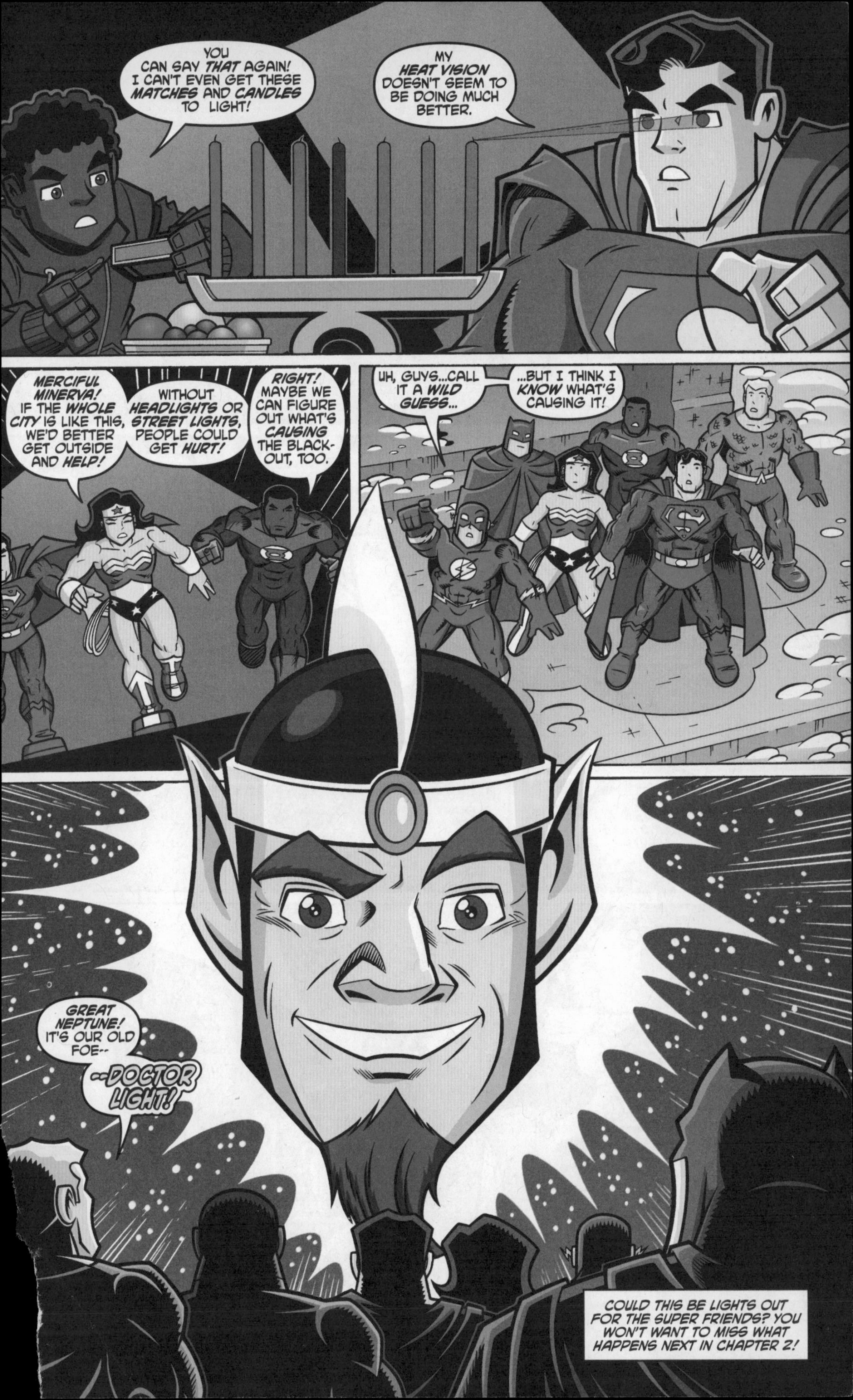
YOU CAN SAY THAT AGAIN! I CAN'T EVEN GET THESE MATCHES AND CANDLES TO LIGHT!
MY HEAT VISION DOESN'T SEEM TO BE DOING MUCH BETTER.
MERCIFUL MINERVA! IF THE WHOLE CITY IS LIKE THIS, WE'D BETTER GET OUTSIDE AND HELP!
WITHOUT HEADLIGHTS OR STREET LIGHTS, PEOPLE COULD GET HURT!
RIGHT! MAYBE WE CAN FIGURE OUT WHAT'S CAUSING THE BLACK-OUT, TOO.
UH, GUYS...CALL IT A WILD GUESS...
...BUT I THINK I KNOW WHAT'S CAUSING IT!
GREAT NEPTUNE! IT'S OUR OLD FOE--
--DOCTOR LIGHT!
COULD THIS BE LIGHTS OUT FOR THE SUPER FRIENDS? YOU WON'T WANT TO MISS WHAT HAPPENS NEXT IN CHAPTER 2!

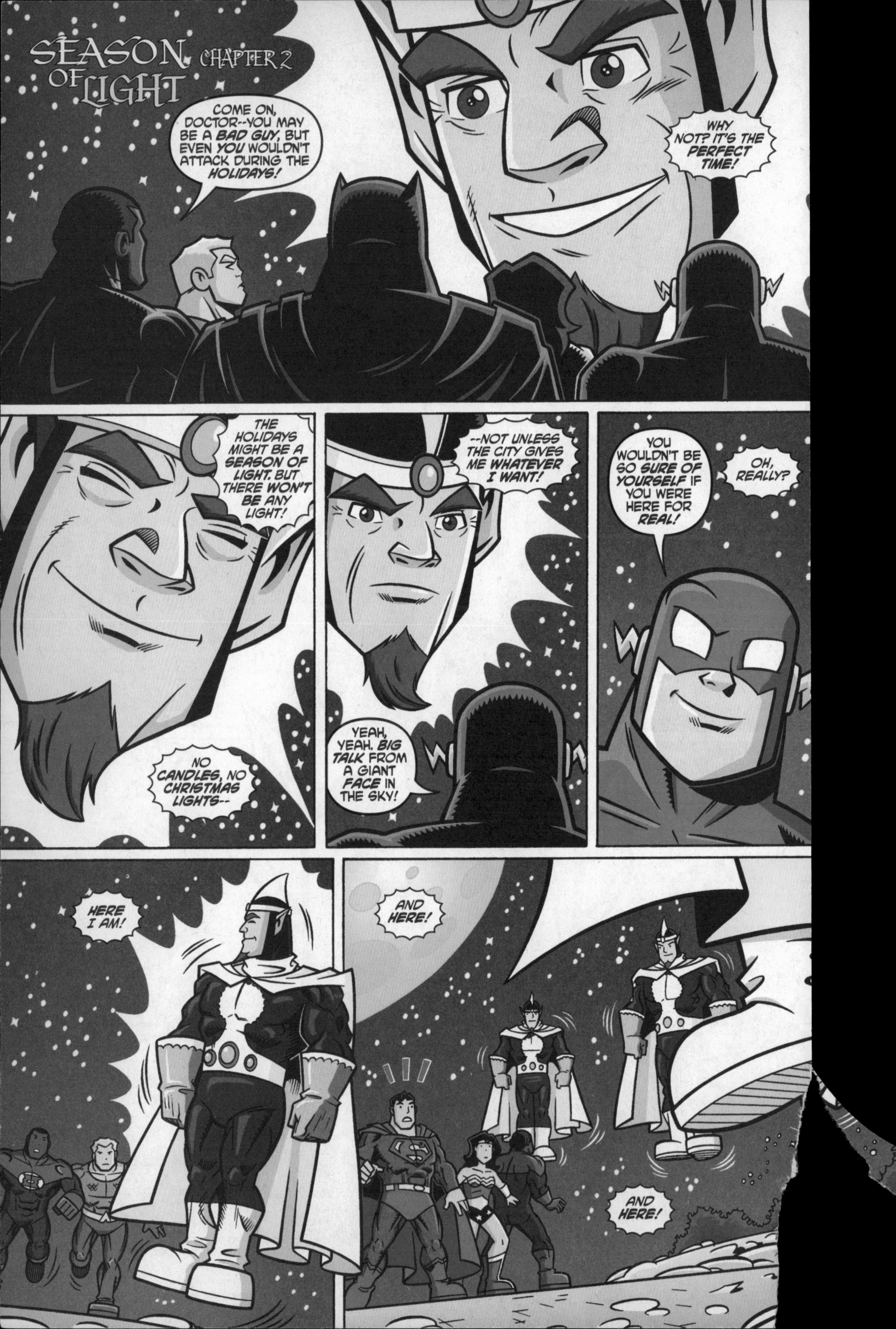
SEASON OF LIGHT CHAPTER 2
COME ON, DOCTOR--YOU MAY BE A BAD GUY, BUT EVEN YOU WOULDN'T ATTACK DURING THE HOLIDAYS!
WHY NOT? IT'S THE PERFECT TIME!
THE HOLIDAYS MIGHT BE A SEASON OF LIGHT. BUT THERE WON'T BE ANY LIGHT!
NO CANDLES, NO CHRISTMAS LIGHTS--
--NOT UNLESS THE CITY GIVES ME WHATEVER I WANT!
YEAH, YEAH. BIG TALK FROM A GIANT FACE IN THE SKY!
YOU WOULDN'T BE SO SURE OF YOURSELF IF YOU WERE HERE FOR REAL!
OH, REALLY?
HERE I AM!
AND HERE!
AND HERE!

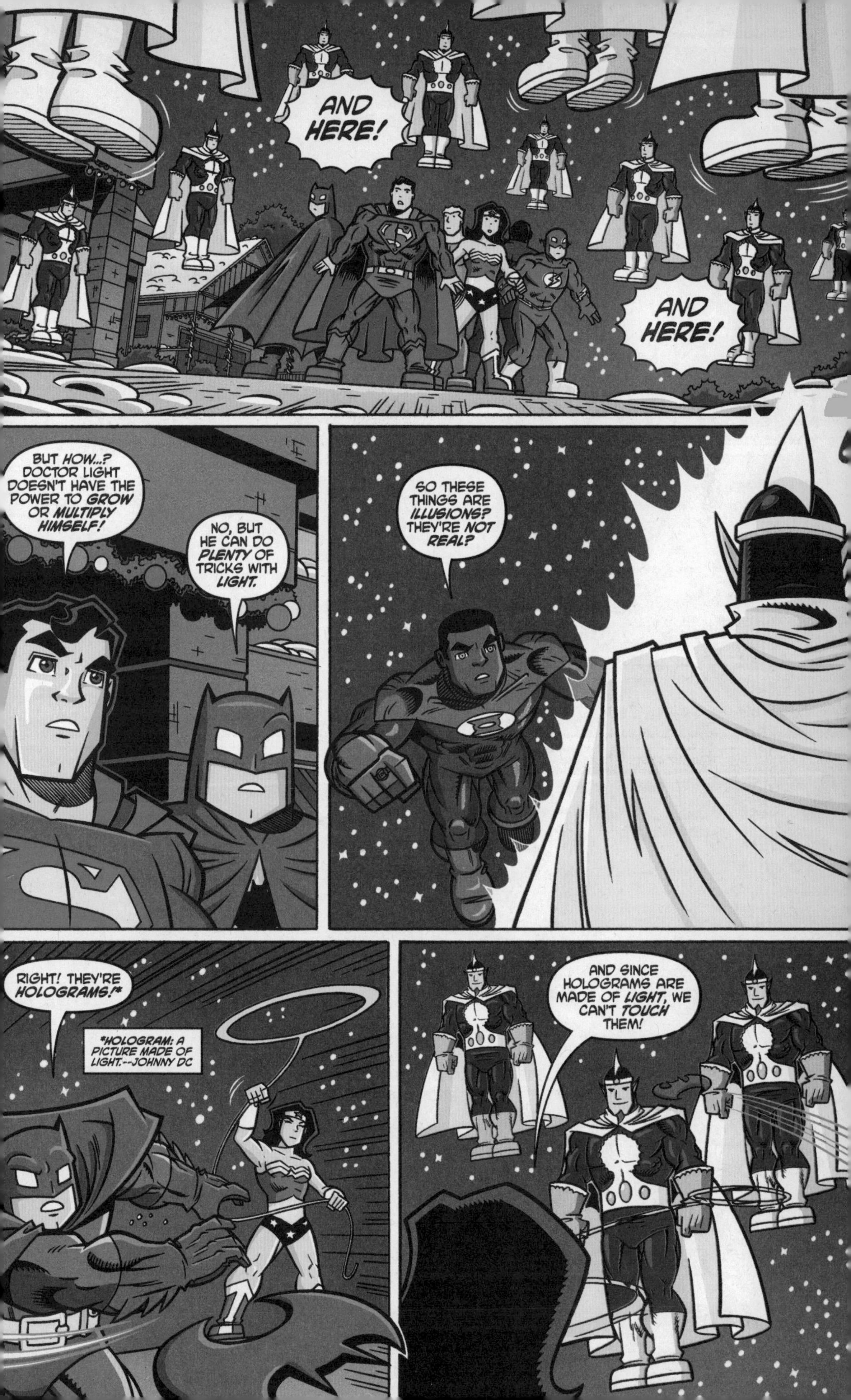
AND HERE!
AND HERE!
BUT HOW...? DOCTOR LIGHT DOESN'T HAVE THE POWER TO GROW OR MULTIPLY HIMSELF!
NO, BUT HE CAN DO PLENTY OF TRICKS WITH LIGHT.
SO THESE THINGS ARE ILLUSIONS? THEY'RE NOT REAL?
RIGHT! THEY'RE HOLOGRAMS!*
*HOLOGRAM: A PICTURE MADE OF LIGHT.--JOHNNY DC
AND SINCE HOLOGRAMS ARE MADE OF LIGHT, WE CAN'T TOUCH THEM!

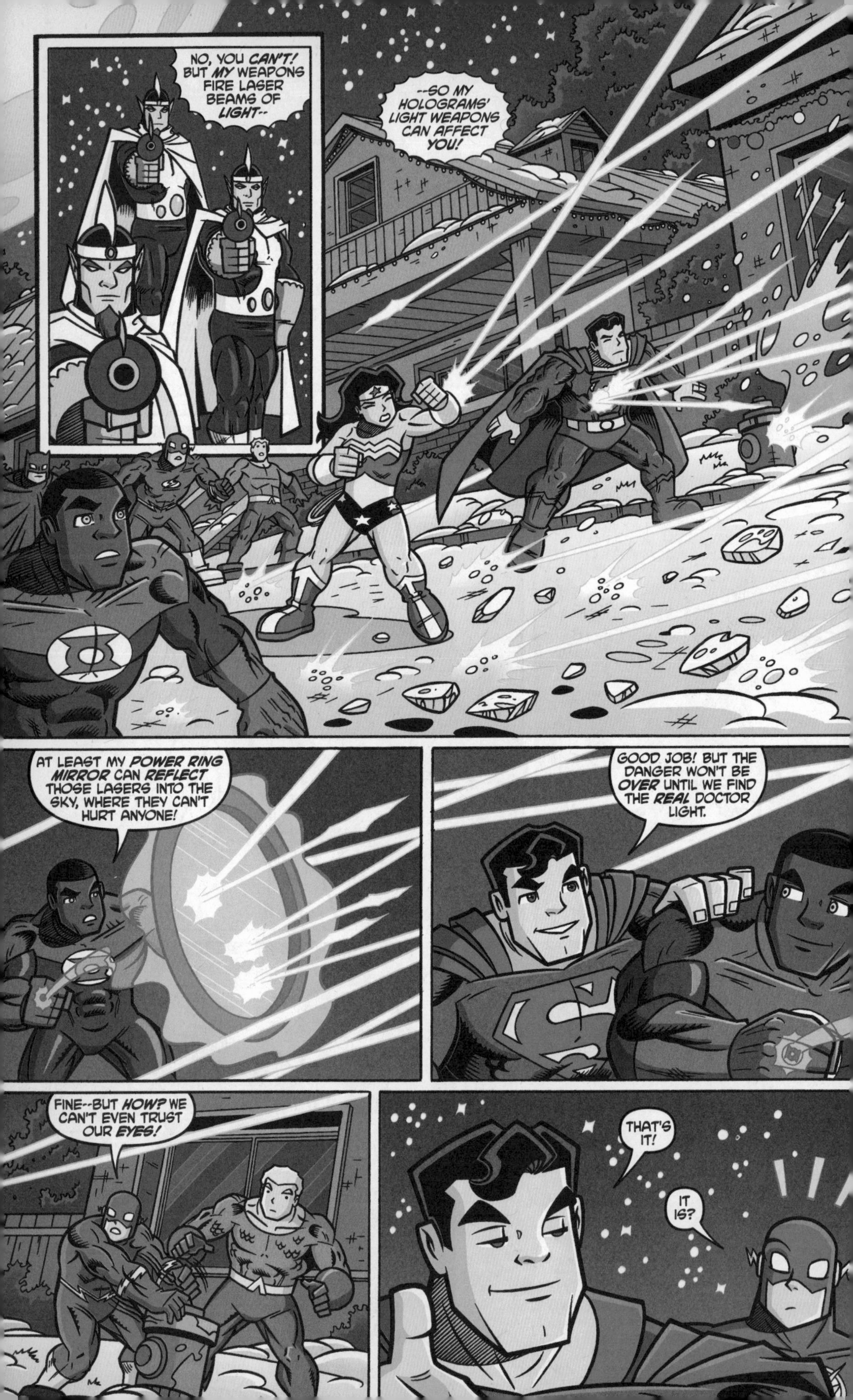
NO, YOU CAN'T! BUT MY WEAPONS FIRE LASER BEAMS OF LIGHT--
--SO MY HOLOGRAMS' LIGHT WEAPONS CAN AFFECT YOU!
AT LEAST MY POWER RING MIRROR CAN REFLECT THOSE LASERS INTO THE SKY, WHERE THEY CAN'T HURT ANYONE!
GOOD JOB! BUT THE DANGER WON'T BE OVER UNTIL WE FIND THE REAL DOCTOR LIGHT.
FINE--BUT HOW? WE CAN'T EVEN TRUST OUR EYES!
THAT'S IT!
IT IS?

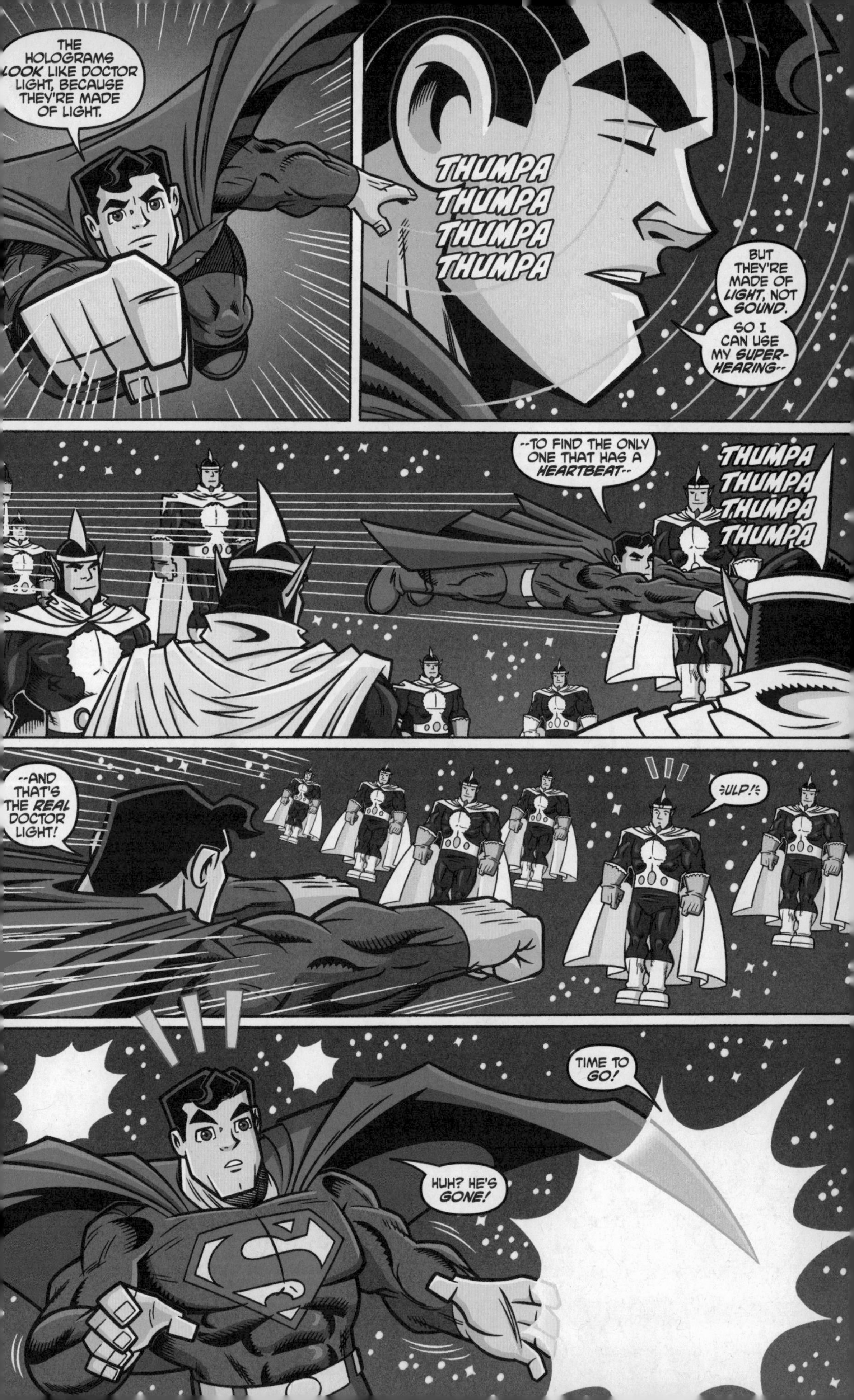
THE HOLOGRAMS LOOK LIKE DOCTOR LIGHT, BECAUSE THEY'RE MADE OF LIGHT.
THUMPA THUMPA THUMPA THUMPA
BUT THEY'RE MADE OF LIGHT, NOT SOUND.
SO I CAN USE MY SUPER-HEARING--
--TO FIND THE ONLY ONE THAT HAS A HEARTBEAT--
THUMPA THUMPA THUMPA THUMPA
--AND THAT'S THE REAL DOCTOR LIGHT!
ULP!
TIME TO GO!
HUH? HE'S GONE!

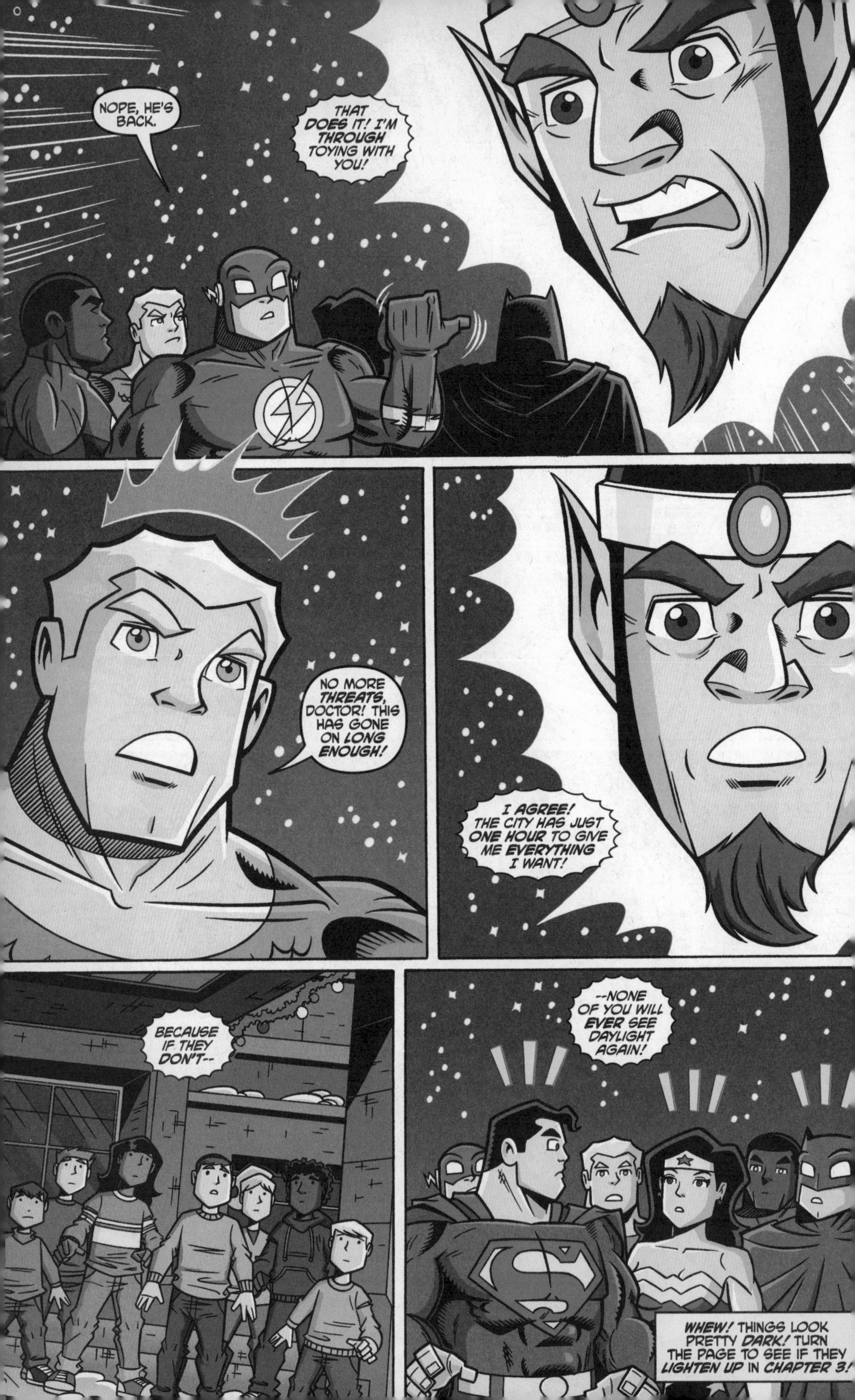
NOPE, HE'S BACK.
THAT DOES IT! I'M THROUGH TOYING WITH YOU!
NO MORE THREATS, DOCTOR! THIS HAS GONE ON LONG ENOUGH!
I AGREE! THE CITY HAS JUST ONE HOUR TO GIVE ME EVERYTHING I WANT!
BECAUSE IF THEY DON'T--
--NONE OF YOU WILL EVER SEE DAYLIGHT AGAIN!
WHEW! THINGS LOOK PRETTY DARK! TURN THE PAGE TO SEE IF THEY LIGHTEN UP IN CHAPTER 3!

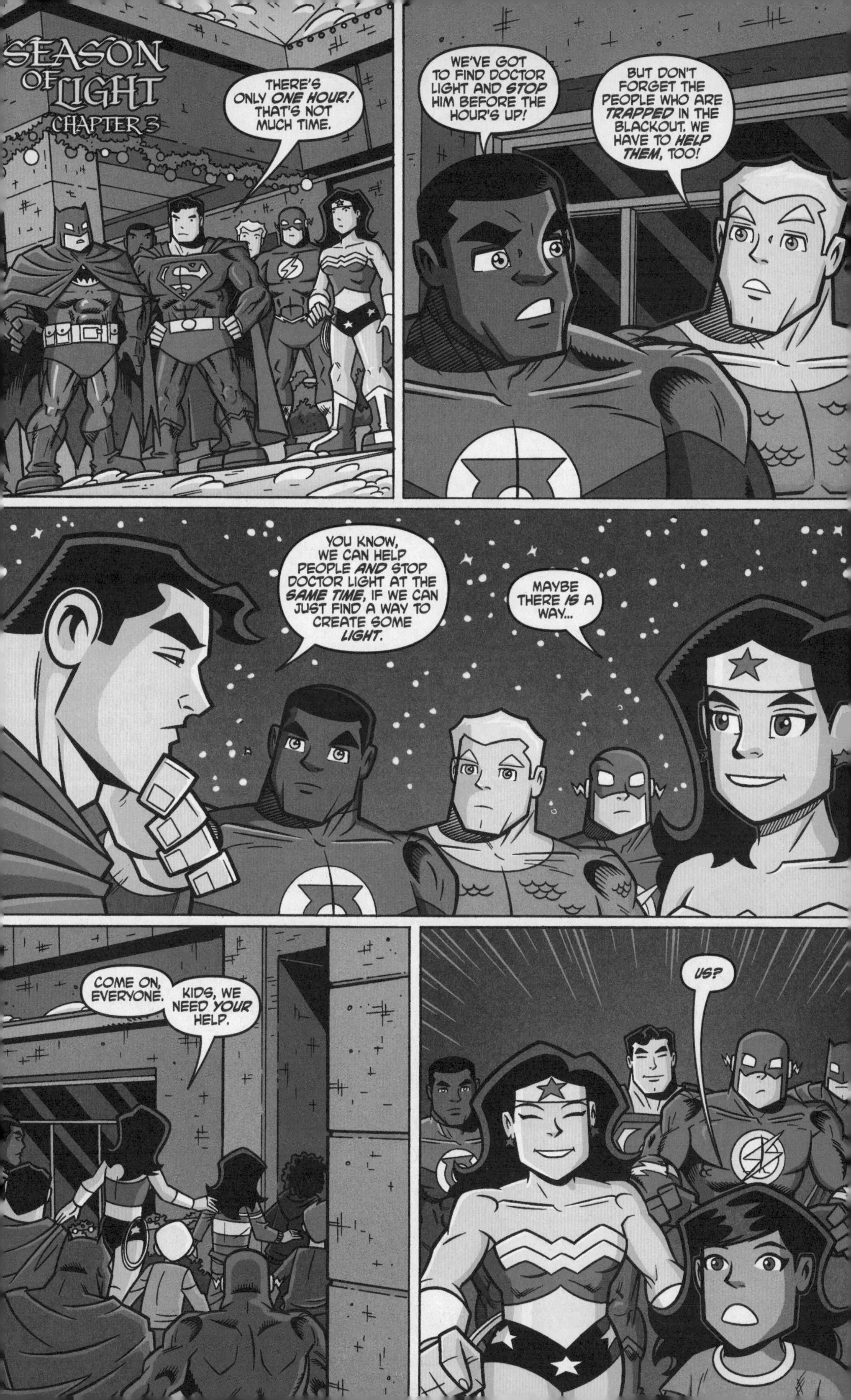
SEASON OF LIGHT
CHAPTER 3
THERE'S ONLY ONE HOUR! THAT'S NOT MUCH TIME.
WE'VE GOT TO FIND DOCTOR LIGHT AND STOP HIM BEFORE THE HOUR'S UP!
BUT DON'T FORGET THE PEOPLE WHO ARE TRAPPED IN THE BLACKOUT. WE HAVE TO HELP THEM, TOO!
YOU KNOW, WE CAN HELP PEOPLE AND STOP DOCTOR LIGHT AT THE SAME TIME, IF WE CAN JUST FIND A WAY TO CREATE SOME LIGHT.
MAYBE THERE IS A WAY...
COME ON, EVERYONE.
KIDS, WE NEED YOUR HELP.
US?

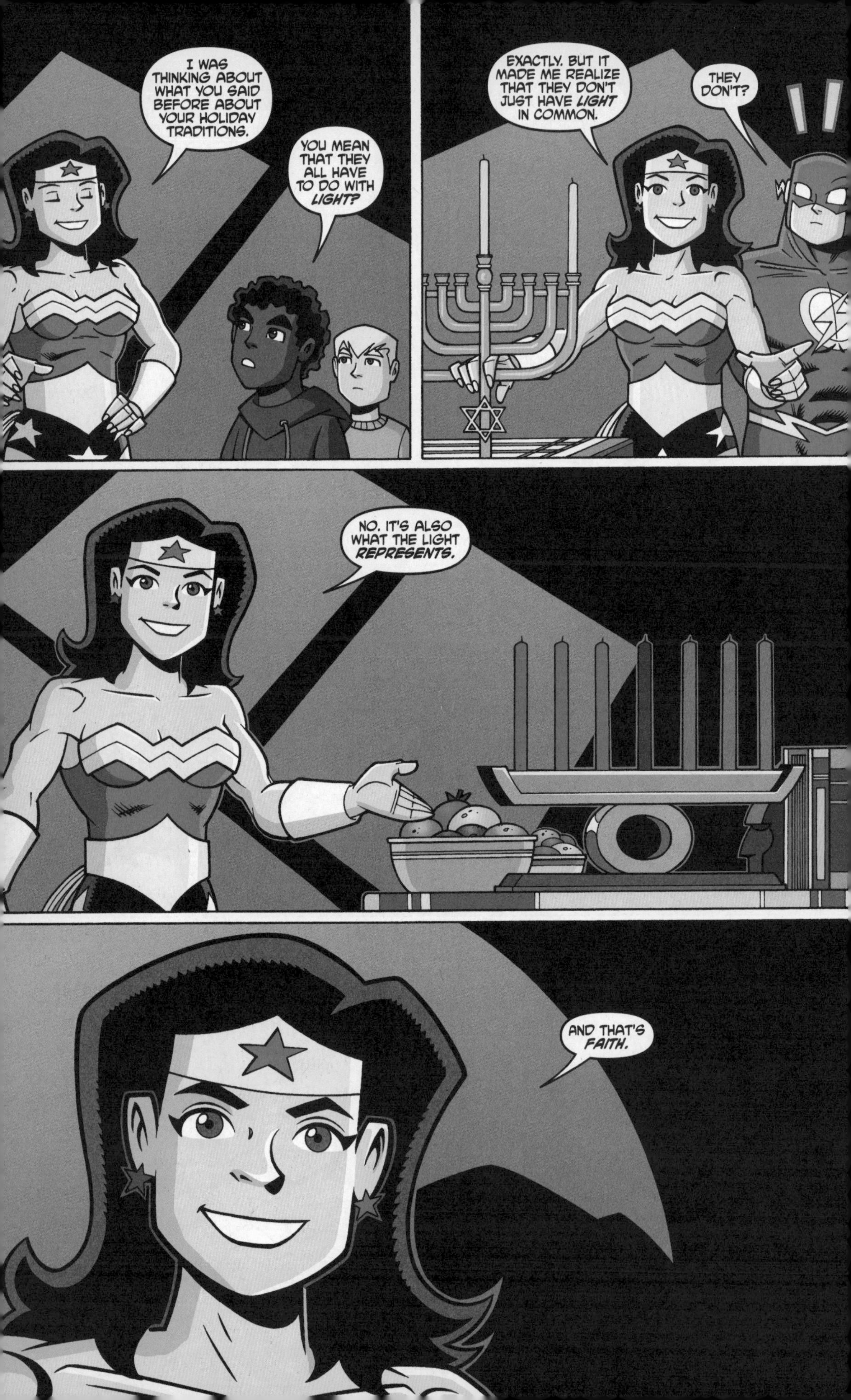
I WAS THINKING ABOUT WHAT YOU SAID BEFORE ABOUT YOUR HOLIDAY TRADITIONS.
YOU MEAN THAT THEY ALL HAVE TO DO WITH *LIGHT?*
EXACTLY. BUT IT MADE ME REALIZE THAT THEY DON'T JUST HAVE *LIGHT* IN COMMON.
THEY DON'T?
NO. IT'S ALSO WHAT THE LIGHT *REPRESENTS.*
AND THAT'S *FAITH.*

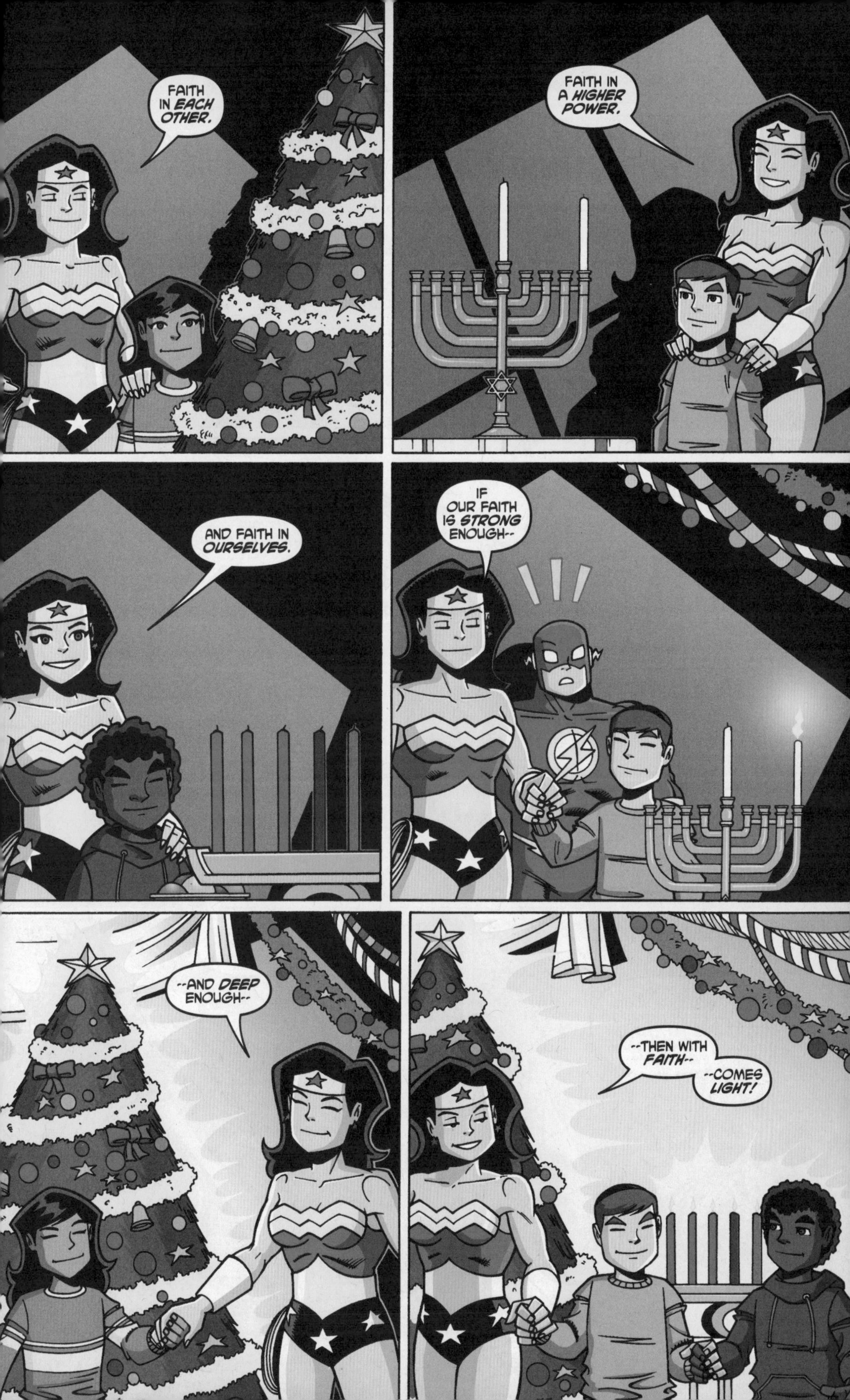
FAITH IN EACH OTHER.
FAITH IN A HIGHER POWER.
AND FAITH IN OURSELVES.
IF OUR FAITH IS STRONG ENOUGH--
--AND DEEP ENOUGH--
--THEN WITH FAITH--
--COMES LIGHT!

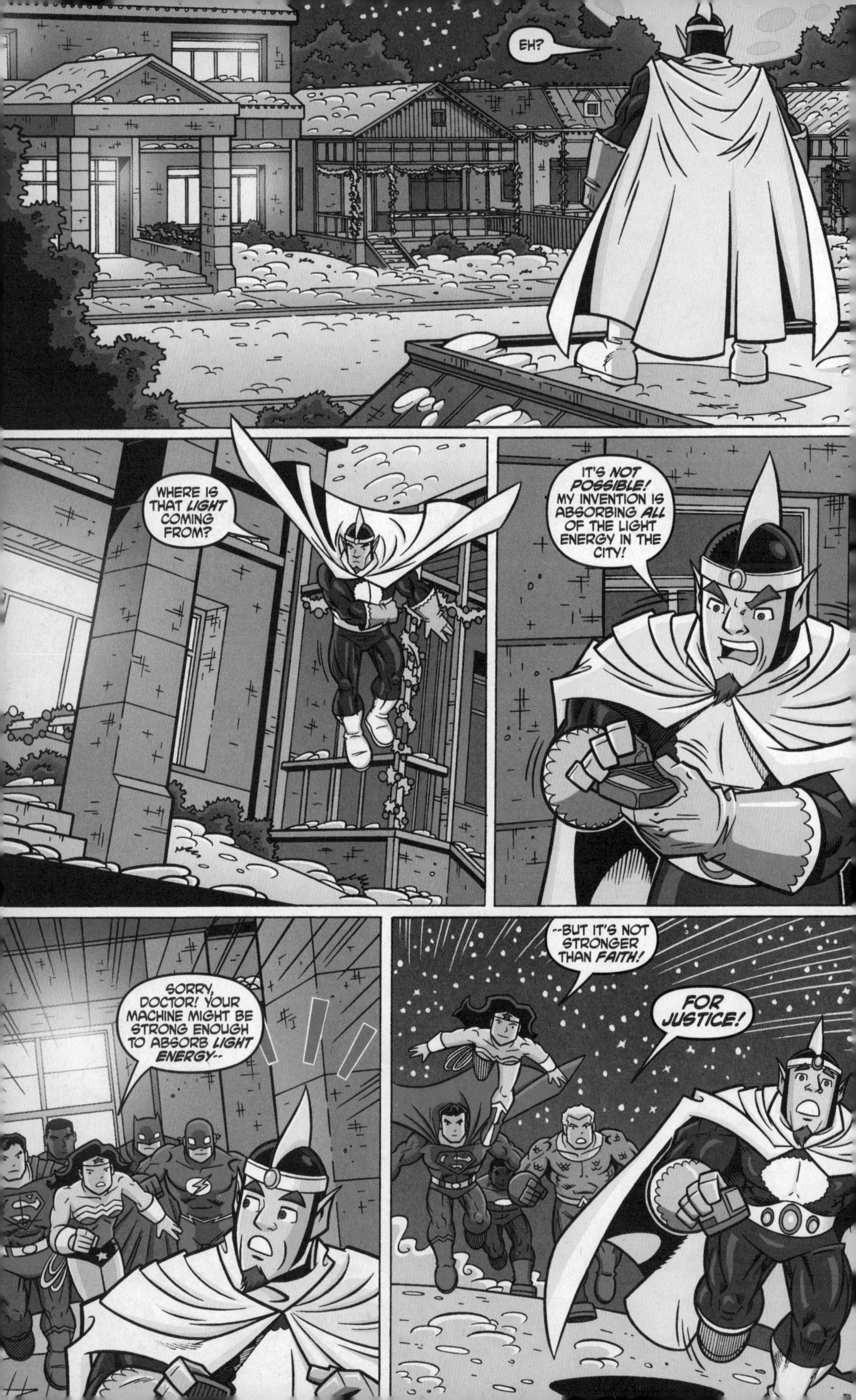
EH?
WHERE IS THAT LIGHT COMING FROM?
IT'S NOT POSSIBLE! MY INVENTION IS ABSORBING ALL OF THE LIGHT ENERGY IN THE CITY!
SORRY, DOCTOR! YOUR MACHINE MIGHT BE STRONG ENOUGH TO ABSORB LIGHT ENERGY--
--BUT IT'S NOT STRONGER THAN FAITH!
FOR JUSTICE!

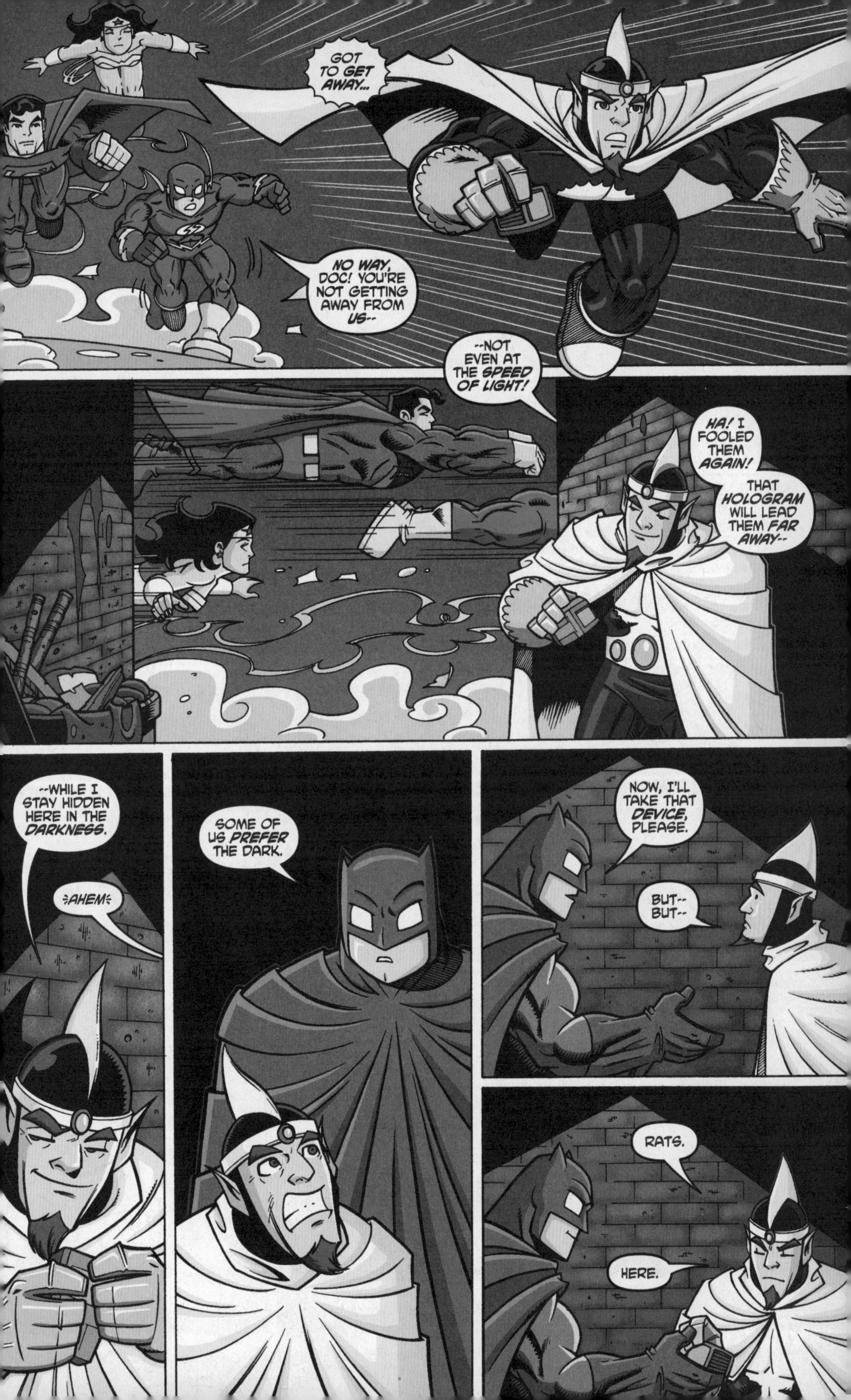
GOT TO GET AWAY...
NO WAY, DOC! YOU'RE NOT GETTING AWAY FROM US--
--NOT EVEN AT THE SPEED OF LIGHT!
HA! I FOOLED THEM AGAIN!
THAT HOLOGRAM WILL LEAD THEM FAR AWAY--
--WHILE I STAY HIDDEN HERE IN THE DARKNESS.
AHEM
SOME OF US PREFER THE DARK.
NOW, I'LL TAKE THAT DEVICE, PLEASE.
BUT-- BUT--
RATS.
HERE.

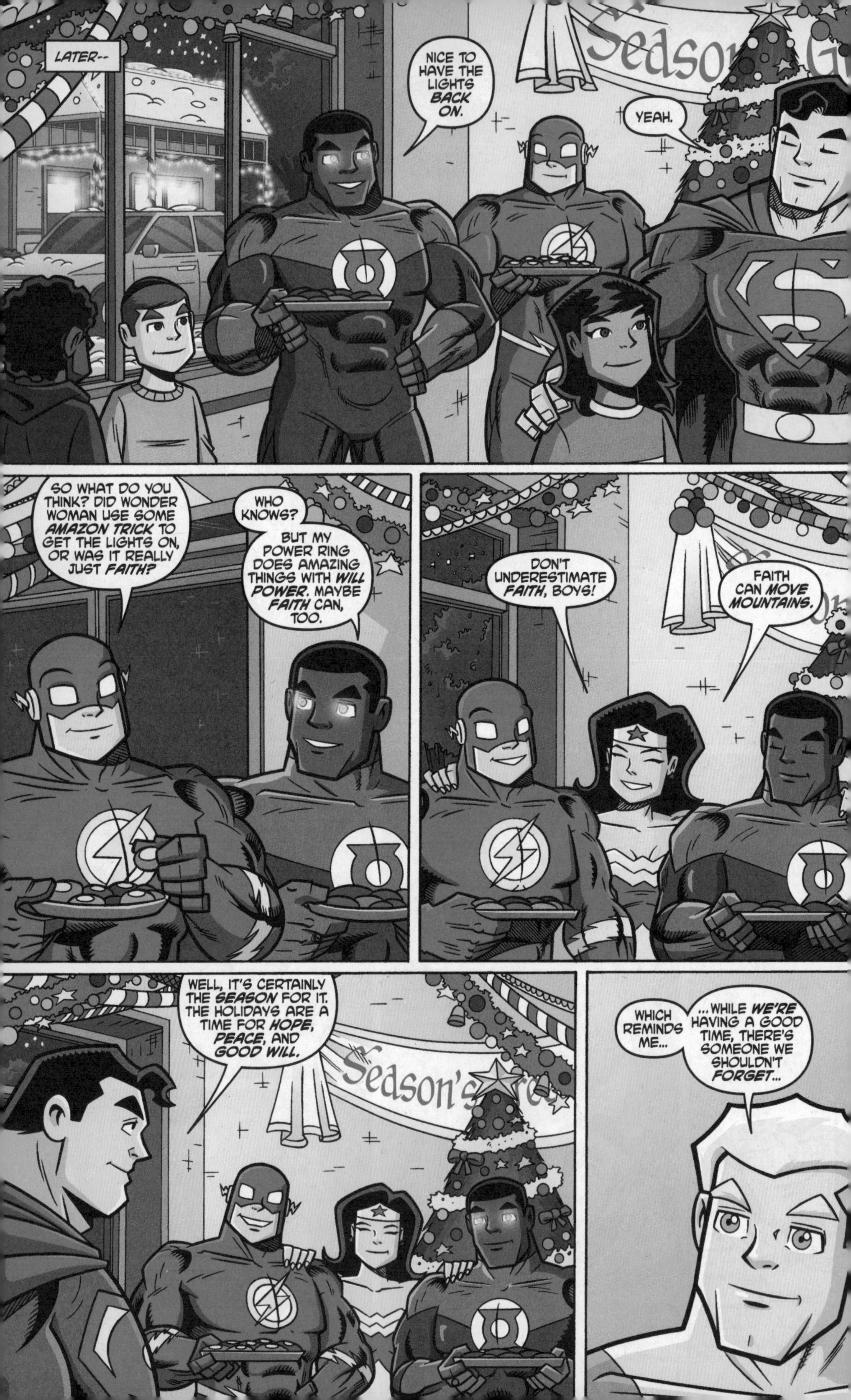
LATER--
NICE TO HAVE THE LIGHTS BACK ON.
YEAH.
SO WHAT DO YOU THINK? DID WONDER WOMAN USE SOME AMAZON TRICK TO GET THE LIGHTS ON, OR WAS IT REALLY JUST FAITH?
WHO KNOWS?
BUT MY POWER RING DOES AMAZING THINGS WITH WILL POWER. MAYBE FAITH CAN, TOO.
DON'T UNDERESTIMATE FAITH, BOYS!
FAITH CAN MOVE MOUNTAINS.
WELL, IT'S CERTAINLY THE SEASON FOR IT. THE HOLIDAYS ARE A TIME FOR HOPE, PEACE, AND GOOD WILL.
WHICH REMINDS ME...
...WHILE WE'RE HAVING A GOOD TIME, THERE'S SOMEONE WE SHOULDN'T FORGET...

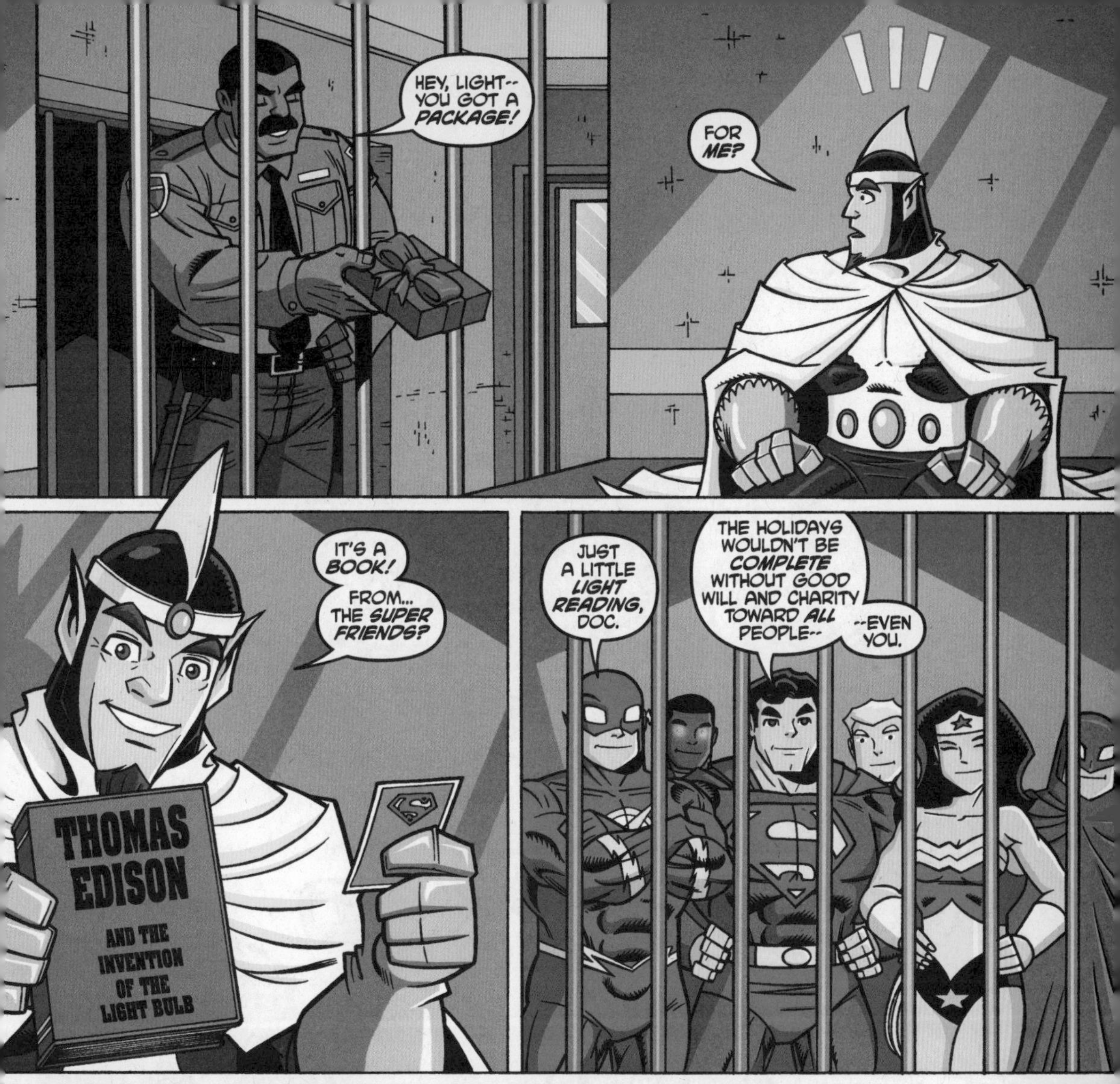
HEY, LIGHT-- YOU GOT A PACKAGE!
FOR ME?
IT'S A BOOK! FROM... THE SUPER FRIENDS?
THOMAS EDISON AND THE INVENTION OF THE LIGHT BULB
JUST A LITTLE LIGHT READING, DOC.
THE HOLIDAYS WOULDN'T BE COMPLETE WITHOUT GOOD WILL AND CHARITY TOWARD ALL PEOPLE--
--EVEN YOU.

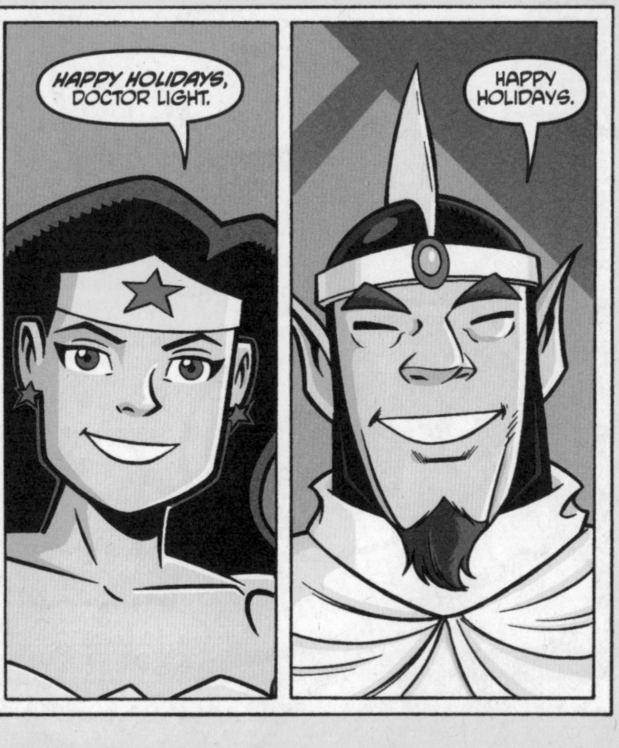
HAPPY HOLIDAYS, DOCTOR LIGHT.
HAPPY HOLIDAYS.

CALLING ALL SUPER FRIENDS!

HERE'S ANOTHER SECRET MESSAGE:

XOLI DBXIN: QOI YOKRW CBY DSPMNSOC KXR CEX GSIN HKI-DSIO!

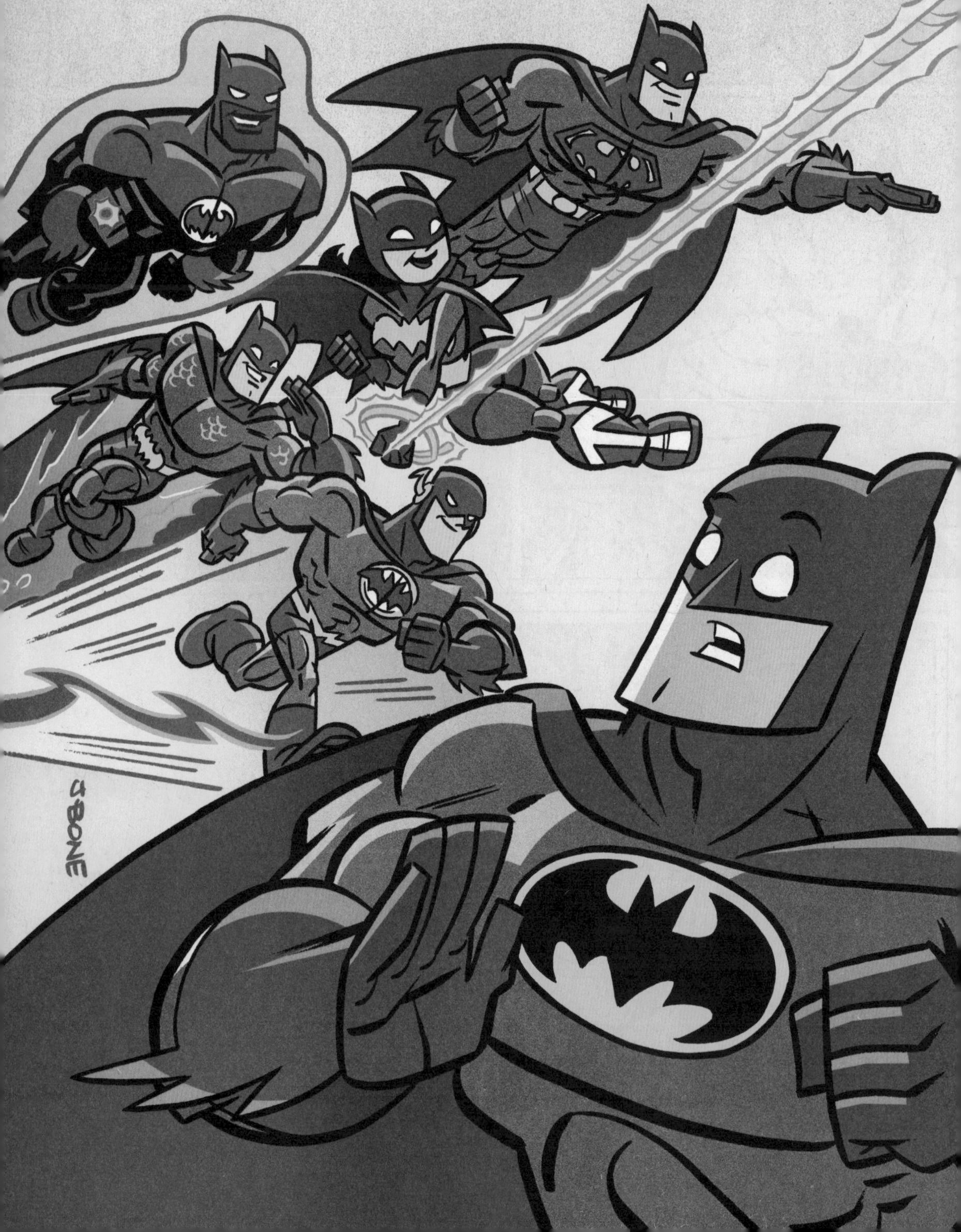

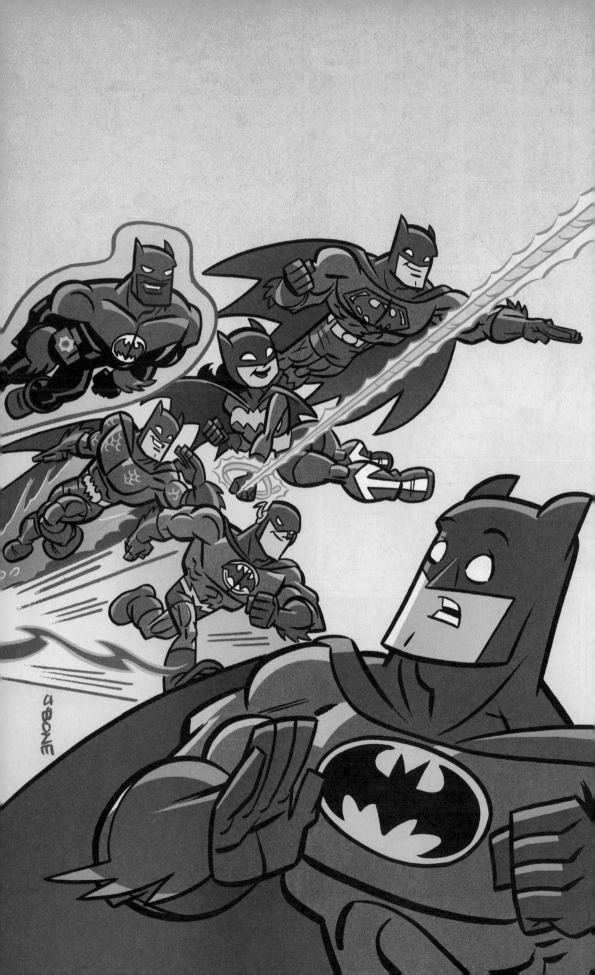

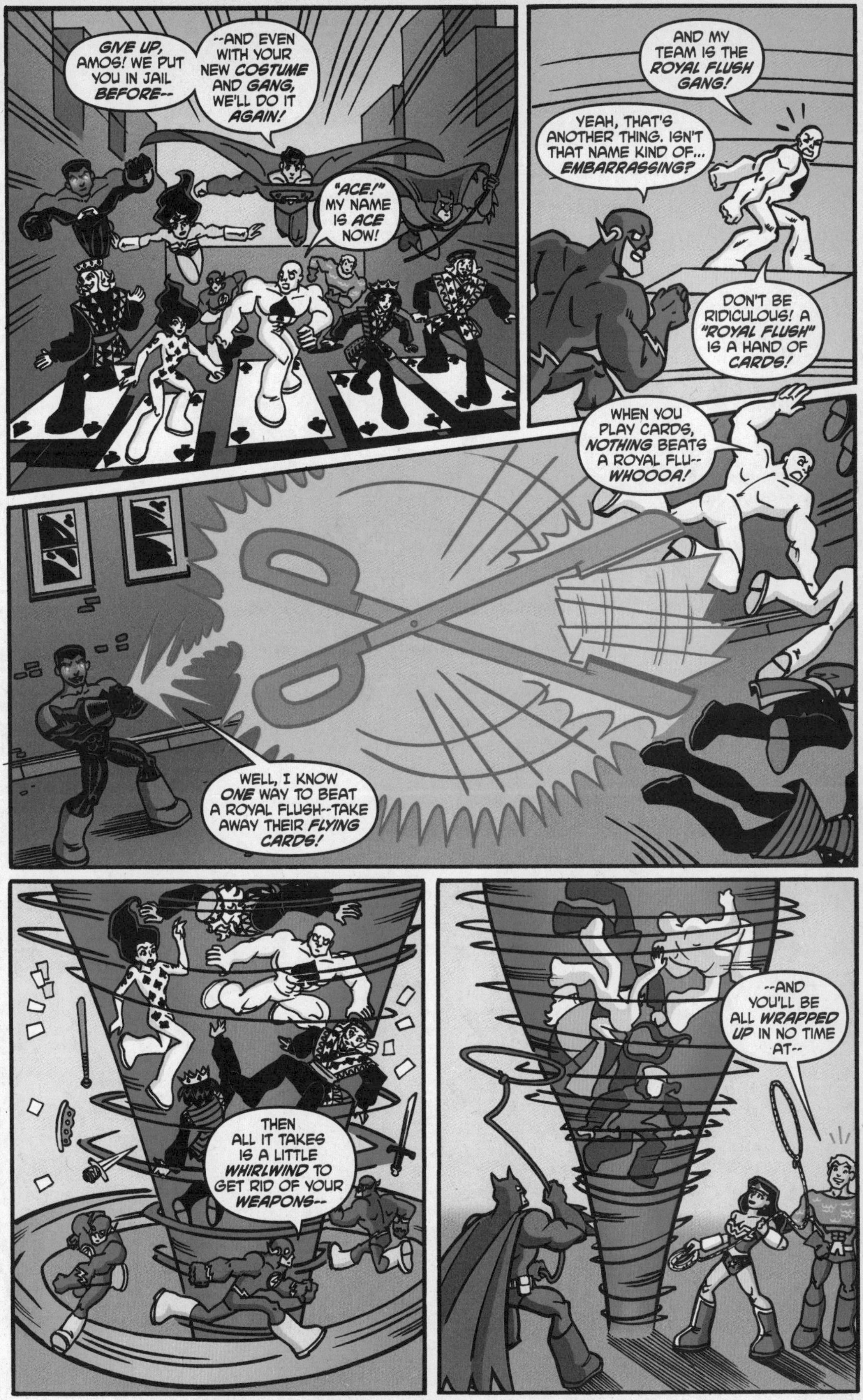
GIVE UP, AMOS! WE PUT YOU IN JAIL BEFORE--
--AND EVEN WITH YOUR NEW COSTUME AND GANG, WE'LL DO IT AGAIN!
"ACE!" MY NAME IS ACE NOW!
AND MY TEAM IS THE ROYAL FLUSH GANG!
YEAH, THAT'S ANOTHER THING. ISN'T THAT NAME KIND OF... EMBARRASSING?
DON'T BE RIDICULOUS! A "ROYAL FLUSH" IS A HAND OF CARDS!
WHEN YOU PLAY CARDS, NOTHING BEATS A ROYAL FLU-- WHOOOA!
WELL, I KNOW ONE WAY TO BEAT A ROYAL FLUSH--TAKE AWAY THEIR FLYING CARDS!
THEN ALL IT TAKES IS A LITTLE WHIRLWIND TO GET RID OF YOUR WEAPONS--
--AND YOU'LL BE ALL WRAPPED UP IN NO TIME AT--

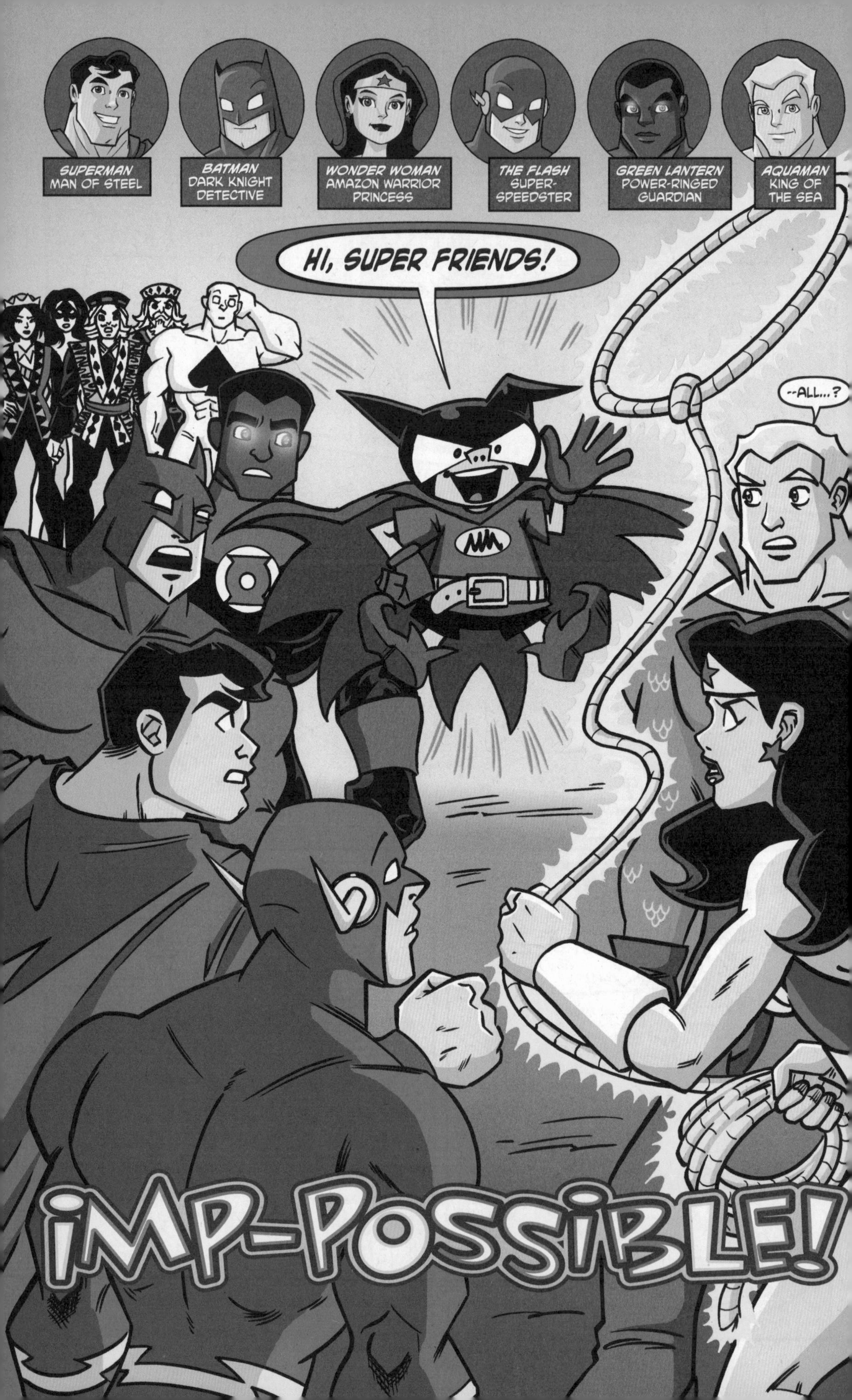
SUPERMAN
MAN OF STEEL
BATMAN
DARK KNIGHT DETECTIVE
WONDER WOMAN
AMAZON WARRIOR PRINCESS
THE FLASH
SUPER-SPEEDSTER
GREEN LANTERN
POWER-RINGED GUARDIAN
AQUAMAN
KING OF THE SEA
HI, SUPER FRIENDS!
--ALL...?
IMP-POSSIBLE!

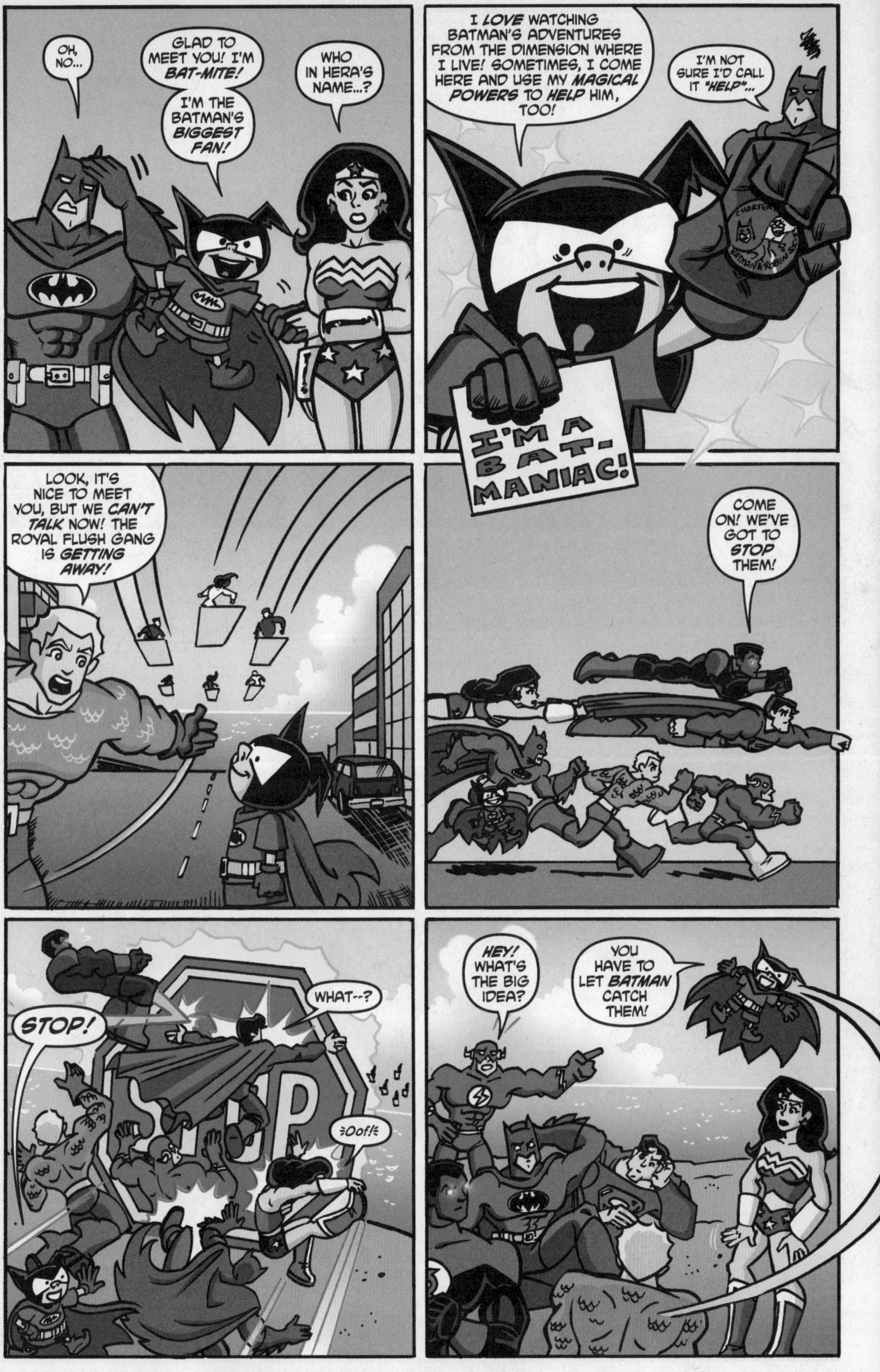
OH, NO...
GLAD TO MEET YOU! I'M BAT-MITE!
I'M THE BATMAN'S BIGGEST FAN!
WHO IN HERA'S NAME...?
I LOVE WATCHING BATMAN'S ADVENTURES FROM THE DIMENSION WHERE I LIVE! SOMETIMES, I COME HERE AND USE MY MAGICAL POWERS TO HELP HIM, TOO!
I'M NOT SURE I'D CALL IT "HELP"...
I'M A BAT-MANIAC!
LOOK, IT'S NICE TO MEET YOU, BUT WE CAN'T TALK NOW! THE ROYAL FLUSH GANG IS GETTING AWAY!
COME ON! WE'VE GOT TO STOP THEM!
STOP!
WHAT--?
OOF!
HEY! WHAT'S THE BIG IDEA?
YOU HAVE TO LET BATMAN CATCH THEM!

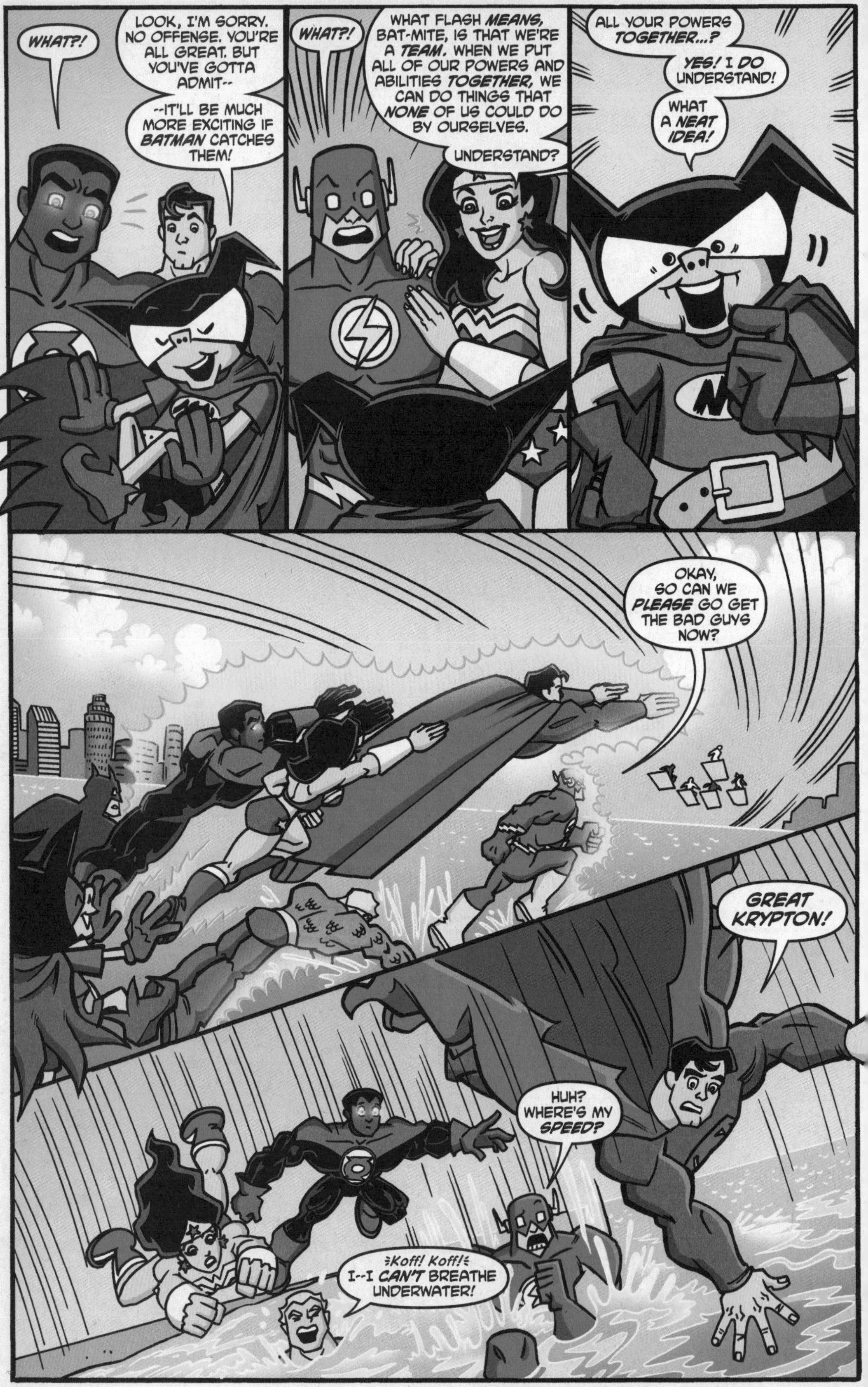
WHAT?!
LOOK, I'M SORRY. NO OFFENSE. YOU'RE ALL GREAT. BUT YOU'VE GOTTA ADMIT--
--IT'LL BE MUCH MORE EXCITING IF BATMAN CATCHES THEM!
WHAT?!
WHAT FLASH MEANS, BAT-MITE, IS THAT WE'RE A TEAM. WHEN WE PUT ALL OF OUR POWERS AND ABILITIES TOGETHER, WE CAN DO THINGS THAT NONE OF US COULD DO BY OURSELVES.
UNDERSTAND?
ALL YOUR POWERS TOGETHER...?
YES! I DO UNDERSTAND!
WHAT A NEAT IDEA!
OKAY, SO CAN WE PLEASE GO GET THE BAD GUYS NOW?
GREAT KRYPTON!
HUH? WHERE'S MY SPEED?
Koff! Koff! I--I CAN'T BREATHE UNDERWATER!

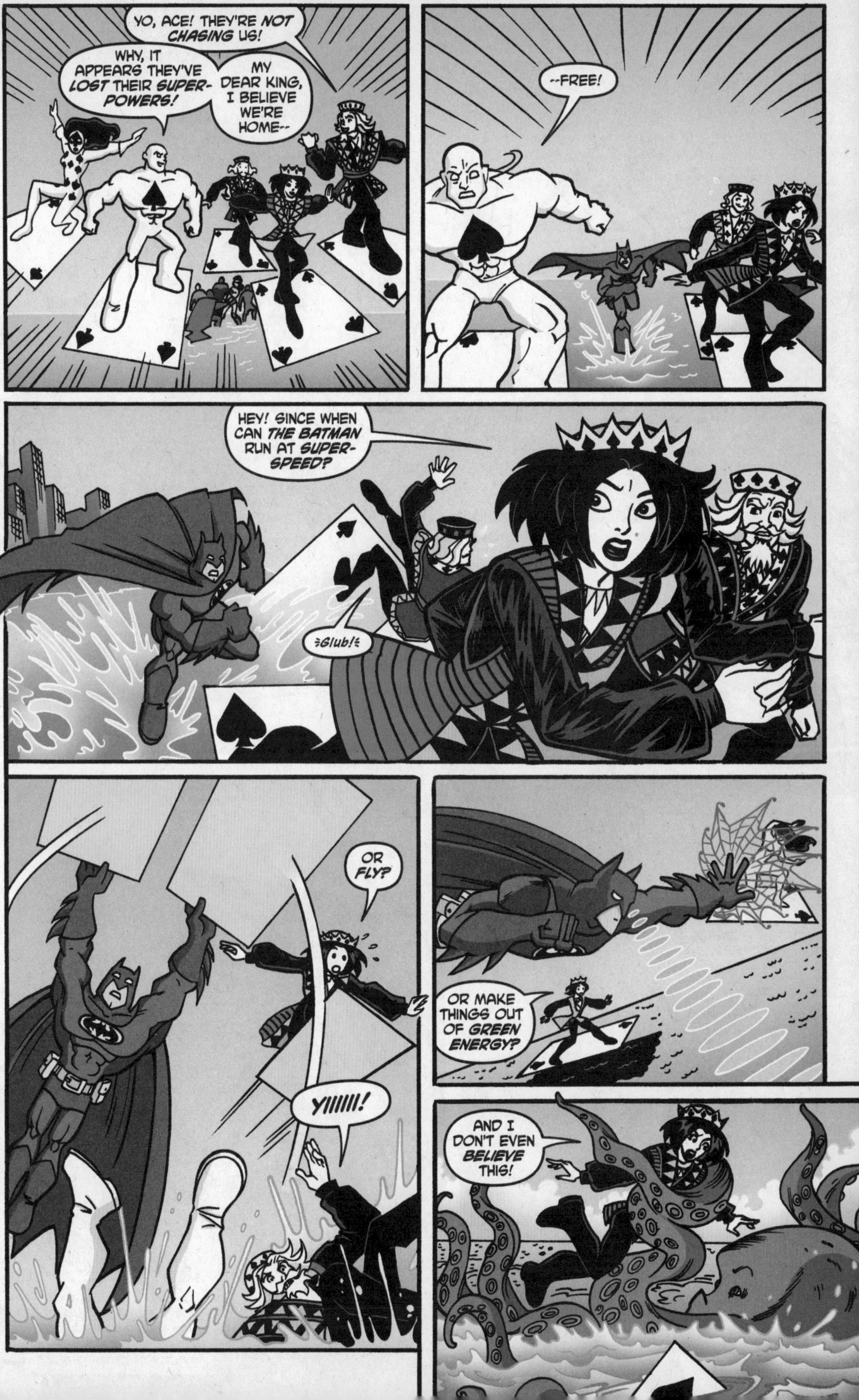
YO, ACE! THEY'RE NOT CHASING US!
WHY, IT APPEARS THEY'VE LOST THEIR SUPER-POWERS!
MY DEAR KING, I BELIEVE WE'RE HOME--
--FREE!
HEY! SINCE WHEN CAN THE BATMAN RUN AT SUPER-SPEED?
Glub!
OR FLY?
YIIIIII!
OR MAKE THINGS OUT OF GREEN ENERGY?
AND I DON'T EVEN BELIEVE THIS!

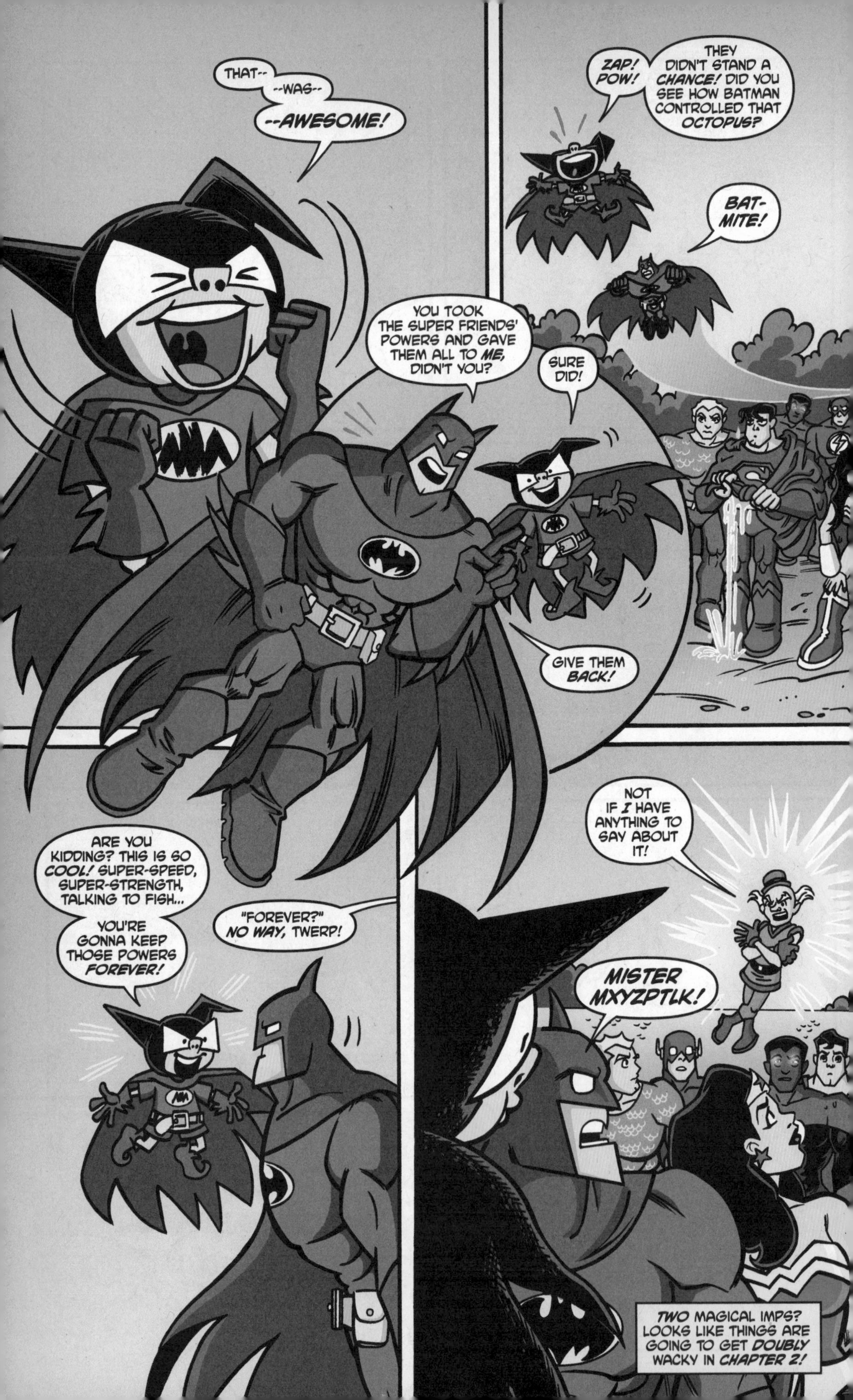

THAT--
--WAS--
--AWESOME!
ZAP! POW!
THEY DIDN'T STAND A CHANCE! DID YOU SEE HOW BATMAN CONTROLLED THAT OCTOPUS?
BAT-MITE!
YOU TOOK THE SUPER FRIENDS' POWERS AND GAVE THEM ALL TO ME, DIDN'T YOU?
SURE DID!
GIVE THEM BACK!
ARE YOU KIDDING? THIS IS SO COOL! SUPER-SPEED, SUPER-STRENGTH, TALKING TO FISH...
YOU'RE GONNA KEEP THOSE POWERS FOREVER!
"FOREVER?" NO WAY, TWERP!
NOT IF I HAVE ANYTHING TO SAY ABOUT IT!
MISTER MXYZPTLK!
TWO MAGICAL IMPS? LOOKS LIKE THINGS ARE GOING TO GET DOUBLY WACKY IN CHAPTER 2!

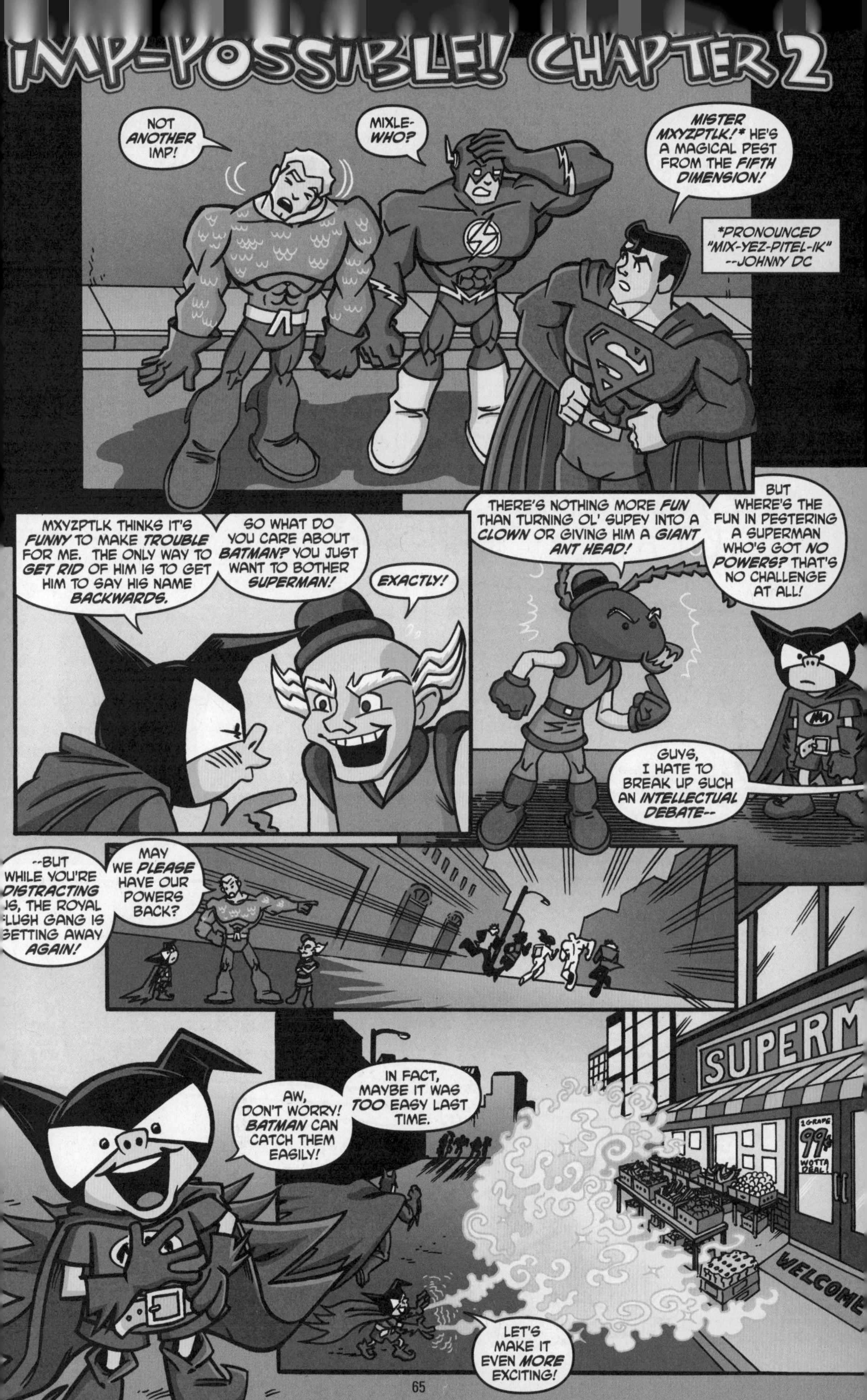
IMP-POSSIBLE! CHAPTER 2
NOT ANOTHER IMP!
MIXLE-WHO?
MISTER MXYZPTLK!* HE'S A MAGICAL PEST FROM THE FIFTH DIMENSION!
*PRONOUNCED "MIX-YEZ-PITEL-IK" --JOHNNY DC
MXYZPTLK THINKS IT'S FUNNY TO MAKE TROUBLE FOR ME. THE ONLY WAY TO GET RID OF HIM IS TO GET HIM TO SAY HIS NAME BACKWARDS.
SO WHAT DO YOU CARE ABOUT BATMAN? YOU JUST WANT TO BOTHER SUPERMAN!
EXACTLY!
THERE'S NOTHING MORE FUN THAN TURNING OL' SUPEY INTO A CLOWN OR GIVING HIM A GIANT ANT HEAD!
BUT WHERE'S THE FUN IN PESTERING A SUPERMAN WHO'S GOT NO POWERS? THAT'S NO CHALLENGE AT ALL!
GUYS, I HATE TO BREAK UP SUCH AN INTELLECTUAL DEBATE--
--BUT WHILE YOU'RE DISTRACTING US, THE ROYAL FLUSH GANG IS GETTING AWAY AGAIN!
MAY WE PLEASE HAVE OUR POWERS BACK?
AW, DON'T WORRY! BATMAN CAN CATCH THEM EASILY!
IN FACT, MAYBE IT WAS TOO EASY LAST TIME.
LET'S MAKE IT EVEN MORE EXCITING!
SUPERM
GRAPE 99¢ WOTTA DEAL!
WELCOME

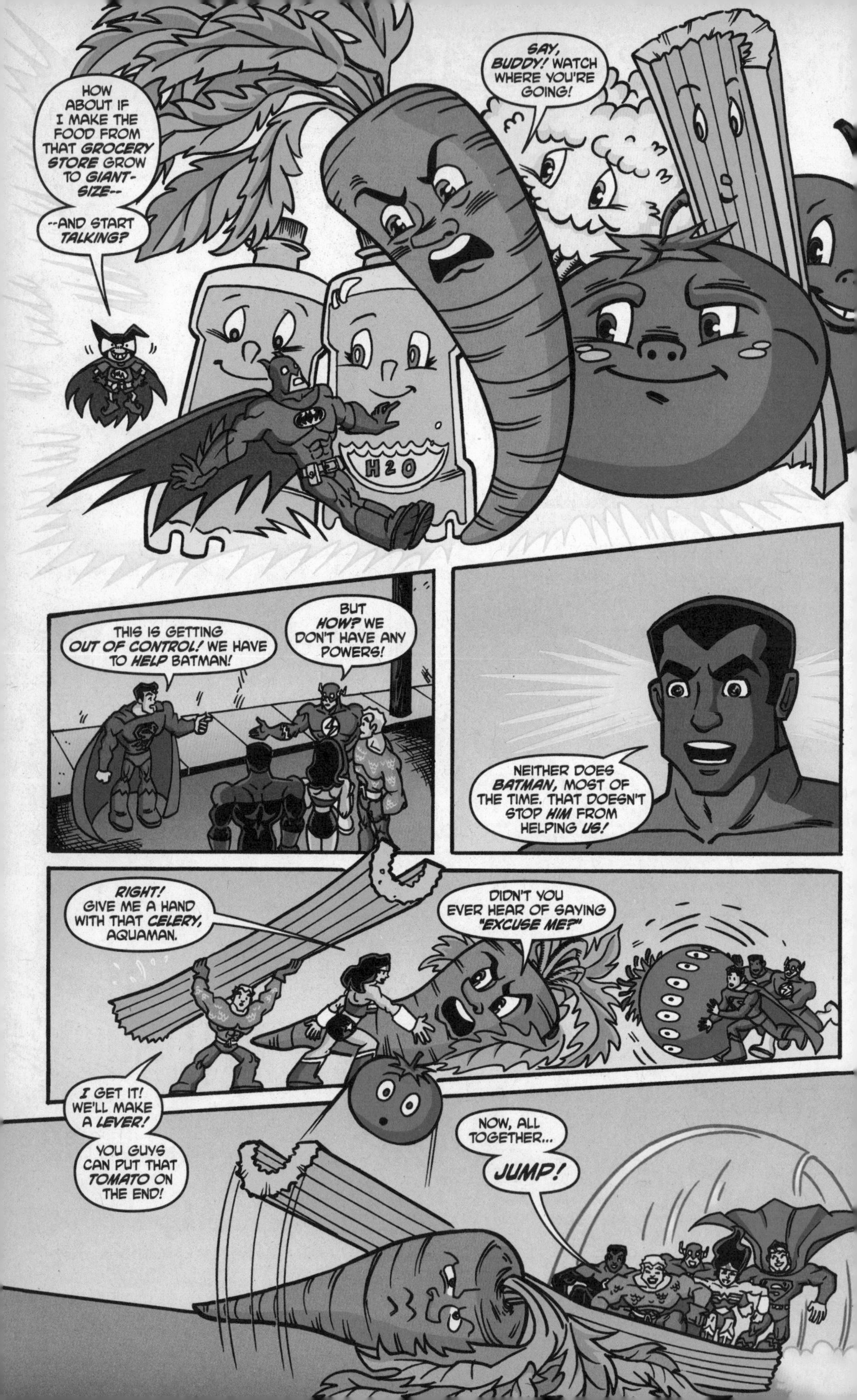
HOW ABOUT IF I MAKE THE FOOD FROM THAT GROCERY STORE GROW TO GIANT-SIZE--
--AND START TALKING?
SAY, BUDDY! WATCH WHERE YOU'RE GOING!
THIS IS GETTING OUT OF CONTROL! WE HAVE TO HELP BATMAN!
BUT HOW? WE DON'T HAVE ANY POWERS!
NEITHER DOES BATMAN, MOST OF THE TIME. THAT DOESN'T STOP HIM FROM HELPING US!
RIGHT! GIVE ME A HAND WITH THAT CELERY, AQUAMAN.
DIDN'T YOU EVER HEAR OF SAYING "EXCUSE ME?"
I GET IT! WE'LL MAKE A LEVER!
YOU GUYS CAN PUT THAT TOMATO ON THE END!
NOW, ALL TOGETHER...
JUMP!

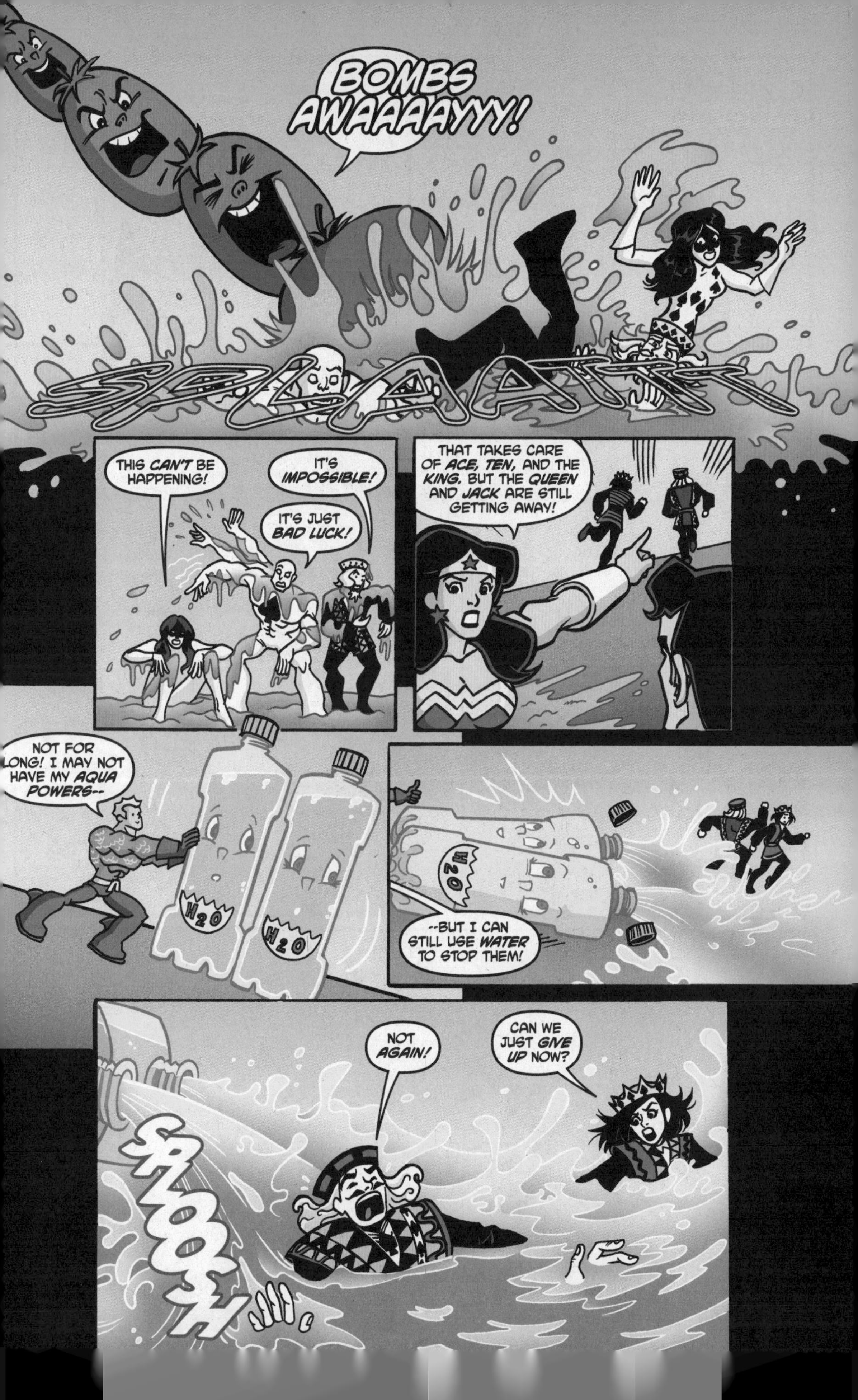
BOMBS AWAAAAAYYY!
SPLAATTT
THIS CAN'T BE HAPPENING!
IT'S IMPOSSIBLE!
IT'S JUST BAD LUCK!
THAT TAKES CARE OF ACE, TEN, AND THE KING. BUT THE QUEEN AND JACK ARE STILL GETTING AWAY!
NOT FOR LONG! I MAY NOT HAVE MY AQUA POWERS--
H2O
H2O
H2O
--BUT I CAN STILL USE WATER TO STOP THEM!
NOT AGAIN!
CAN WE JUST GIVE UP NOW?
SPLOOSH

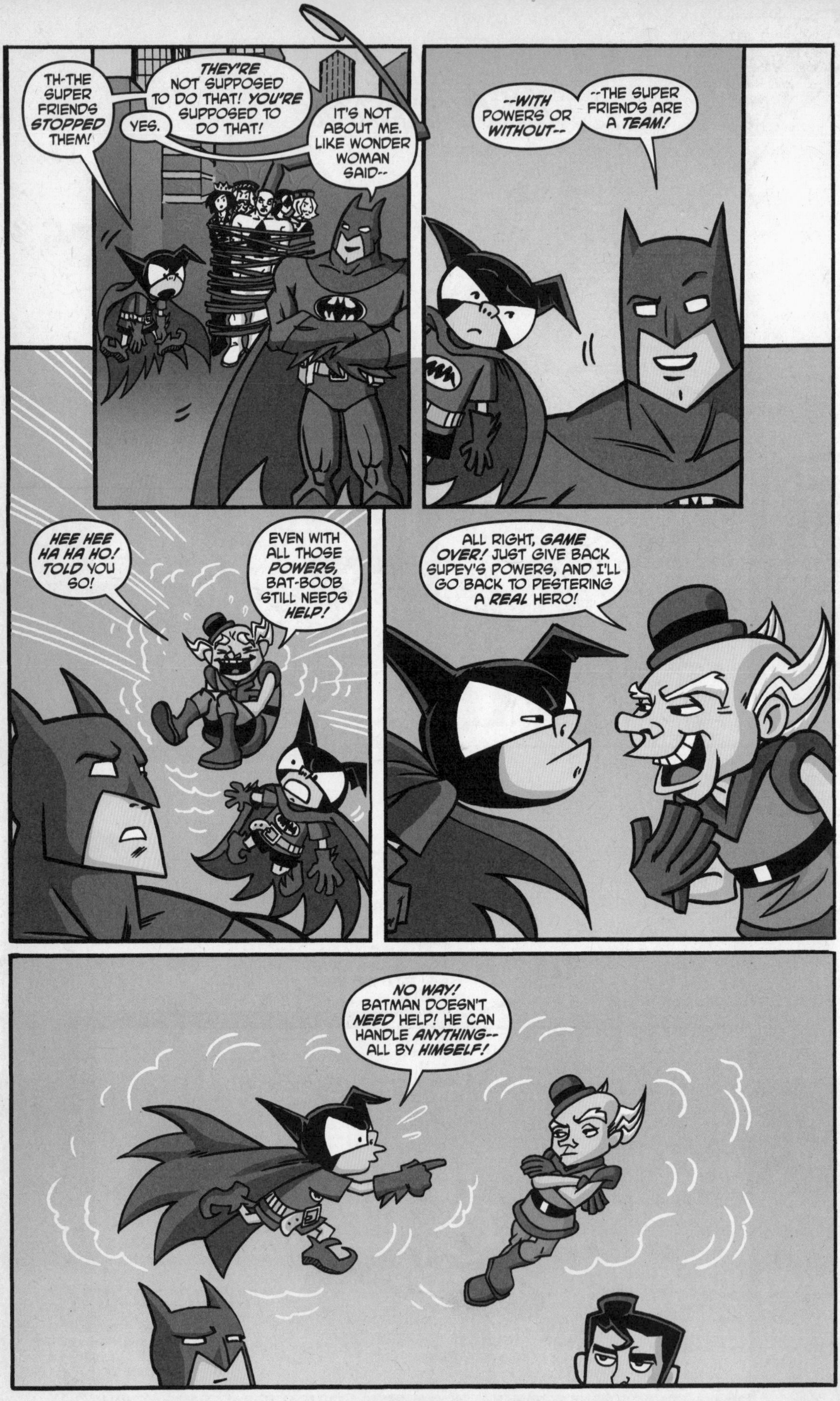
TH-THE SUPER FRIENDS STOPPED THEM!
THEY'RE NOT SUPPOSED TO DO THAT! YOU'RE SUPPOSED TO DO THAT!
YES.
IT'S NOT ABOUT ME. LIKE WONDER WOMAN SAID--
--WITH POWERS OR WITHOUT--
--THE SUPER FRIENDS ARE A TEAM!
HEE HEE HA HA HO! TOLD YOU SO!
EVEN WITH ALL THOSE POWERS, BAT-BOOB STILL NEEDS HELP!
ALL RIGHT, GAME OVER! JUST GIVE BACK SUPEY'S POWERS, AND I'LL GO BACK TO PESTERING A REAL HERO!
NO WAY! BATMAN DOESN'T NEED HELP! HE CAN HANDLE ANYTHING-- ALL BY HIMSELF!

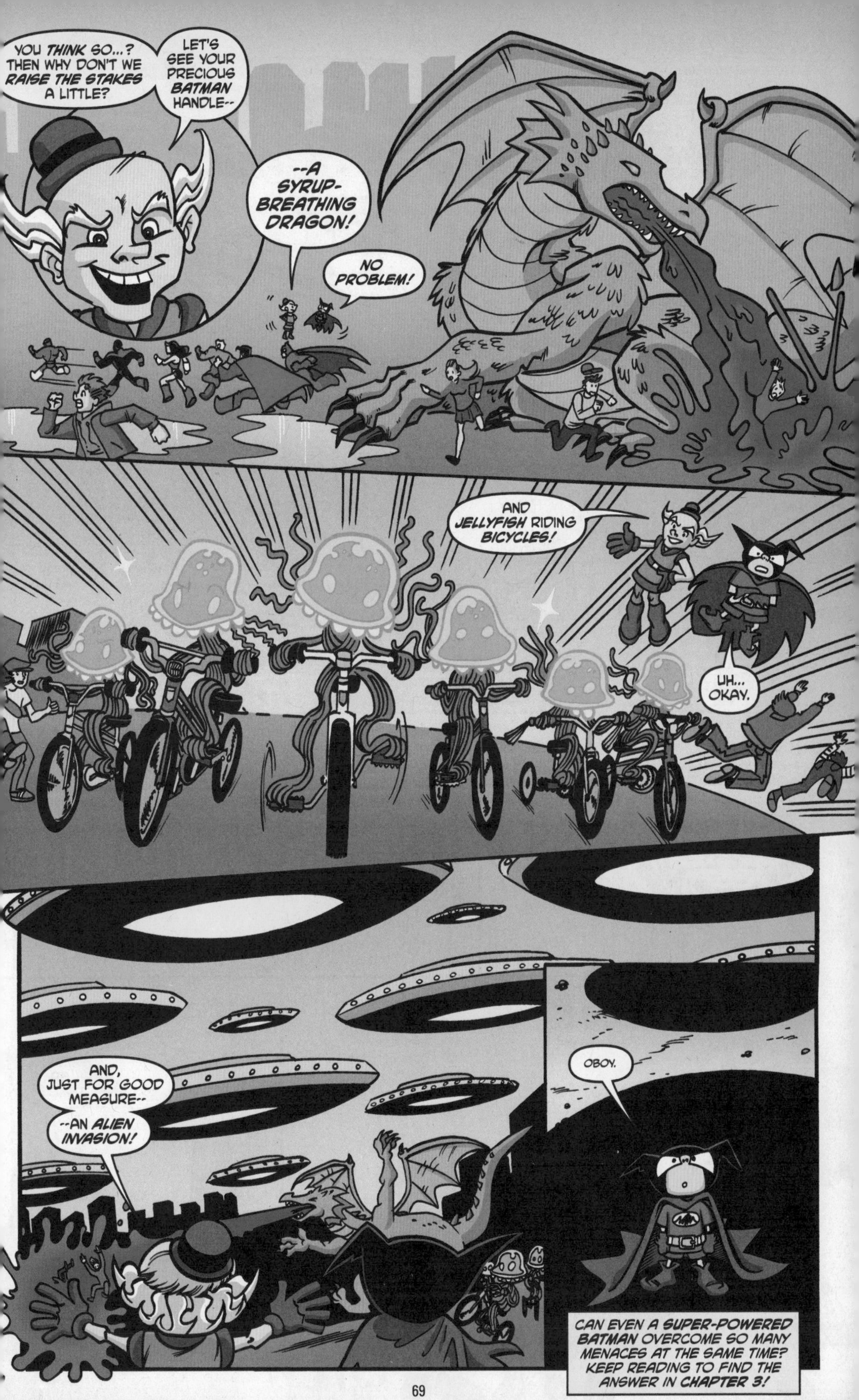

YOU THINK SO...? THEN WHY DON'T WE RAISE THE STAKES A LITTLE?
LET'S SEE YOUR PRECIOUS BATMAN HANDLE--
--A SYRUP-BREATHING DRAGON!
NO PROBLEM!
AND JELLYFISH RIDING BICYCLES!
UH... OKAY.
AND, JUST FOR GOOD MEASURE--
--AN ALIEN INVASION!
OBOY.
CAN EVEN A SUPER-POWERED BATMAN OVERCOME SO MANY MENACES AT THE SAME TIME? KEEP READING TO FIND THE ANSWER IN CHAPTER 3!

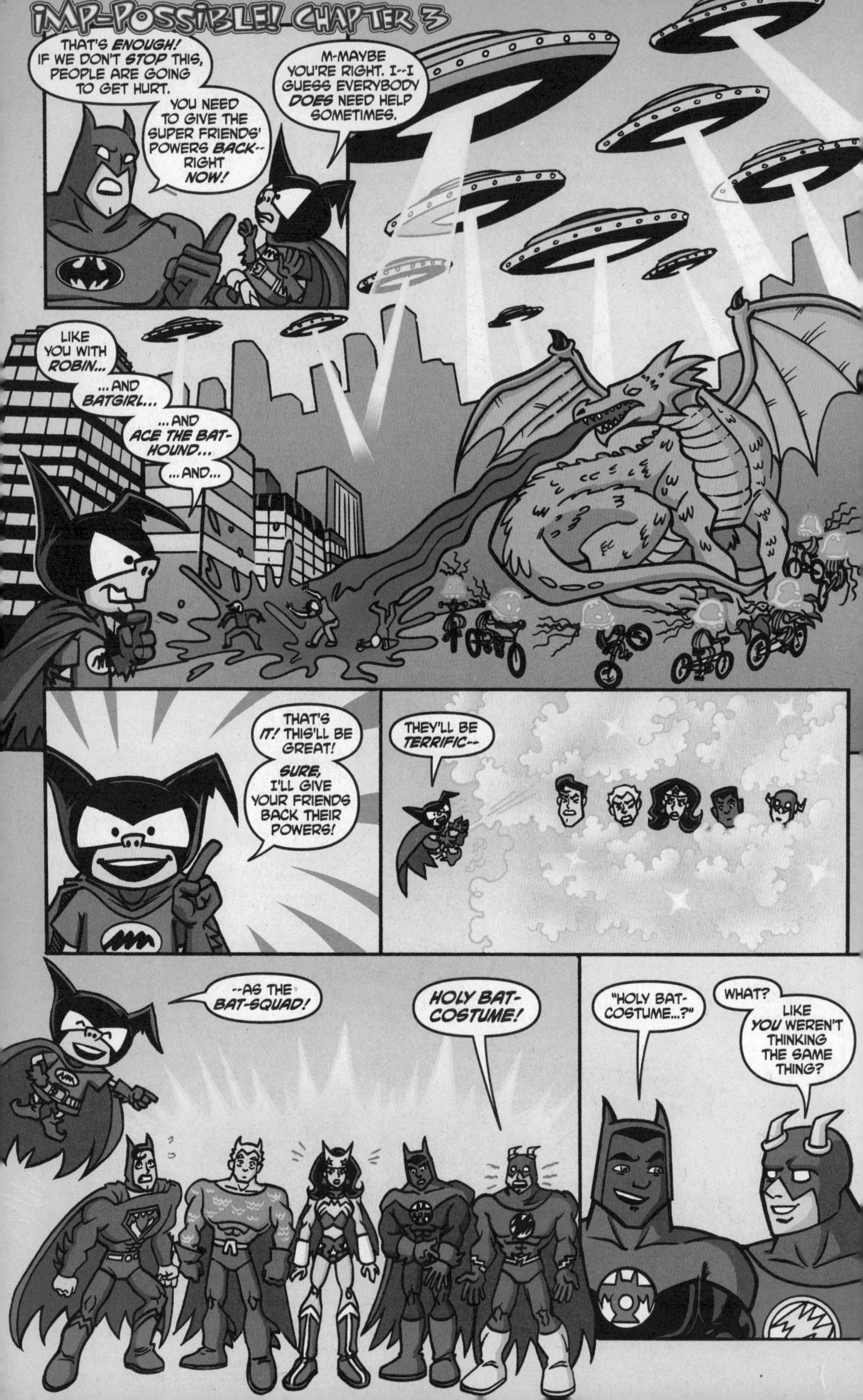
iMP-POSSIBLE! CHAPTER 3
THAT'S ENOUGH! IF WE DON'T STOP THIS, PEOPLE ARE GOING TO GET HURT.
YOU NEED TO GIVE THE SUPER FRIENDS' POWERS BACK-- RIGHT NOW!
M-MAYBE YOU'RE RIGHT. I--I GUESS EVERYBODY DOES NEED HELP SOMETIMES.
LIKE YOU WITH ROBIN...
...AND BATGIRL...
...AND ACE THE BAT-HOUND...
...AND...
THAT'S IT! THIS'LL BE GREAT!
SURE, I'LL GIVE YOUR FRIENDS BACK THEIR POWERS!
THEY'LL BE TERRIFIC--
--AS THE BAT-SQUAD!
HOLY BAT-COSTUME!
"HOLY BAT-COSTUME...?"
WHAT?
LIKE YOU WEREN'T THINKING THE SAME THING?

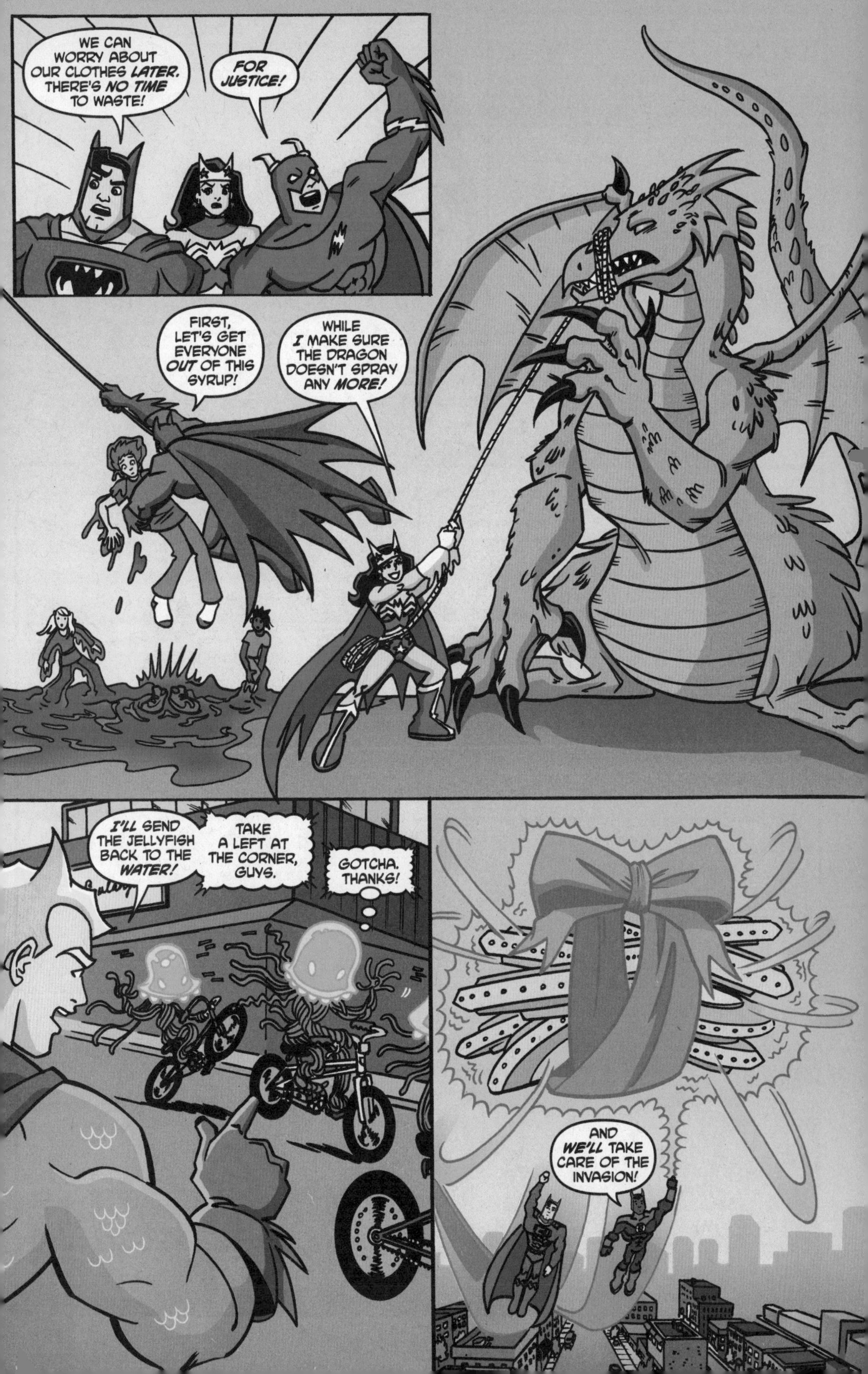
WE CAN WORRY ABOUT OUR CLOTHES *LATER*. THERE'S *NO TIME* TO WASTE!
FOR JUSTICE!
FIRST, LET'S GET EVERYONE *OUT* OF THIS SYRUP!
WHILE *I* MAKE SURE THE DRAGON DOESN'T SPRAY ANY *MORE!*
I'LL SEND THE JELLYFISH BACK TO THE *WATER!*
TAKE A LEFT AT THE CORNER, GUYS.
GOTCHA. THANKS!
AND *WE'LL* TAKE CARE OF THE INVASION!

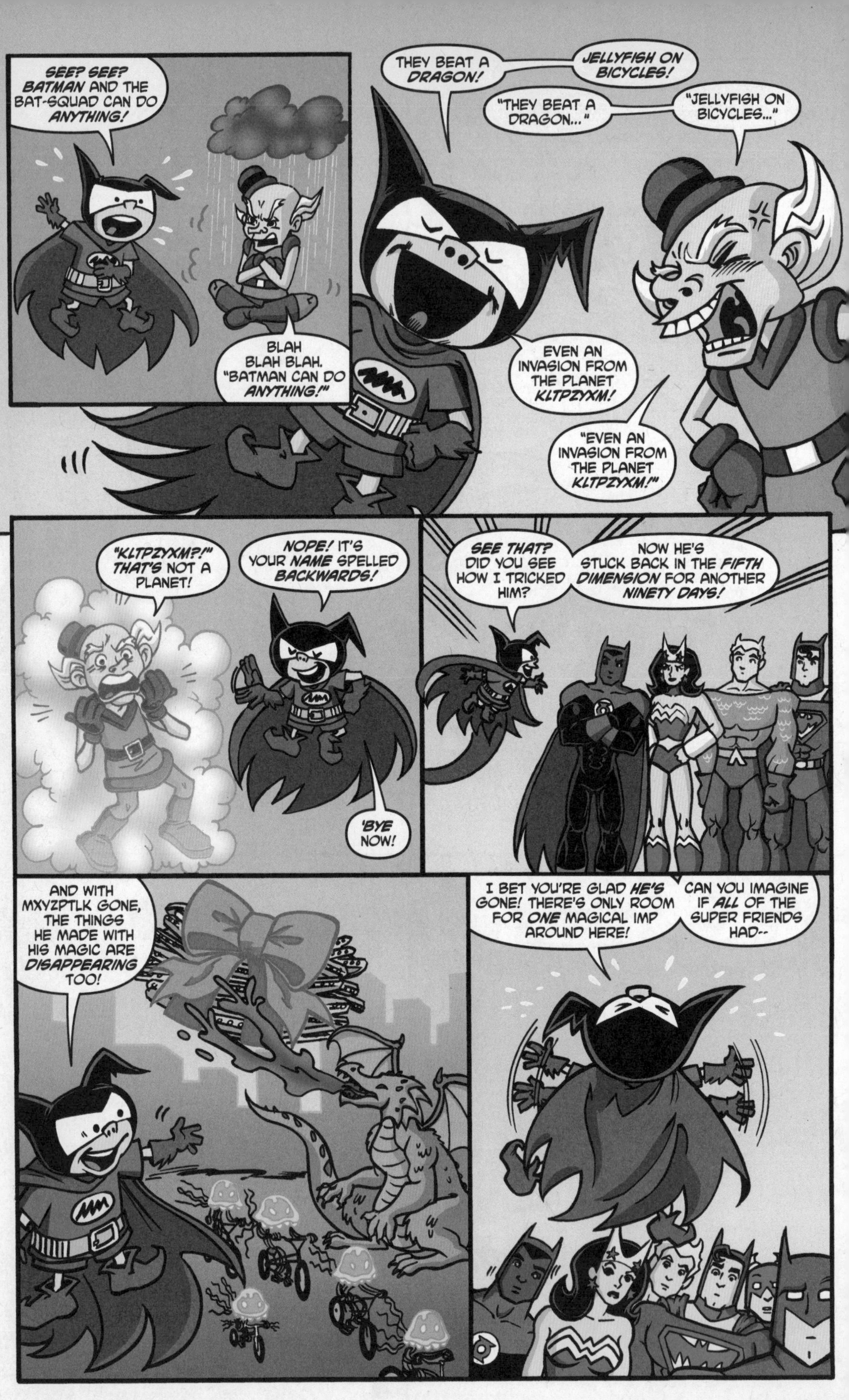

SEE? SEE? BATMAN AND THE BAT-SQUAD CAN DO ANYTHING!
BLAH BLAH BLAH. "BATMAN CAN DO ANYTHING!"
THEY BEAT A DRAGON!
JELLYFISH ON BICYCLES!
"THEY BEAT A DRAGON..."
"JELLYFISH ON BICYCLES..."
EVEN AN INVASION FROM THE PLANET KLTPZYXM!
"EVEN AN INVASION FROM THE PLANET KLTPZYXM!"
"KLTPZYXM?!" THAT'S NOT A PLANET!
NOPE! IT'S YOUR NAME SPELLED BACKWARDS!
'BYE NOW!
SEE THAT? DID YOU SEE HOW I TRICKED HIM?
NOW HE'S STUCK BACK IN THE FIFTH DIMENSION FOR ANOTHER NINETY DAYS!
AND WITH MXYZPTLK GONE, THE THINGS HE MADE WITH HIS MAGIC ARE DISAPPEARING TOO!
I BET YOU'RE GLAD HE'S GONE! THERE'S ONLY ROOM FOR ONE MAGICAL IMP AROUND HERE!
CAN YOU IMAGINE IF ALL OF THE SUPER FRIENDS HAD--

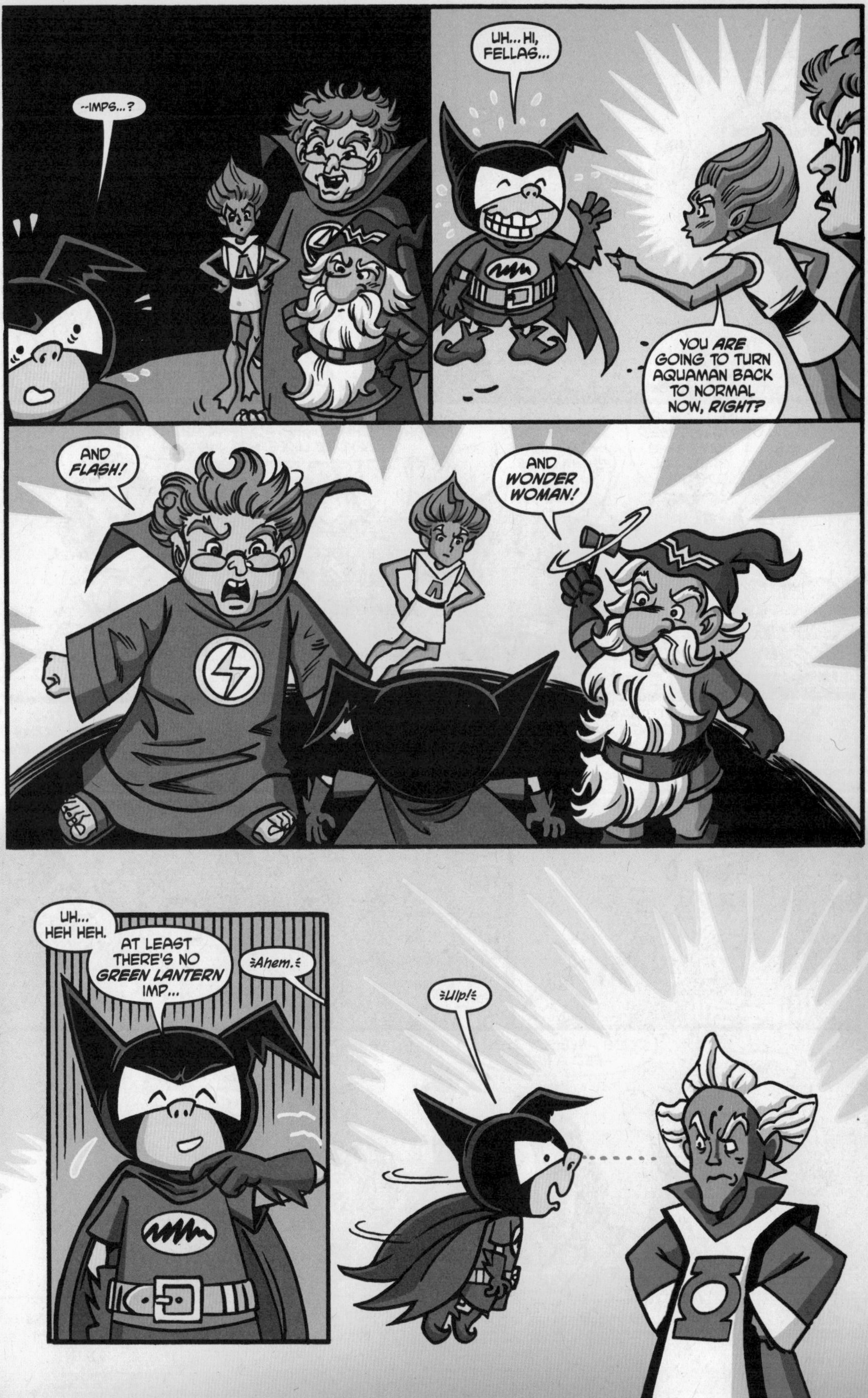

--IMPS...?
UH... HI, FELLAS...
YOU *ARE* GOING TO TURN AQUAMAN BACK TO NORMAL NOW, *RIGHT?*
AND *FLASH!*
AND *WONDER WOMAN!*
UH... HEH HEH.
AT LEAST THERE'S NO *GREEN LANTERN* IMP...
Ahem.
Ulp!

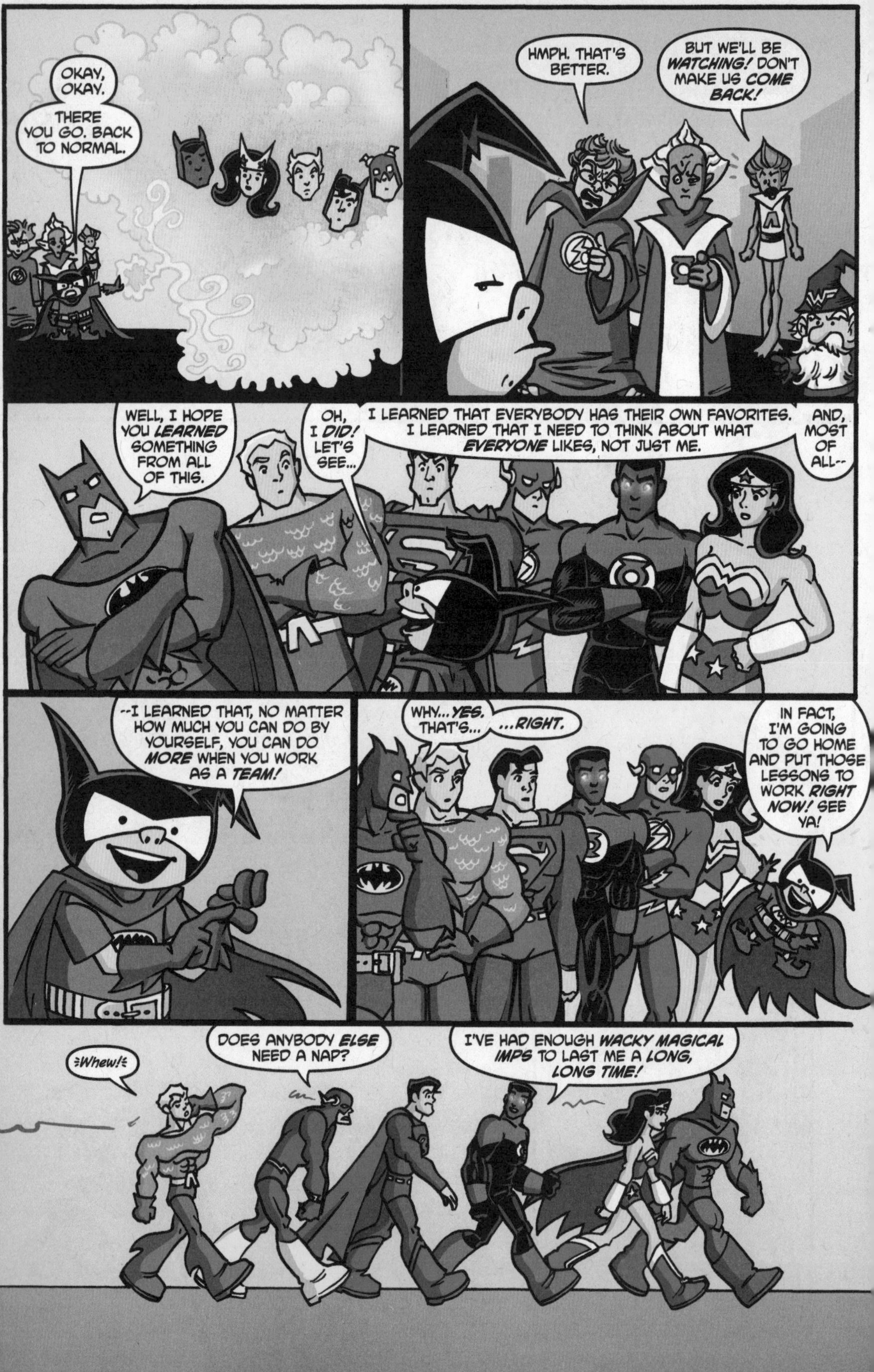
OKAY, OKAY.
THERE YOU GO. BACK TO NORMAL.
HMPH. THAT'S BETTER.
BUT WE'LL BE *WATCHING!* DON'T MAKE US *COME BACK!*
WELL, I HOPE YOU *LEARNED* SOMETHING FROM ALL OF THIS.
OH, I *DID!* LET'S SEE...
I LEARNED THAT EVERYBODY HAS THEIR OWN FAVORITES. I LEARNED THAT I NEED TO THINK ABOUT WHAT *EVERYONE* LIKES, NOT JUST ME.
AND, MOST OF ALL--
--I LEARNED THAT, NO MATTER HOW MUCH YOU CAN DO BY YOURSELF, YOU CAN DO *MORE* WHEN YOU WORK AS A *TEAM!*
WHY... *YES.* THAT'S...
...*RIGHT.*
IN FACT, I'M GOING TO GO HOME AND PUT THOSE LESSONS TO WORK *RIGHT NOW!* SEE YA!
Whew!
DOES ANYBODY *ELSE* NEED A NAP?
I'VE HAD ENOUGH *WACKY MAGICAL IMPS* TO LAST ME A *LONG, LONG TIME!*

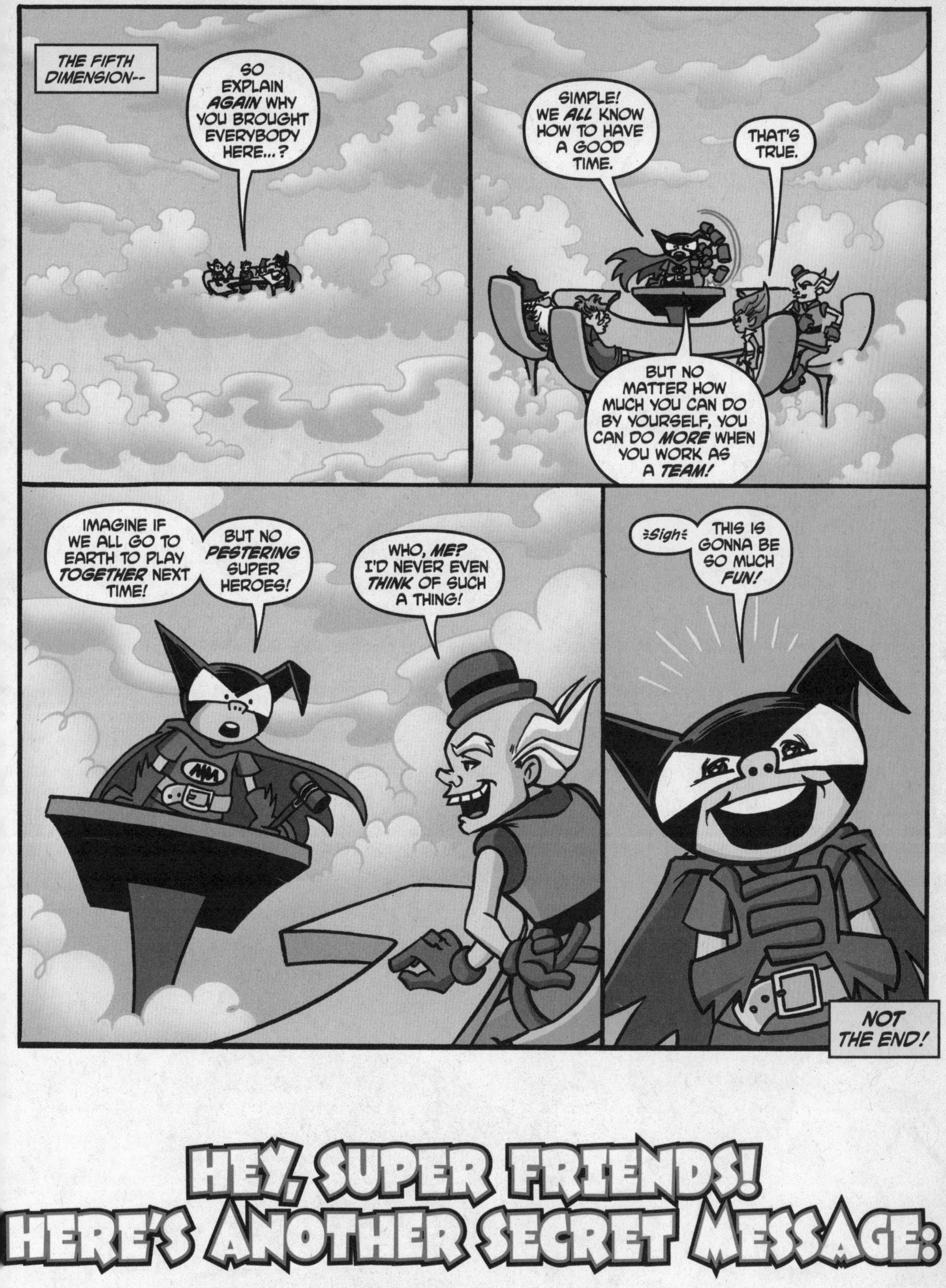
THE FIFTH DIMENSION--
SO EXPLAIN AGAIN WHY YOU BROUGHT EVERYBODY HERE...?
SIMPLE! WE ALL KNOW HOW TO HAVE A GOOD TIME.
THAT'S TRUE.
BUT NO MATTER HOW MUCH YOU CAN DO BY YOURSELF, YOU CAN DO MORE WHEN YOU WORK AS A TEAM!
IMAGINE IF WE ALL GO TO EARTH TO PLAY TOGETHER NEXT TIME!
BUT NO PESTERING SUPER HEROES!
WHO, ME? I'D NEVER EVEN THINK OF SUCH A THING!
Sigh
THIS IS GONNA BE SO MUCH FUN!
NOT THE END!

HEY, SUPER FRIENDS! HERE'S ANOTHER SECRET MESSAGE:

XOLI DBXIN, PIKYYB INO MBXAEYBY KIIKMUP CYBD HOXOKIN INO POK!

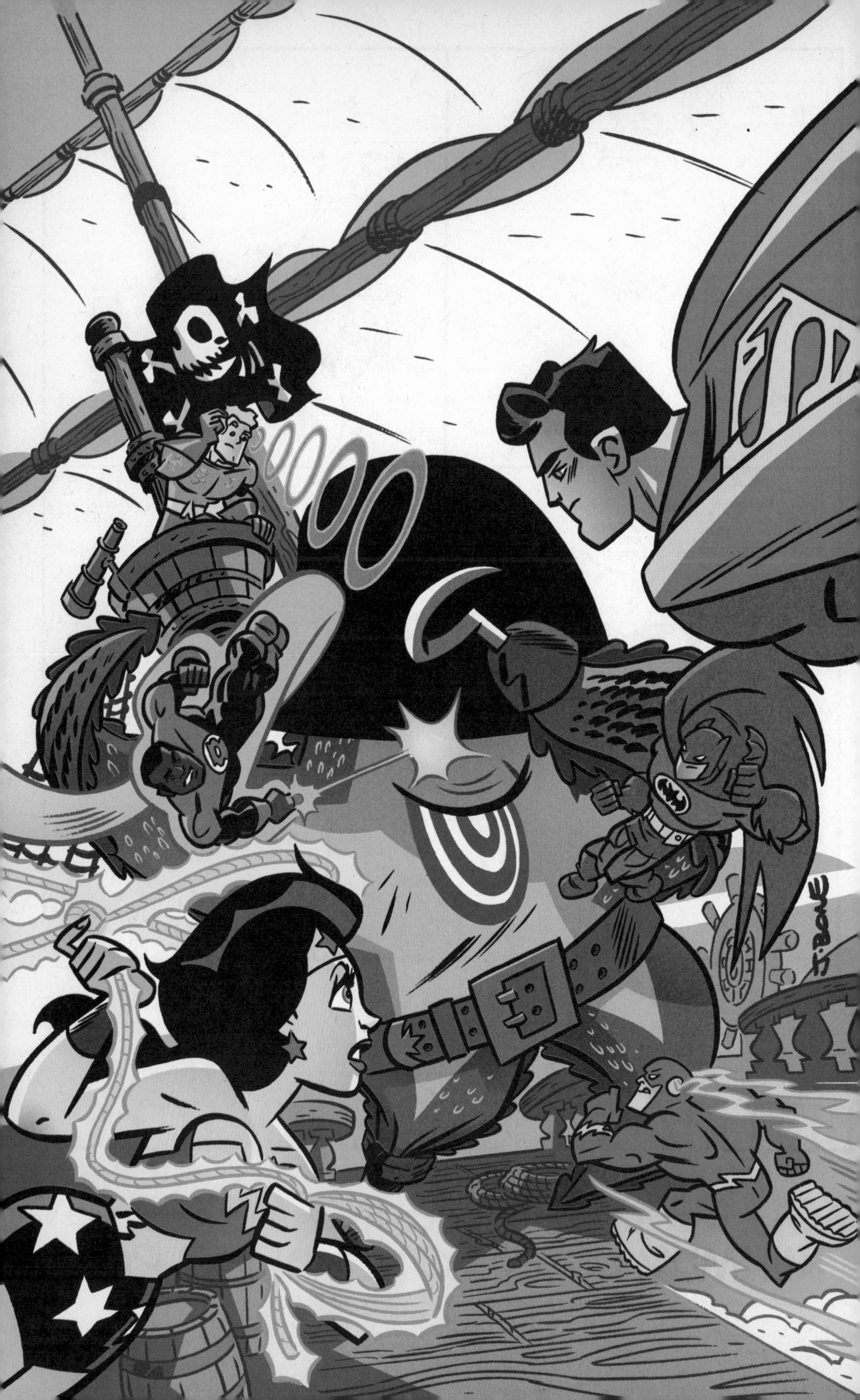
J.BONE

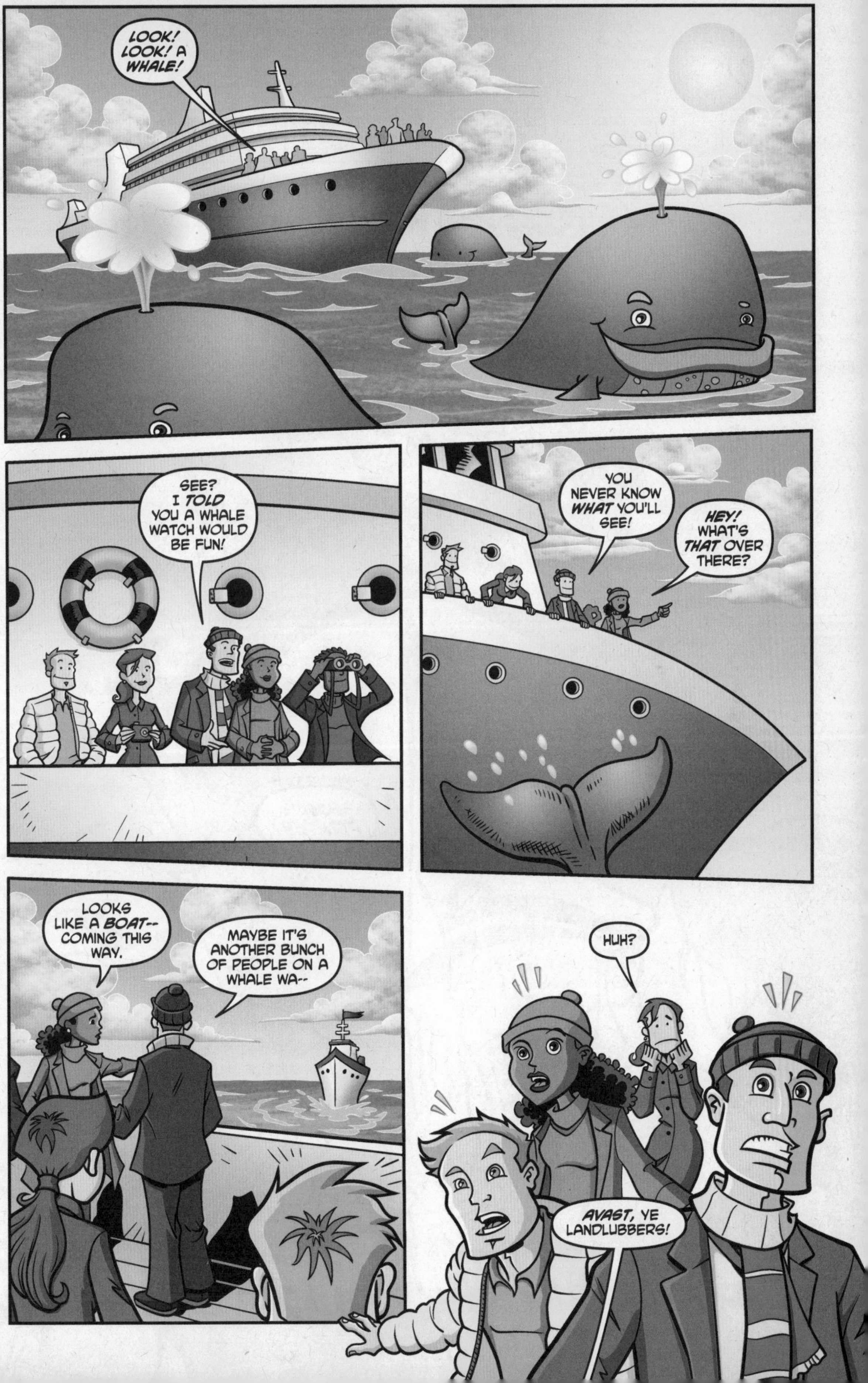
LOOK! LOOK! A WHALE!
SEE? I TOLD YOU A WHALE WATCH WOULD BE FUN!
YOU NEVER KNOW WHAT YOU'LL SEE!
HEY! WHAT'S THAT OVER THERE?
LOOKS LIKE A BOAT-- COMING THIS WAY.
MAYBE IT'S ANOTHER BUNCH OF PEOPLE ON A WHALE WA--
HUH?
AVAST, YE LANDLUBBERS!

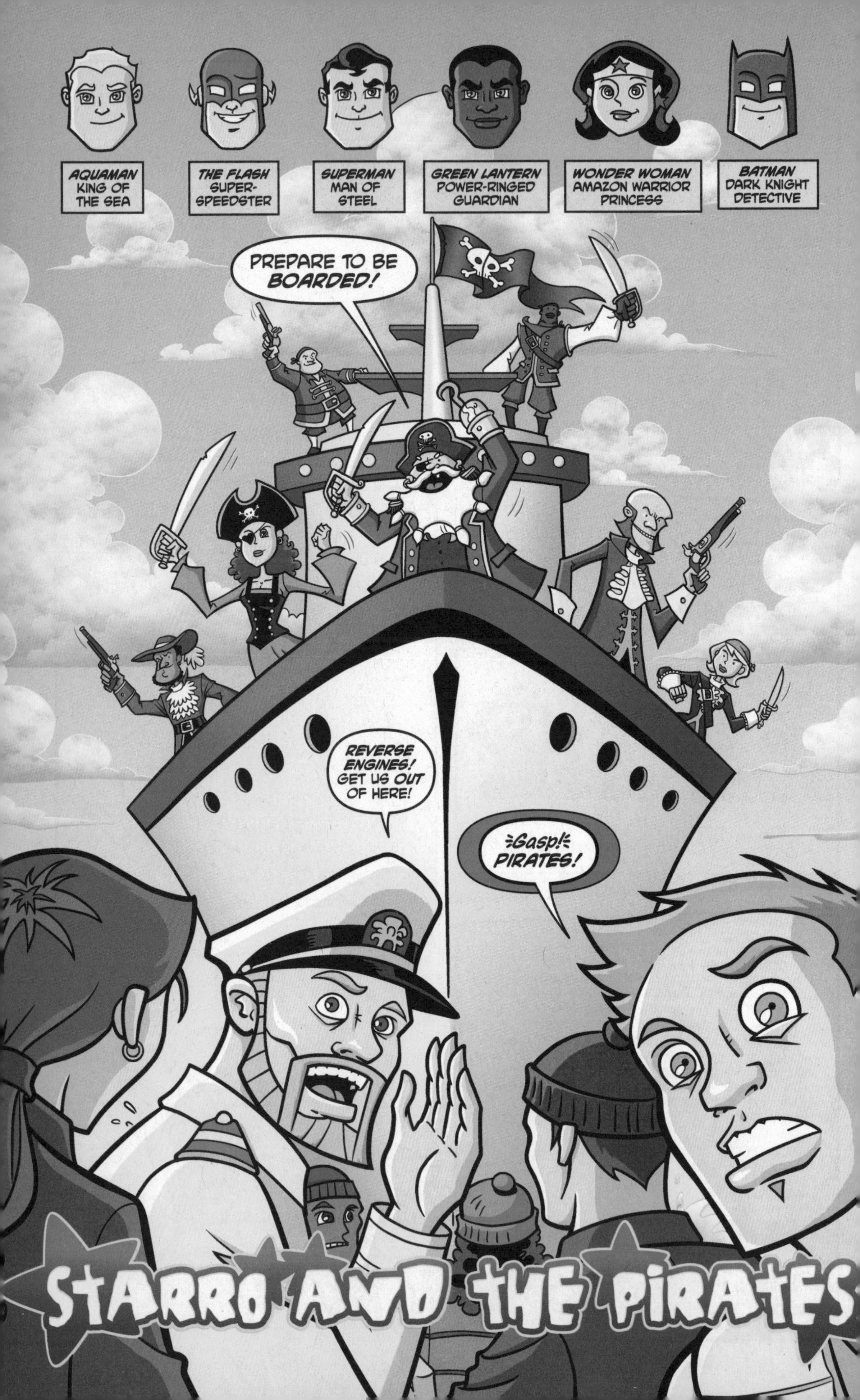
AQUAMAN
KING OF THE SEA
THE FLASH
SUPER-SPEEDSTER
SUPERMAN
MAN OF STEEL
GREEN LANTERN
POWER-RINGED GUARDIAN
WONDER WOMAN
AMAZON WARRIOR PRINCESS
BATMAN
DARK KNIGHT DETECTIVE
PREPARE TO BE BOARDED!
REVERSE ENGINES! GET US OUT OF HERE!
Gasp! PIRATES!
STARRO AND THE PIRATES

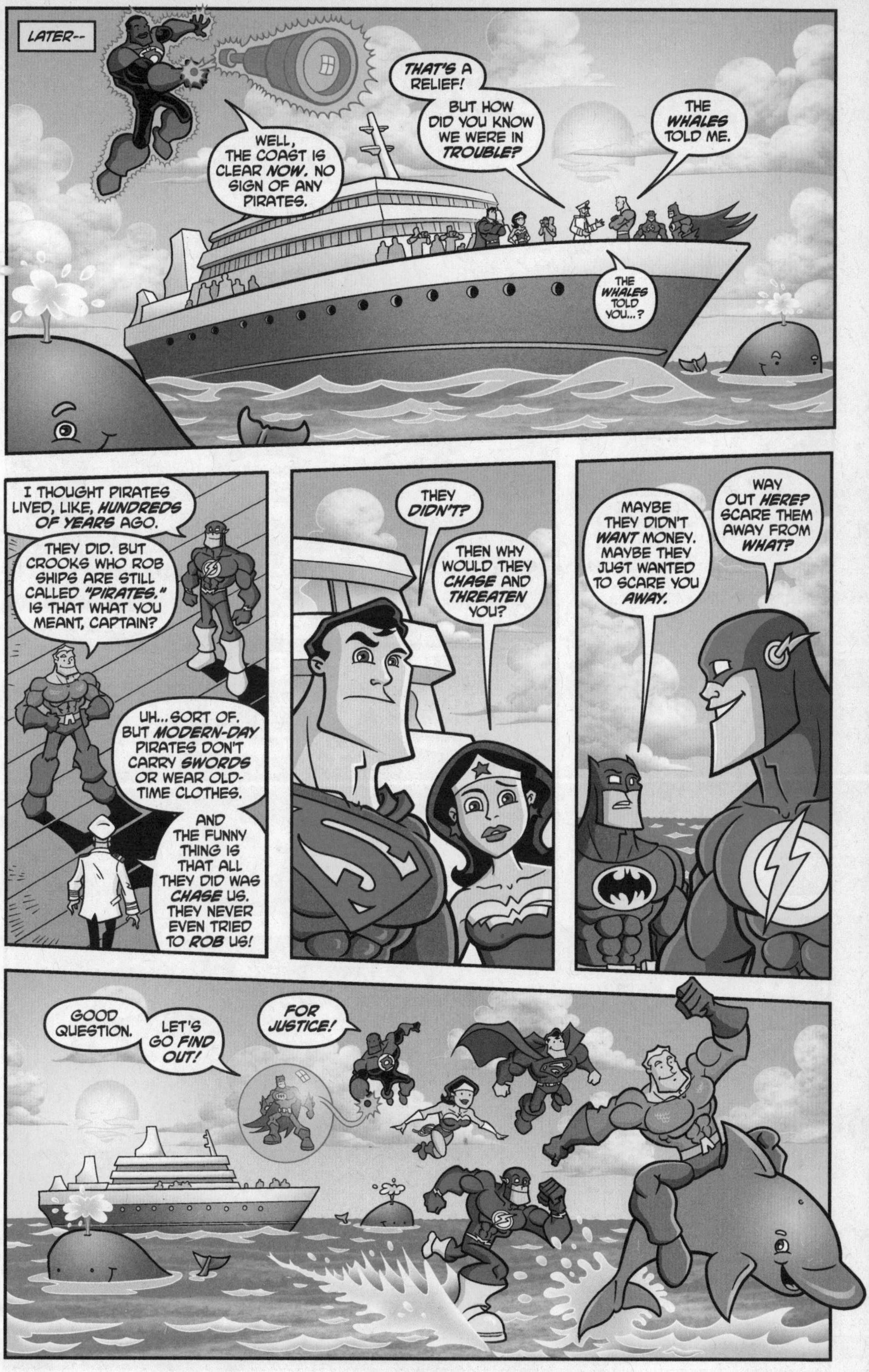
LATER--
WELL, THE COAST IS CLEAR NOW. NO SIGN OF ANY PIRATES.
THAT'S A RELIEF!
BUT HOW DID YOU KNOW WE WERE IN TROUBLE?
THE WHALES TOLD ME.
THE WHALES TOLD YOU...?
I THOUGHT PIRATES LIVED, LIKE, HUNDREDS OF YEARS AGO.
THEY DID. BUT CROOKS WHO ROB SHIPS ARE STILL CALLED "PIRATES." IS THAT WHAT YOU MEANT, CAPTAIN?
UH... SORT OF. BUT MODERN-DAY PIRATES DON'T CARRY SWORDS OR WEAR OLD-TIME CLOTHES.
AND THE FUNNY THING IS THAT ALL THEY DID WAS CHASE US. THEY NEVER EVEN TRIED TO ROB US!
THEY DIDN'T?
THEN WHY WOULD THEY CHASE AND THREATEN YOU?
MAYBE THEY DIDN'T WANT MONEY. MAYBE THEY JUST WANTED TO SCARE YOU AWAY.
WAY OUT HERE? SCARE THEM AWAY FROM WHAT?
GOOD QUESTION.
LET'S GO FIND OUT!
FOR JUSTICE!

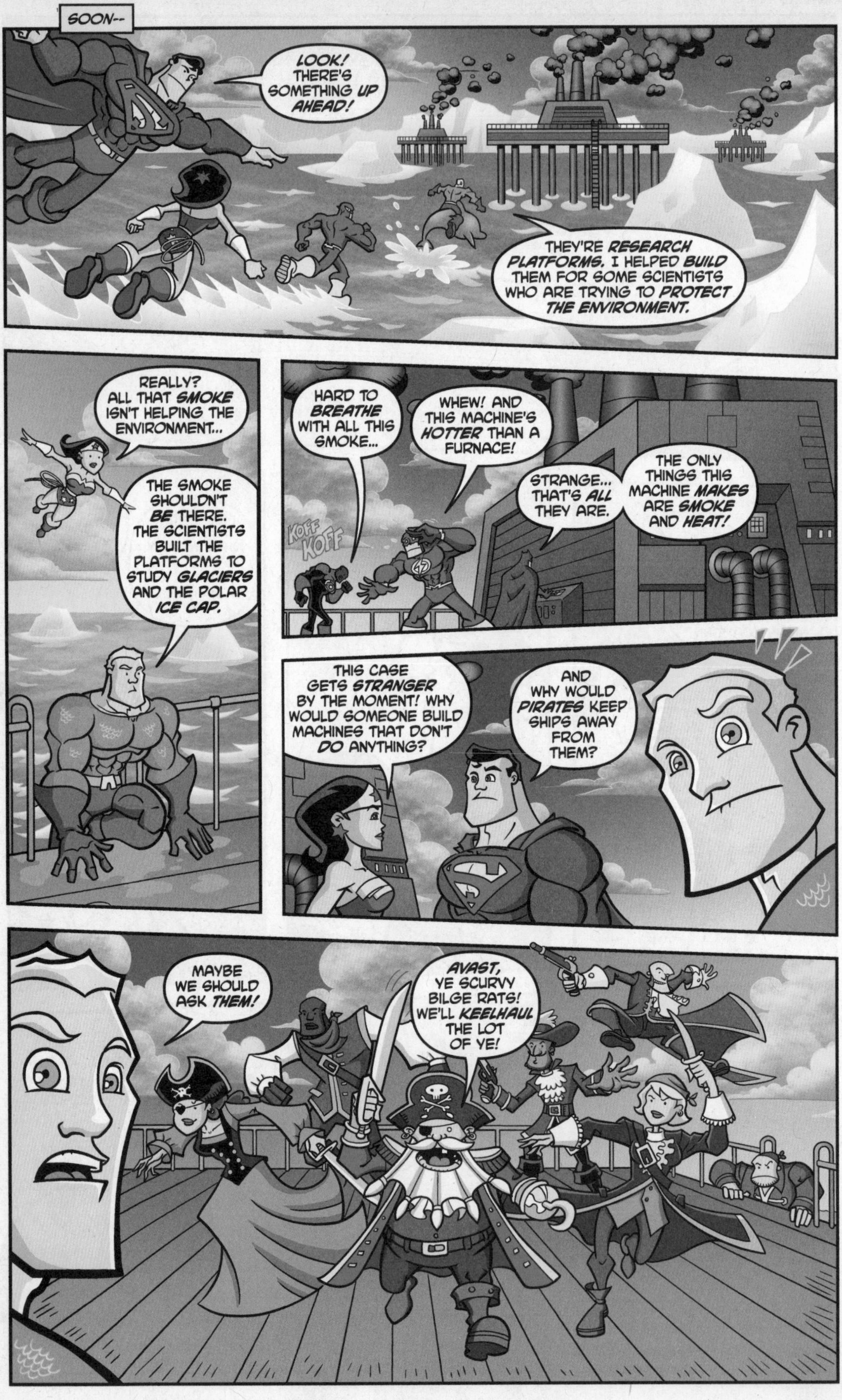
SOON--
LOOK! THERE'S SOMETHING UP AHEAD!
THEY'RE RESEARCH PLATFORMS. I HELPED BUILD THEM FOR SOME SCIENTISTS WHO ARE TRYING TO PROTECT THE ENVIRONMENT.
REALLY? ALL THAT SMOKE ISN'T HELPING THE ENVIRONMENT...
THE SMOKE SHOULDN'T BE THERE. THE SCIENTISTS BUILT THE PLATFORMS TO STUDY GLACIERS AND THE POLAR ICE CAP.
HARD TO BREATHE WITH ALL THIS SMOKE...
KOFF KOFF
WHEW! AND THIS MACHINE'S HOTTER THAN A FURNACE!
STRANGE... THAT'S ALL THEY ARE.
THE ONLY THINGS THIS MACHINE MAKES ARE SMOKE AND HEAT!
THIS CASE GETS STRANGER BY THE MOMENT! WHY WOULD SOMEONE BUILD MACHINES THAT DON'T DO ANYTHING?
AND WHY WOULD PIRATES KEEP SHIPS AWAY FROM THEM?
MAYBE WE SHOULD ASK THEM!
AVAST, YE SCURVY BILGE RATS! WE'LL KEELHAUL THE LOT OF YE!

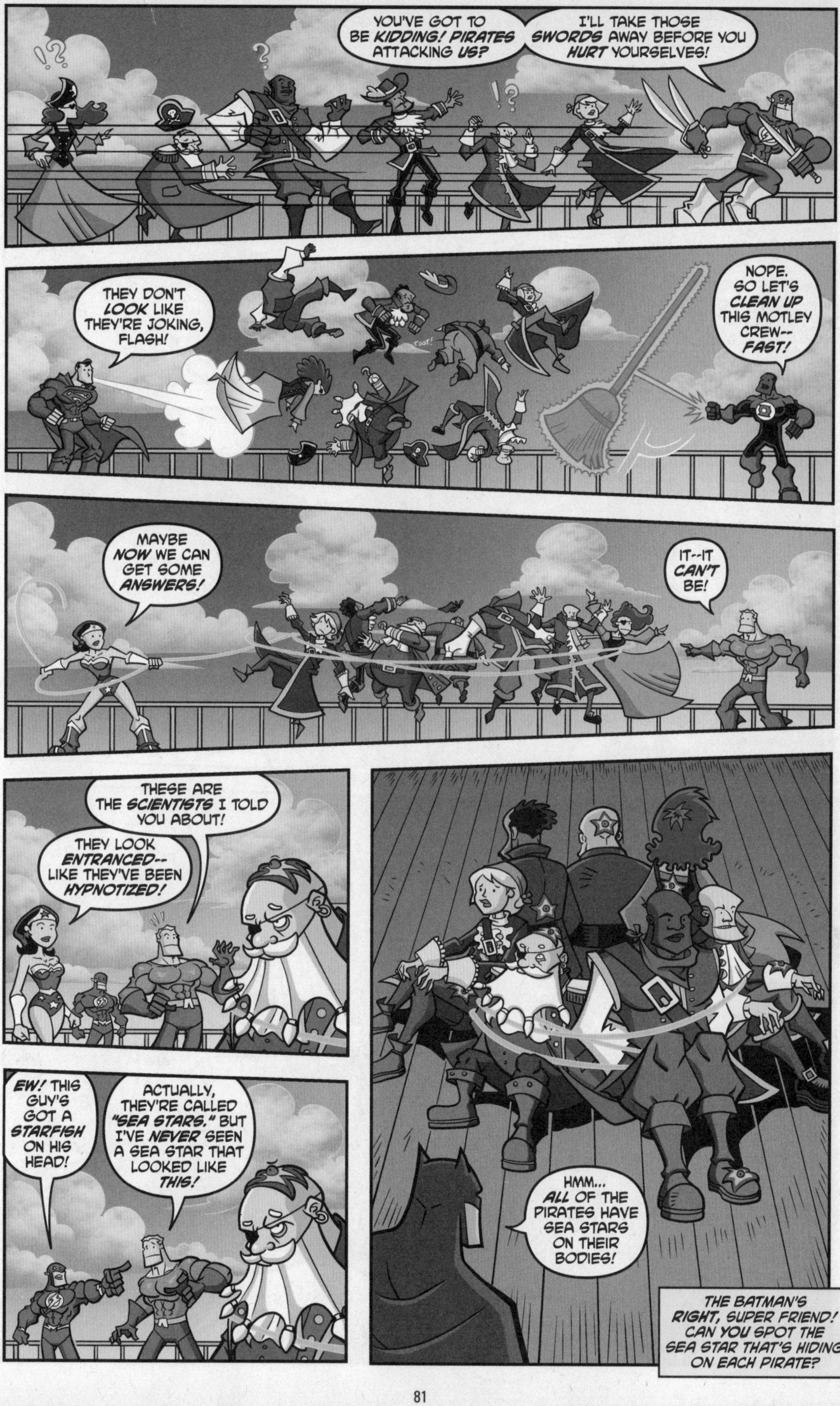

!??
?
!?
YOU'VE GOT TO BE KIDDING! PIRATES ATTACKING US?
I'LL TAKE THOSE SWORDS AWAY BEFORE YOU HURT YOURSELVES!
THEY DON'T LOOK LIKE THEY'RE JOKING, FLASH!
NOPE. SO LET'S CLEAN UP THIS MOTLEY CREW--FAST!
MAYBE NOW WE CAN GET SOME ANSWERS!
IT--IT CAN'T BE!
THESE ARE THE SCIENTISTS I TOLD YOU ABOUT!
THEY LOOK ENTRANCED--LIKE THEY'VE BEEN HYPNOTIZED!
EW! THIS GUY'S GOT A STARFISH ON HIS HEAD!
ACTUALLY, THEY'RE CALLED "SEA STARS." BUT I'VE NEVER SEEN A SEA STAR THAT LOOKED LIKE THIS!
HMM... ALL OF THE PIRATES HAVE SEA STARS ON THEIR BODIES!
THE BATMAN'S RIGHT, SUPER FRIEND! CAN YOU SPOT THE SEA STAR THAT'S HIDING ON EACH PIRATE?

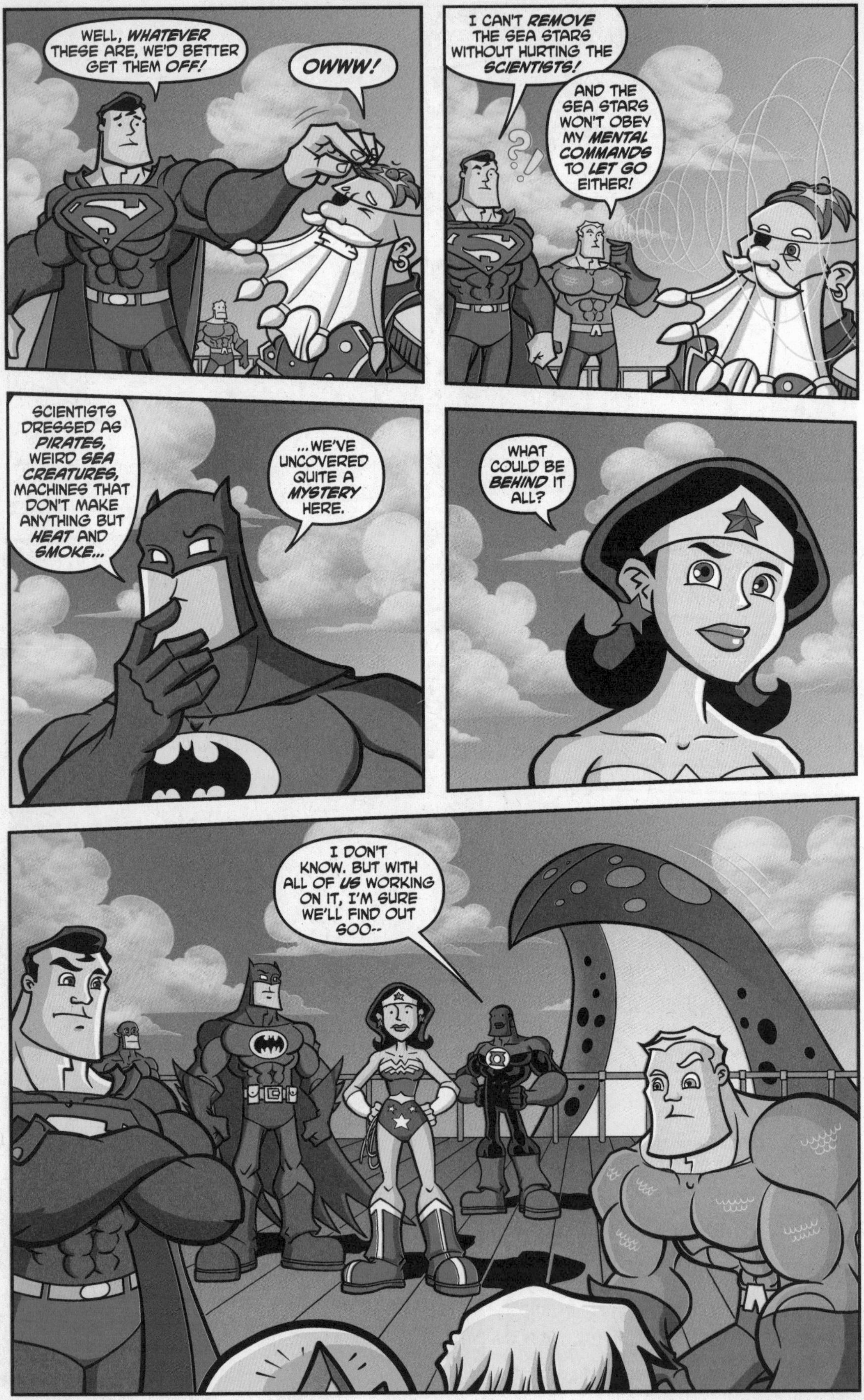
WELL, WHATEVER THESE ARE, WE'D BETTER GET THEM OFF!
OWWW!
I CAN'T REMOVE THE SEA STARS WITHOUT HURTING THE SCIENTISTS!
AND THE SEA STARS WON'T OBEY MY MENTAL COMMANDS TO LET GO EITHER!
SCIENTISTS DRESSED AS PIRATES, WEIRD SEA CREATURES, MACHINES THAT DON'T MAKE ANYTHING BUT HEAT AND SMOKE...
...WE'VE UNCOVERED QUITE A MYSTERY HERE.
WHAT COULD BE BEHIND IT ALL?
I DON'T KNOW. BUT WITH ALL OF US WORKING ON IT, I'M SURE WE'LL FIND OUT SOO--

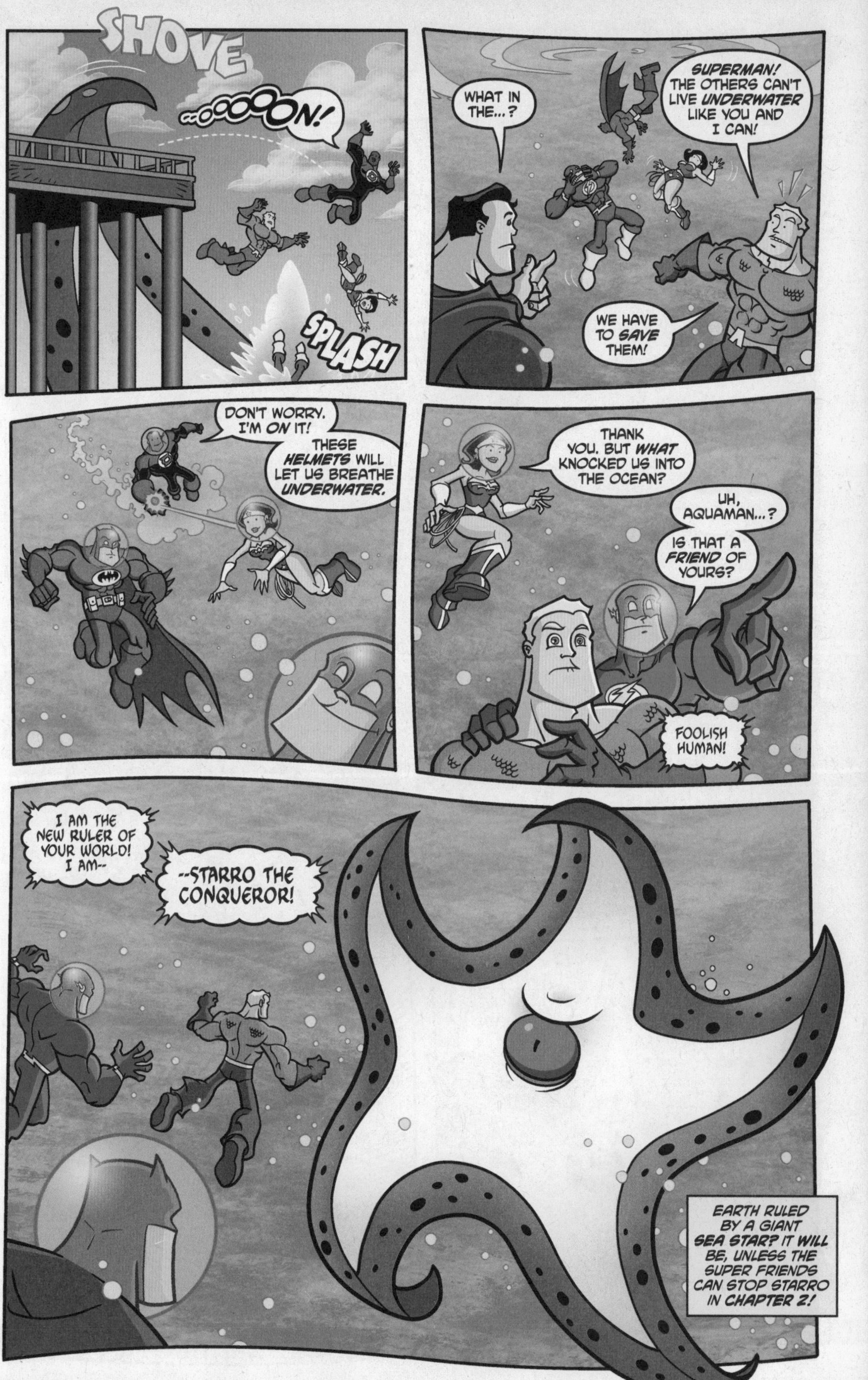

SHOVE
--OOOOOON!
SPLASH
WHAT IN THE...?
SUPERMAN! THE OTHERS CAN'T LIVE UNDERWATER LIKE YOU AND I CAN!
WE HAVE TO SAVE THEM!
DON'T WORRY. I'M ON IT!
THESE HELMETS WILL LET US BREATHE UNDERWATER.
THANK YOU. BUT WHAT KNOCKED US INTO THE OCEAN?
UH, AQUAMAN...?
IS THAT A FRIEND OF YOURS?
FOOLISH HUMAN!
I AM THE NEW RULER OF YOUR WORLD! I AM--
--STARRO THE CONQUEROR!
EARTH RULED BY A GIANT SEA STAR? IT WILL BE, UNLESS THE SUPER FRIENDS CAN STOP STARRO IN CHAPTER 2!

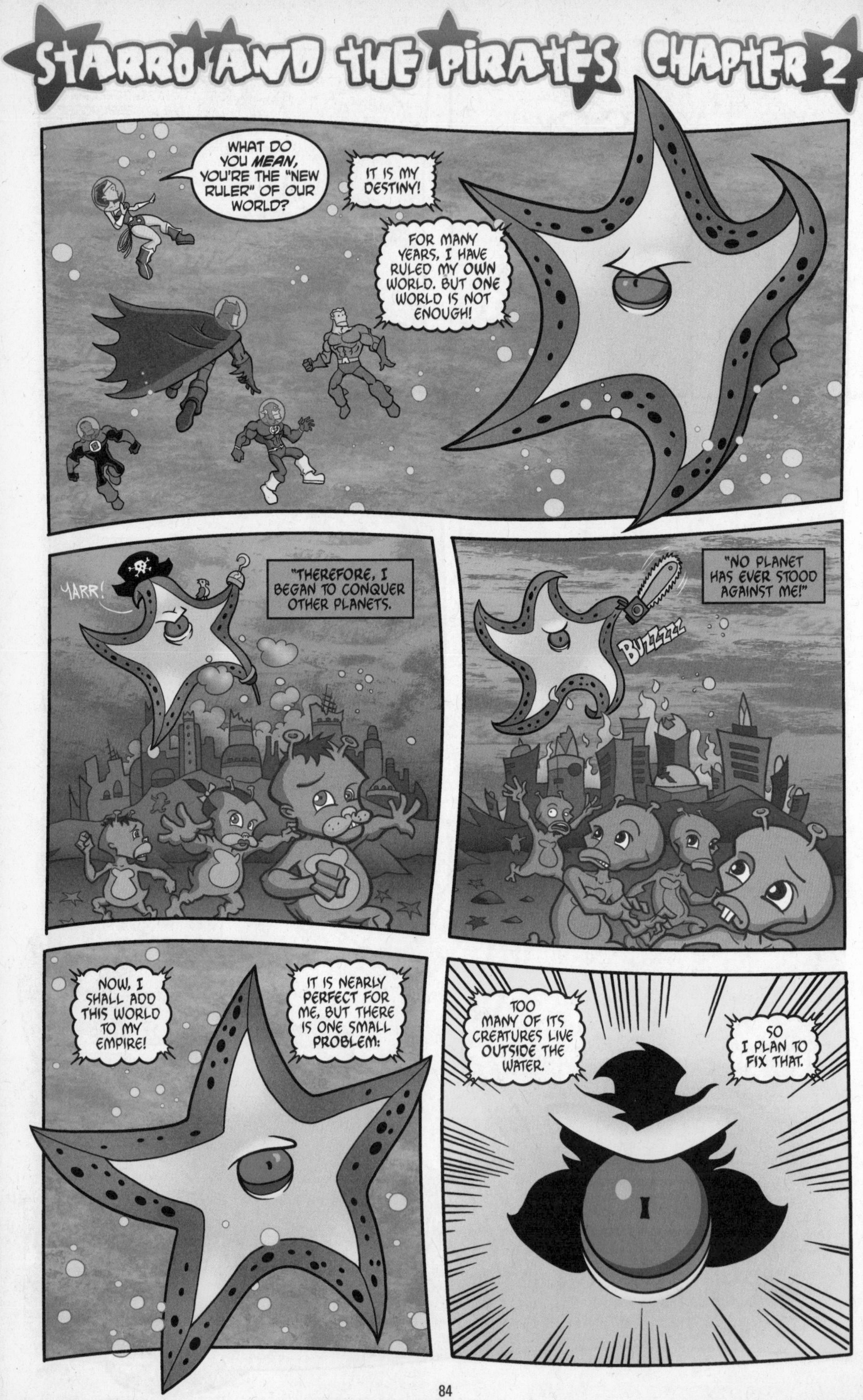
STARRO AND THE PIRATES CHAPTER 2
WHAT DO YOU MEAN, YOU'RE THE "NEW RULER" OF OUR WORLD?
IT IS MY DESTINY!
FOR MANY YEARS, I HAVE RULED MY OWN WORLD. BUT ONE WORLD IS NOT ENOUGH!
"THEREFORE, I BEGAN TO CONQUER OTHER PLANETS.
YARR!
"NO PLANET HAS EVER STOOD AGAINST ME!"
BUZZZZZ
NOW, I SHALL ADD THIS WORLD TO MY EMPIRE!
IT IS NEARLY PERFECT FOR ME, BUT THERE IS ONE SMALL PROBLEM:
TOO MANY OF ITS CREATURES LIVE OUTSIDE THE WATER.
SO I PLAN TO FIX THAT.

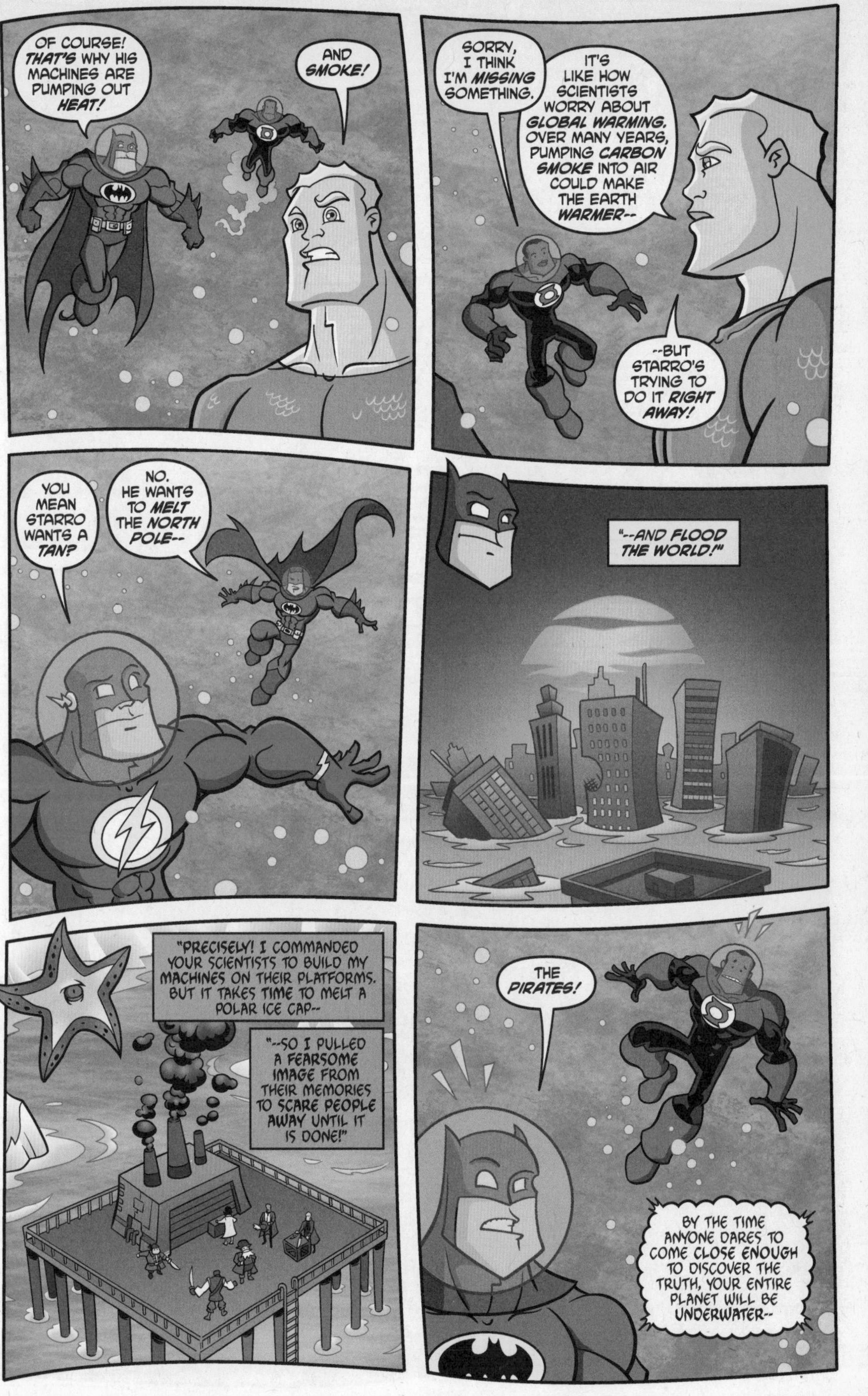

OF COURSE! THAT'S WHY HIS MACHINES ARE PUMPING OUT HEAT!
AND SMOKE!
SORRY, I THINK I'M MISSING SOMETHING.
IT'S LIKE HOW SCIENTISTS WORRY ABOUT GLOBAL WARMING. OVER MANY YEARS, PUMPING CARBON SMOKE INTO AIR COULD MAKE THE EARTH WARMER--
--BUT STARRO'S TRYING TO DO IT RIGHT AWAY!
YOU MEAN STARRO WANTS A TAN?
NO. HE WANTS TO MELT THE NORTH POLE--
"--AND FLOOD THE WORLD!"
"PRECISELY! I COMMANDED YOUR SCIENTISTS TO BUILD MY MACHINES ON THEIR PLATFORMS. BUT IT TAKES TIME TO MELT A POLAR ICE CAP--
"--SO I PULLED A FEARSOME IMAGE FROM THEIR MEMORIES TO SCARE PEOPLE AWAY UNTIL IT IS DONE!"
THE PIRATES!
BY THE TIME ANYONE DARES TO COME CLOSE ENOUGH TO DISCOVER THE TRUTH, YOUR ENTIRE PLANET WILL BE UNDERWATER--

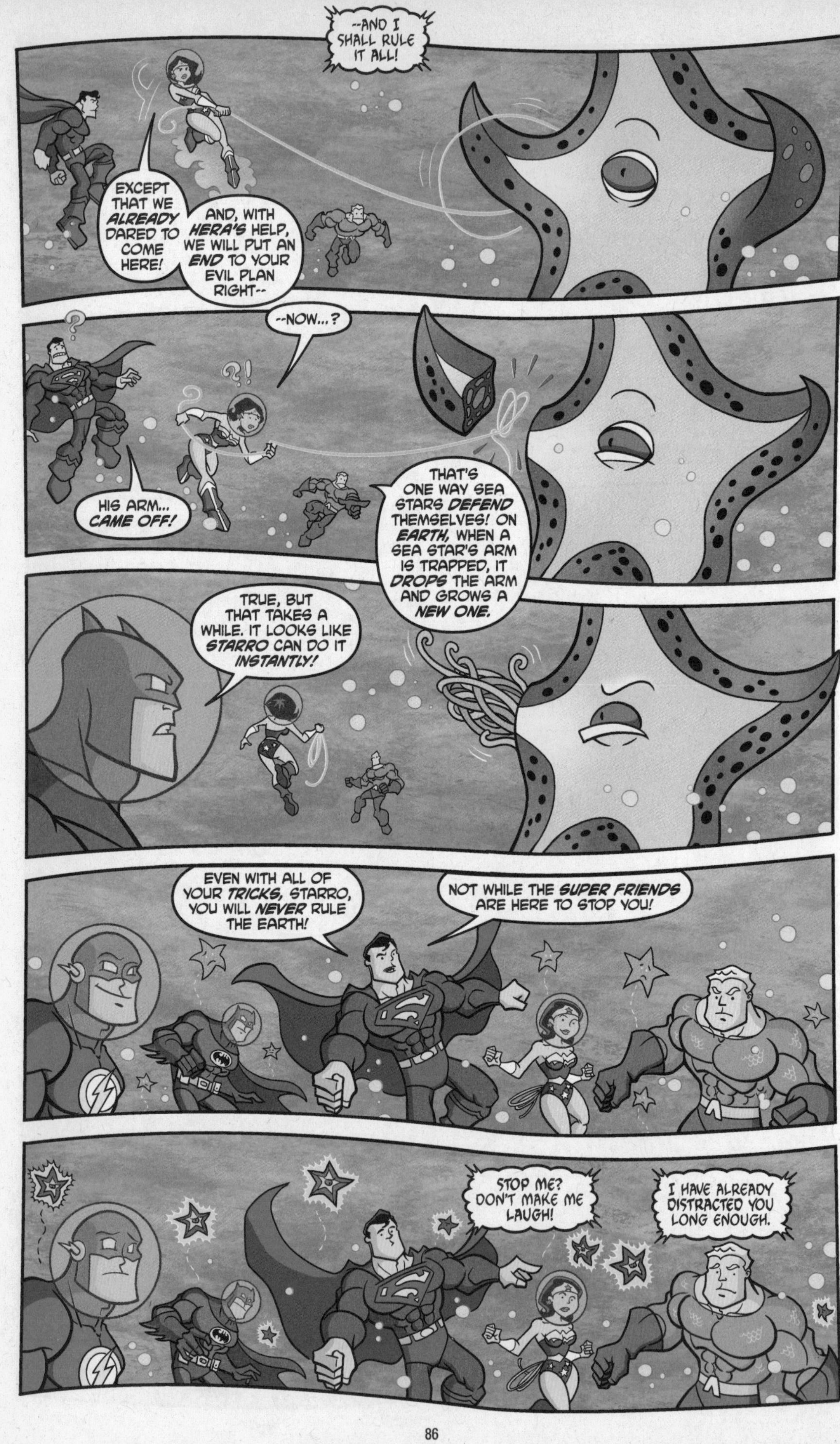
--AND I SHALL RULE IT ALL!
EXCEPT THAT WE ALREADY DARED TO COME HERE!
AND, WITH HERA'S HELP, WE WILL PUT AN END TO YOUR EVIL PLAN RIGHT--
--NOW...?
HIS ARM... CAME OFF!
THAT'S ONE WAY SEA STARS DEFEND THEMSELVES! ON EARTH, WHEN A SEA STAR'S ARM IS TRAPPED, IT DROPS THE ARM AND GROWS A NEW ONE.
TRUE, BUT THAT TAKES A WHILE. IT LOOKS LIKE STARRO CAN DO IT INSTANTLY!
EVEN WITH ALL OF YOUR TRICKS, STARRO, YOU WILL NEVER RULE THE EARTH!
NOT WHILE THE SUPER FRIENDS ARE HERE TO STOP YOU!
STOP ME? DON'T MAKE ME LAUGH!
I HAVE ALREADY DISTRACTED YOU LONG ENOUGH.

ONCE MY SEA STARS ATTACH THEMSELVES TO YOUR BODIES--

--YOU'LL HELP ME!

GOT TO USE MY *MENTAL* POWERS...

COMMAND THEM TO *STAY AWAY*...

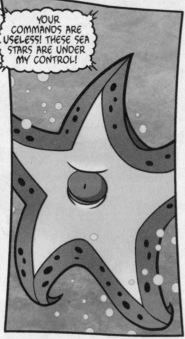

YOUR COMMANDS ARE USELESS! THESE SEA STARS ARE UNDER MY CONTROL!

OH... *REALLY?*

THEN I'LL JUST HAVE TO...

...TRY *HARDER!*

THANK NEPTUNE! THE SEA STARS ARE RETURNING TO *NORMAL!*

I *DID* IT!

SO YOU DID. TOO BAD YOUR MENTAL POWERS DON'T WORK ON YOUR FRIENDS--

--NOW THAT THEY ARE UNDER MY CONTROL!

AQUAMAN--ALONE AGAINST THE *SUPER FRIENDS?* YOU WON'T WANT TO MISS WHAT HAPPENS IN *CHAPTER 3!*

STARRO AND THE PIRATES CHAPTER 3

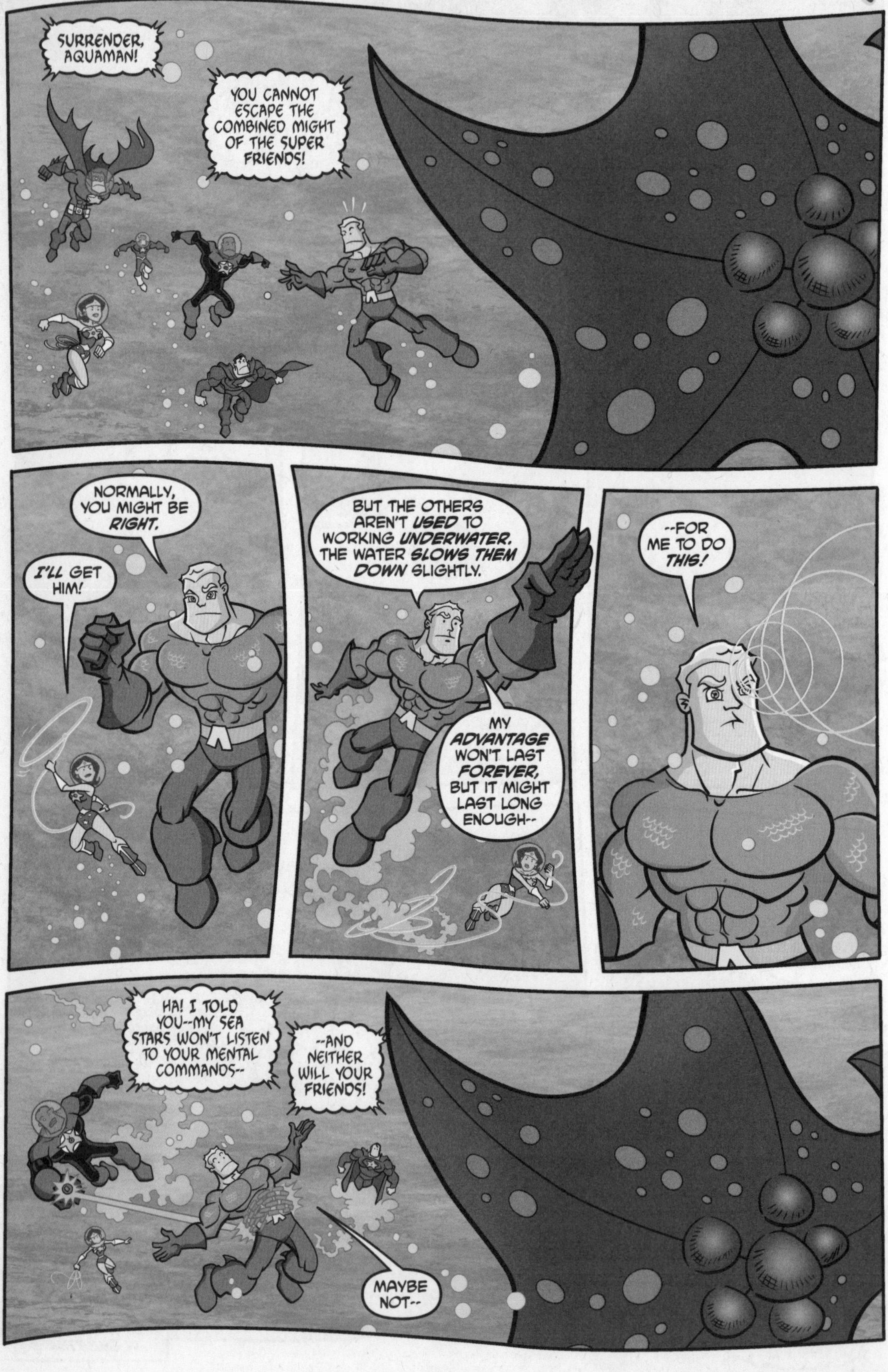

SURRENDER, AQUAMAN!
YOU CANNOT ESCAPE THE COMBINED MIGHT OF THE SUPER FRIENDS!
NORMALLY, YOU MIGHT BE RIGHT.
I'LL GET HIM!
BUT THE OTHERS AREN'T USED TO WORKING UNDERWATER. THE WATER SLOWS THEM DOWN SLIGHTLY.
MY ADVANTAGE WON'T LAST FOREVER, BUT IT MIGHT LAST LONG ENOUGH--
--FOR ME TO DO THIS!
HA! I TOLD YOU--MY SEA STARS WON'T LISTEN TO YOUR MENTAL COMMANDS--
--AND NEITHER WILL YOUR FRIENDS!
MAYBE NOT--

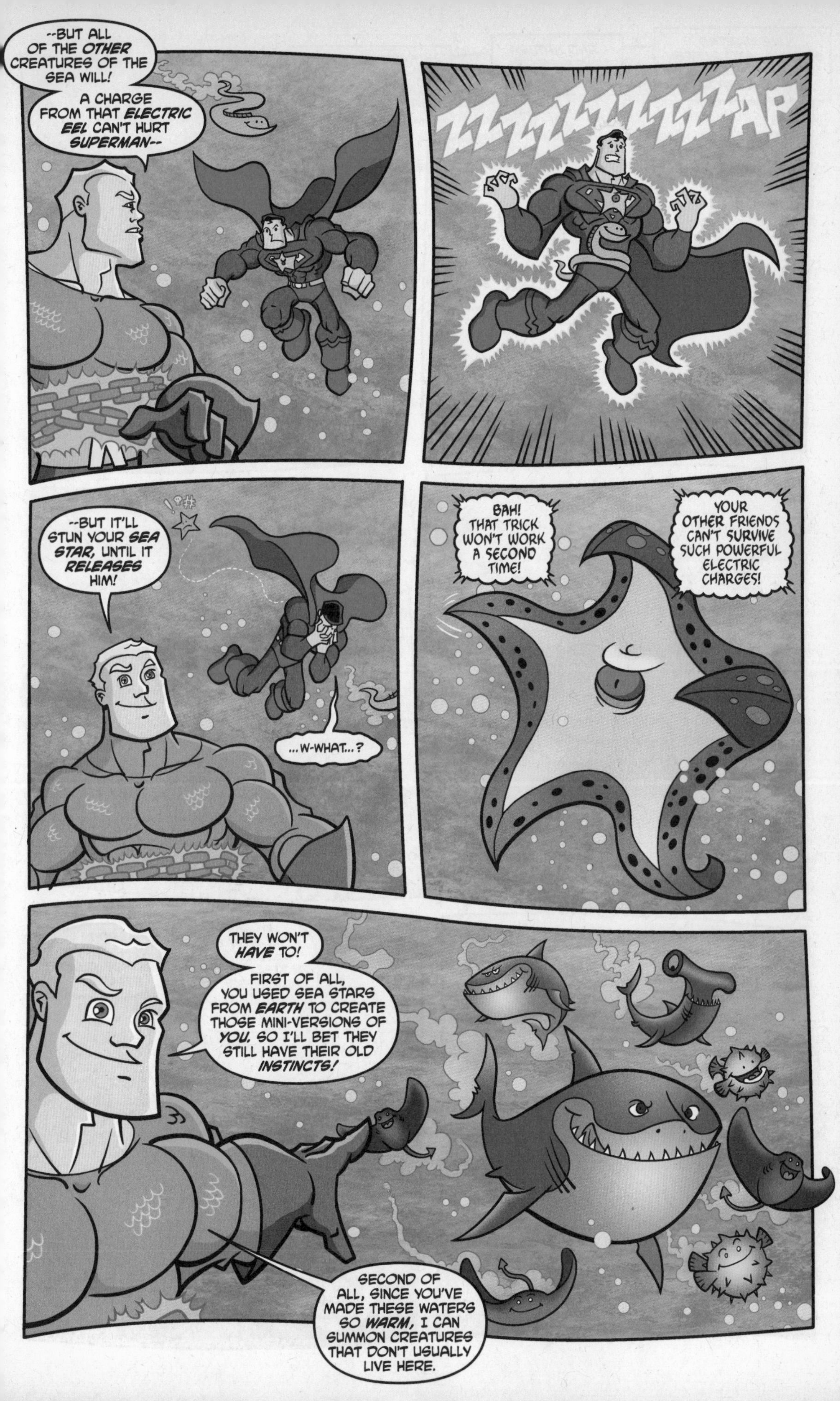
--BUT ALL OF THE OTHER CREATURES OF THE SEA WILL!
A CHARGE FROM THAT ELECTRIC EEL CAN'T HURT SUPERMAN--
ZZZZZZZZZZZAP
--BUT IT'LL STUN YOUR SEA STAR, UNTIL IT RELEASES HIM!
...W-WHAT...?
BAH! THAT TRICK WON'T WORK A SECOND TIME!
YOUR OTHER FRIENDS CAN'T SURVIVE SUCH POWERFUL ELECTRIC CHARGES!
THEY WON'T HAVE TO!
FIRST OF ALL, YOU USED SEA STARS FROM EARTH TO CREATE THOSE MINI-VERSIONS OF YOU, SO I'LL BET THEY STILL HAVE THEIR OLD INSTINCTS!
SECOND OF ALL, SINCE YOU'VE MADE THESE WATERS SO WARM, I CAN SUMMON CREATURES THAT DON'T USUALLY LIVE HERE.

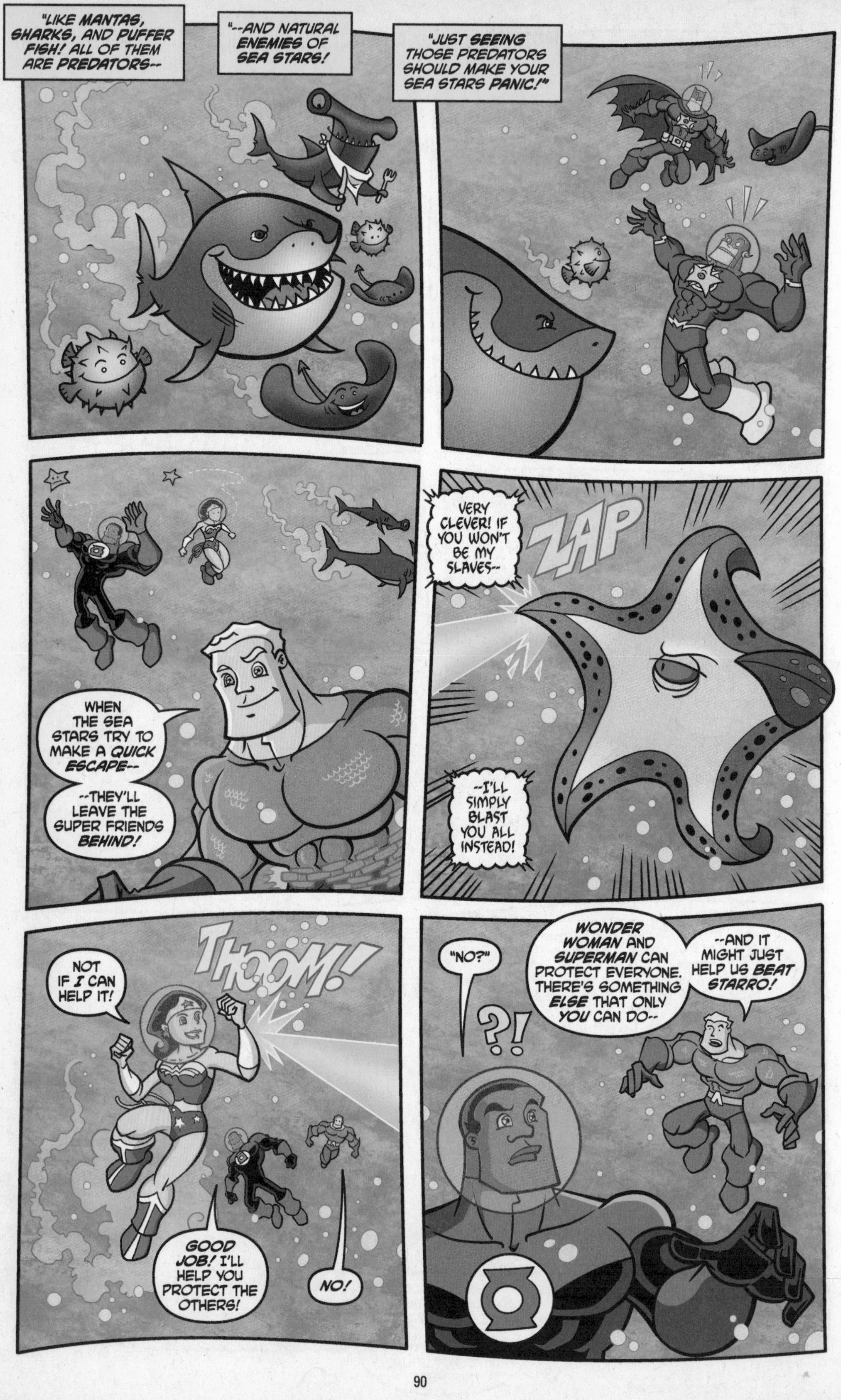
"LIKE MANTAS, SHARKS, AND PUFFER FISH! ALL OF THEM ARE PREDATORS--
"--AND NATURAL ENEMIES OF SEA STARS!
"JUST SEEING THOSE PREDATORS SHOULD MAKE YOUR SEA STARS PANIC!"
WHEN THE SEA STARS TRY TO MAKE A QUICK ESCAPE--
--THEY'LL LEAVE THE SUPER FRIENDS BEHIND!
VERY CLEVER! IF YOU WON'T BE MY SLAVES--
ZAP
--I'LL SIMPLY BLAST YOU ALL INSTEAD!
NOT IF I CAN HELP IT!
THOOM!
GOOD JOB! I'LL HELP YOU PROTECT THE OTHERS!
NO!
"NO?"
?!
WONDER WOMAN AND SUPERMAN CAN PROTECT EVERYONE. THERE'S SOMETHING ELSE THAT ONLY YOU CAN DO--
--AND IT MIGHT JUST HELP US BEAT STARRO!

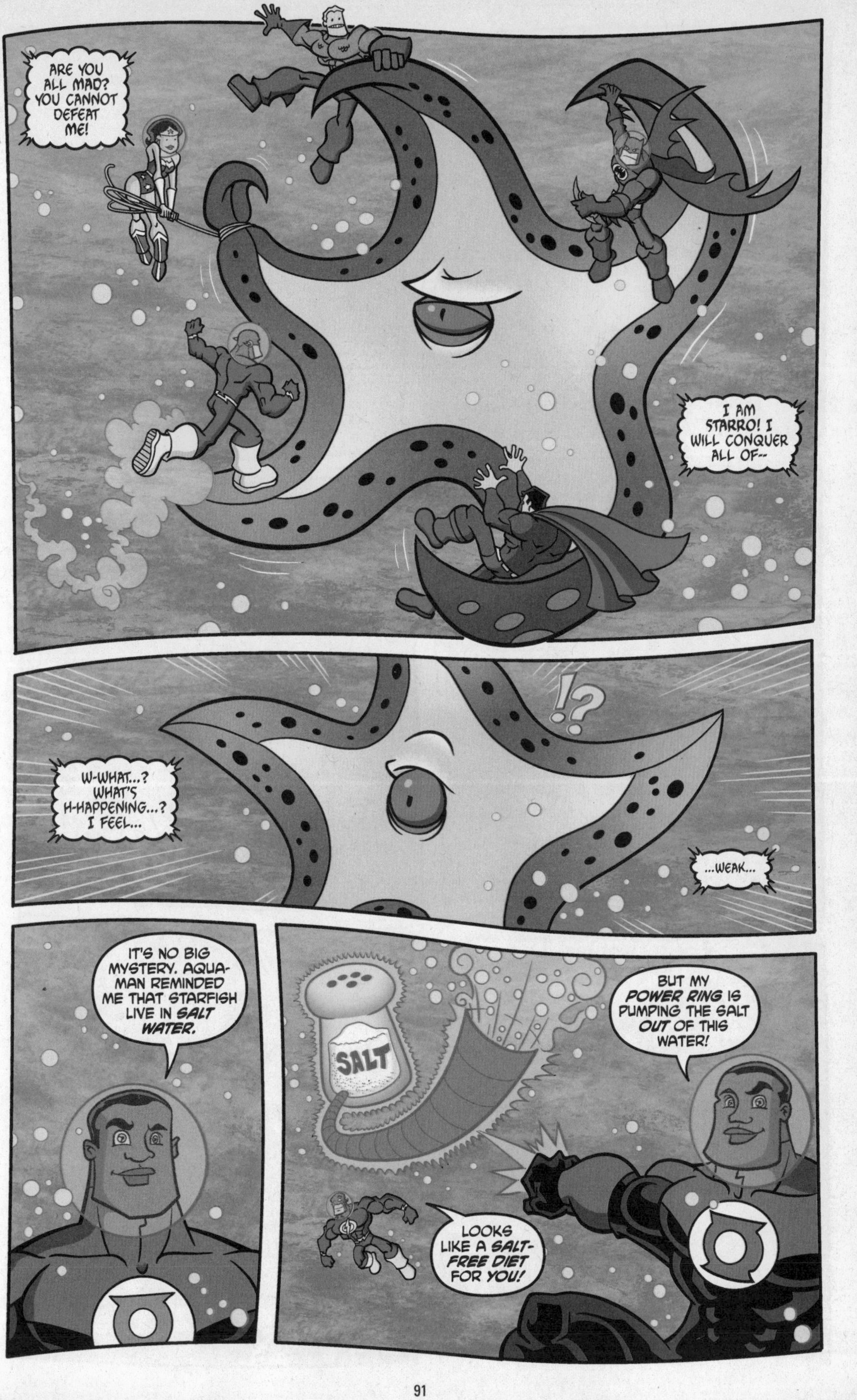
ARE YOU ALL MAD? YOU CANNOT DEFEAT ME!
I AM STARRO! I WILL CONQUER ALL OF--
!?
W-WHAT...? WHAT'S H-HAPPENING...? I FEEL...
...WEAK...
IT'S NO BIG MYSTERY. AQUAMAN REMINDED ME THAT STARFISH LIVE IN SALT WATER.
SALT
BUT MY POWER RING IS PUMPING THE SALT OUT OF THIS WATER!
LOOKS LIKE A SALT-FREE DIET FOR YOU!

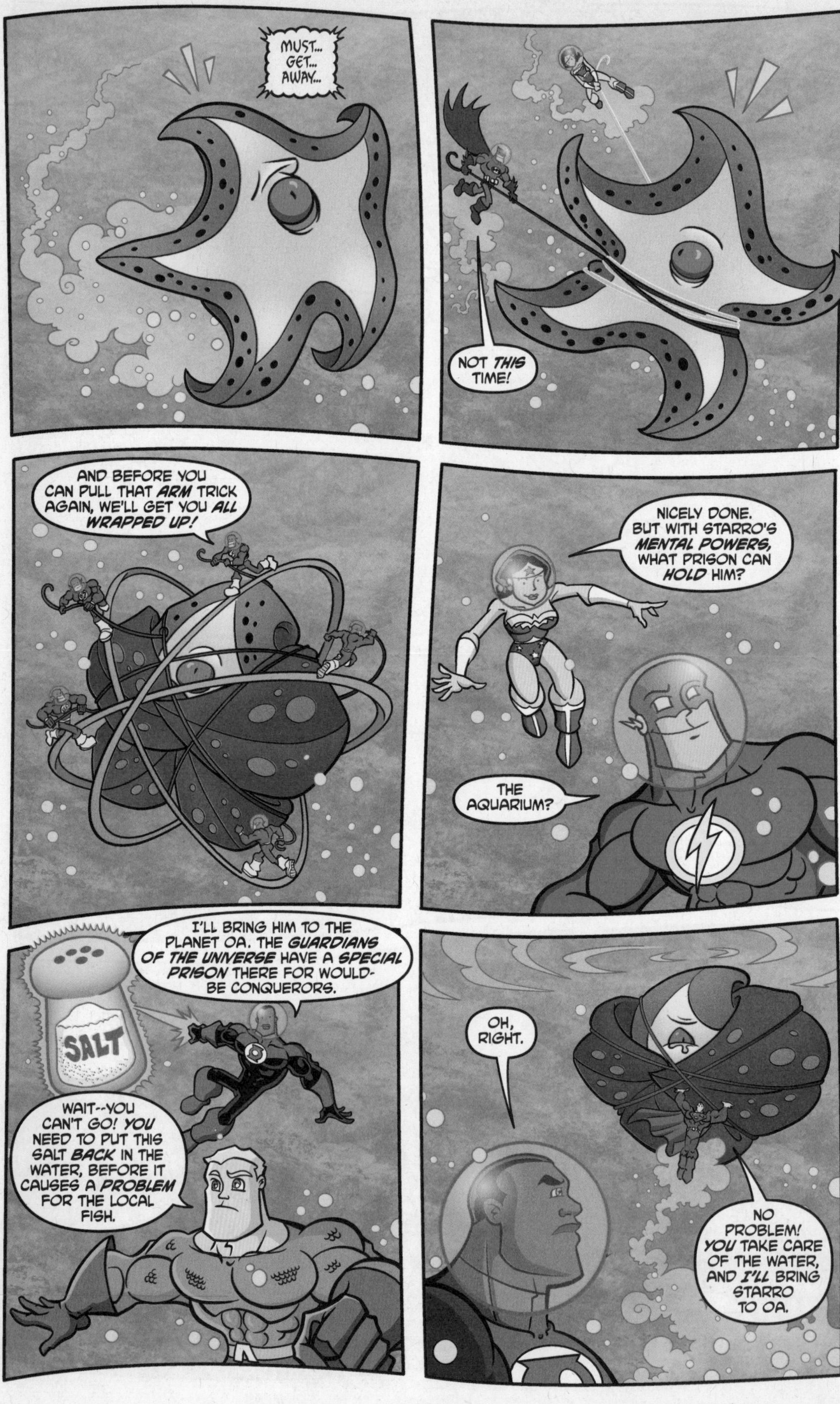

MUST... GET... AWAY...
NOT THIS TIME!
AND BEFORE YOU CAN PULL THAT ARM TRICK AGAIN, WE'LL GET YOU ALL WRAPPED UP!
NICELY DONE. BUT WITH STARRO'S MENTAL POWERS, WHAT PRISON CAN HOLD HIM?
THE AQUARIUM?
SALT
I'LL BRING HIM TO THE PLANET OA. THE GUARDIANS OF THE UNIVERSE HAVE A SPECIAL PRISON THERE FOR WOULD-BE CONQUERORS.
WAIT--YOU CAN'T GO! YOU NEED TO PUT THIS SALT BACK IN THE WATER, BEFORE IT CAUSES A PROBLEM FOR THE LOCAL FISH.
OH, RIGHT.
NO PROBLEM! YOU TAKE CARE OF THE WATER, AND I'LL BRING STARRO TO OA.

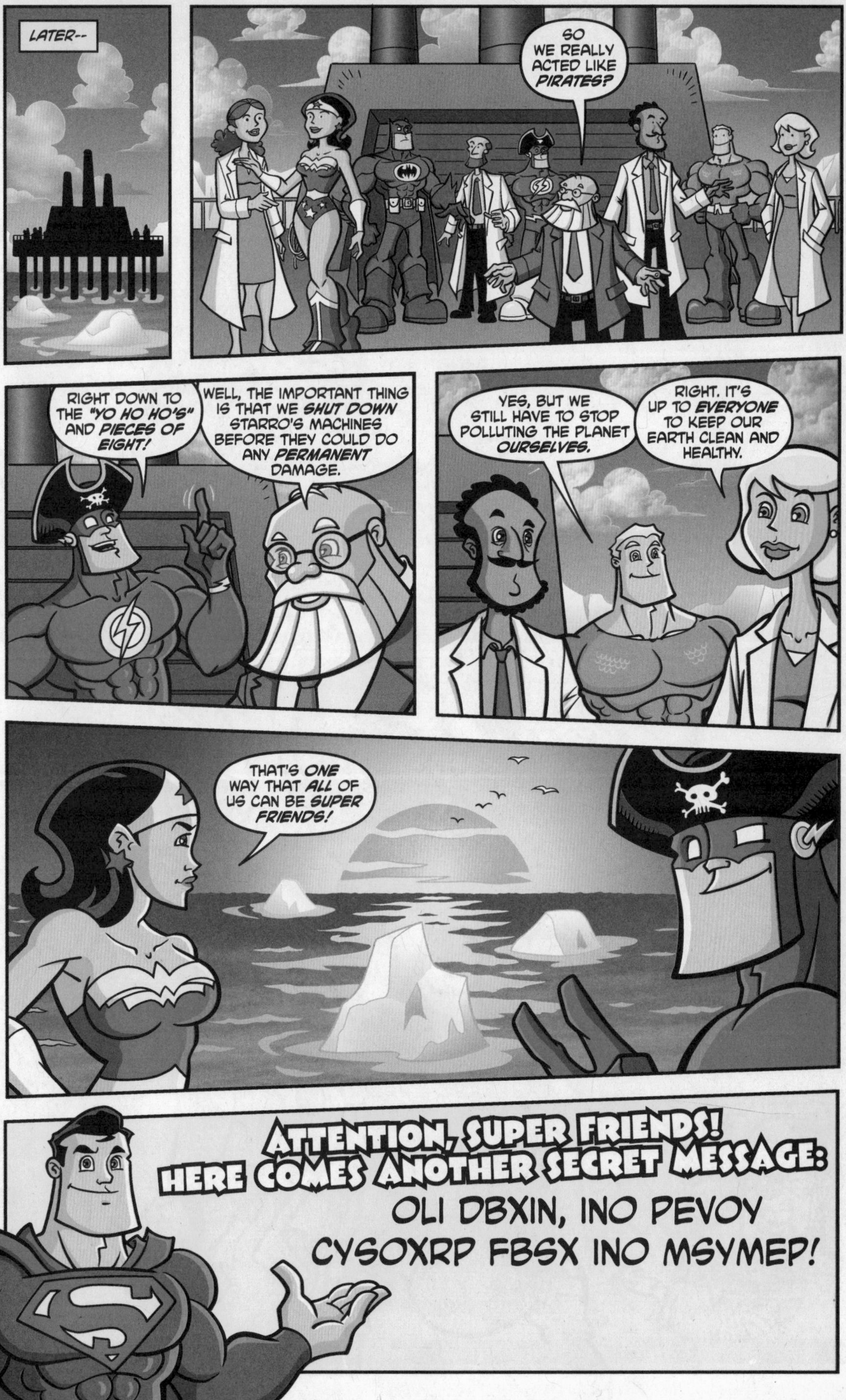
LATER--
SO WE REALLY ACTED LIKE PIRATES?
RIGHT DOWN TO THE "YO HO HO'S" AND PIECES OF EIGHT!
WELL, THE IMPORTANT THING IS THAT WE SHUT DOWN STARRO'S MACHINES BEFORE THEY COULD DO ANY PERMANENT DAMAGE.
YES, BUT WE STILL HAVE TO STOP POLLUTING THE PLANET OURSELVES.
RIGHT. IT'S UP TO EVERYONE TO KEEP OUR EARTH CLEAN AND HEALTHY.
THAT'S ONE WAY THAT ALL OF US CAN BE SUPER FRIENDS!
ATTENTION, SUPER FRIENDS!
HERE COMES ANOTHER SECRET MESSAGE:
OLI DBXIN, INO PEVOY
CYSOXRP FBSX INO MSYMEP!

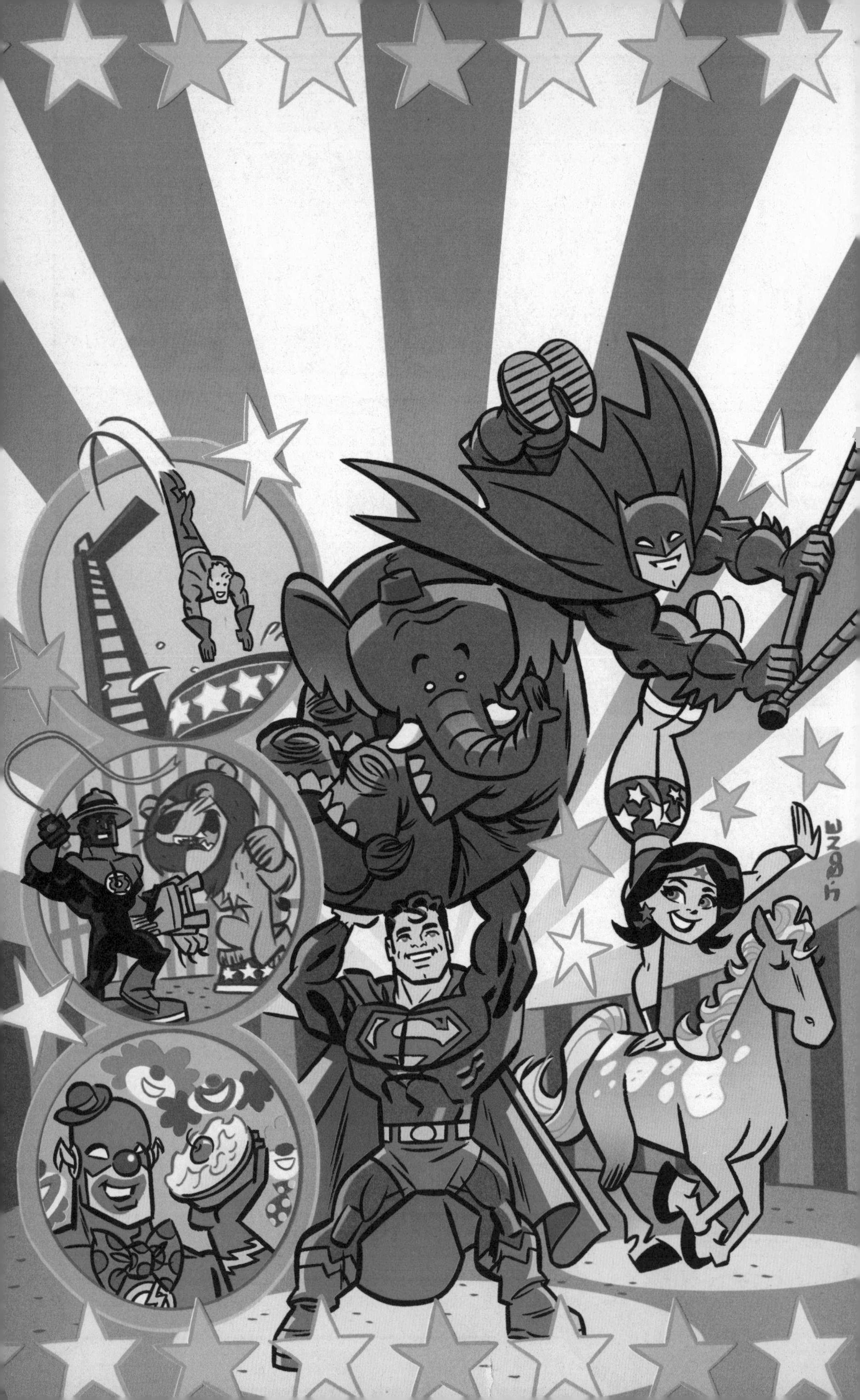

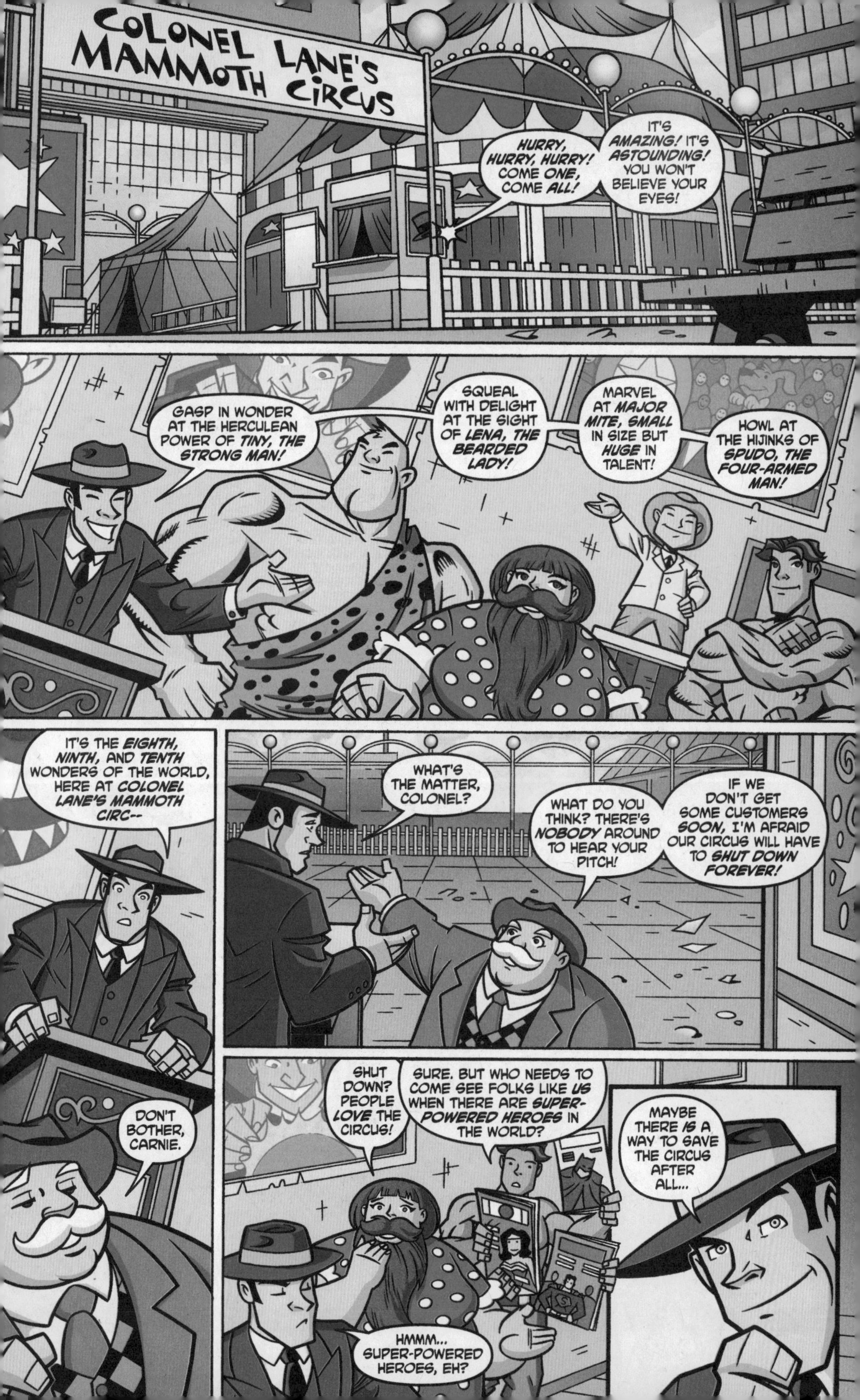
COLONEL LANE'S MAMMOTH CIRCUS
HURRY, HURRY, HURRY! COME ONE, COME ALL!
IT'S AMAZING! IT'S ASTOUNDING! YOU WON'T BELIEVE YOUR EYES!
GASP IN WONDER AT THE HERCULEAN POWER OF TINY, THE STRONG MAN!
SQUEAL WITH DELIGHT AT THE SIGHT OF LENA, THE BEARDED LADY!
MARVEL AT MAJOR MITE, SMALL IN SIZE BUT HUGE IN TALENT!
HOWL AT THE HIJINKS OF SPUDO, THE FOUR-ARMED MAN!
IT'S THE EIGHTH, NINTH, AND TENTH WONDERS OF THE WORLD, HERE AT COLONEL LANE'S MAMMOTH CIRC--
WHAT'S THE MATTER, COLONEL?
WHAT DO YOU THINK? THERE'S NOBODY AROUND TO HEAR YOUR PITCH!
IF WE DON'T GET SOME CUSTOMERS SOON, I'M AFRAID OUR CIRCUS WILL HAVE TO SHUT DOWN FOREVER!
DON'T BOTHER, CARNIE.
SHUT DOWN? PEOPLE LOVE THE CIRCUS!
SURE. BUT WHO NEEDS TO COME SEE FOLKS LIKE US WHEN THERE ARE SUPER-POWERED HEROES IN THE WORLD?
HMMM... SUPER-POWERED HEROES, EH?
MAYBE THERE IS A WAY TO SAVE THE CIRCUS AFTER ALL...

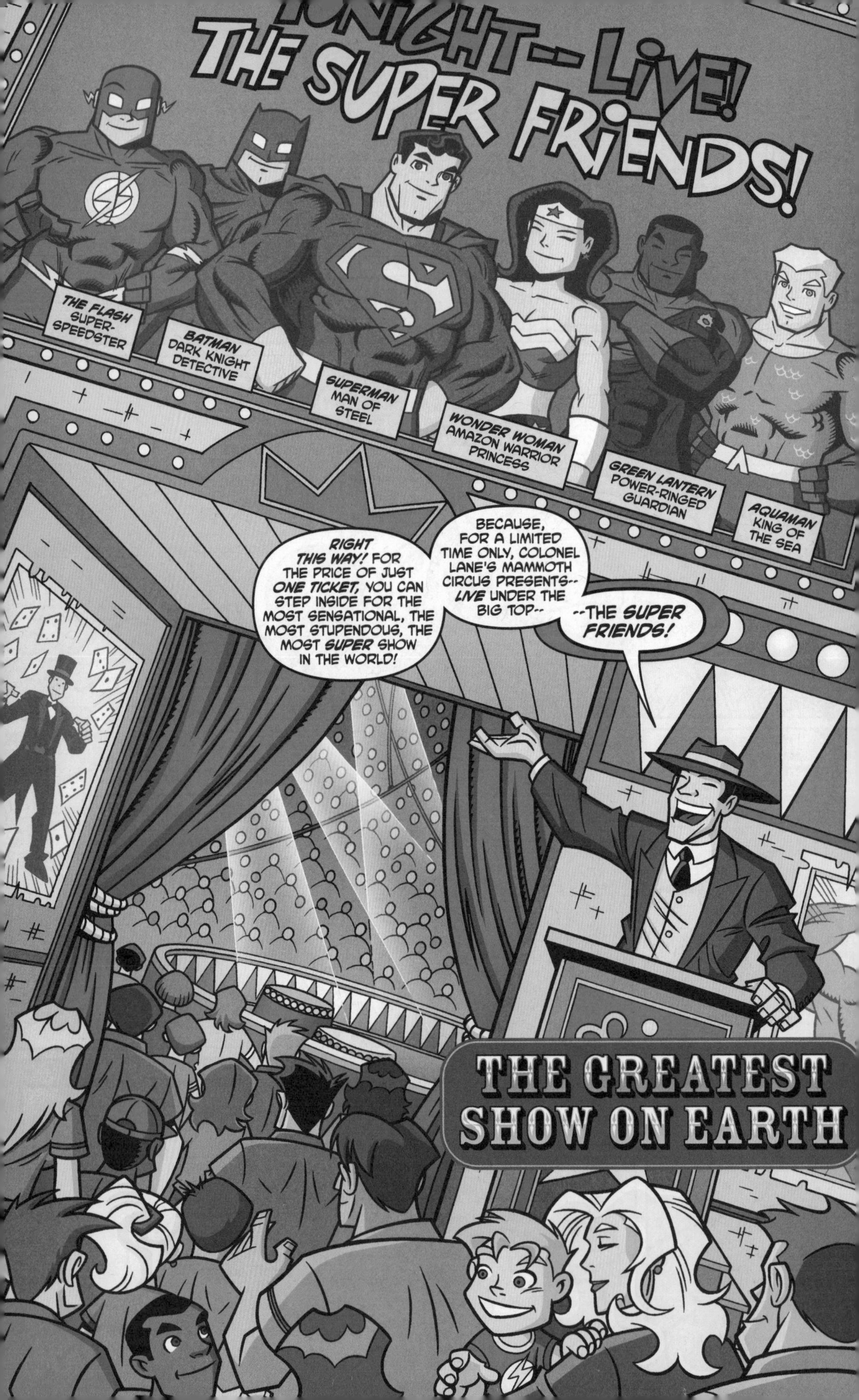
TONIGHT -- LIVE! THE SUPER FRIENDS!
THE FLASH SUPER-SPEEDSTER
BATMAN DARK KNIGHT DETECTIVE
SUPERMAN MAN OF STEEL
WONDER WOMAN AMAZON WARRIOR PRINCESS
GREEN LANTERN POWER-RINGED GUARDIAN
AQUAMAN KING OF THE SEA
RIGHT THIS WAY! FOR THE PRICE OF JUST ONE TICKET, YOU CAN STEP INSIDE FOR THE MOST SENSATIONAL, THE MOST STUPENDOUS, THE MOST SUPER SHOW IN THE WORLD!
BECAUSE, FOR A LIMITED TIME ONLY, COLONEL LANE'S MAMMOTH CIRCUS PRESENTS-- LIVE UNDER THE BIG TOP--
--THE SUPER FRIENDS!
THE GREATEST SHOW ON EARTH

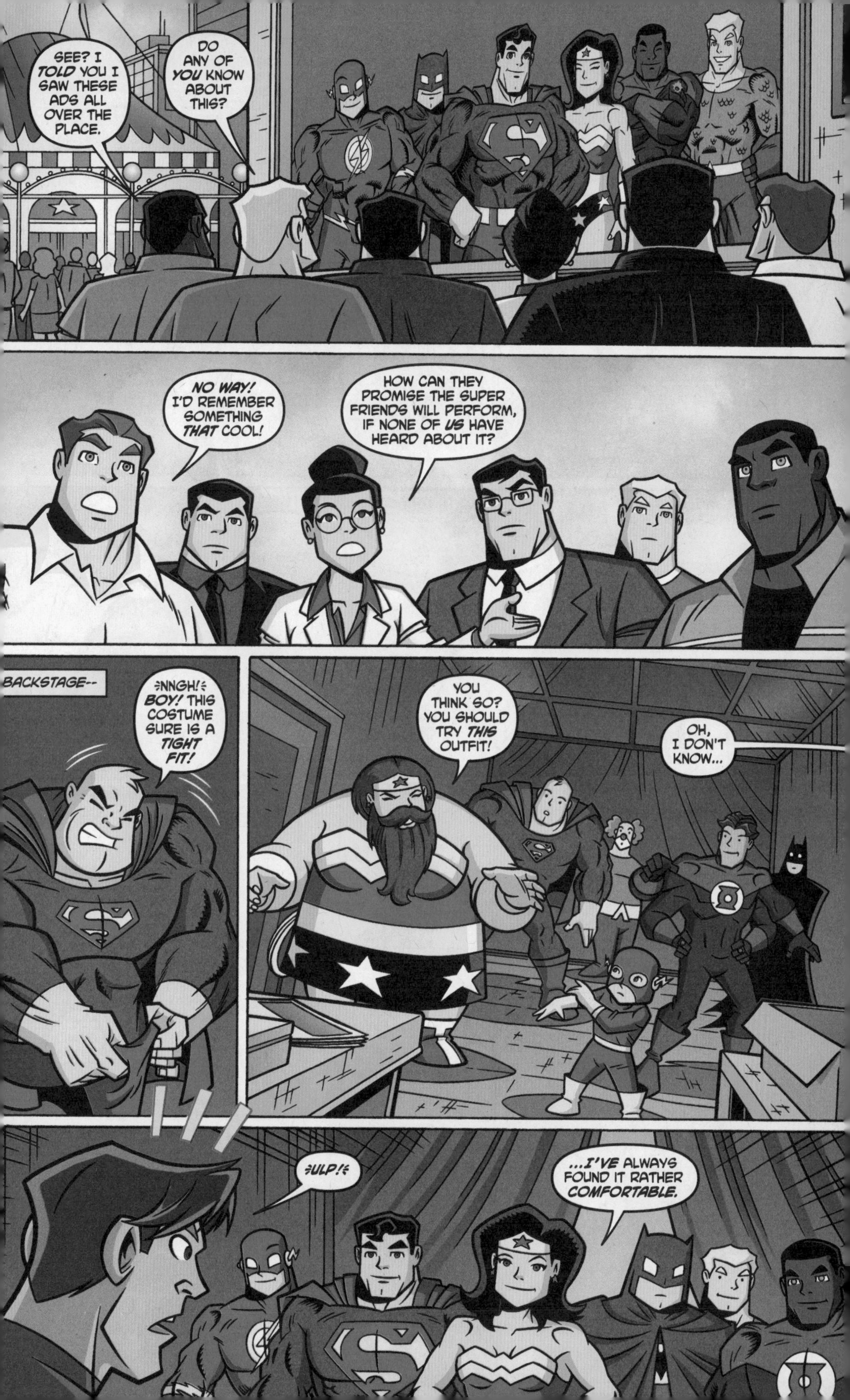

SEE? I TOLD YOU I SAW THESE ADS ALL OVER THE PLACE.
DO ANY OF YOU KNOW ABOUT THIS?
NO WAY! I'D REMEMBER SOMETHING THAT COOL!
HOW CAN THEY PROMISE THE SUPER FRIENDS WILL PERFORM, IF NONE OF US HAVE HEARD ABOUT IT?
BACKSTAGE--
NNGH! BOY! THIS COSTUME SURE IS A TIGHT FIT!
YOU THINK SO? YOU SHOULD TRY THIS OUTFIT!
OH, I DON'T KNOW...
ULP!
...I'VE ALWAYS FOUND IT RATHER COMFORTABLE.

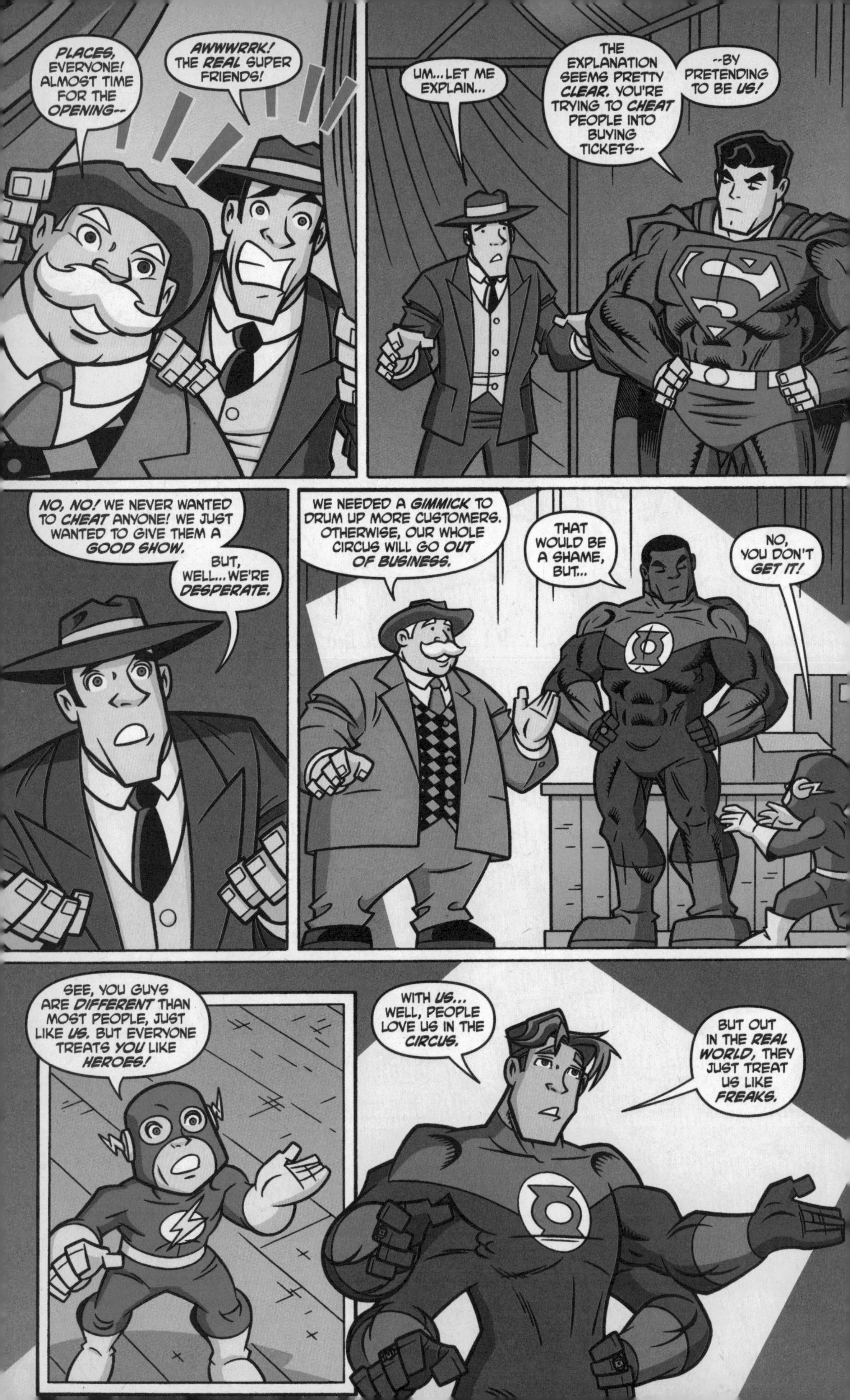

PLACES, EVERYONE! ALMOST TIME FOR THE OPENING--
AWWWRRK! THE REAL SUPER FRIENDS!
UM...LET ME EXPLAIN...
THE EXPLANATION SEEMS PRETTY CLEAR. YOU'RE TRYING TO CHEAT PEOPLE INTO BUYING TICKETS--
--BY PRETENDING TO BE US!
NO, NO! WE NEVER WANTED TO CHEAT ANYONE! WE JUST WANTED TO GIVE THEM A GOOD SHOW.
BUT, WELL...WE'RE DESPERATE.
WE NEEDED A GIMMICK TO DRUM UP MORE CUSTOMERS. OTHERWISE, OUR WHOLE CIRCUS WILL GO OUT OF BUSINESS.
THAT WOULD BE A SHAME, BUT...
NO, YOU DON'T GET IT!
SEE, YOU GUYS ARE DIFFERENT THAN MOST PEOPLE, JUST LIKE US. BUT EVERYONE TREATS YOU LIKE HEROES!
WITH US... WELL, PEOPLE LOVE US IN THE CIRCUS.
BUT OUT IN THE REAL WORLD, THEY JUST TREAT US LIKE FREAKS.

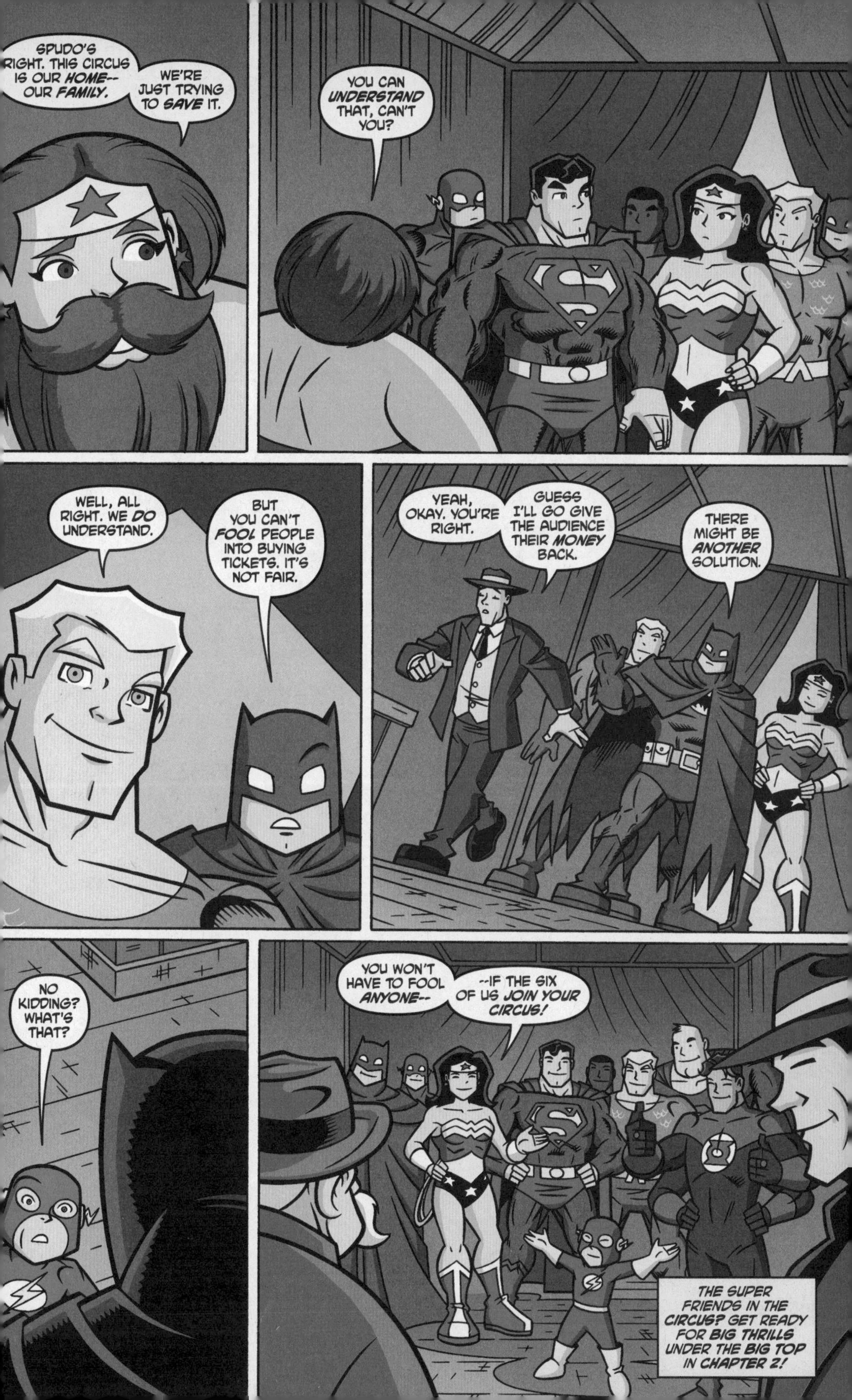
SPUDO'S RIGHT. THIS CIRCUS IS OUR HOME-- OUR FAMILY.
WE'RE JUST TRYING TO SAVE IT.
YOU CAN UNDERSTAND THAT, CAN'T YOU?
WELL, ALL RIGHT. WE DO UNDERSTAND.
BUT YOU CAN'T FOOL PEOPLE INTO BUYING TICKETS. IT'S NOT FAIR.
YEAH, OKAY. YOU'RE RIGHT.
GUESS I'LL GO GIVE THE AUDIENCE THEIR MONEY BACK.
THERE MIGHT BE ANOTHER SOLUTION.
NO KIDDING? WHAT'S THAT?
YOU WON'T HAVE TO FOOL ANYONE--
--IF THE SIX OF US JOIN YOUR CIRCUS!
THE SUPER FRIENDS IN THE CIRCUS? GET READY FOR BIG THRILLS UNDER THE BIG TOP IN CHAPTER 2!

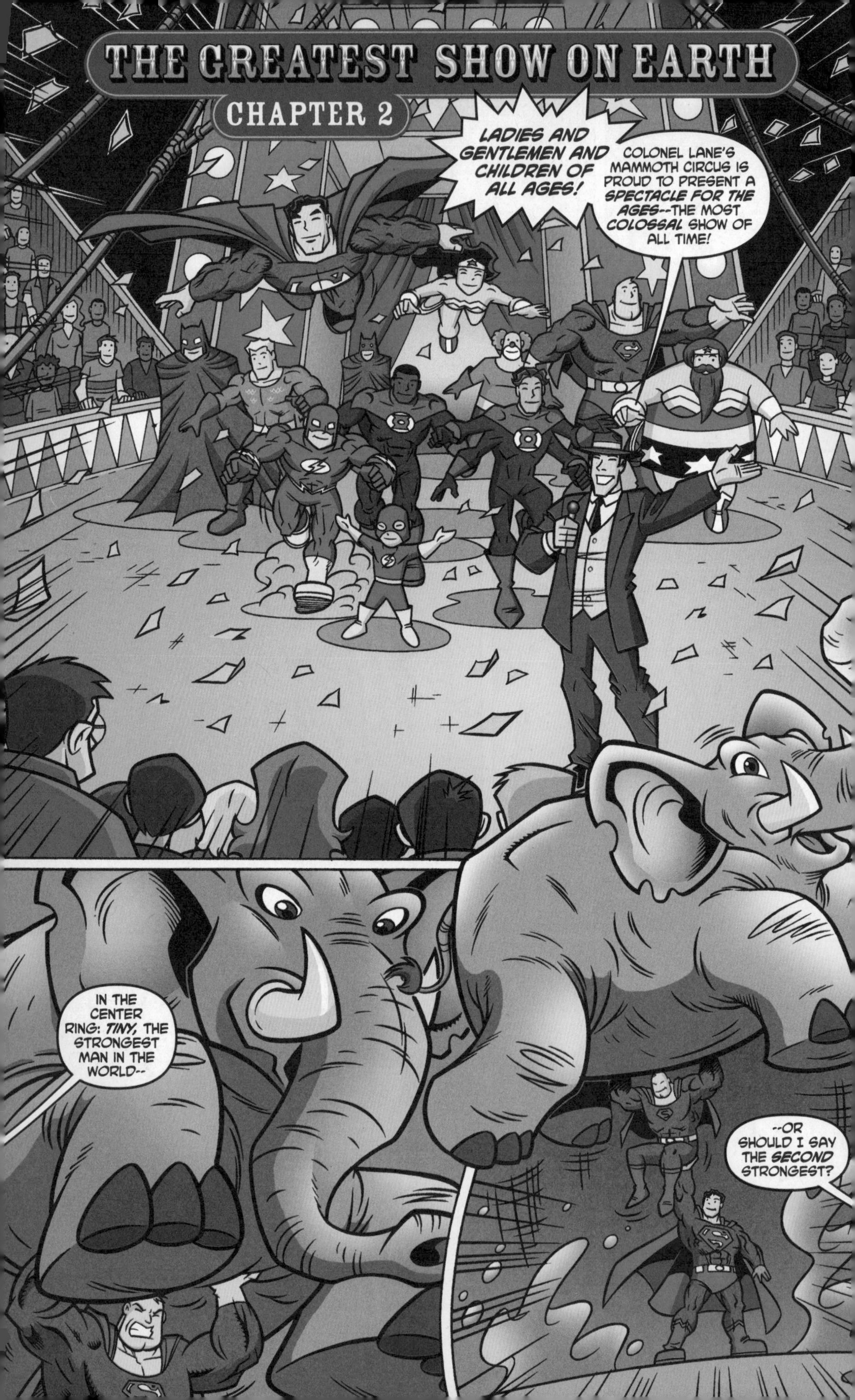
THE GREATEST SHOW ON EARTH
CHAPTER 2
LADIES AND GENTLEMEN AND CHILDREN OF ALL AGES!
COLONEL LANE'S MAMMOTH CIRCUS IS PROUD TO PRESENT A SPECTACLE FOR THE AGES--THE MOST COLOSSAL SHOW OF ALL TIME!
IN THE CENTER RING: TINY, THE STRONGEST MAN IN THE WORLD--
--OR SHOULD I SAY THE SECOND STRONGEST?

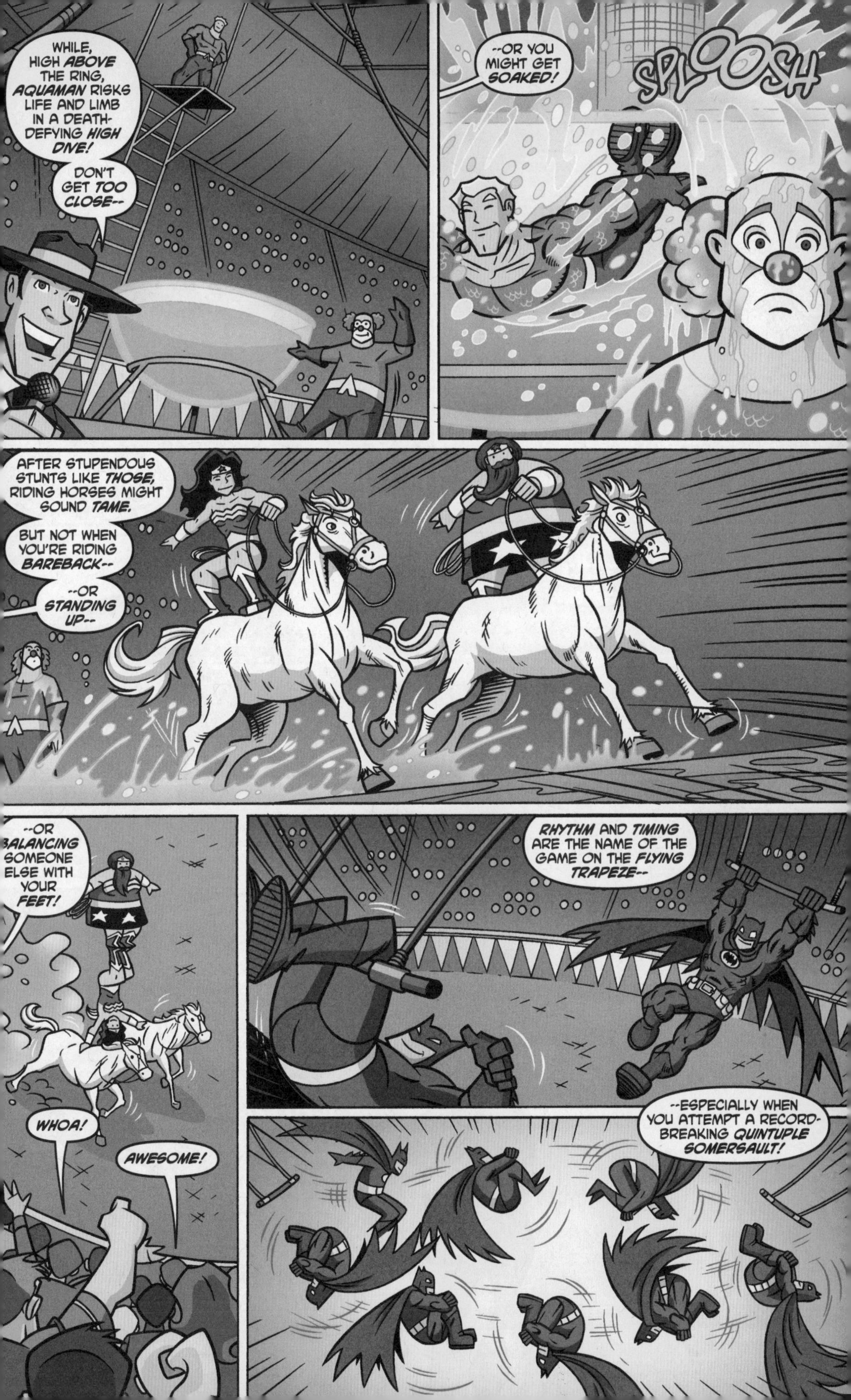
WHILE, HIGH ABOVE THE RING, AQUAMAN RISKS LIFE AND LIMB IN A DEATH-DEFYING HIGH DIVE!
DON'T GET TOO CLOSE--
--OR YOU MIGHT GET SOAKED!
SPLOOSH
AFTER STUPENDOUS STUNTS LIKE THOSE, RIDING HORSES MIGHT SOUND TAME.
BUT NOT WHEN YOU'RE RIDING BAREBACK--
--OR STANDING UP--
--OR BALANCING SOMEONE ELSE WITH YOUR FEET!
WHOA!
AWESOME!
RHYTHM AND TIMING ARE THE NAME OF THE GAME ON THE FLYING TRAPEZE--
--ESPECIALLY WHEN YOU ATTEMPT A RECORD-BREAKING QUINTUPLE SOMERSAULT!

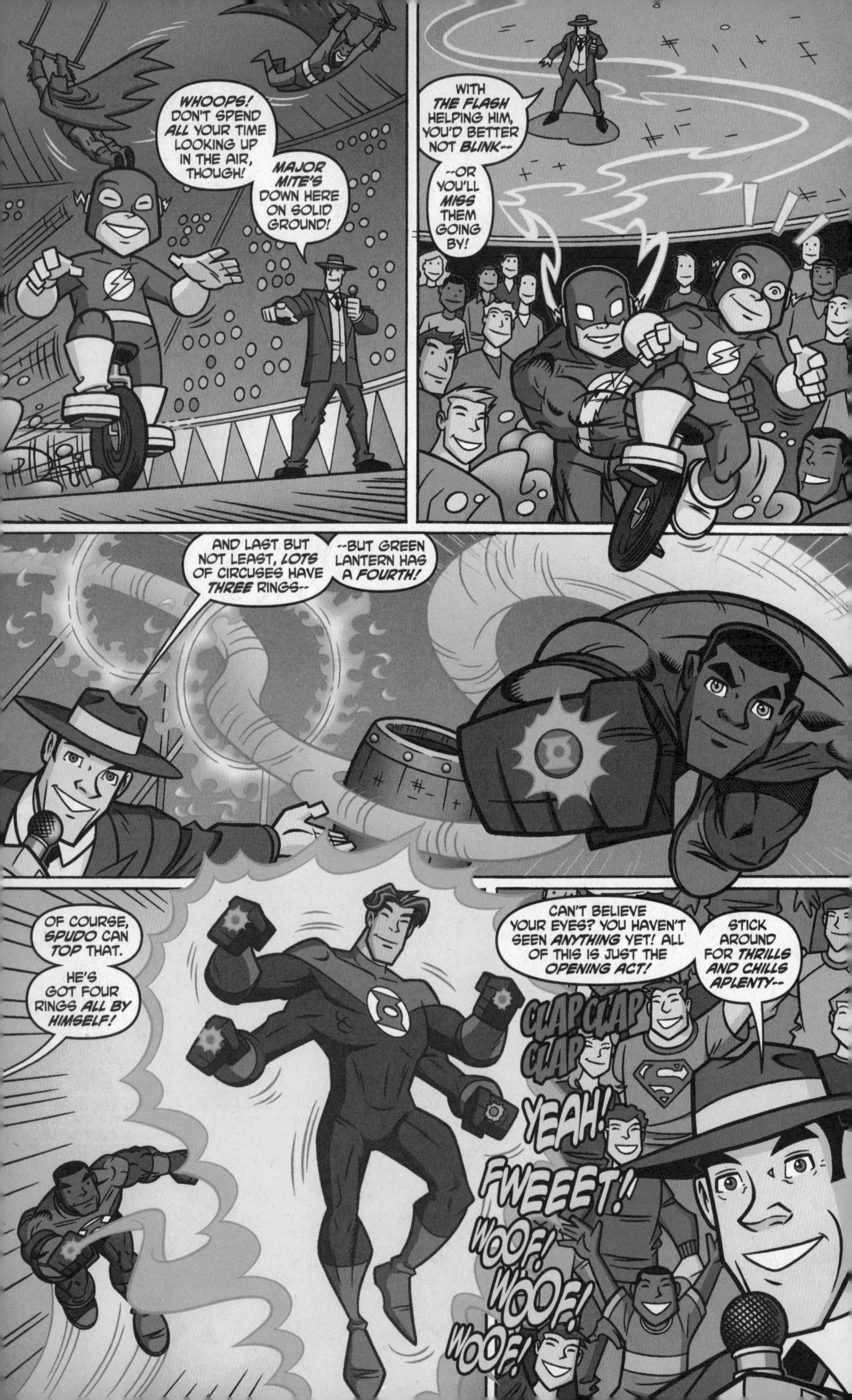
WHOOPS! DON'T SPEND ALL YOUR TIME LOOKING UP IN THE AIR, THOUGH!
MAJOR MITE'S DOWN HERE ON SOLID GROUND!
WITH THE FLASH HELPING HIM, YOU'D BETTER NOT BLINK--
--OR YOU'LL MISS THEM GOING BY!
AND LAST BUT NOT LEAST, LOTS OF CIRCUSES HAVE THREE RINGS--
--BUT GREEN LANTERN HAS A FOURTH!
OF COURSE, SPUDO CAN TOP THAT.
HE'S GOT FOUR RINGS ALL BY HIMSELF!
CAN'T BELIEVE YOUR EYES? YOU HAVEN'T SEEN ANYTHING YET! ALL OF THIS IS JUST THE OPENING ACT!
STICK AROUND FOR THRILLS AND CHILLS APLENTY--
CLAP CLAP CLAP
YEAH!
FWEEEET!!
WOOF! WOOF! WOOF!

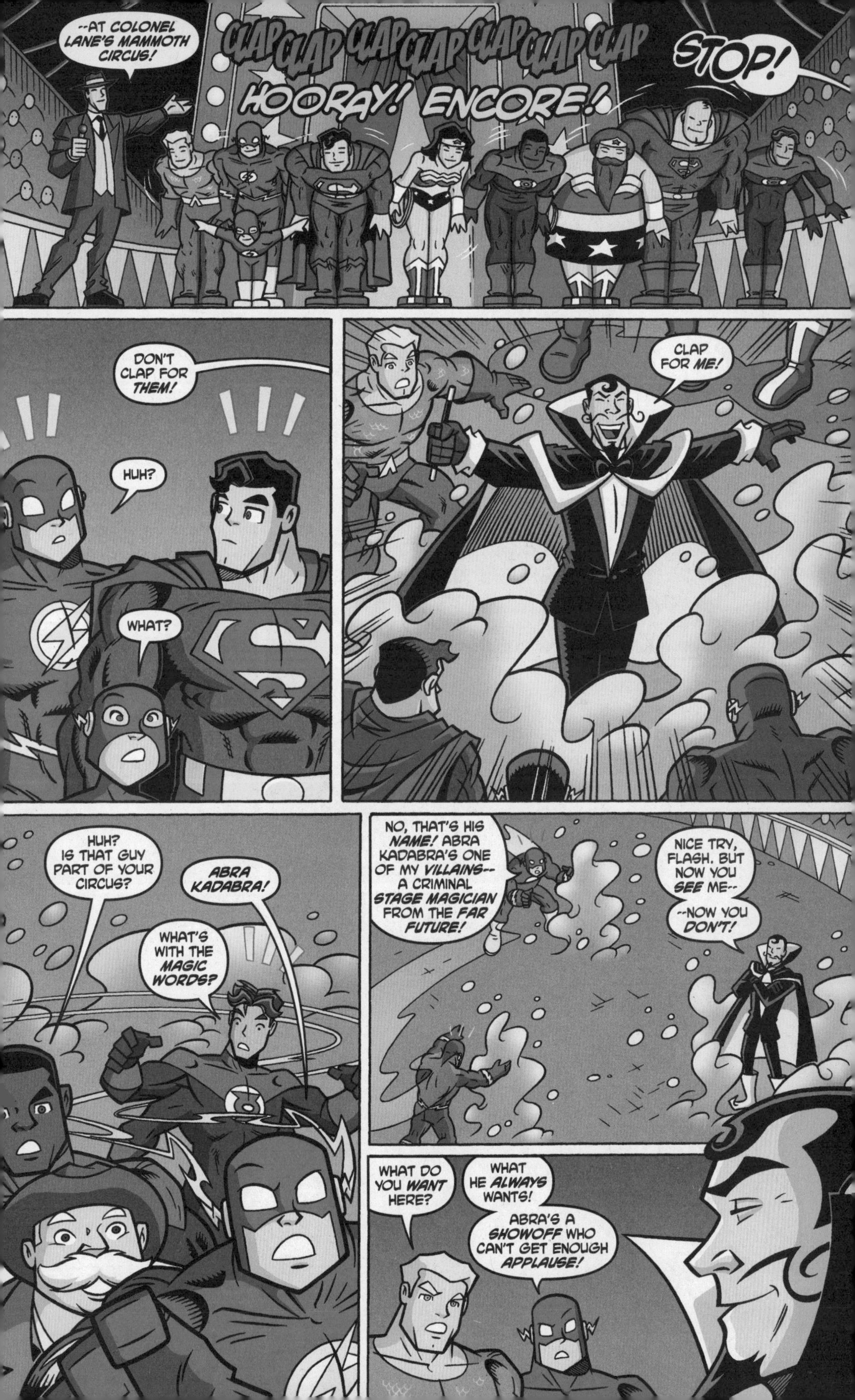
--AT COLONEL LANE'S MAMMOTH CIRCUS!
CLAP CLAP CLAP CLAP CLAP CLAP CLAP
HOORAY! ENCORE!
STOP!
DON'T CLAP FOR THEM!
HUH?
WHAT?
CLAP FOR ME!
HUH? IS THAT GUY PART OF YOUR CIRCUS?
ABRA KADABRA!
WHAT'S WITH THE MAGIC WORDS?
NO, THAT'S HIS NAME! ABRA KADABRA'S ONE OF MY VILLAINS-- A CRIMINAL STAGE MAGICIAN FROM THE FAR FUTURE!
NICE TRY, FLASH. BUT NOW YOU SEE ME--
--NOW YOU DON'T!
WHAT DO YOU WANT HERE?
WHAT HE ALWAYS WANTS!
ABRA'S A SHOWOFF WHO CAN'T GET ENOUGH APPLAUSE!

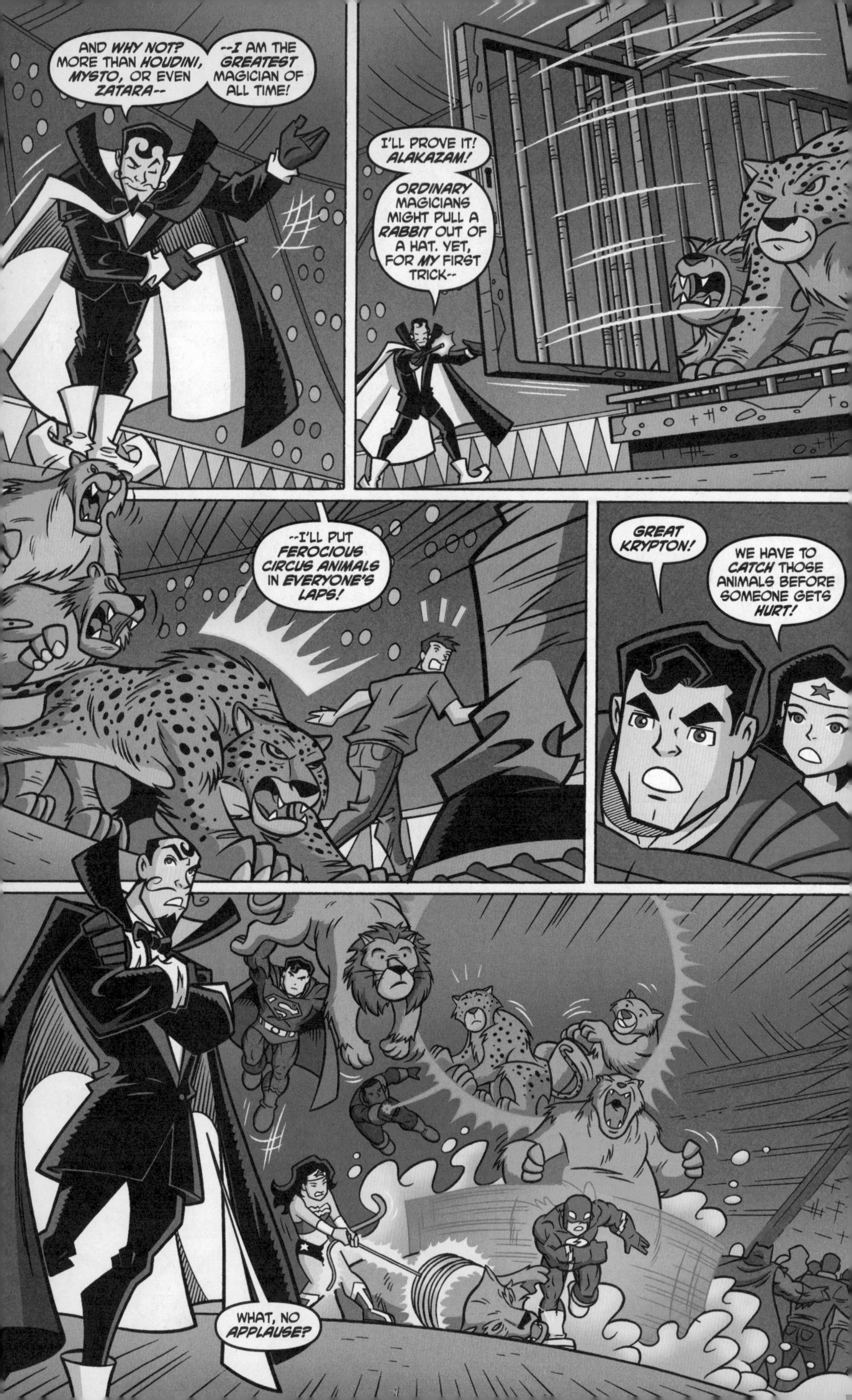
AND WHY NOT? MORE THAN HOUDINI, MYSTO, OR EVEN ZATARA--
--I AM THE GREATEST MAGICIAN OF ALL TIME!
I'LL PROVE IT! ALAKAZAM!
ORDINARY MAGICIANS MIGHT PULL A RABBIT OUT OF A HAT. YET, FOR MY FIRST TRICK--
--I'LL PUT FEROCIOUS CIRCUS ANIMALS IN EVERYONE'S LAPS!
GREAT KRYPTON!
WE HAVE TO CATCH THOSE ANIMALS BEFORE SOMEONE GETS HURT!
WHAT, NO APPLAUSE?

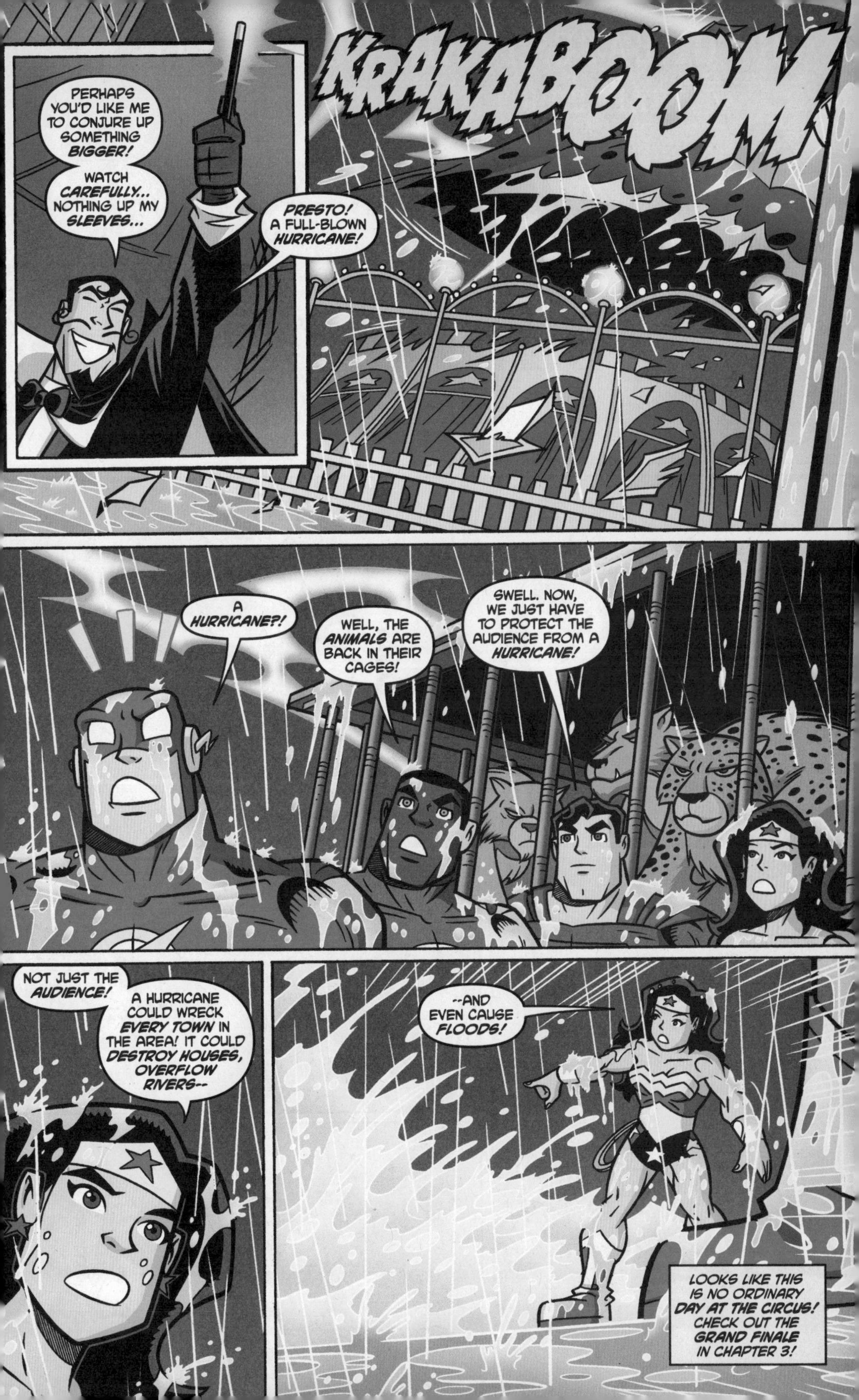
KRAKABOOM
PERHAPS YOU'D LIKE ME TO CONJURE UP SOMETHING BIGGER!
WATCH CAREFULLY... NOTHING UP MY SLEEVES...
PRESTO! A FULL-BLOWN HURRICANE!
A HURRICANE?!
WELL, THE ANIMALS ARE BACK IN THEIR CAGES!
SWELL. NOW, WE JUST HAVE TO PROTECT THE AUDIENCE FROM A HURRICANE!
NOT JUST THE AUDIENCE!
A HURRICANE COULD WRECK EVERY TOWN IN THE AREA! IT COULD DESTROY HOUSES, OVERFLOW RIVERS--
--AND EVEN CAUSE FLOODS!
LOOKS LIKE THIS IS NO ORDINARY DAY AT THE CIRCUS! CHECK OUT THE GRAND FINALE IN CHAPTER 3!

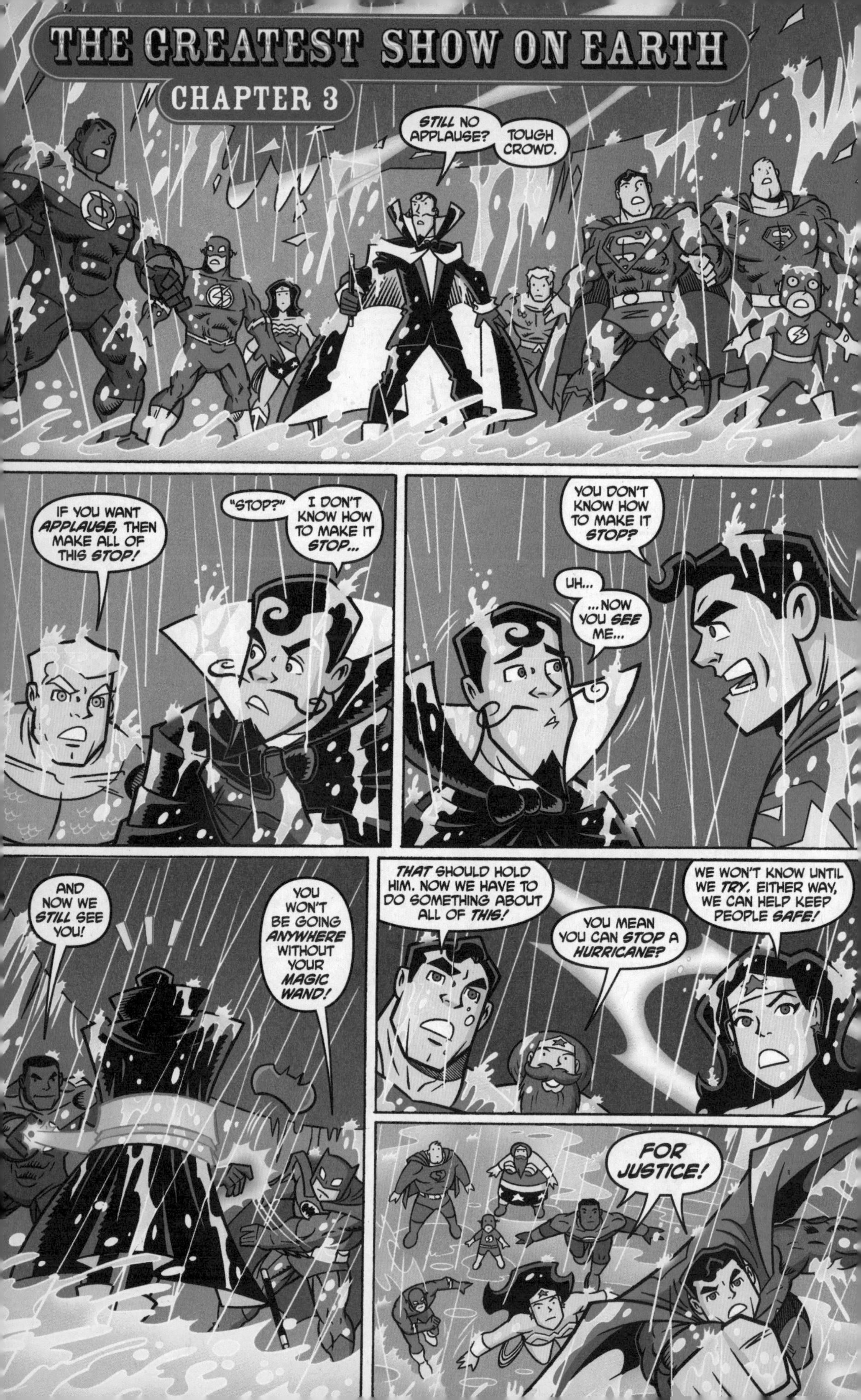
THE GREATEST SHOW ON EARTH
CHAPTER 3
STILL NO APPLAUSE?
TOUGH CROWD.
IF YOU WANT APPLAUSE, THEN MAKE ALL OF THIS STOP!
"STOP?"
I DON'T KNOW HOW TO MAKE IT STOP...
YOU DON'T KNOW HOW TO MAKE IT STOP?
UH...
...NOW YOU SEE ME...
AND NOW WE STILL SEE YOU!
YOU WON'T BE GOING ANYWHERE WITHOUT YOUR MAGIC WAND!
THAT SHOULD HOLD HIM. NOW WE HAVE TO DO SOMETHING ABOUT ALL OF THIS!
YOU MEAN YOU CAN STOP A HURRICANE?
WE WON'T KNOW UNTIL WE TRY. EITHER WAY, WE CAN HELP KEEP PEOPLE SAFE!
FOR JUSTICE!

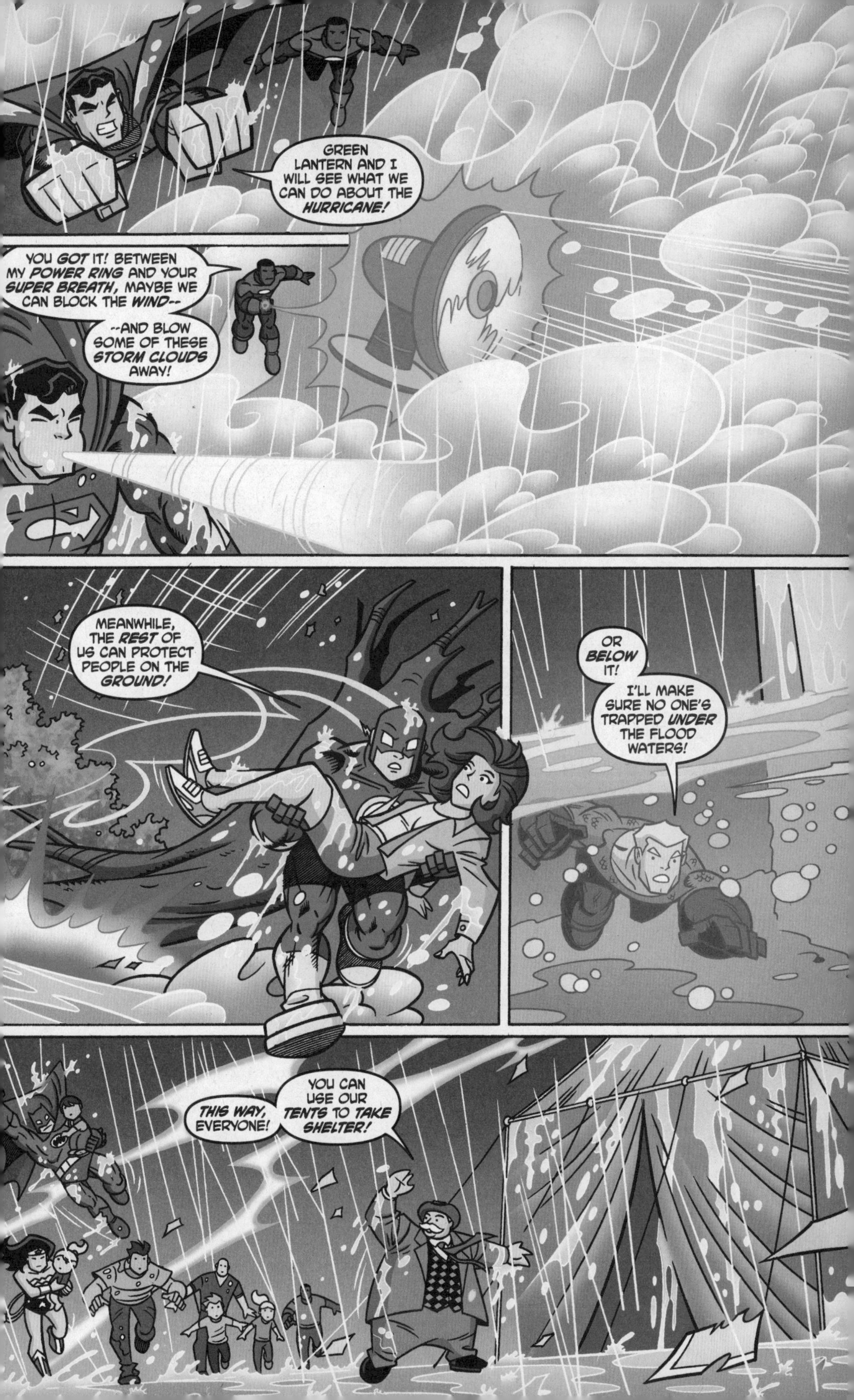
GREEN LANTERN AND I WILL SEE WHAT WE CAN DO ABOUT THE HURRICANE!
YOU GOT IT! BETWEEN MY POWER RING AND YOUR SUPER BREATH, MAYBE WE CAN BLOCK THE WIND--
--AND BLOW SOME OF THESE STORM CLOUDS AWAY!
MEANWHILE, THE REST OF US CAN PROTECT PEOPLE ON THE GROUND!
OR BELOW IT!
I'LL MAKE SURE NO ONE'S TRAPPED UNDER THE FLOOD WATERS!
THIS WAY, EVERYONE!
YOU CAN USE OUR TENTS TO TAKE SHELTER!

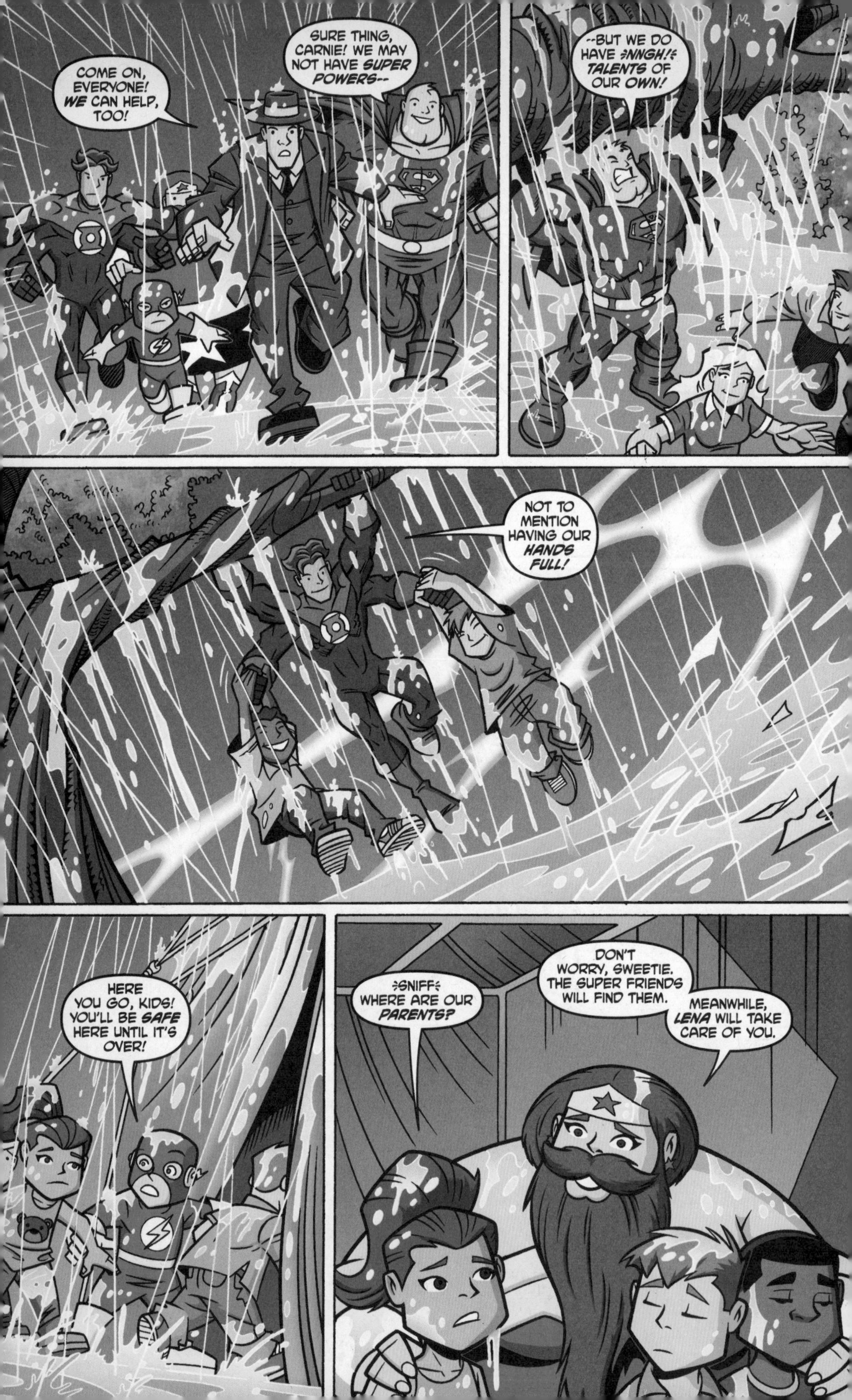
COME ON, EVERYONE! WE CAN HELP, TOO!
SURE THING, CARNIE! WE MAY NOT HAVE SUPER POWERS--
--BUT WE DO HAVE ≈NNGH!≈ TALENTS OF OUR OWN!
NOT TO MENTION HAVING OUR HANDS FULL!
HERE YOU GO, KIDS! YOU'LL BE SAFE HERE UNTIL IT'S OVER!
≈SNIFF≈ WHERE ARE OUR PARENTS?
DON'T WORRY, SWEETIE. THE SUPER FRIENDS WILL FIND THEM.
MEANWHILE, LENA WILL TAKE CARE OF YOU.

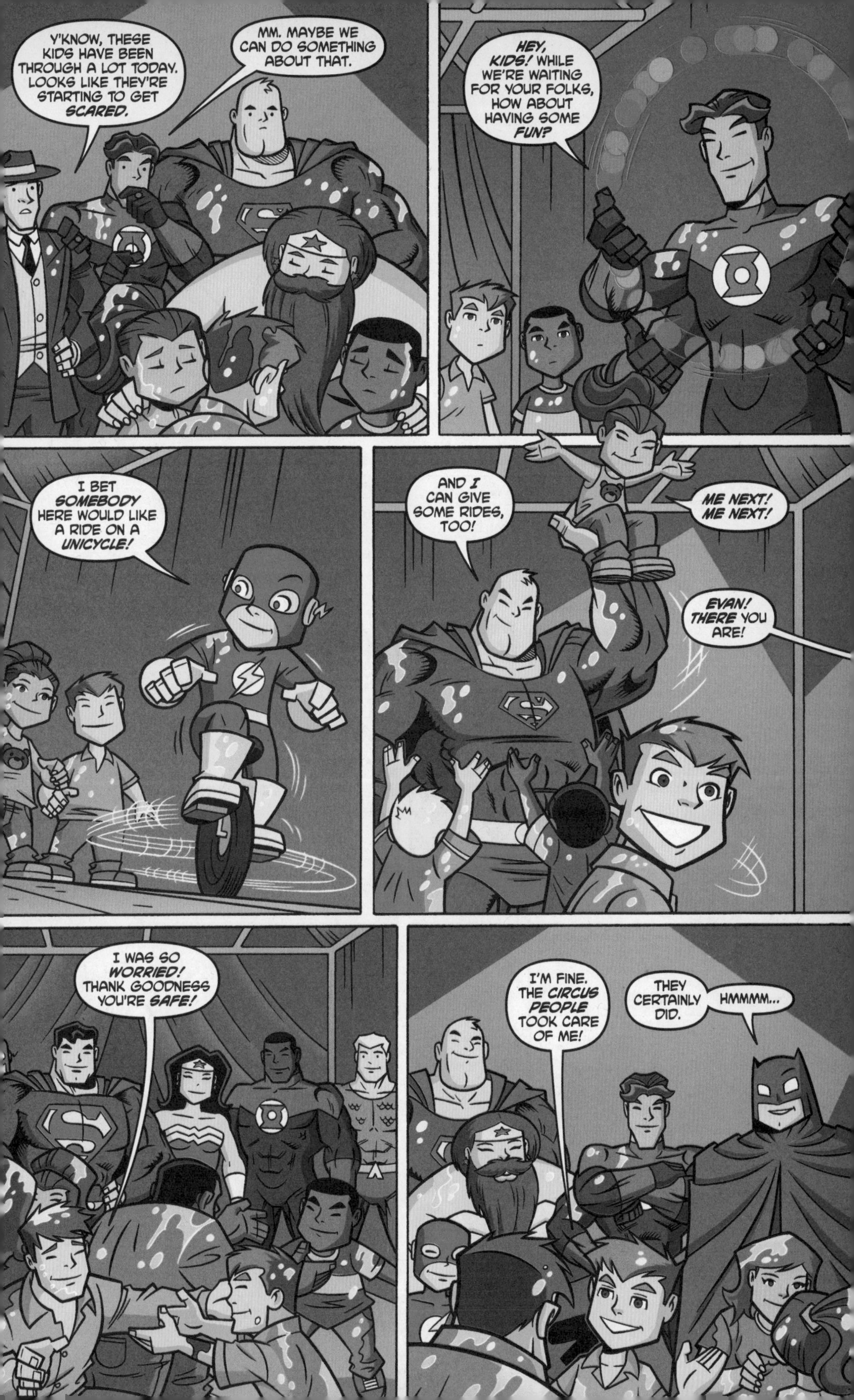

Y'KNOW, THESE KIDS HAVE BEEN THROUGH A LOT TODAY. LOOKS LIKE THEY'RE STARTING TO GET SCARED.
MM. MAYBE WE CAN DO SOMETHING ABOUT THAT.
HEY, KIDS! WHILE WE'RE WAITING FOR YOUR FOLKS, HOW ABOUT HAVING SOME FUN?
I BET SOMEBODY HERE WOULD LIKE A RIDE ON A UNICYCLE!
AND I CAN GIVE SOME RIDES, TOO!
ME NEXT! ME NEXT!
EVAN! THERE YOU ARE!
I WAS SO WORRIED! THANK GOODNESS YOU'RE SAFE!
I'M FINE. THE CIRCUS PEOPLE TOOK CARE OF ME!
THEY CERTAINLY DID.
HMMMM...

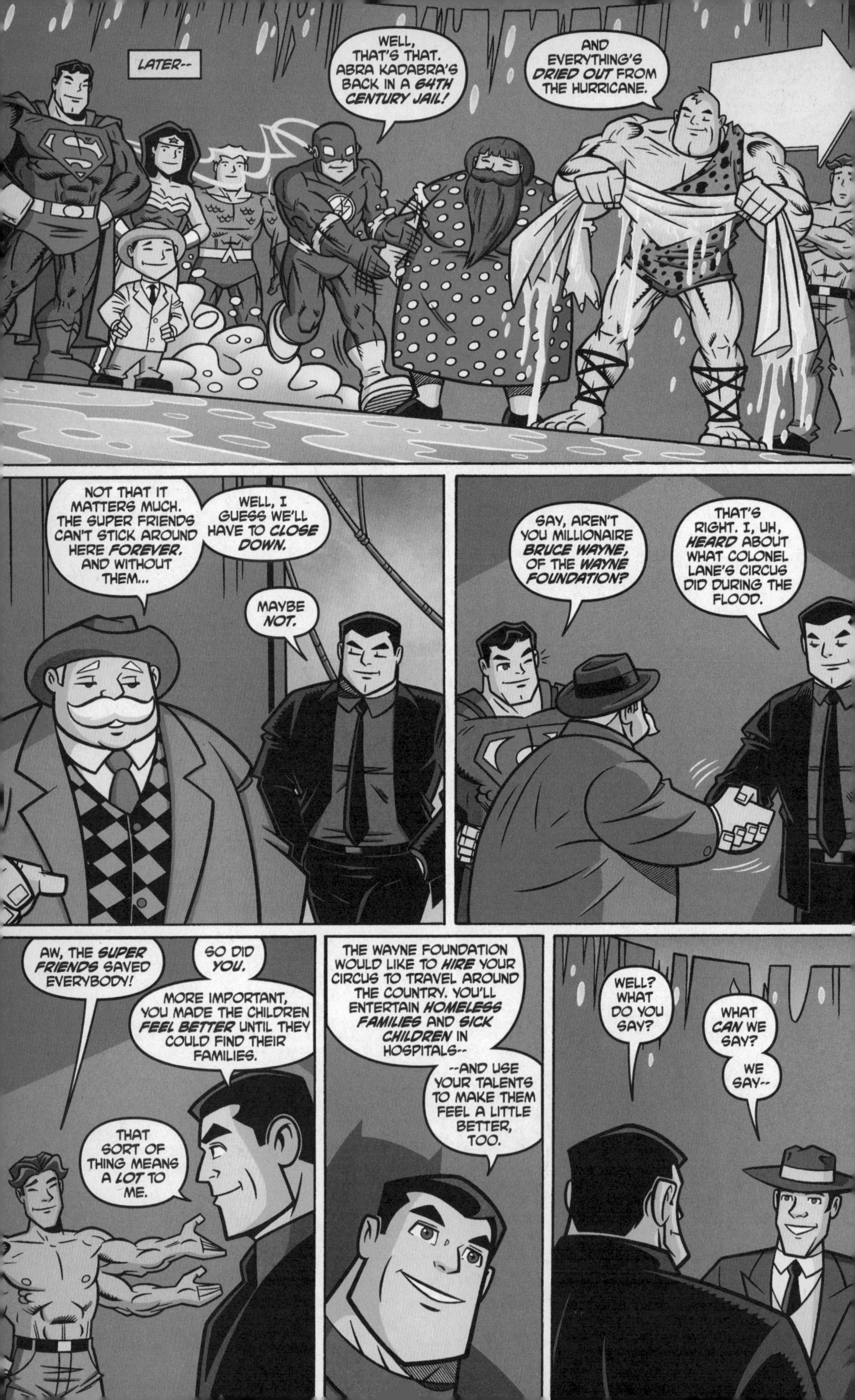
LATER--
WELL, THAT'S THAT. ABRA KADABRA'S BACK IN A 64TH CENTURY JAIL!
AND EVERYTHING'S DRIED OUT FROM THE HURRICANE.
NOT THAT IT MATTERS MUCH. THE SUPER FRIENDS CAN'T STICK AROUND HERE FOREVER. AND WITHOUT THEM...
WELL, I GUESS WE'LL HAVE TO CLOSE DOWN.
MAYBE NOT.
SAY, AREN'T YOU MILLIONAIRE BRUCE WAYNE, OF THE WAYNE FOUNDATION?
THAT'S RIGHT. I, UH, HEARD ABOUT WHAT COLONEL LANE'S CIRCUS DID DURING THE FLOOD.
AW, THE SUPER FRIENDS SAVED EVERYBODY!
SO DID YOU.
MORE IMPORTANT, YOU MADE THE CHILDREN FEEL BETTER UNTIL THEY COULD FIND THEIR FAMILIES.
THAT SORT OF THING MEANS A LOT TO ME.
THE WAYNE FOUNDATION WOULD LIKE TO HIRE YOUR CIRCUS TO TRAVEL AROUND THE COUNTRY. YOU'LL ENTERTAIN HOMELESS FAMILIES AND SICK CHILDREN IN HOSPITALS--
--AND USE YOUR TALENTS TO MAKE THEM FEEL A LITTLE BETTER, TOO.
WELL? WHAT DO YOU SAY?
WHAT CAN WE SAY?
WE SAY--

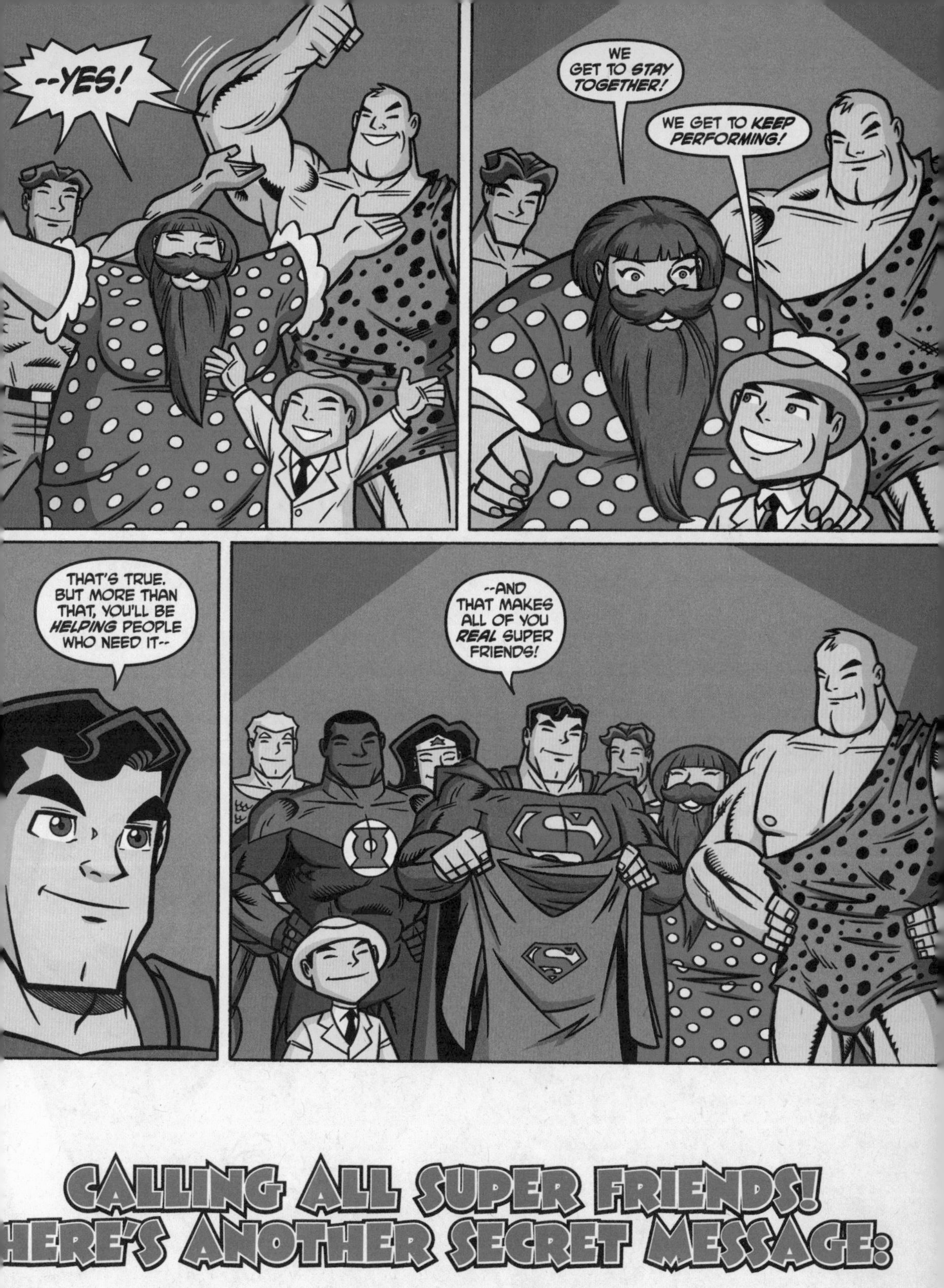
--YES!
WE GET TO STAY TOGETHER!
WE GET TO KEEP PERFORMING!
THAT'S TRUE. BUT MORE THAN THAT, YOU'LL BE HELPING PEOPLE WHO NEED IT--
--AND THAT MAKES ALL OF YOU REAL SUPER FRIENDS!

CALLING ALL SUPER FRIENDS! HERE'S ANOTHER SECRET MESSAGE:

XOLI ISDO, INO PEVOY CYSOXRP QOI
NOZV--CYBD INO PEVOY VOIP!

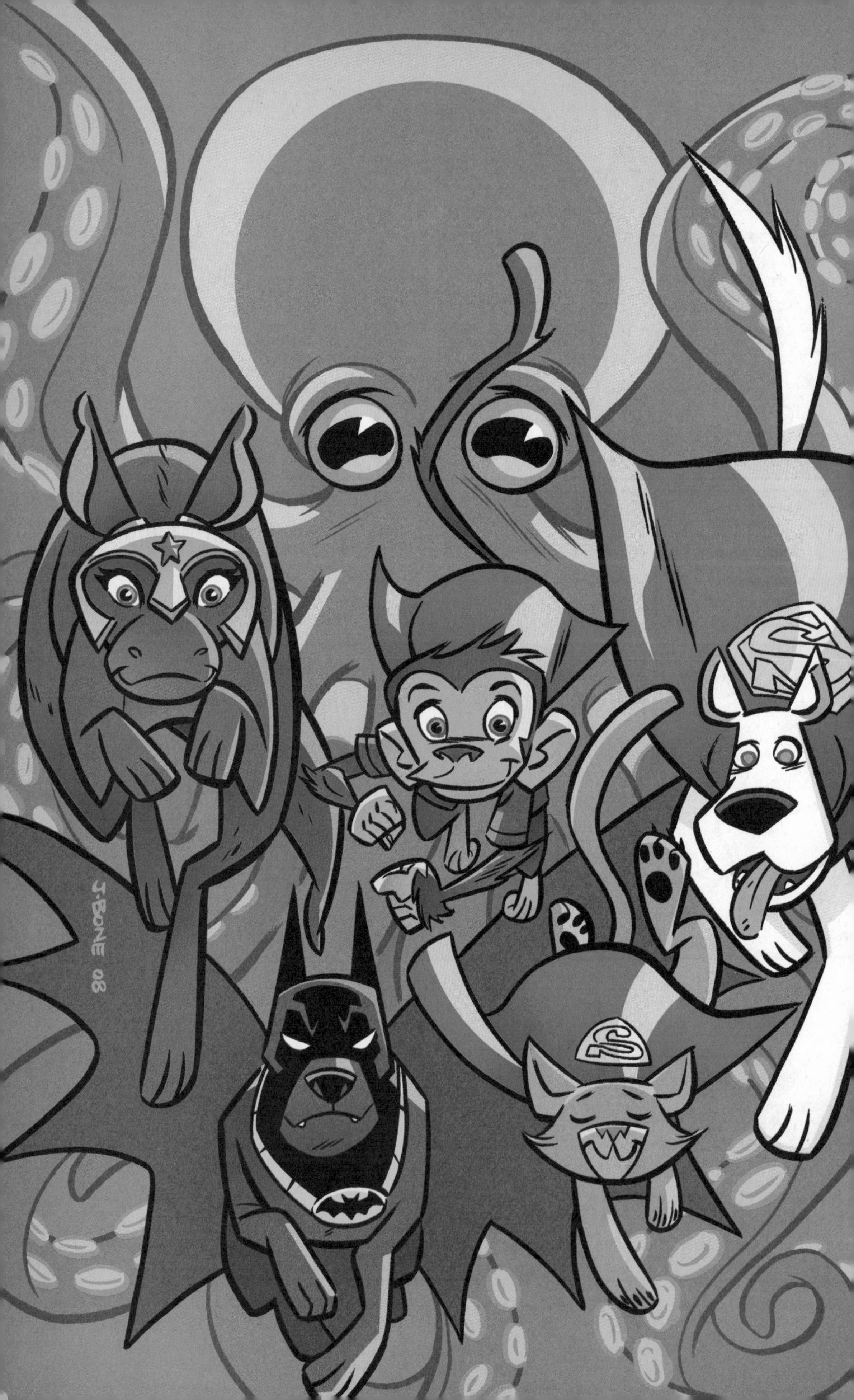
J-BONE 08

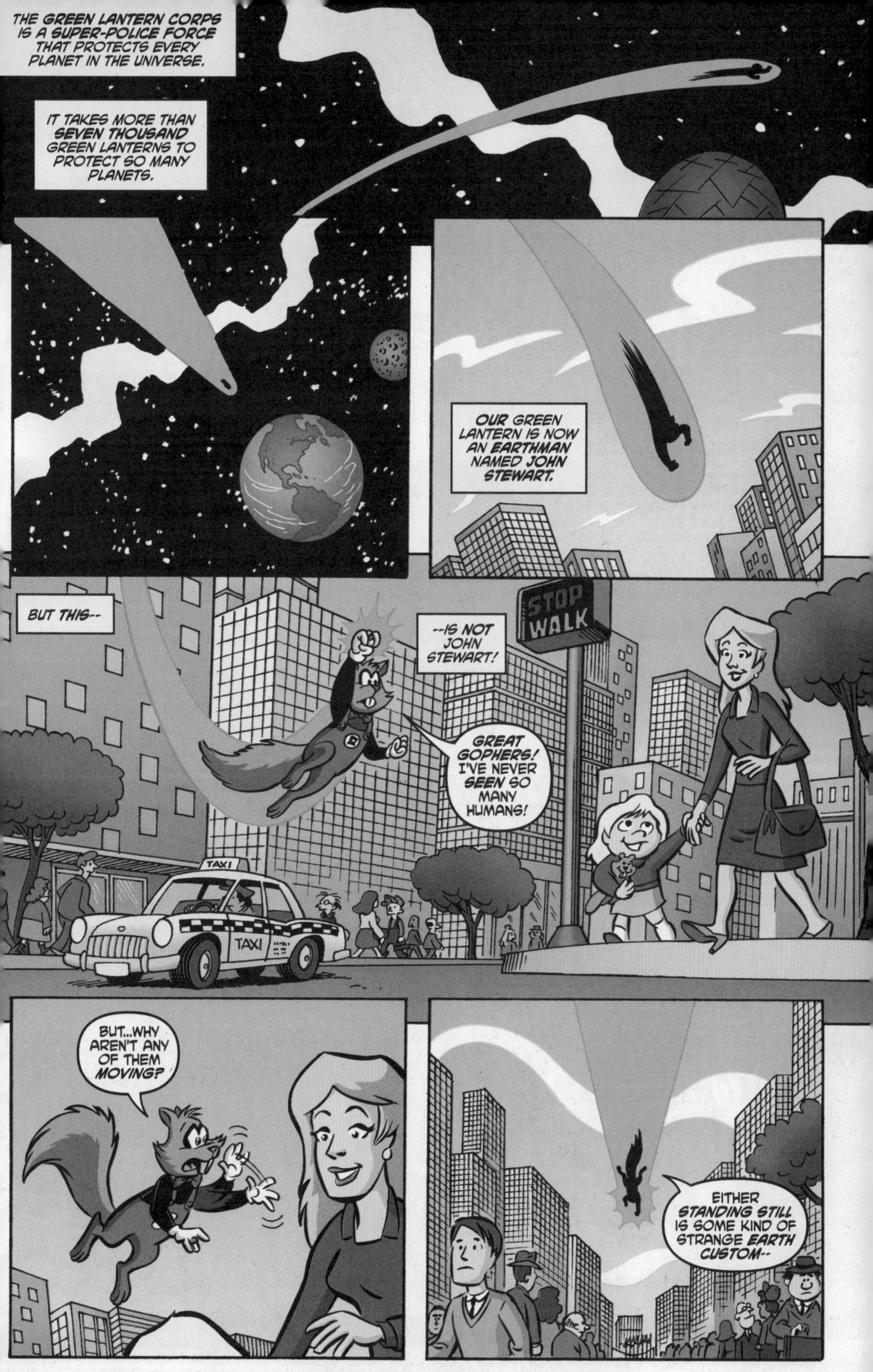
THE GREEN LANTERN CORPS IS A SUPER-POLICE FORCE THAT PROTECTS EVERY PLANET IN THE UNIVERSE.
IT TAKES MORE THAN SEVEN THOUSAND GREEN LANTERNS TO PROTECT SO MANY PLANETS.
OUR GREEN LANTERN IS NOW AN EARTHMAN NAMED JOHN STEWART.
BUT THIS--
--IS NOT JOHN STEWART!
STOP
WALK
GREAT GOPHERS! I'VE NEVER SEEN SO MANY HUMANS!
TAXI
TAXI
BUT...WHY AREN'T ANY OF THEM MOVING?
EITHER STANDING STILL IS SOME KIND OF STRANGE EARTH CUSTOM--

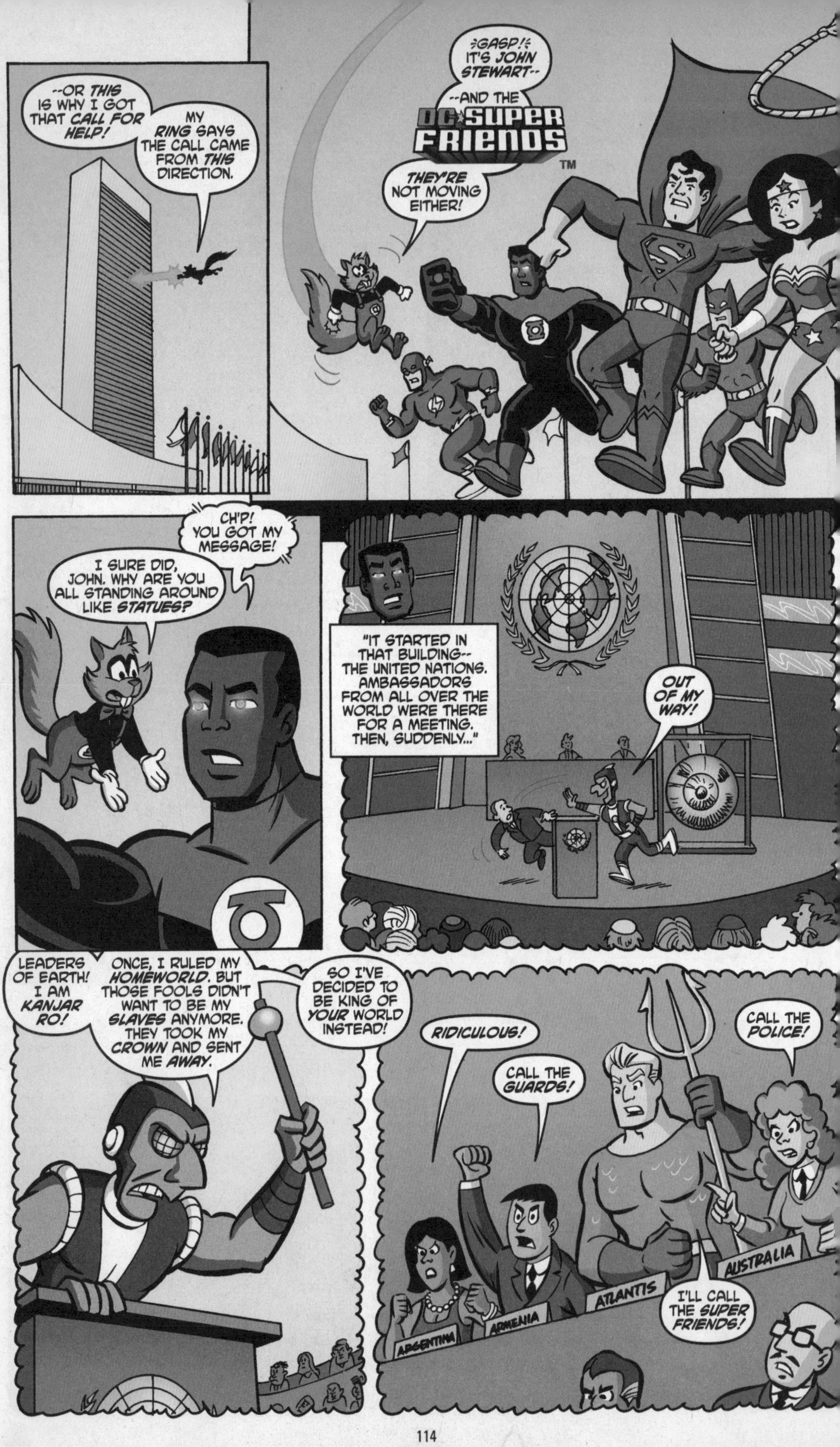
--OR THIS IS WHY I GOT THAT CALL FOR HELP!
MY RING SAYS THE CALL CAME FROM THIS DIRECTION.
GASP! IT'S JOHN STEWART--
--AND THE
DC SUPER FRIENDS
TM
THEY'RE NOT MOVING EITHER!
CH'P! YOU GOT MY MESSAGE!
I SURE DID, JOHN. WHY ARE YOU ALL STANDING AROUND LIKE STATUES?
"IT STARTED IN THAT BUILDING-- THE UNITED NATIONS. AMBASSADORS FROM ALL OVER THE WORLD WERE THERE FOR A MEETING. THEN, SUDDENLY..."
OUT OF MY WAY!
LEADERS OF EARTH! I AM KANJAR RO!
ONCE, I RULED MY HOMEWORLD. BUT THOSE FOOLS DIDN'T WANT TO BE MY SLAVES ANYMORE. THEY TOOK MY CROWN AND SENT ME AWAY.
SO I'VE DECIDED TO BE KING OF YOUR WORLD INSTEAD!
RIDICULOUS!
CALL THE GUARDS!
CALL THE POLICE!
ARGENTINA
ARMENIA
ATLANTIS
AUSTRALIA
I'LL CALL THE SUPER FRIENDS!

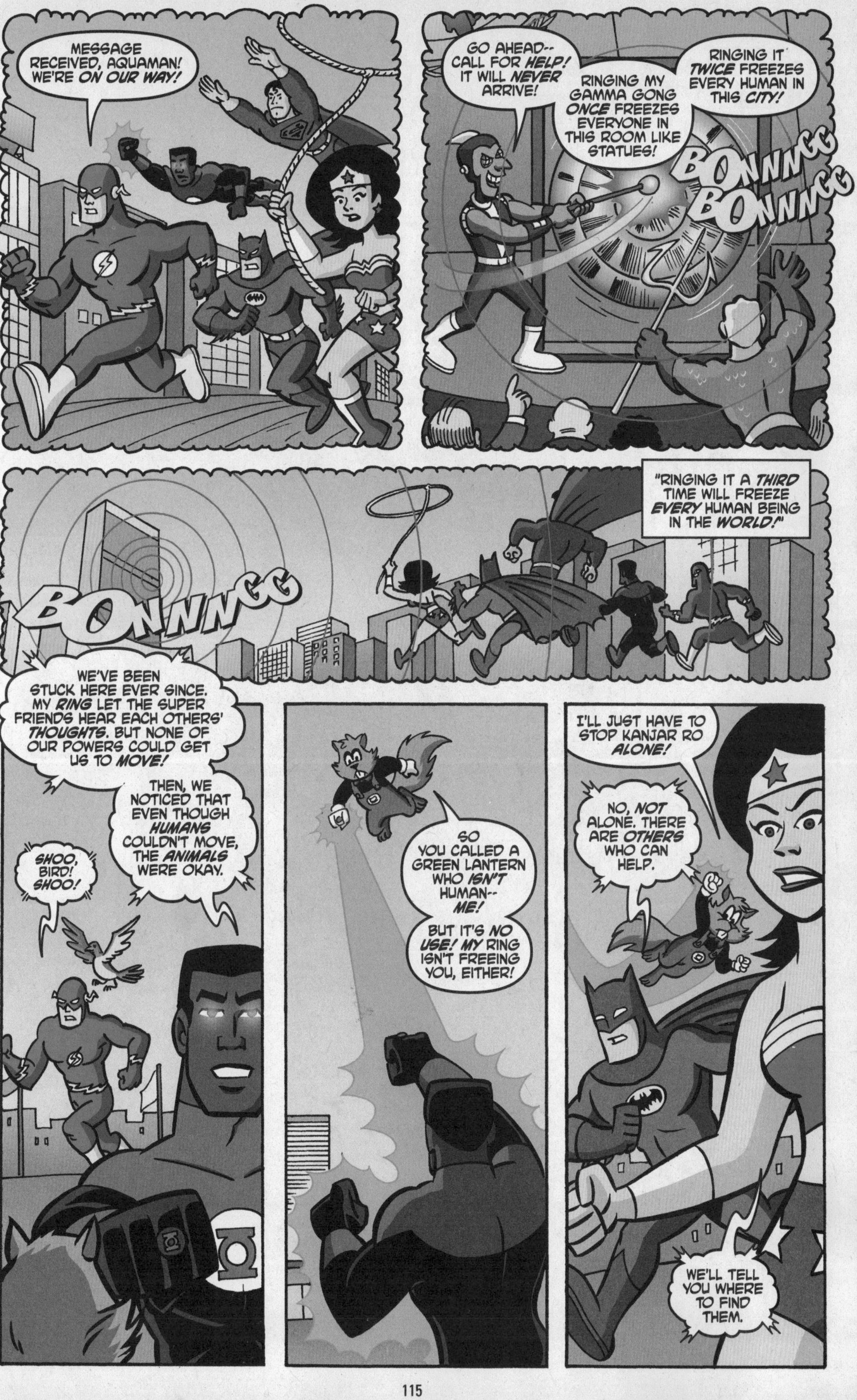
MESSAGE RECEIVED, AQUAMAN! WE'RE ON OUR WAY!
GO AHEAD-- CALL FOR HELP! IT WILL NEVER ARRIVE!
RINGING MY GAMMA GONG ONCE FREEZES EVERYONE IN THIS ROOM LIKE STATUES!
RINGING IT TWICE FREEZES EVERY HUMAN IN THIS CITY!
BONNNGG
BONNNGG
"RINGING IT A THIRD TIME WILL FREEZE EVERY HUMAN BEING IN THE WORLD!"
BONNNGG
WE'VE BEEN STUCK HERE EVER SINCE. MY RING LET THE SUPER FRIENDS HEAR EACH OTHERS' THOUGHTS. BUT NONE OF OUR POWERS COULD GET US TO MOVE!
THEN, WE NOTICED THAT EVEN THOUGH HUMANS COULDN'T MOVE, THE ANIMALS WERE OKAY.
SHOO, BIRD! SHOO!
SO YOU CALLED A GREEN LANTERN WHO ISN'T HUMAN-- ME!
BUT IT'S NO USE! MY RING ISN'T FREEING YOU, EITHER!
I'LL JUST HAVE TO STOP KANJAR RO ALONE!
NO, NOT ALONE. THERE ARE OTHERS WHO CAN HELP.
WE'LL TELL YOU WHERE TO FIND THEM.

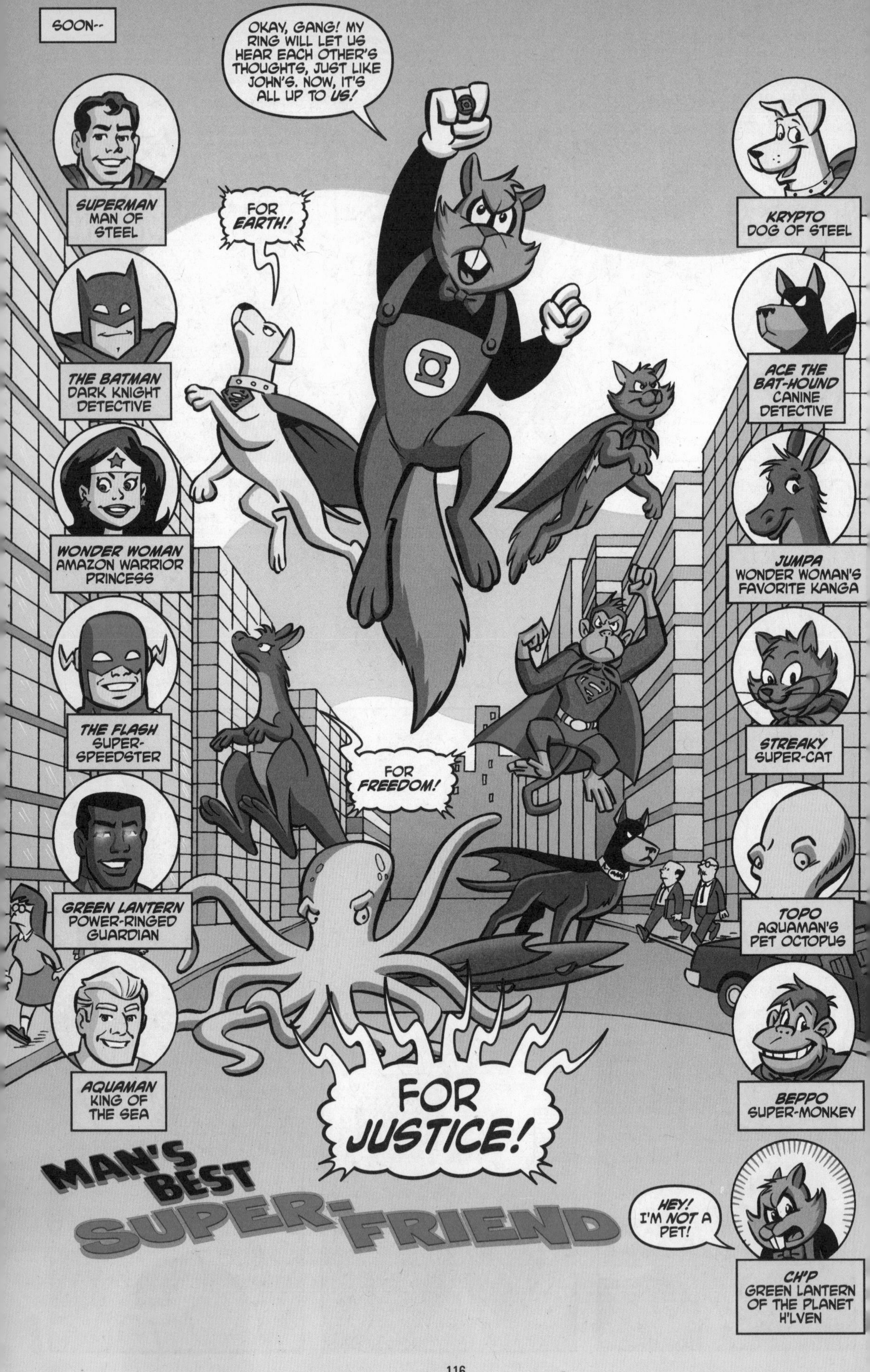

SOON--
OKAY, GANG! MY RING WILL LET US HEAR EACH OTHER'S THOUGHTS, JUST LIKE JOHN'S. NOW, IT'S ALL UP TO US!
SUPERMAN MAN OF STEEL
KRYPTO DOG OF STEEL
FOR EARTH!
THE BATMAN DARK KNIGHT DETECTIVE
ACE THE BAT-HOUND CANINE DETECTIVE
WONDER WOMAN AMAZON WARRIOR PRINCESS
JUMPA WONDER WOMAN'S FAVORITE KANGA
THE FLASH SUPER-SPEEDSTER
STREAKY SUPER-CAT
FOR FREEDOM!
GREEN LANTERN POWER-RINGED GUARDIAN
TOPO AQUAMAN'S PET OCTOPUS
AQUAMAN KING OF THE SEA
BEPPO SUPER-MONKEY
FOR JUSTICE!
MAN'S BEST SUPER-FRIEND
HEY! I'M NOT A PET!
CH'P GREEN LANTERN OF THE PLANET H'LVEN

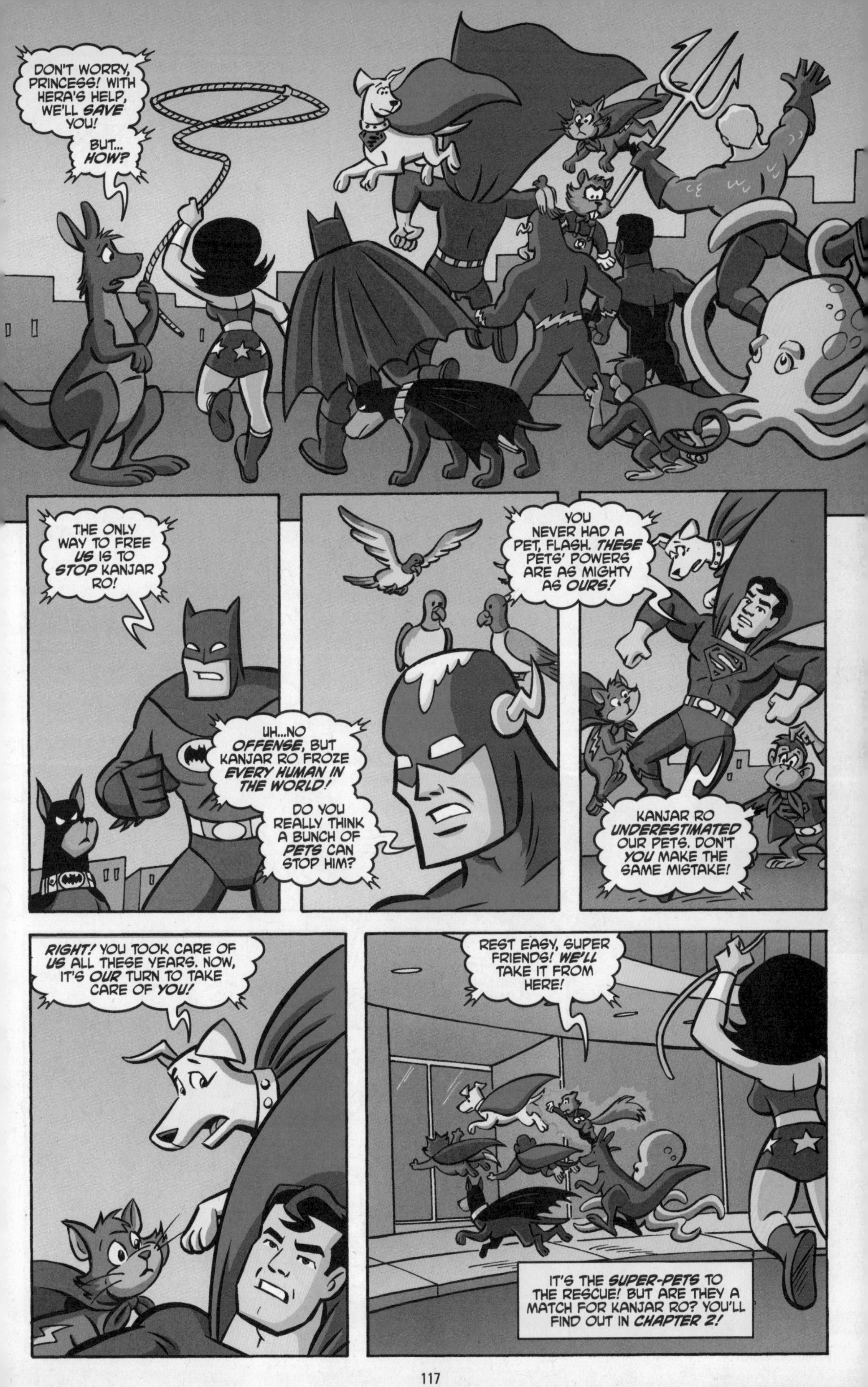
DON'T WORRY, PRINCESS! WITH HERA'S HELP, WE'LL SAVE YOU!
BUT... HOW?
THE ONLY WAY TO FREE US IS TO STOP KANJAR RO!
UH...NO OFFENSE, BUT KANJAR RO FROZE EVERY HUMAN IN THE WORLD!
DO YOU REALLY THINK A BUNCH OF PETS CAN STOP HIM?
YOU NEVER HAD A PET, FLASH. THESE PETS' POWERS ARE AS MIGHTY AS OURS!
KANJAR RO UNDERESTIMATED OUR PETS. DON'T YOU MAKE THE SAME MISTAKE!
RIGHT! YOU TOOK CARE OF US ALL THESE YEARS. NOW, IT'S OUR TURN TO TAKE CARE OF YOU!
REST EASY, SUPER FRIENDS! WE'LL TAKE IT FROM HERE!
IT'S THE SUPER-PETS TO THE RESCUE! BUT ARE THEY A MATCH FOR KANJAR RO? YOU'LL FIND OUT IN CHAPTER 2!

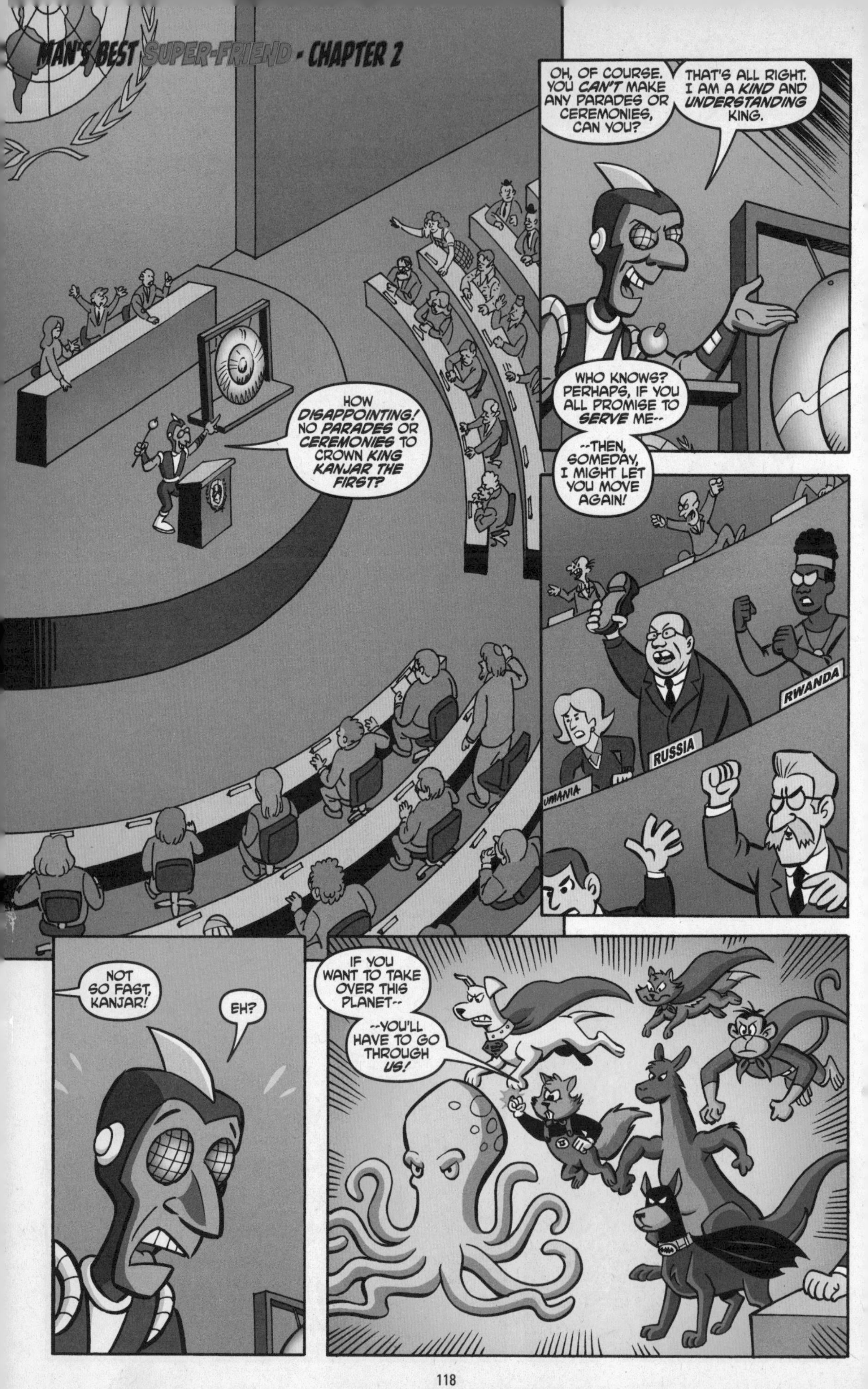
MAN'S BEST SUPER-FRIEND - CHAPTER 2
HOW DISAPPOINTING! NO PARADES OR CEREMONIES TO CROWN KING KANJAR THE FIRST?
OH, OF COURSE. YOU CAN'T MAKE ANY PARADES OR CEREMONIES, CAN YOU?
THAT'S ALL RIGHT. I AM A KIND AND UNDERSTANDING KING.
WHO KNOWS? PERHAPS, IF YOU ALL PROMISE TO SERVE ME--
--THEN, SOMEDAY, I MIGHT LET YOU MOVE AGAIN!
RWANDA
RUSSIA
UMANIA
NOT SO FAST, KANJAR!
EH?
IF YOU WANT TO TAKE OVER THIS PLANET--
--YOU'LL HAVE TO GO THROUGH US!

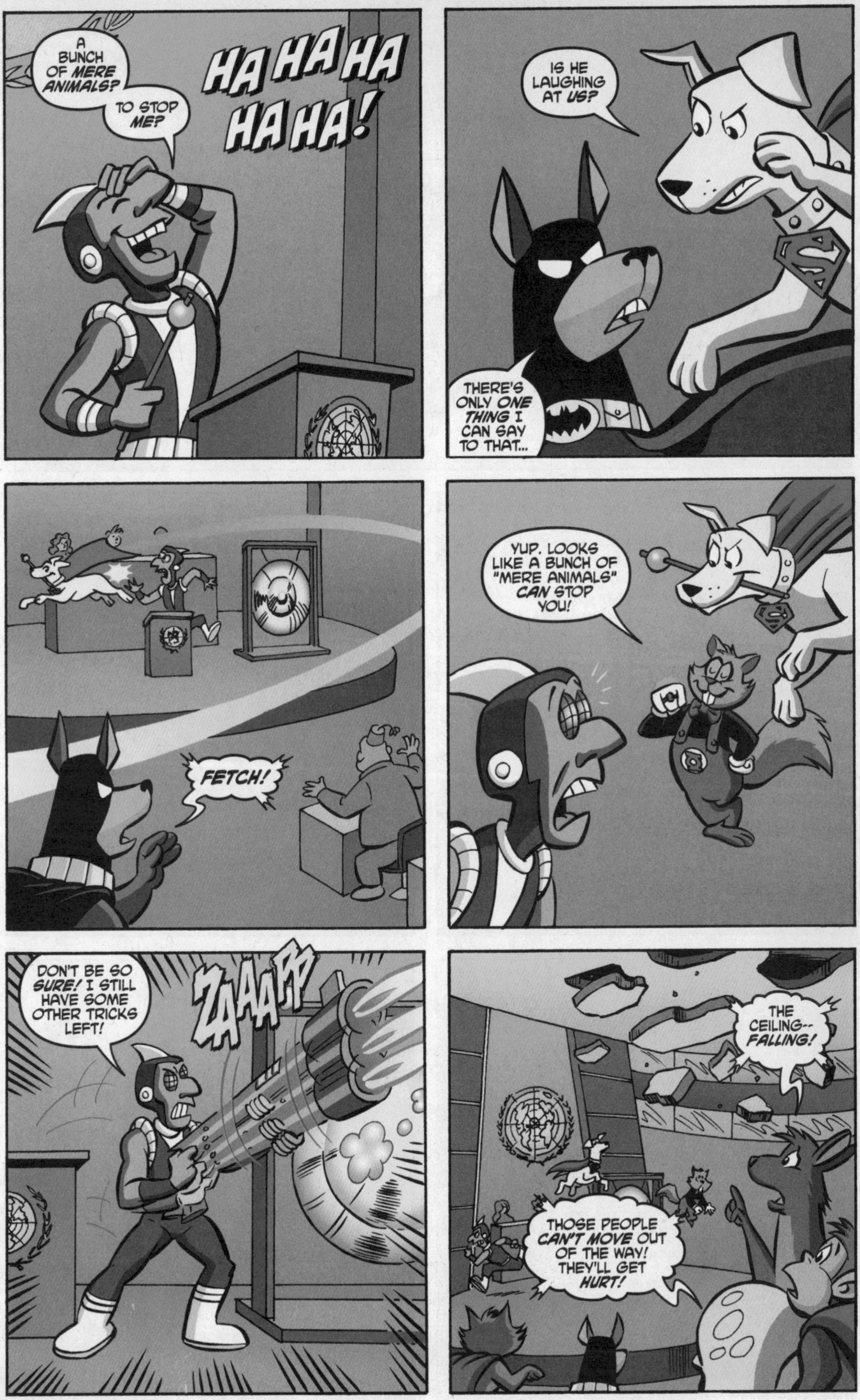
A BUNCH OF MERE ANIMALS?
TO STOP ME?
HA HA HA HA HA HA!
IS HE LAUGHING AT US?
THERE'S ONLY ONE THING I CAN SAY TO THAT...
FETCH!
YUP. LOOKS LIKE A BUNCH OF "MERE ANIMALS" CAN STOP YOU!
DON'T BE SO SURE! I STILL HAVE SOME OTHER TRICKS LEFT!
ZAAARR
THE CEILING-- FALLING!
THOSE PEOPLE CAN'T MOVE OUT OF THE WAY! THEY'LL GET HURT!

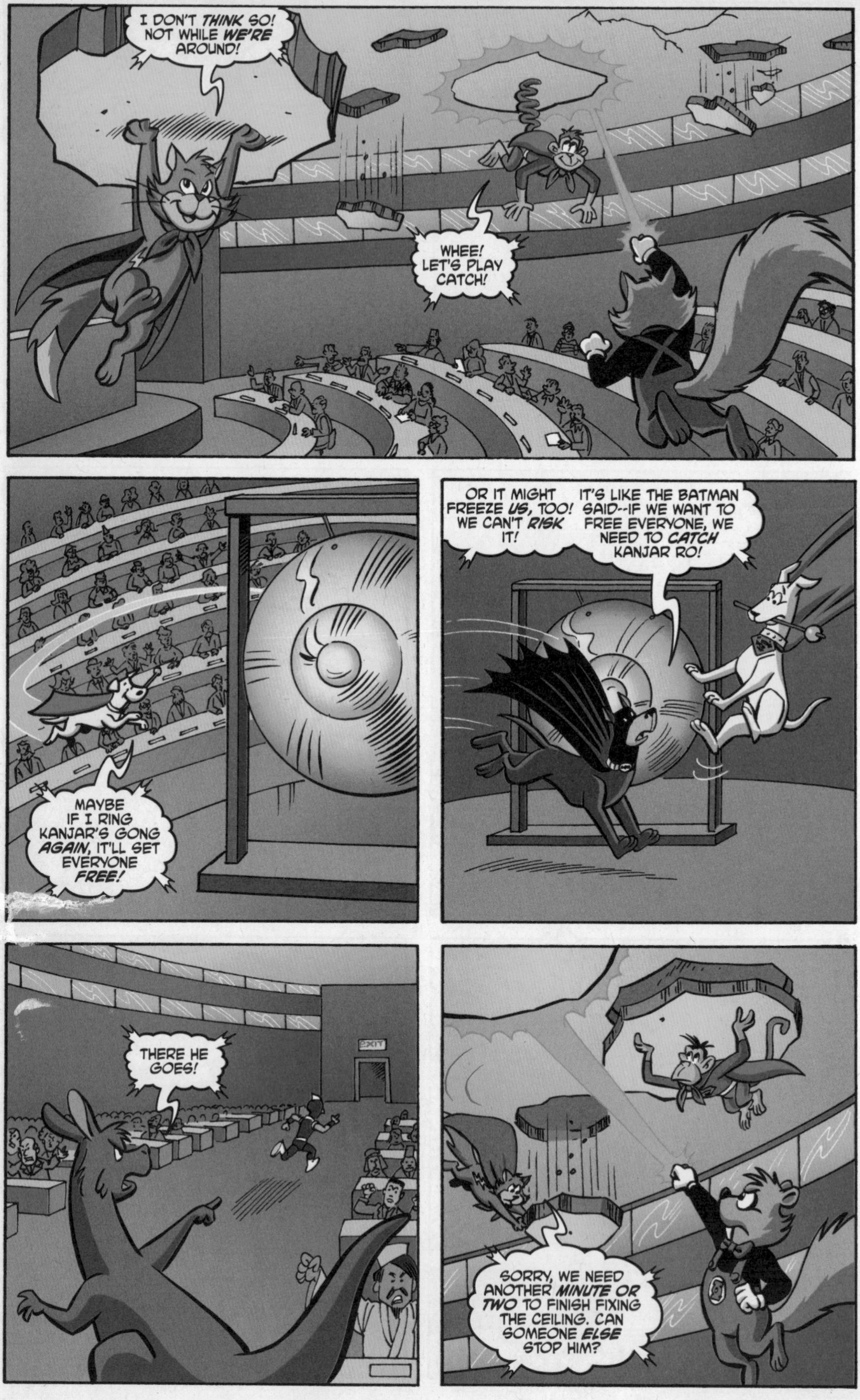
I DON'T THINK SO! NOT WHILE WE'RE AROUND!
WHEE! LET'S PLAY CATCH!
MAYBE IF I RING KANJAR'S GONG AGAIN, IT'LL SET EVERYONE FREE!
OR IT MIGHT FREEZE US, TOO! WE CAN'T RISK IT!
IT'S LIKE THE BATMAN SAID--IF WE WANT TO FREE EVERYONE, WE NEED TO CATCH KANJAR RO!
EXIT
THERE HE GOES!
SORRY, WE NEED ANOTHER MINUTE OR TWO TO FINISH FIXING THE CEILING. CAN SOMEONE ELSE STOP HIM?

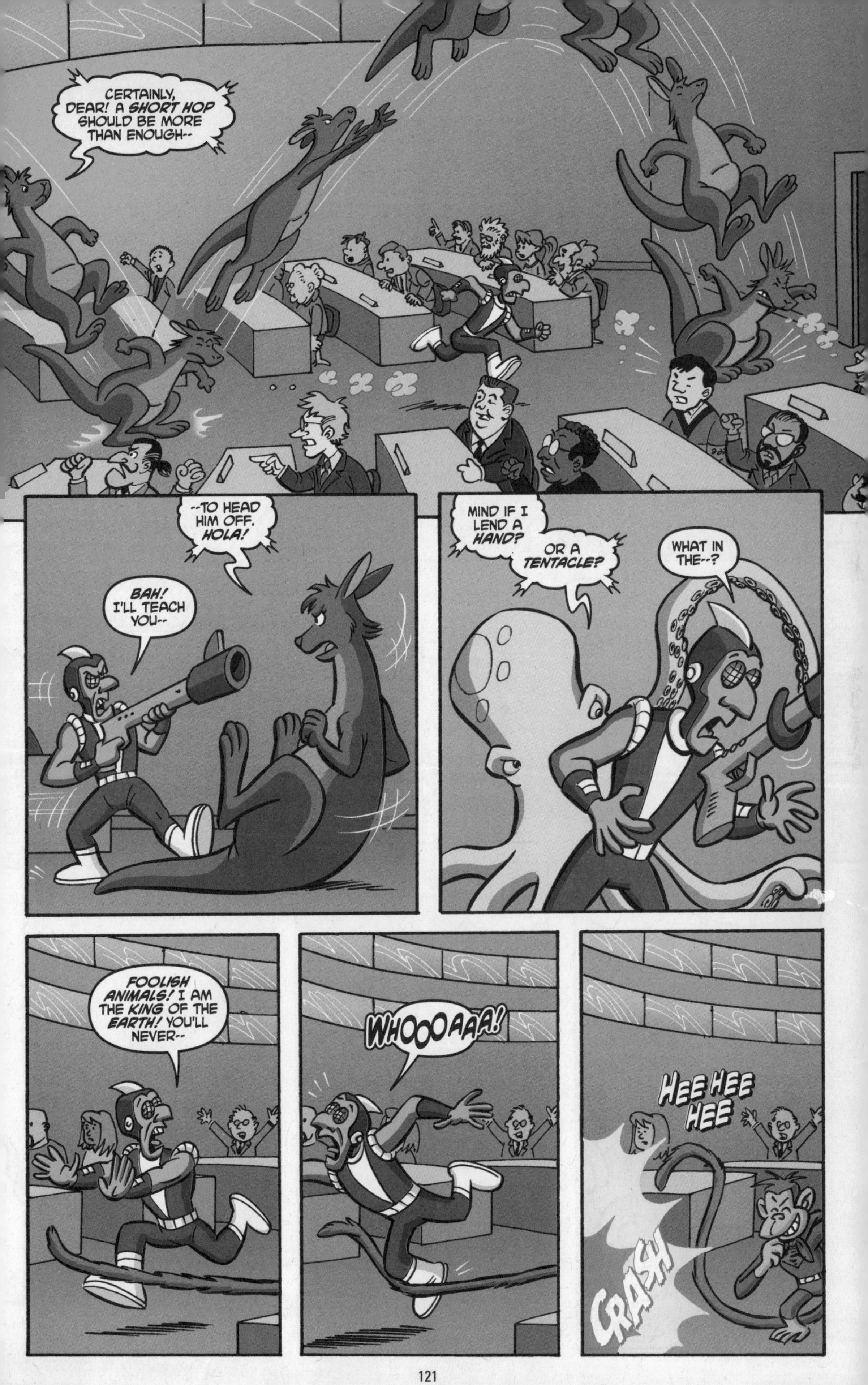

CERTAINLY, DEAR! A SHORT HOP SHOULD BE MORE THAN ENOUGH--
--TO HEAD HIM OFF. HOLA!
BAH! I'LL TEACH YOU--
MIND IF I LEND A HAND?
OR A TENTACLE?
WHAT IN THE--?
FOOLISH ANIMALS! I AM THE KING OF THE EARTH! YOU'LL NEVER--
WHOOOAAA!
HEE HEE HEE
CRASH

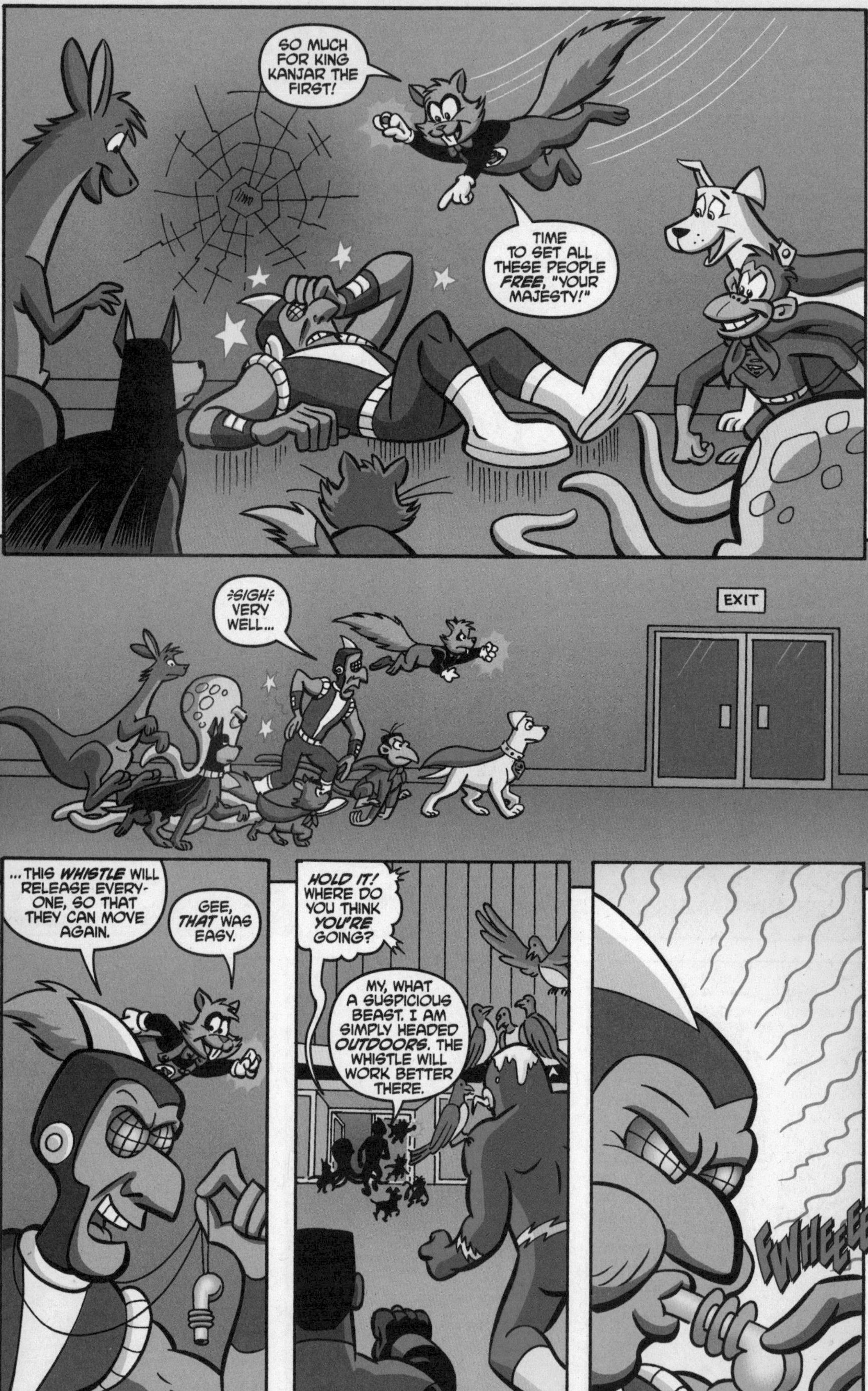
SO MUCH FOR KING KANJAR THE FIRST!
TIME TO SET ALL THESE PEOPLE *FREE*, "YOUR MAJESTY!"
SIGH VERY WELL...
EXIT
...THIS *WHISTLE* WILL RELEASE EVERY-ONE, SO THAT THEY CAN MOVE AGAIN.
GEE, *THAT* WAS EASY.
HOLD IT! WHERE DO YOU THINK *YOU'RE* GOING?
MY, WHAT A SUSPICIOUS BEAST. I AM SIMPLY HEADED *OUTDOORS*. THE WHISTLE WILL WORK BETTER THERE.
FWHEEEET

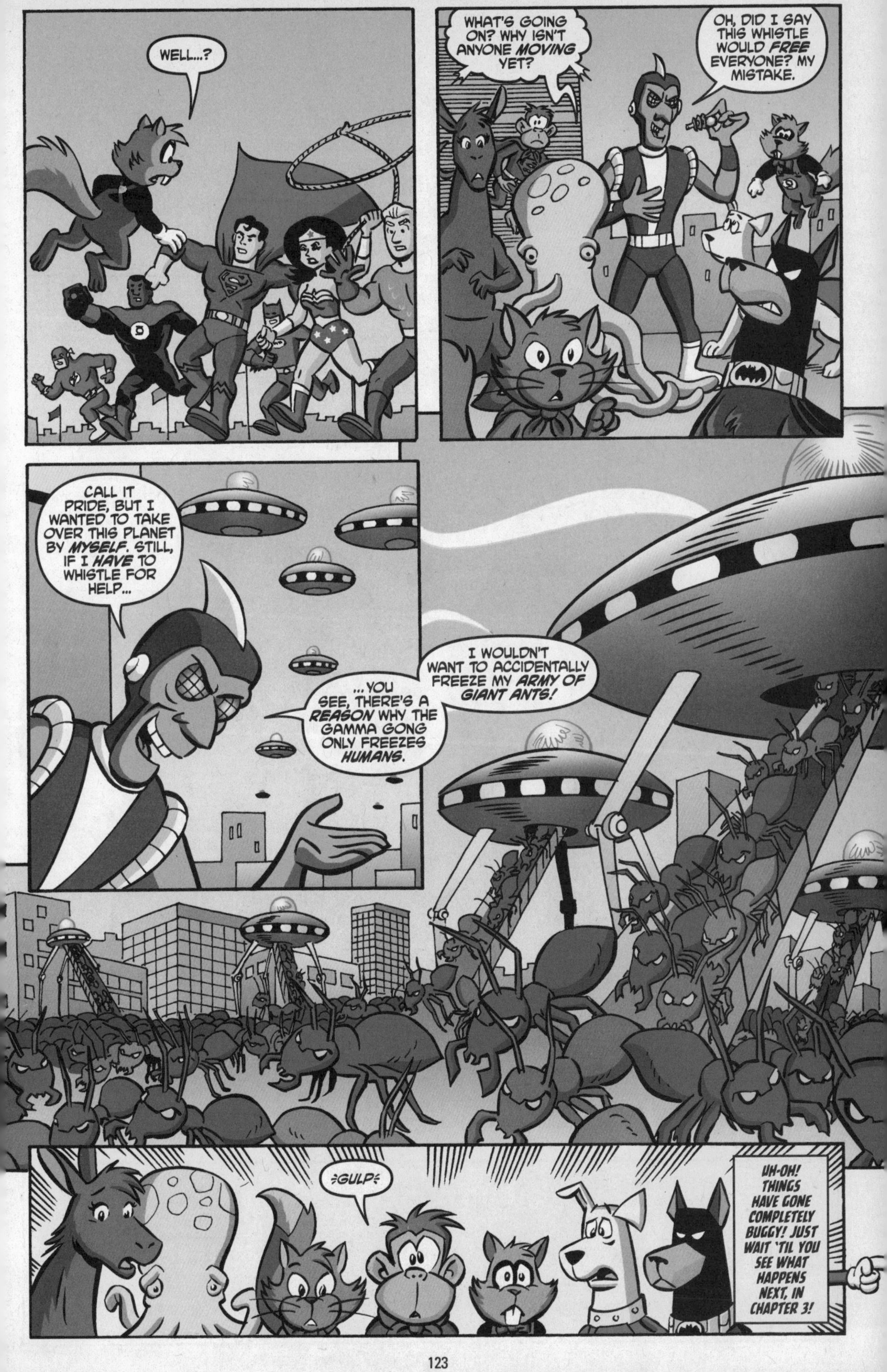
WELL...?
WHAT'S GOING ON? WHY ISN'T ANYONE MOVING YET?
OH, DID I SAY THIS WHISTLE WOULD FREE EVERYONE? MY MISTAKE.
CALL IT PRIDE, BUT I WANTED TO TAKE OVER THIS PLANET BY MYSELF. STILL, IF I HAVE TO WHISTLE FOR HELP...
...YOU SEE, THERE'S A REASON WHY THE GAMMA GONG ONLY FREEZES HUMANS.
I WOULDN'T WANT TO ACCIDENTALLY FREEZE MY ARMY OF GIANT ANTS!
GULP
UH-OH! THINGS HAVE GONE COMPLETELY BUGGY! JUST WAIT 'TIL YOU SEE WHAT HAPPENS NEXT, IN CHAPTER 3!

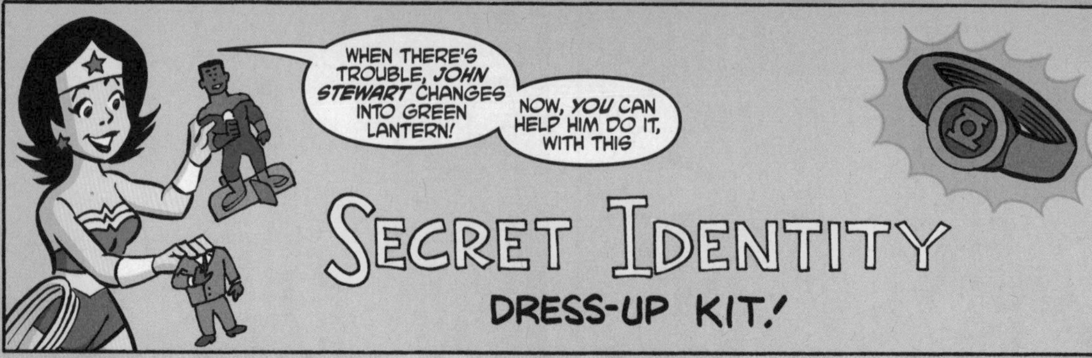
WHEN THERE'S TROUBLE, JOHN STEWART CHANGES INTO GREEN LANTERN!
NOW, YOU CAN HELP HIM DO IT, WITH THIS
SECRET IDENTITY
DRESS-UP KIT!

JOHN STEWART

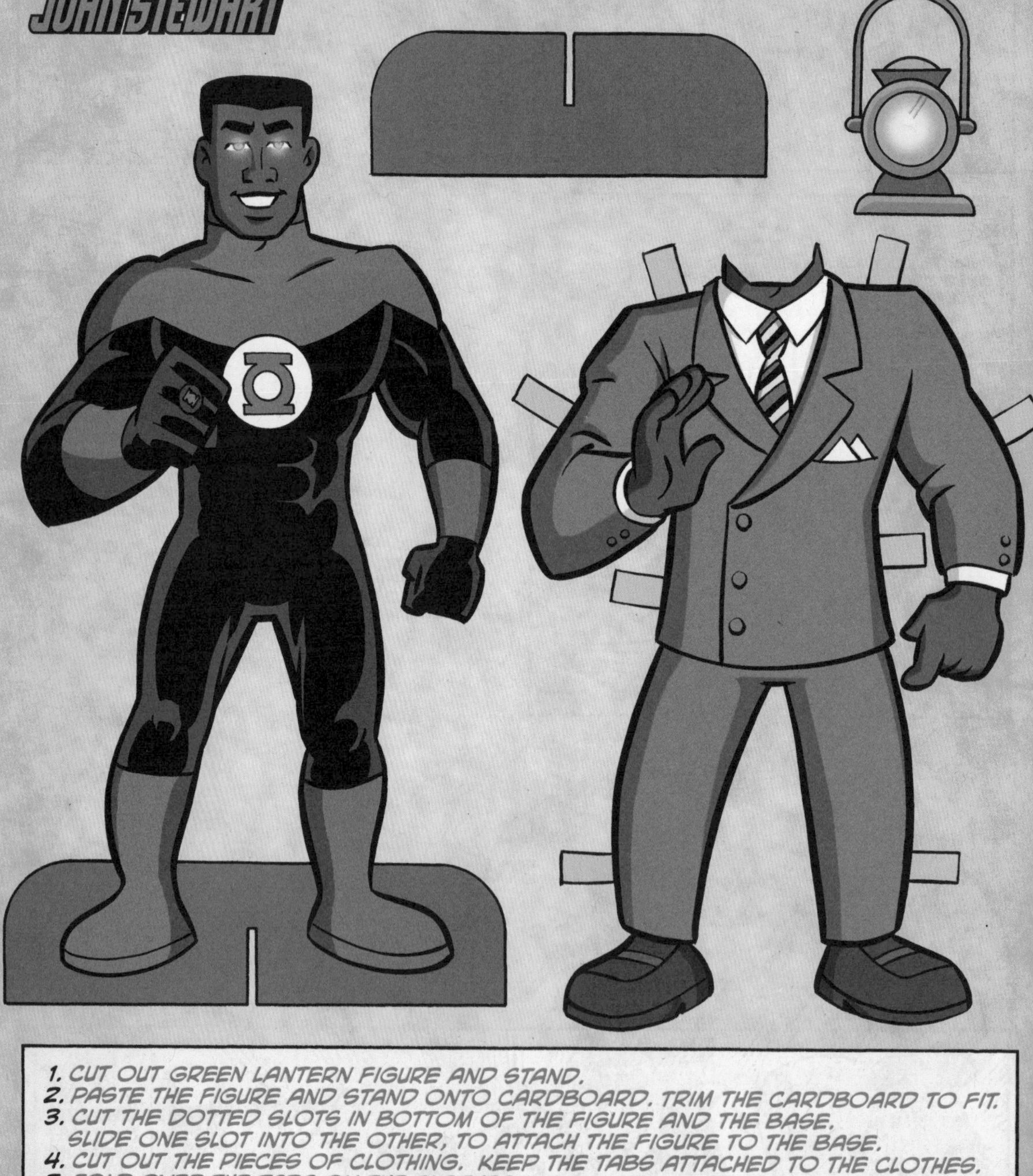

1. CUT OUT GREEN LANTERN FIGURE AND STAND.
2. PASTE THE FIGURE AND STAND ONTO CARDBOARD. TRIM THE CARDBOARD TO FIT.
3. CUT THE DOTTED SLOTS IN BOTTOM OF THE FIGURE AND THE BASE.
   SLIDE ONE SLOT INTO THE OTHER, TO ATTACH THE FIGURE TO THE BASE.
4. CUT OUT THE PIECES OF CLOTHING. KEEP THE TABS ATTACHED TO THE CLOTHES.
5. FOLD OVER THE TABS ON THE CLOTHES.
   USE THEM TO ATTACH THE CLOTHES TO THE FIGURE.
6. PRETEND TO USE THE POWER BATTERY TO CHARGE GREEN LANTERN'S RING.
   NOW HE'S READY TO PROTECT THE UNIVERSE!

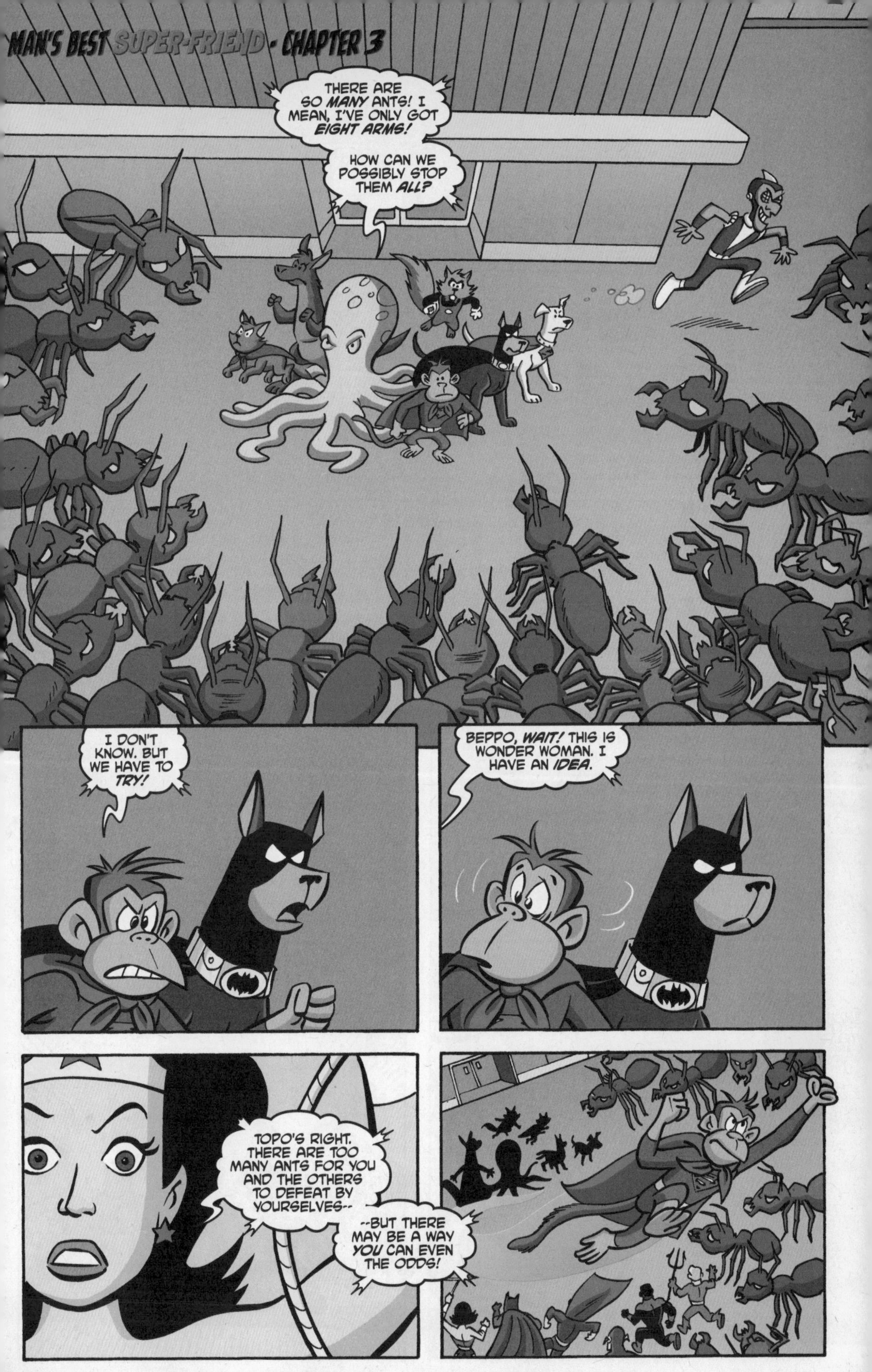
MAN'S BEST SUPER-FRIEND · CHAPTER 3
THERE ARE SO MANY ANTS! I MEAN, I'VE ONLY GOT EIGHT ARMS!
HOW CAN WE POSSIBLY STOP THEM ALL?
I DON'T KNOW. BUT WE HAVE TO TRY!
BEPPO, WAIT! THIS IS WONDER WOMAN. I HAVE AN IDEA.
TOPO'S RIGHT. THERE ARE TOO MANY ANTS FOR YOU AND THE OTHERS TO DEFEAT BY YOURSELVES--
--BUT THERE MAY BE A WAY YOU CAN EVEN THE ODDS!

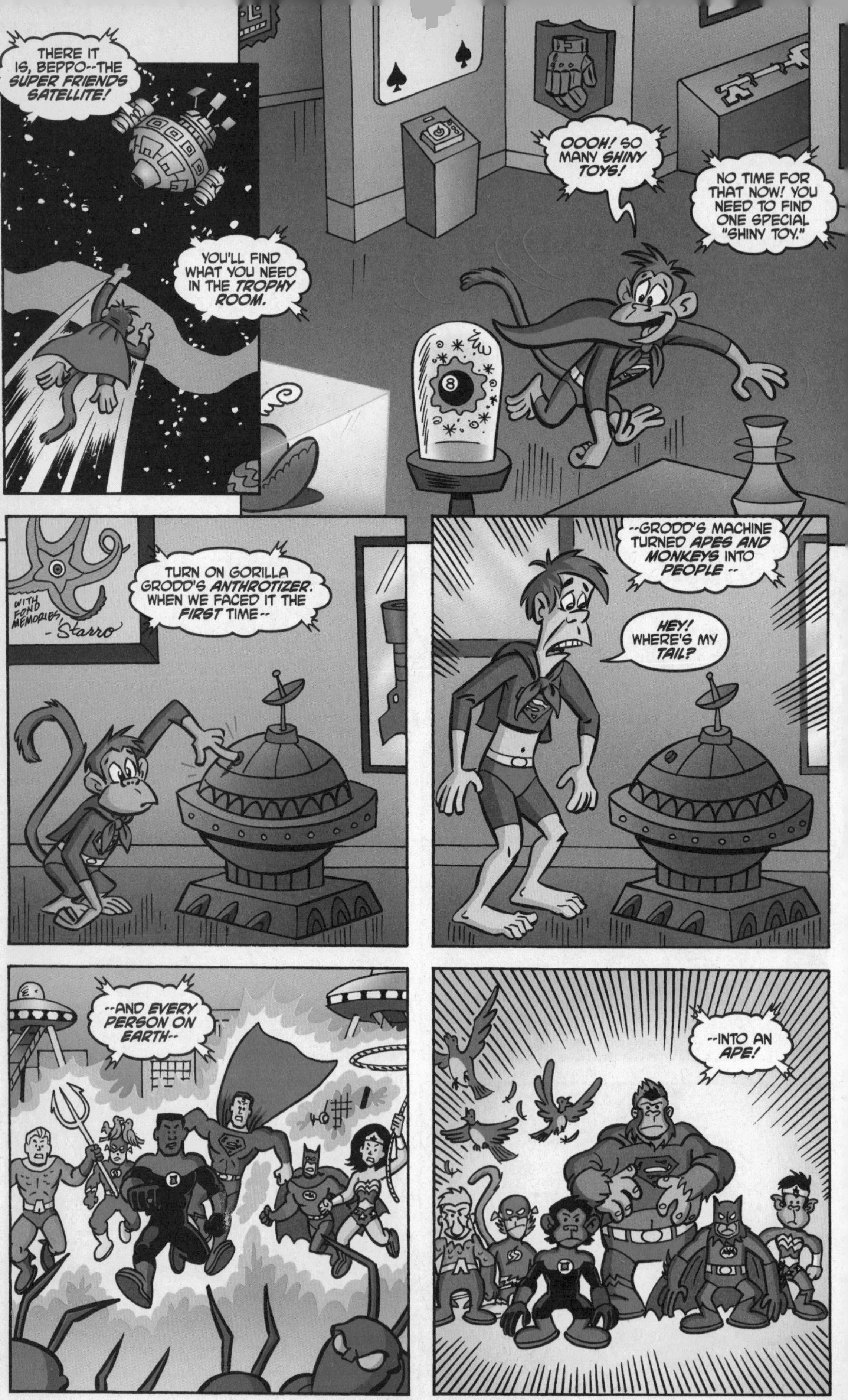
THERE IT IS, BEPPO--THE SUPER FRIENDS SATELLITE!
YOU'LL FIND WHAT YOU NEED IN THE TROPHY ROOM.
OOOH! SO MANY SHINY TOYS!
NO TIME FOR THAT NOW! YOU NEED TO FIND ONE SPECIAL "SHINY TOY."
WITH FOND MEMORIES, -Starro
TURN ON GORILLA GRODD'S ANTHROTIZER. WHEN WE FACED IT THE FIRST TIME--
--GRODD'S MACHINE TURNED APES AND MONKEYS INTO PEOPLE --
HEY! WHERE'S MY TAIL?
--AND EVERY PERSON ON EARTH--
--INTO AN APE!

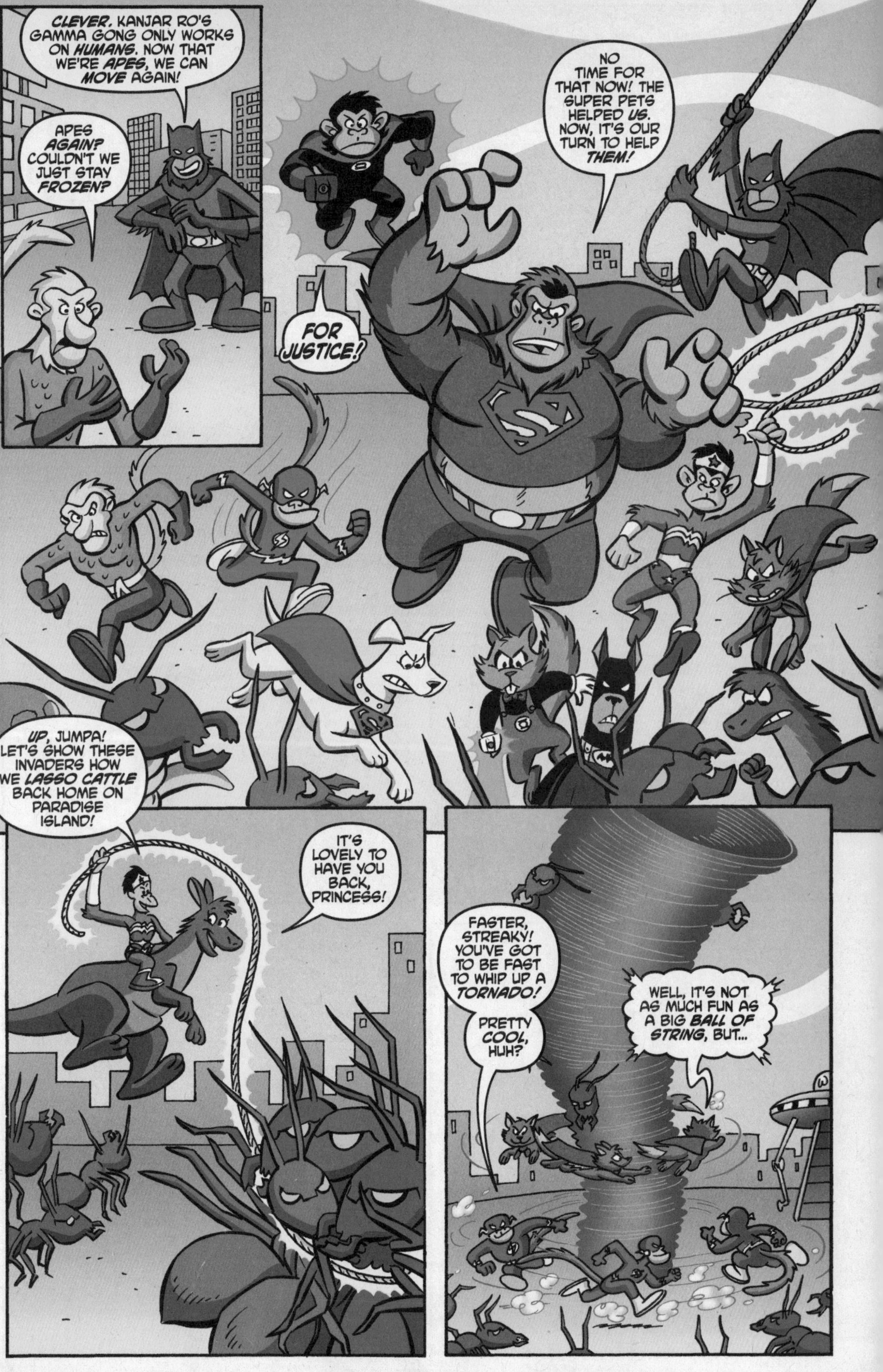

CLEVER. KANJAR RO'S GAMMA GONG ONLY WORKS ON HUMANS. NOW THAT WE'RE APES, WE CAN MOVE AGAIN!
APES AGAIN? COULDN'T WE JUST STAY FROZEN?
NO TIME FOR THAT NOW! THE SUPER PETS HELPED US. NOW, IT'S OUR TURN TO HELP THEM!
FOR JUSTICE!
UP, JUMPA! LET'S SHOW THESE INVADERS HOW WE LASSO CATTLE BACK HOME ON PARADISE ISLAND!
IT'S LOVELY TO HAVE YOU BACK, PRINCESS!
FASTER, STREAKY! YOU'VE GOT TO BE FAST TO WHIP UP A TORNADO!
PRETTY COOL, HUH?
WELL, IT'S NOT AS MUCH FUN AS A BIG BALL OF STRING, BUT...

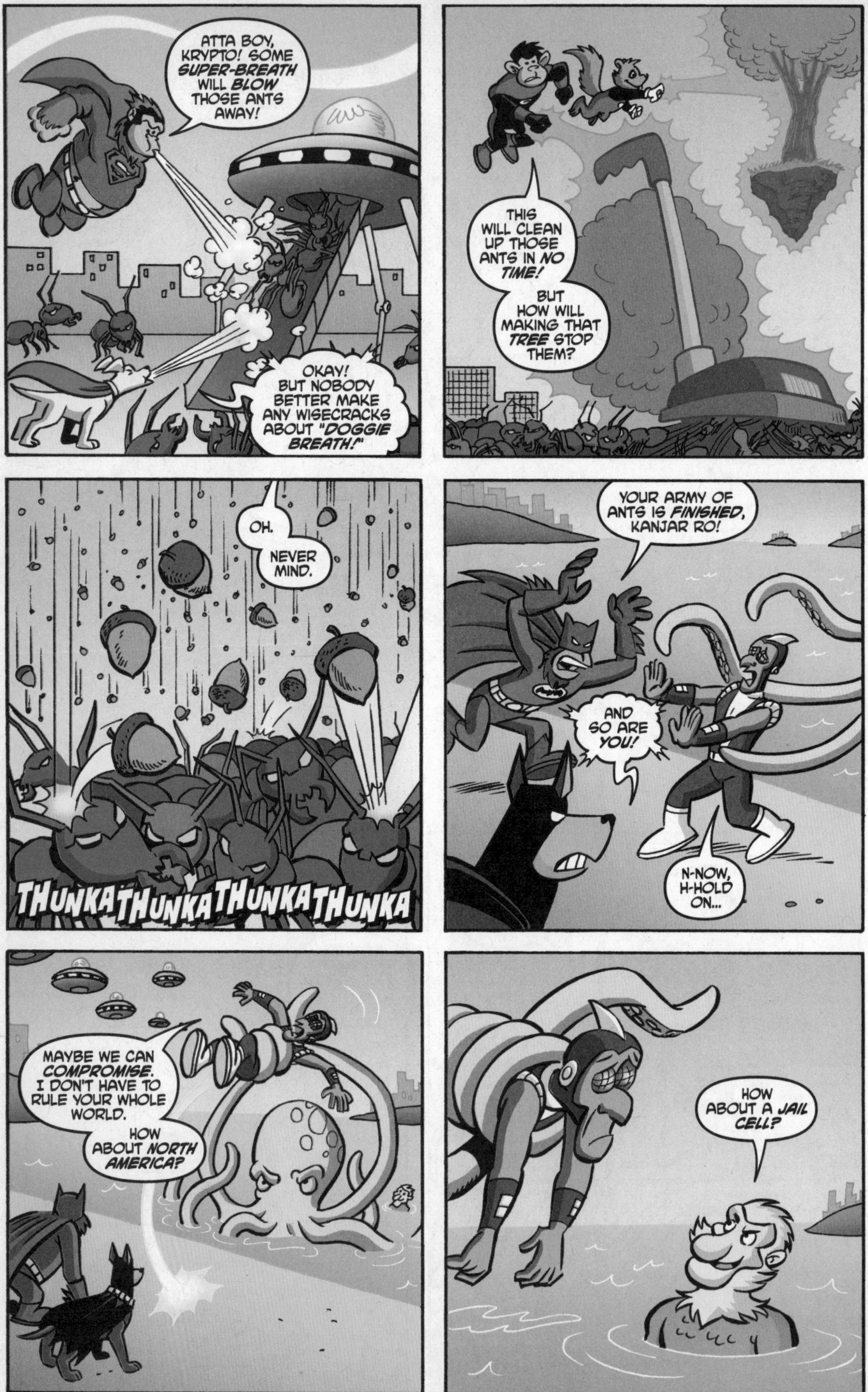
ATTA BOY, KRYPTO! SOME SUPER-BREATH WILL BLOW THOSE ANTS AWAY!
OKAY! BUT NOBODY BETTER MAKE ANY WISECRACKS ABOUT "DOGGIE BREATH!"
THIS WILL CLEAN UP THOSE ANTS IN NO TIME!
BUT HOW WILL MAKING THAT TREE STOP THEM?
OH.
NEVER MIND.
THUNKA THUNKA THUNKA THUNKA
YOUR ARMY OF ANTS IS FINISHED, KANJAR RO!
AND SO ARE YOU!
N-NOW, H-HOLD ON...
MAYBE WE CAN COMPROMISE. I DON'T HAVE TO RULE YOUR WHOLE WORLD.
HOW ABOUT NORTH AMERICA?
HOW ABOUT A JAIL CELL?

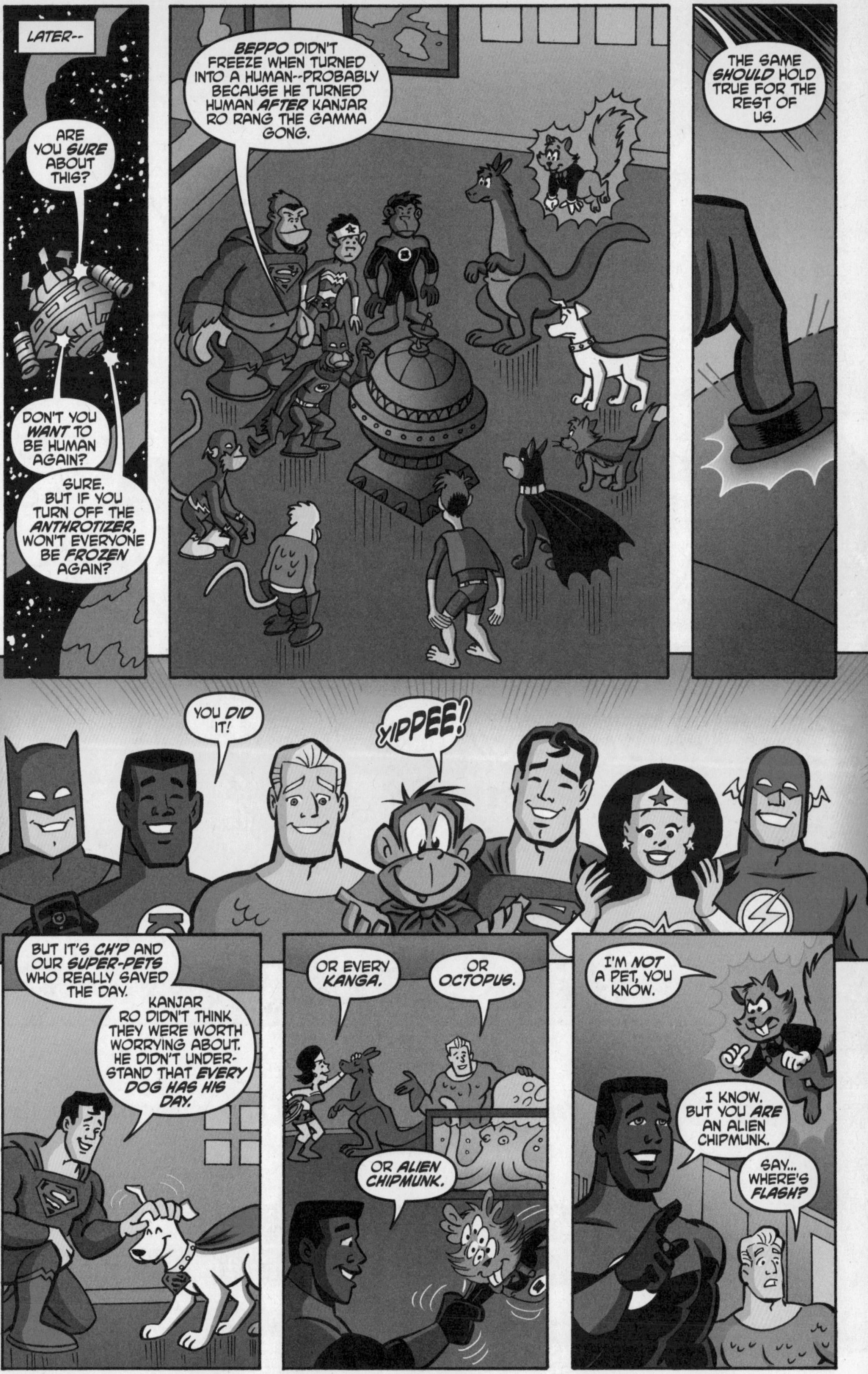
LATER--
ARE YOU SURE ABOUT THIS?
DON'T YOU WANT TO BE HUMAN AGAIN?
SURE. BUT IF YOU TURN OFF THE ANTHROTIZER, WON'T EVERYONE BE FROZEN AGAIN?
BEPPO DIDN'T FREEZE WHEN TURNED INTO A HUMAN--PROBABLY BECAUSE HE TURNED HUMAN AFTER KANJAR RO RANG THE GAMMA GONG.
THE SAME SHOULD HOLD TRUE FOR THE REST OF US.
YOU DID IT!
YIPPEE!
BUT IT'S CH'P AND OUR SUPER-PETS WHO REALLY SAVED THE DAY.
KANJAR RO DIDN'T THINK THEY WERE WORTH WORRYING ABOUT. HE DIDN'T UNDERSTAND THAT EVERY DOG HAS HIS DAY.
OR EVERY KANGA.
OR OCTOPUS.
OR ALIEN CHIPMUNK.
I'M NOT A PET, YOU KNOW.
I KNOW. BUT YOU ARE AN ALIEN CHIPMUNK.
SAY... WHERE'S FLASH?

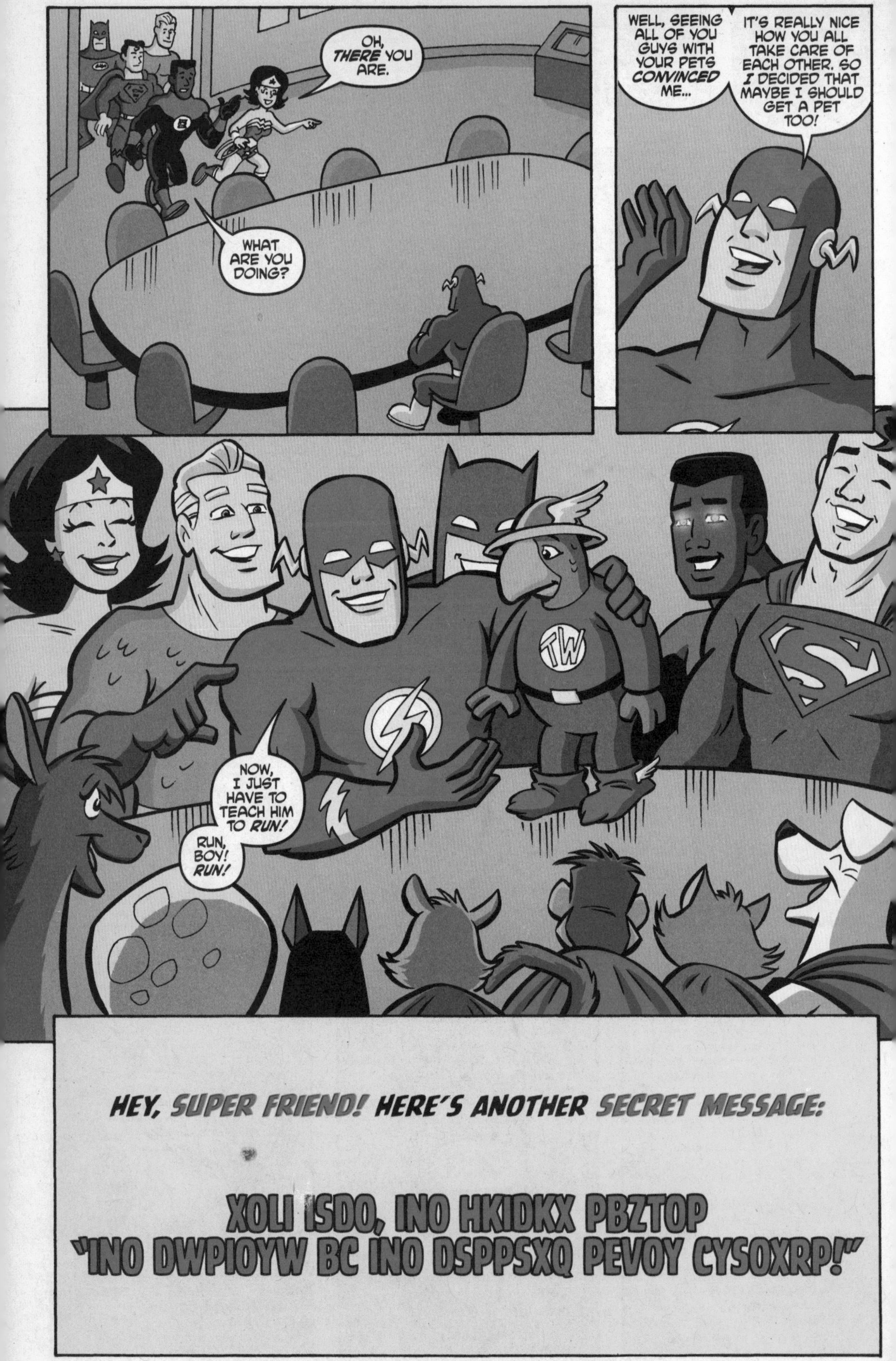
OH, *THERE* YOU ARE.
WHAT ARE YOU DOING?
WELL, SEEING ALL OF YOU GUYS WITH YOUR PETS *CONVINCED* ME...
IT'S REALLY NICE HOW YOU ALL TAKE CARE OF EACH OTHER. SO *I* DECIDED THAT MAYBE I SHOULD GET A PET TOO!
TW
NOW, I JUST HAVE TO TEACH HIM TO *RUN!*
RUN, BOY! *RUN!*

HEY, SUPER FRIEND! HERE'S ANOTHER SECRET MESSAGE:

XOLI ISDO, INO HKIDKX PBZTOP "INO DWPIOYW BC INO DSPPSXQ PEVOY CYSOXRP!"

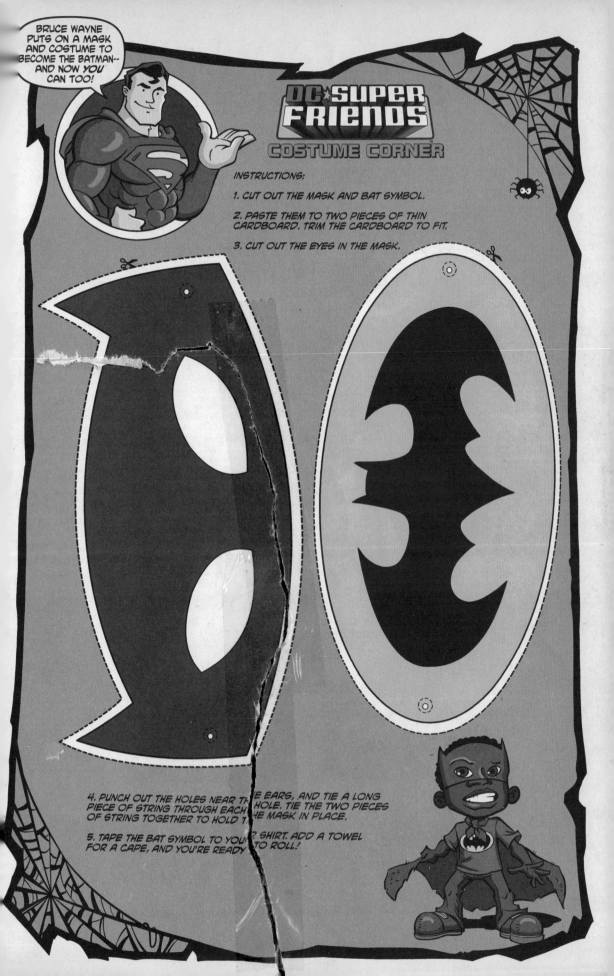

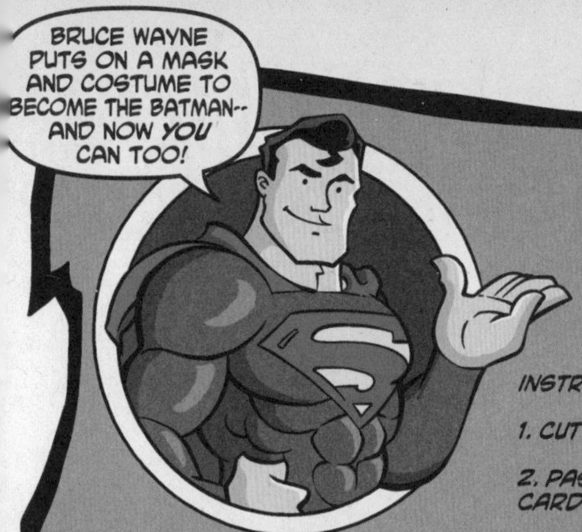
BRUCE WAYNE PUTS ON A MASK AND COSTUME TO BECOME THE BATMAN-- AND NOW *YOU* CAN TOO!

DC SUPER FRIENDS
COSTUME CORNER™

INSTRUCTIONS:

1. CUT OUT THE MASK AND BAT SYMBOL.

2. PASTE THEM TO TWO PIECES OF THIN CARDBOARD. TRIM THE CARDBOARD TO FIT.

3. CUT OUT THE EYES IN THE MASK.

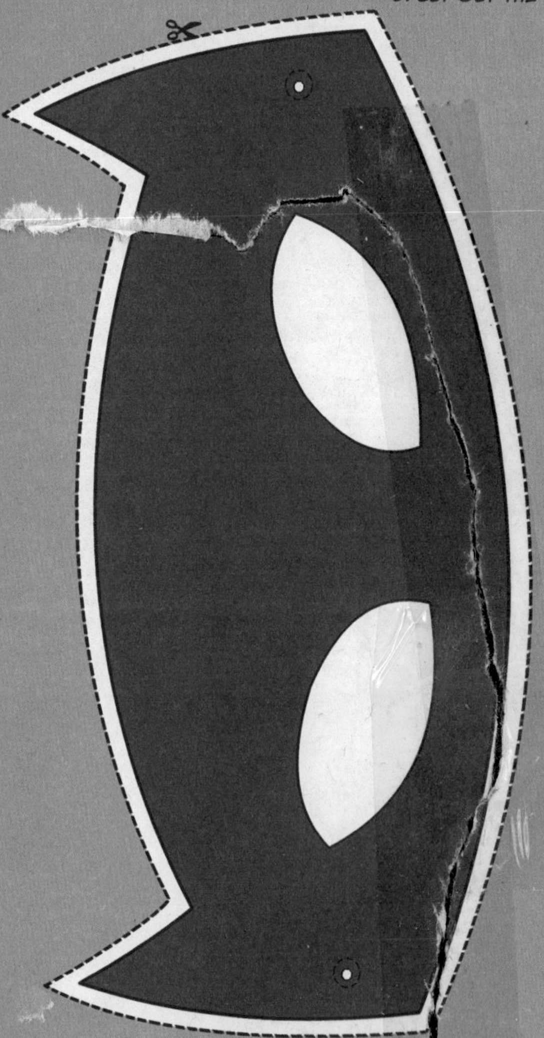

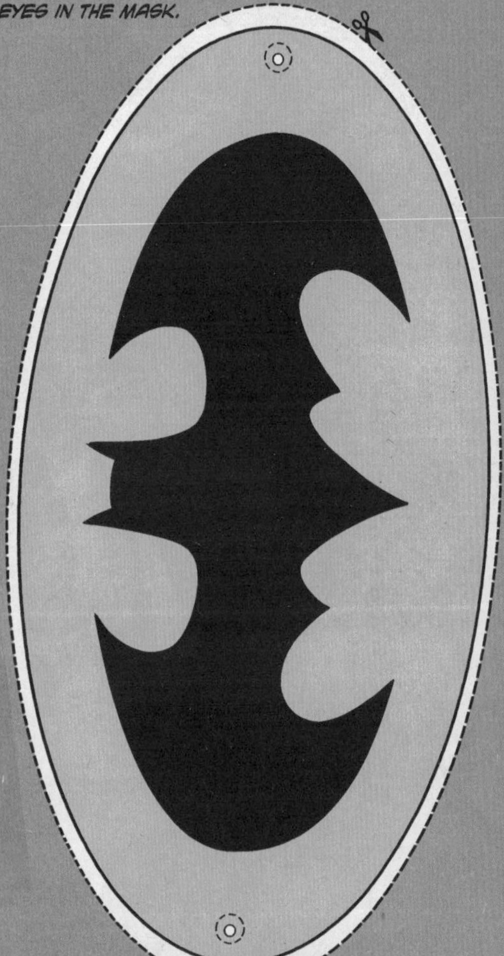

4. PUNCH OUT THE HOLES NEAR THE EARS, AND TIE A LONG PIECE OF STRING THROUGH EACH HOLE. TIE THE TWO PIECES OF STRING TOGETHER TO HOLD THE MASK IN PLACE.

5. TAPE THE BAT SYMBOL TO YOUR SHIRT. ADD A TOWEL FOR A CAPE, AND YOU'RE READY TO ROLL!

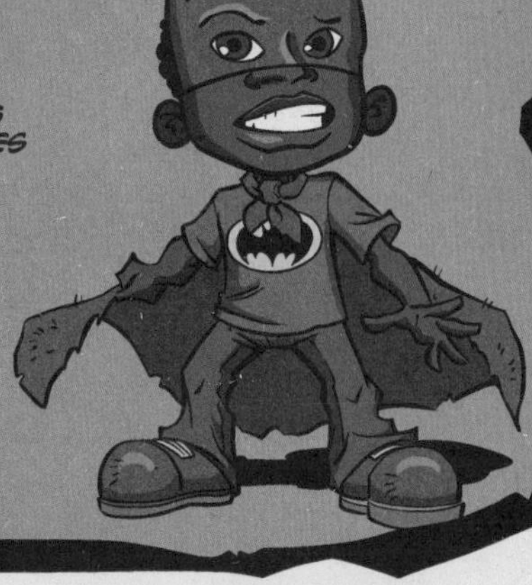

THE SHADOW KNOWS!

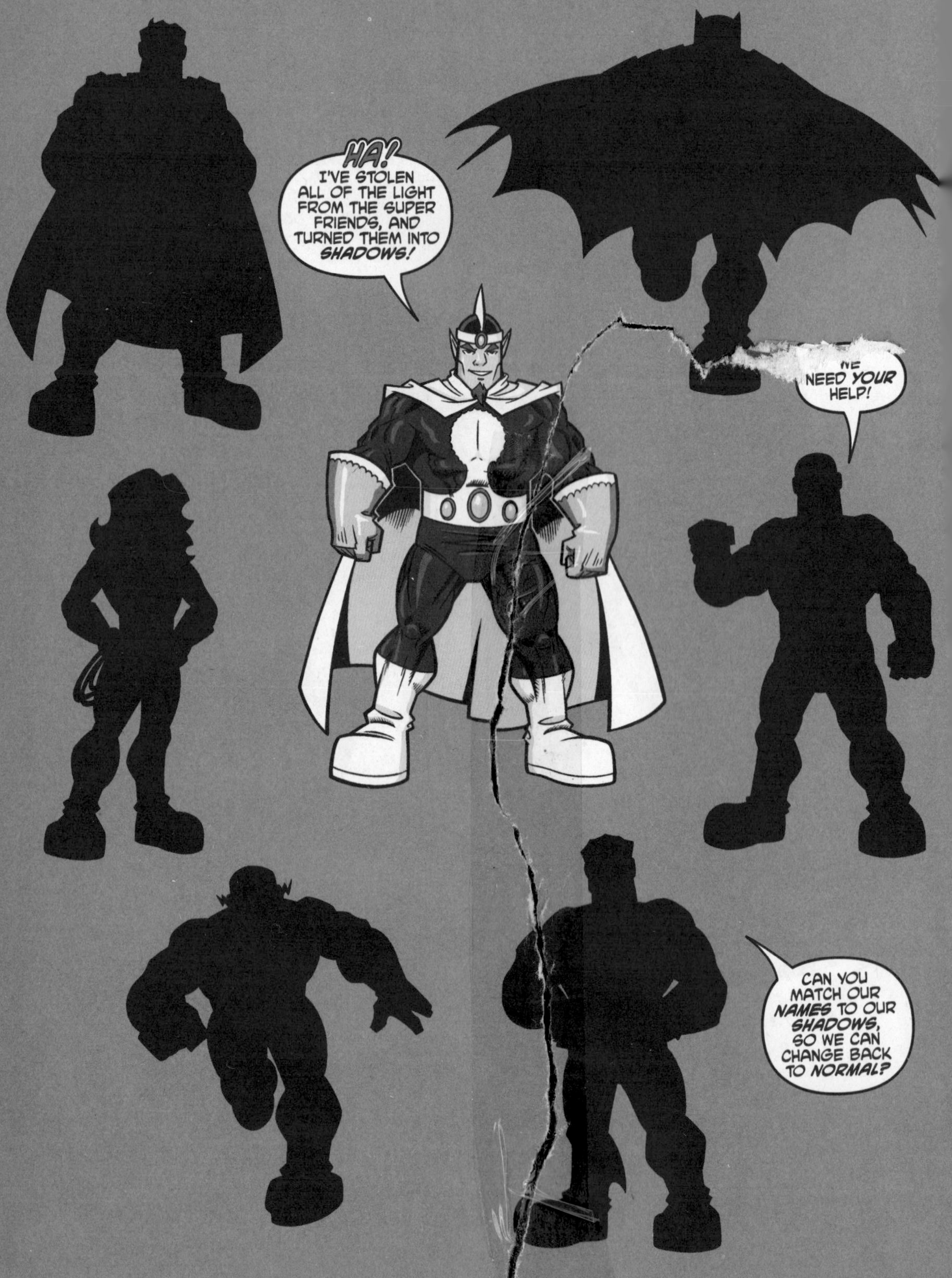
HA! I'VE STOLEN ALL OF THE LIGHT FROM THE SUPER FRIENDS, AND TURNED THEM INTO SHADOWS!
NEED YOUR HELP!
CAN YOU MATCH OUR NAMES TO OUR SHADOWS, SO WE CAN CHANGE BACK TO NORMAL?

SUPERMAN | THE BATMAN | WONDER WOMAN | THE FLASH | GREEN LANTERN | AQUAMAN

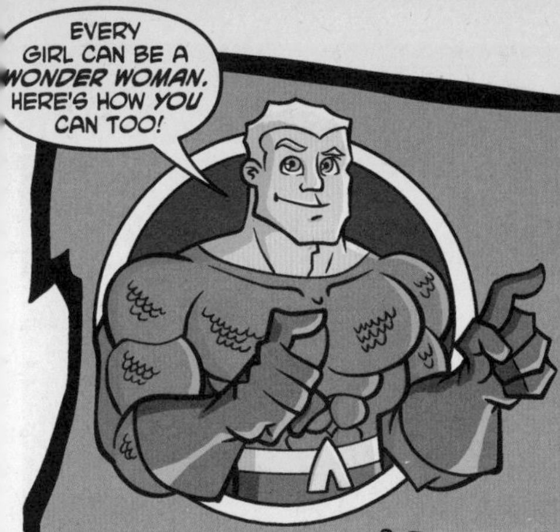

EVERY GIRL CAN BE A *WONDER WOMAN*. HERE'S HOW *YOU* CAN TOO!

DC SUPER FRIENDS
COSTUME CORNER

NSTRUCTIONS:

1. CUT OUT THE TIARA AND BRACELETS.

2. PASTE THEM TO TWO PIECES OF THIN CARDBOARD. TRIM THE CARDBOARD TO FIT.

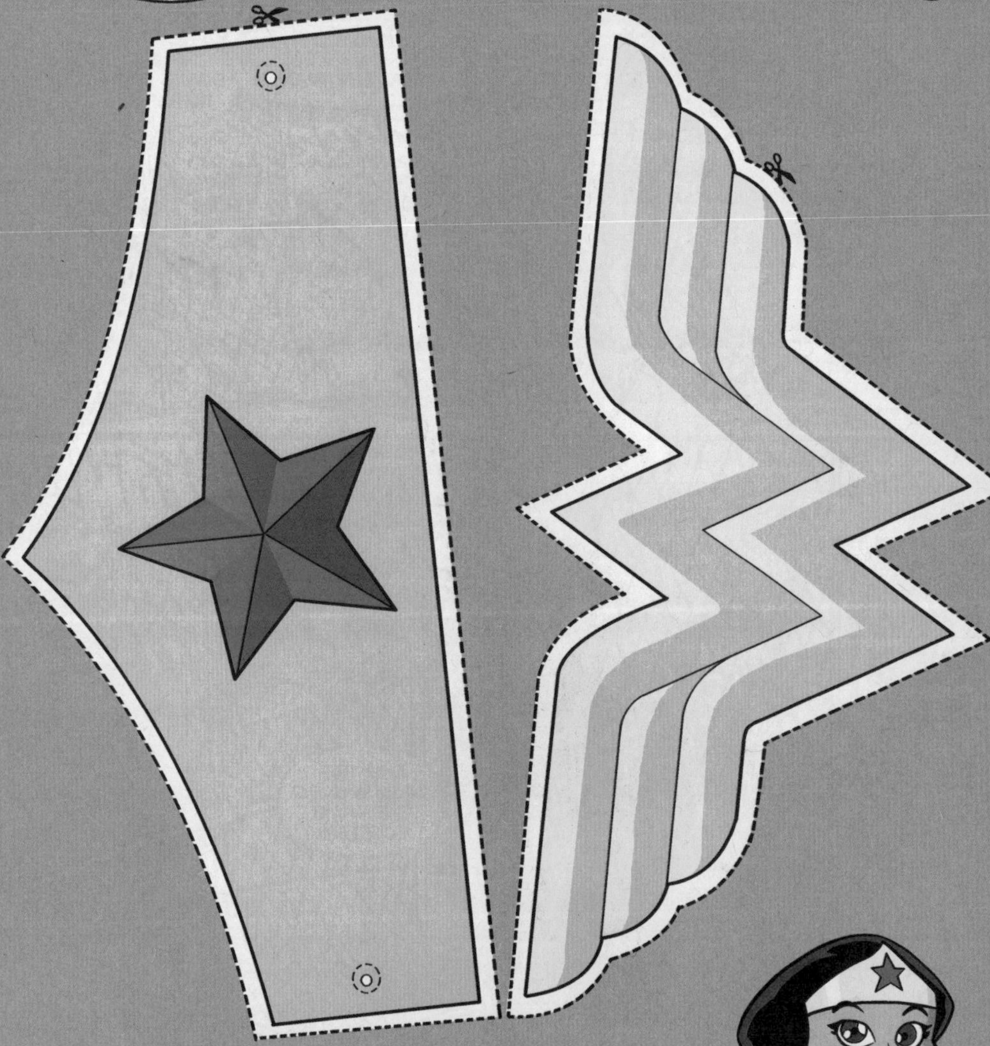

3. PUNCH OUT THE HOLES NEAR THE ENDS OF THE TIARA, AND TIE A LONG PIECE OF STRING THROUGH EACH HOLE.

4. TIE THE PIECES OF STRING TOGETHER BEHIND YOUR HEAD, TO HOLD THE TIARA ON YOUR FOREHEAD.

5. WRAP THE BRACELETS LOOSELY AROUND YOUR WRISTS. TAPE TOGETHER THE ENDS AND CUT OFF ANY EXTRA PAPER ON THE BRACELETS. NOW YOU'RE READY TO BE AN AMAZON PRINCESS!

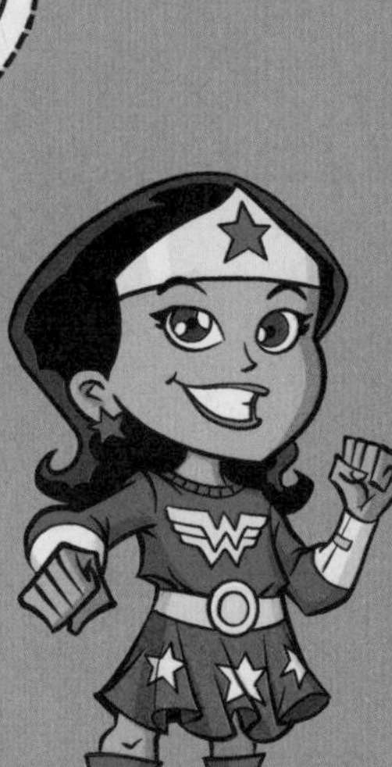

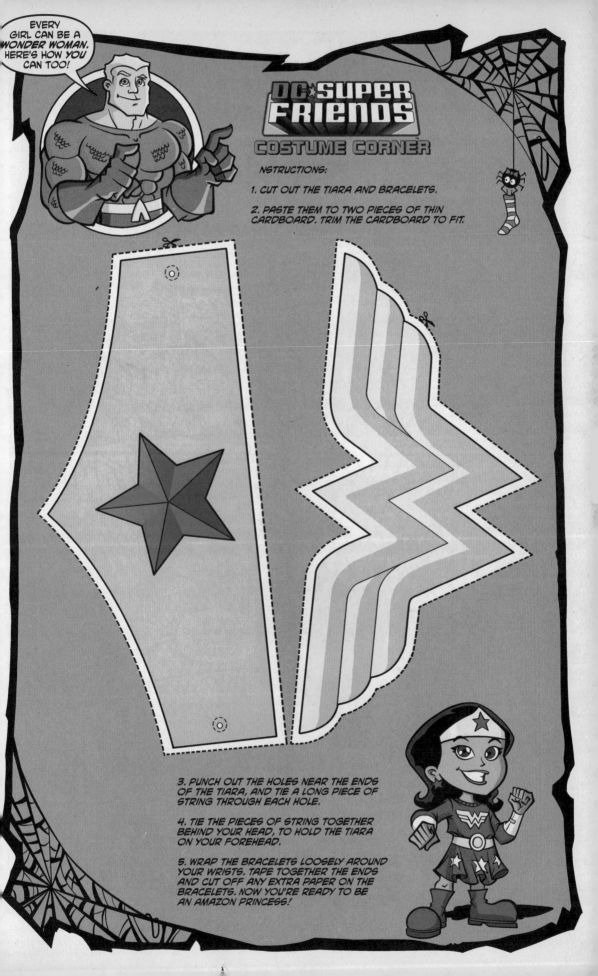

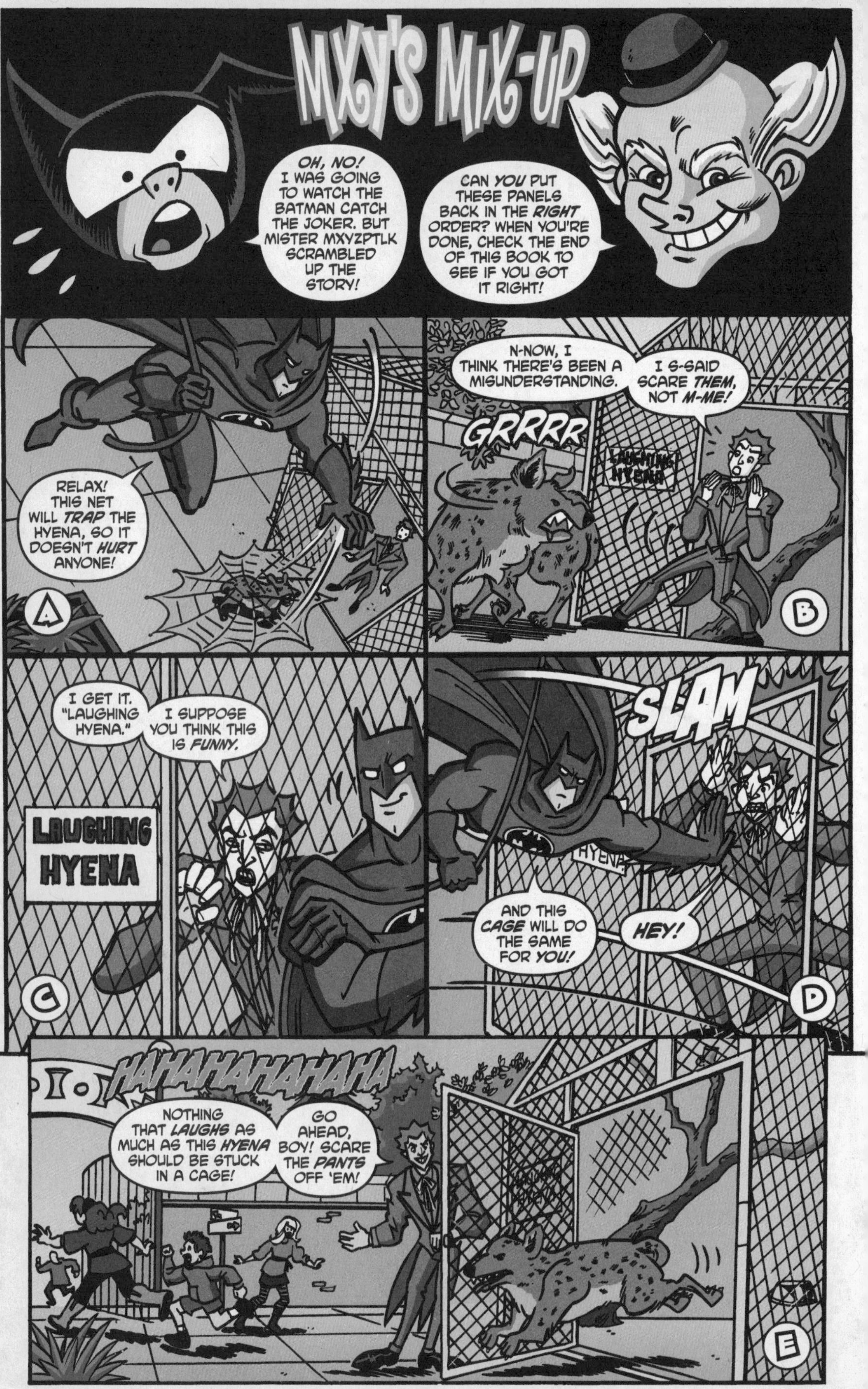

MXY'S MIX-UP
OH, NO! I WAS GOING TO WATCH THE BATMAN CATCH THE JOKER. BUT MISTER MXYZPTLK SCRAMBLED UP THE STORY!
CAN YOU PUT THESE PANELS BACK IN THE RIGHT ORDER? WHEN YOU'RE DONE, CHECK THE END OF THIS BOOK TO SEE IF YOU GOT IT RIGHT!
RELAX! THIS NET WILL TRAP THE HYENA, SO IT DOESN'T HURT ANYONE!
A
N-NOW, I THINK THERE'S BEEN A MISUNDERSTANDING.
I S-SAID SCARE THEM, NOT M-ME!
GRRRR
LAUGHING HYENA
B
I GET IT. "LAUGHING HYENA."
I SUPPOSE YOU THINK THIS IS FUNNY.
LAUGHING HYENA
C
SLAM
HYENA
AND THIS CAGE WILL DO THE SAME FOR YOU!
HEY!
D
HAHAHAHAHAHAHA
NOTHING THAT LAUGHS AS MUCH AS THIS HYENA SHOULD BE STUCK IN A CAGE!
GO AHEAD, BOY! SCARE THE PANTS OFF 'EM!
E

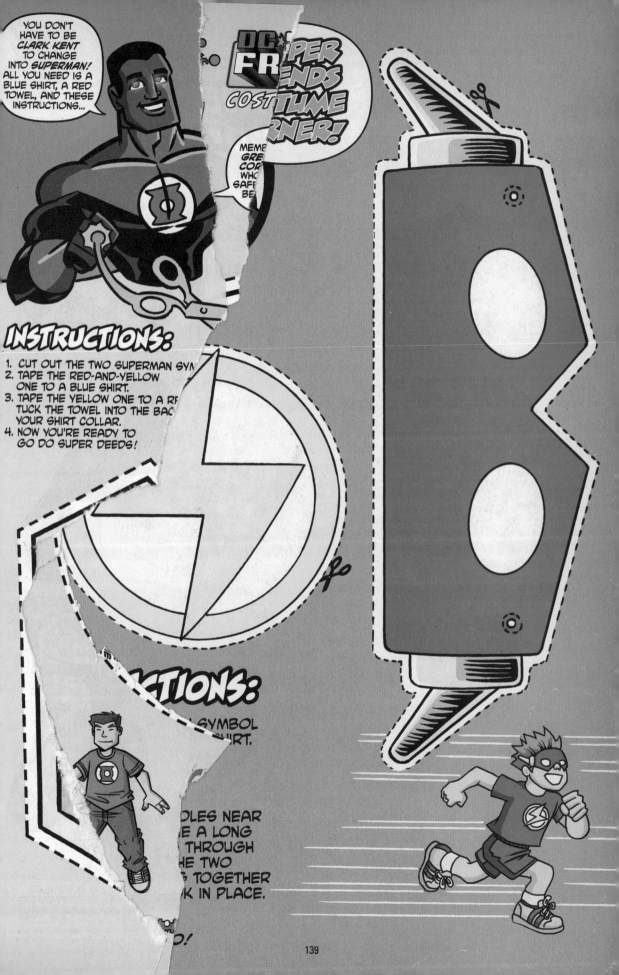

YOU DON'T HAVE TO BE *CLARK KENT* TO CHANGE INTO *SUPERMAN!* ALL YOU NEED IS A BLUE SHIRT, A RED TOWEL, AND THESE INSTRUCTIONS...

DC SUPER FRIENDS COSTUME CORNER!

MEME GRE COR WHO SAFE BE

INSTRUCTIONS:

1. CUT OUT THE TWO SUPERMAN SYM
2. TAPE THE RED-AND-YELLOW ONE TO A BLUE SHIRT.
3. TAPE THE YELLOW ONE TO A RE TUCK THE TOWEL INTO THE BAC YOUR SHIRT COLLAR.
4. NOW YOU'RE READY TO GO DO SUPER DEEDS!

CTIONS:

SYMBOL HIRT.

OLES NEAR E A LONG THROUGH HE TWO G TOGETHER K IN PLACE.

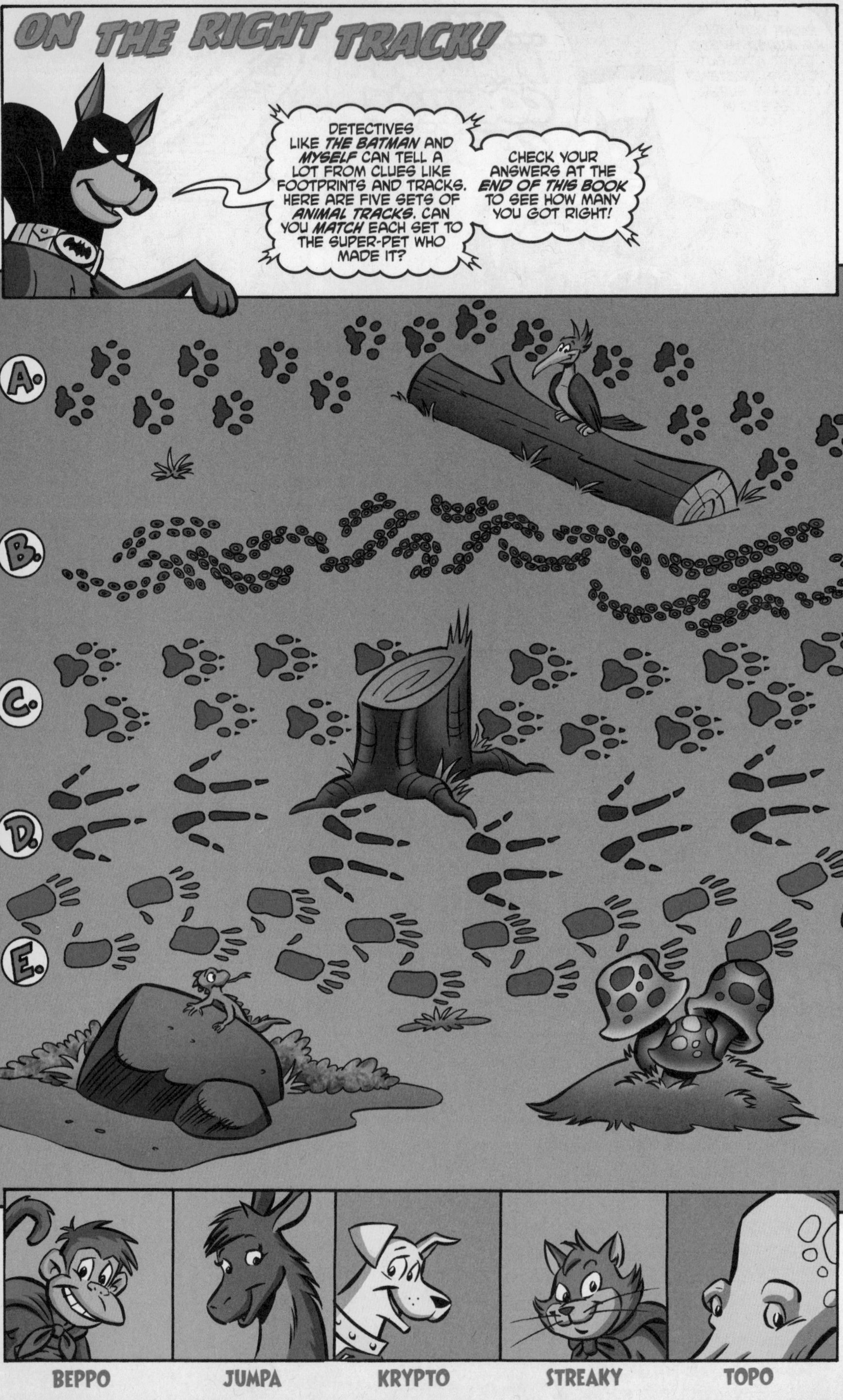
ON THE RIGHT TRACK!
DETECTIVES LIKE THE BATMAN AND MYSELF CAN TELL A LOT FROM CLUES LIKE FOOTPRINTS AND TRACKS. HERE ARE FIVE SETS OF ANIMAL TRACKS. CAN YOU MATCH EACH SET TO THE SUPER-PET WHO MADE IT?
CHECK YOUR ANSWERS AT THE END OF THIS BOOK TO SEE HOW MANY YOU GOT RIGHT!
A.
B.
C.
D.
E.
BEPPO
JUMPA
KRYPTO
STREAKY
TOPO

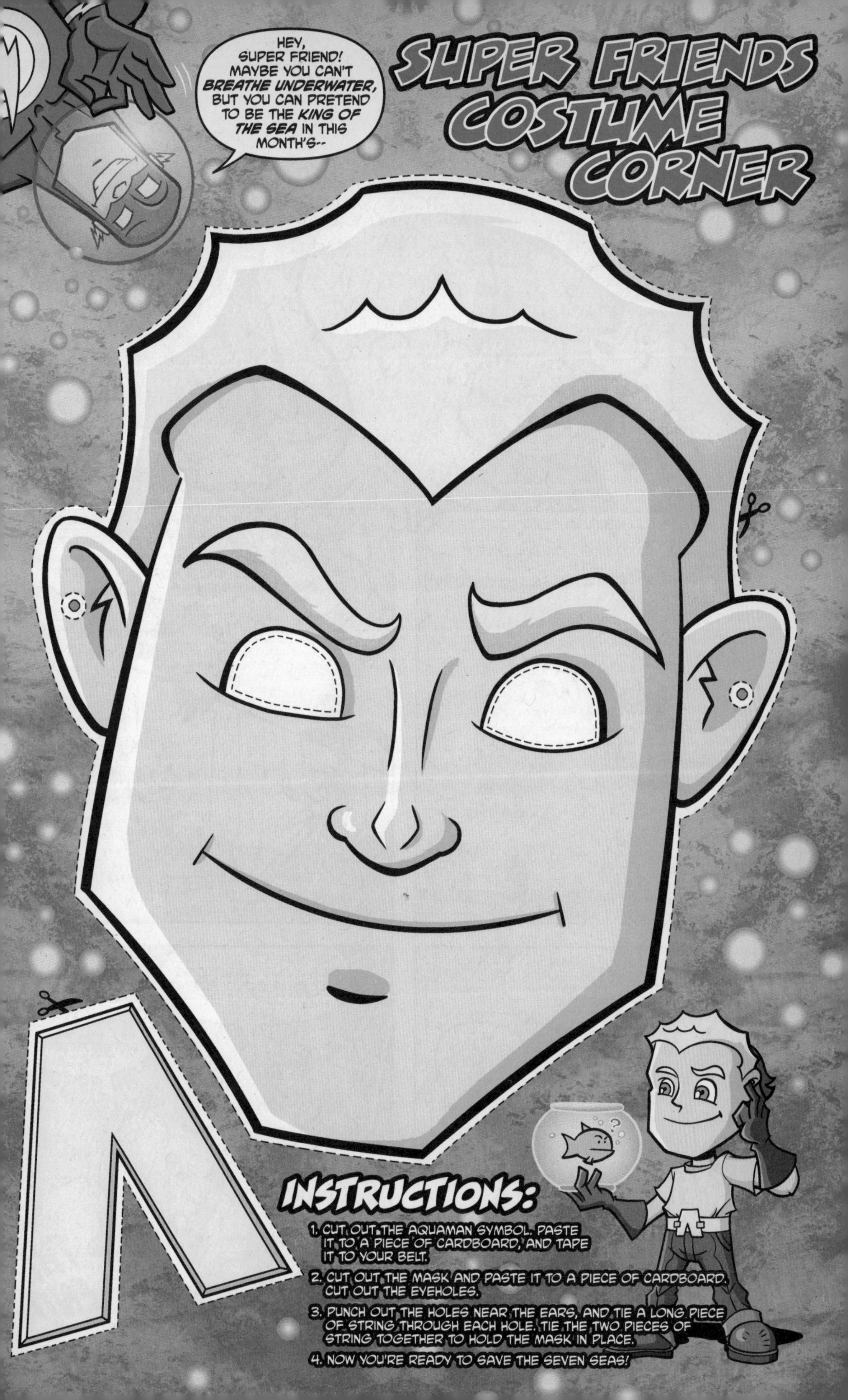
HEY, SUPER FRIEND! MAYBE YOU CAN'T BREATHE UNDERWATER, BUT YOU CAN PRETEND TO BE THE KING OF THE SEA IN THIS MONTH'S--
SUPER FRIENDS COSTUME CORNER
INSTRUCTIONS:
1. CUT OUT THE AQUAMAN SYMBOL. PASTE IT TO A PIECE OF CARDBOARD, AND TAPE IT TO YOUR BELT.
2. CUT OUT THE MASK AND PASTE IT TO A PIECE OF CARDBOARD. CUT OUT THE EYEHOLES.
3. PUNCH OUT THE HOLES NEAR THE EARS, AND TIE A LONG PIECE OF STRING THROUGH EACH HOLE. TIE THE TWO PIECES OF STRING TOGETHER TO HOLD THE MASK IN PLACE.
4. NOW YOU'RE READY TO SAVE THE SEVEN SEAS!

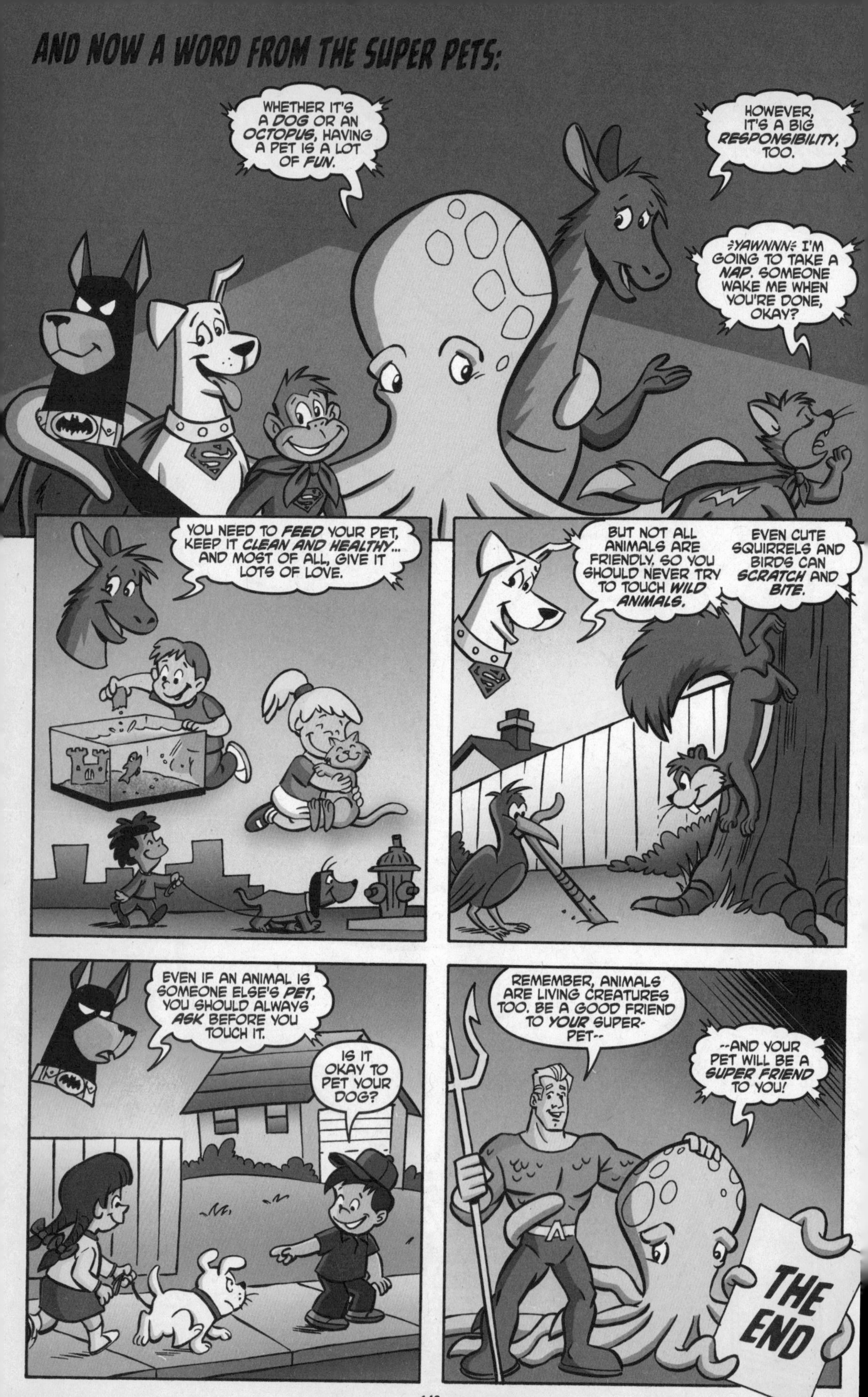
AND NOW A WORD FROM THE SUPER PETS:
WHETHER IT'S A DOG OR AN OCTOPUS, HAVING A PET IS A LOT OF FUN.
HOWEVER, IT'S A BIG RESPONSIBILITY, TOO.
=YAWNNN= I'M GOING TO TAKE A NAP. SOMEONE WAKE ME WHEN YOU'RE DONE, OKAY?
YOU NEED TO FEED YOUR PET, KEEP IT CLEAN AND HEALTHY... AND MOST OF ALL, GIVE IT LOTS OF LOVE.
BUT NOT ALL ANIMALS ARE FRIENDLY. SO YOU SHOULD NEVER TRY TO TOUCH WILD ANIMALS.
EVEN CUTE SQUIRRELS AND BIRDS CAN SCRATCH AND BITE.
EVEN IF AN ANIMAL IS SOMEONE ELSE'S PET, YOU SHOULD ALWAYS ASK BEFORE YOU TOUCH IT.
IS IT OKAY TO PET YOUR DOG?
REMEMBER, ANIMALS ARE LIVING CREATURES TOO. BE A GOOD FRIEND TO YOUR SUPER-PET--
--AND YOUR PET WILL BE A SUPER FRIEND TO YOU!
THE END

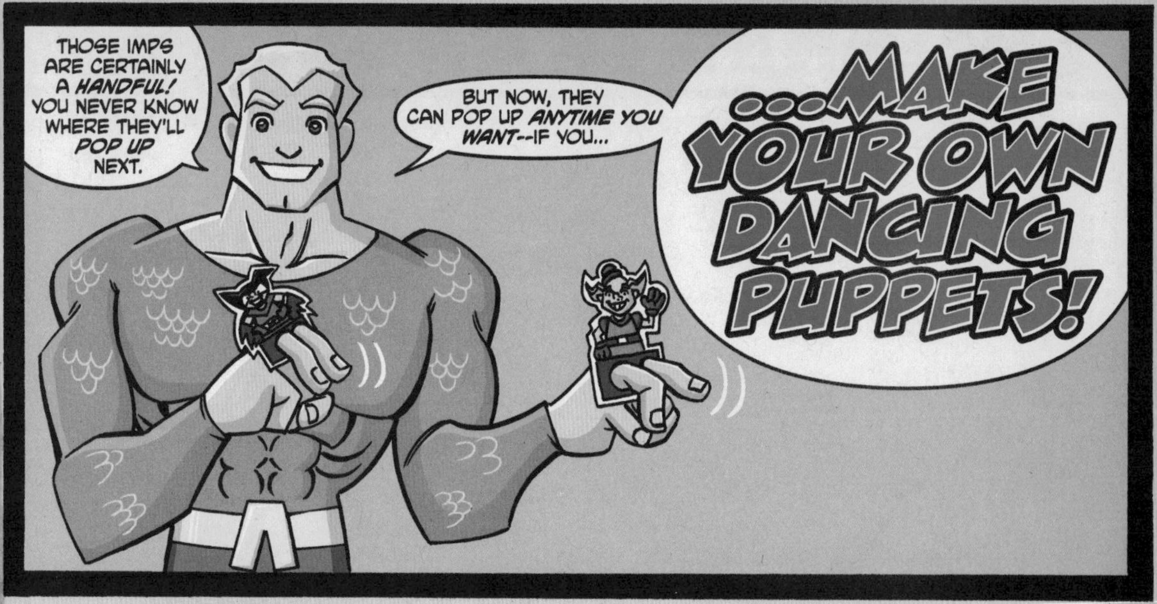
THOSE IMPS ARE CERTAINLY A HANDFUL! YOU NEVER KNOW WHERE THEY'LL POP UP NEXT.
BUT NOW, THEY CAN POP UP ANYTIME YOU WANT--IF YOU...
...MAKE YOUR OWN DANCING PUPPETS!

INSTRUCTIONS:

1.) CUT OUT BAT-MITE AND MR. MXYZPTLK. GLUE EACH ONE TO A PIECE OF CARDBOARD, AND TRIM THE CARDBOARD TO FIT.

2.) CUT OUT THE DOTTED CIRCLES AT THE BOTTOM OF THEIR BODIES.

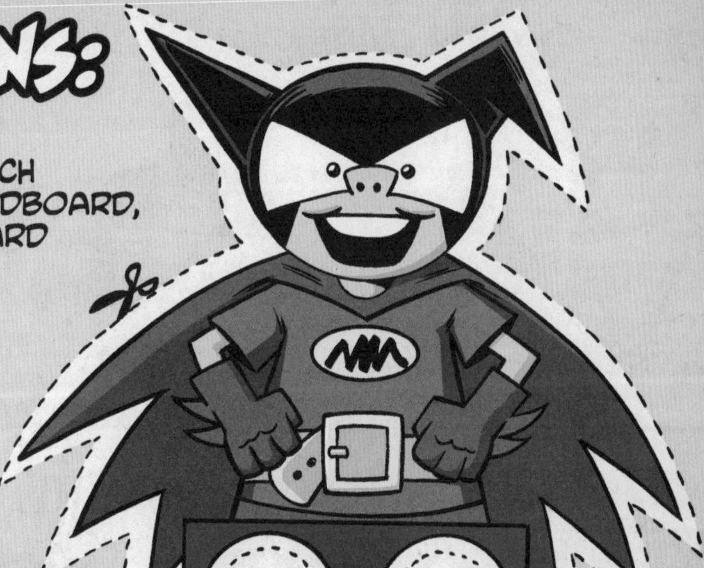

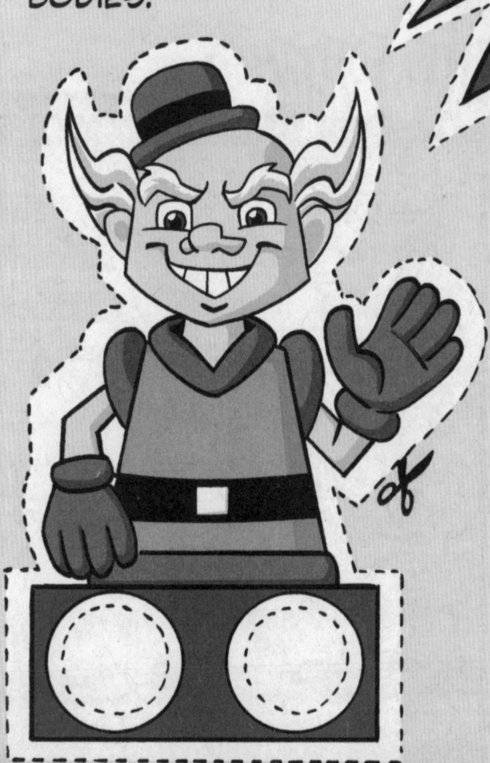

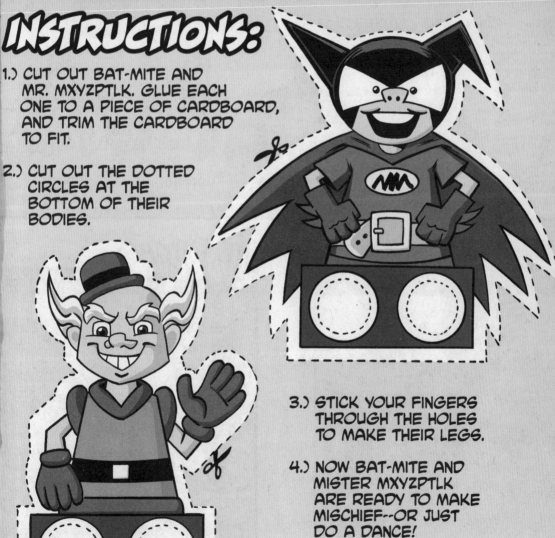

3.) STICK YOUR FINGERS THROUGH THE HOLES TO MAKE THEIR LEGS.

4.) NOW BAT-MITE AND MISTER MXYZPTLK ARE READY TO MAKE MISCHIEF--OR JUST DO A DANCE!

THE ANSWER PAGE!

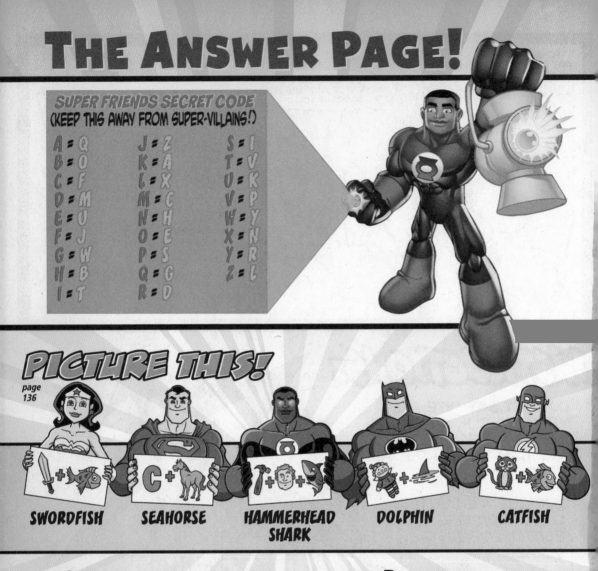

SUPER FRIENDS SECRET CODE
(KEEP THIS AWAY FROM SUPER-VILLAINS!)

A = Q	J = Z	S = I
B = O	K = A	T = V
C = F	L = X	U = K
D = M	M = C	V = P
E = U	N = H	W = Y
F = J	O = E	X = N
G = W	P = S	Y = R
H = B	Q = G	Z = L
I = T	R = D	

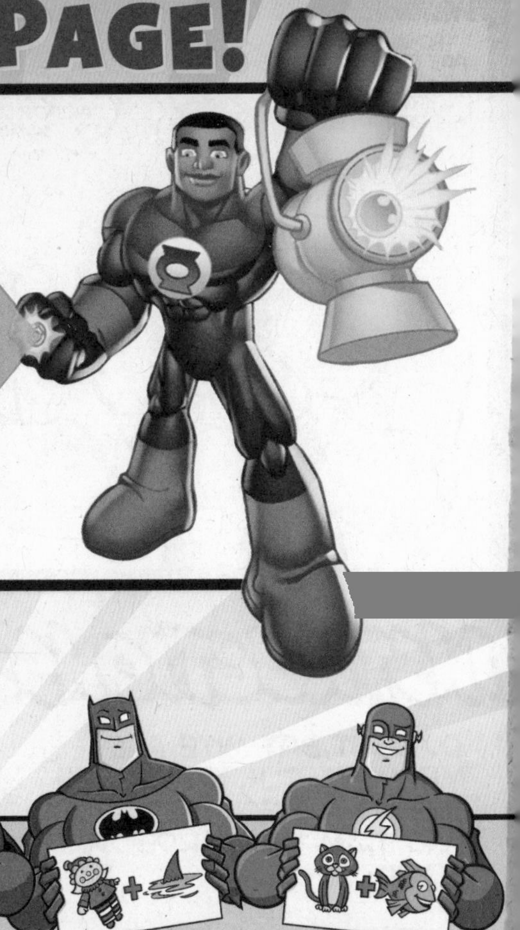

PICTURE THIS!

page 136

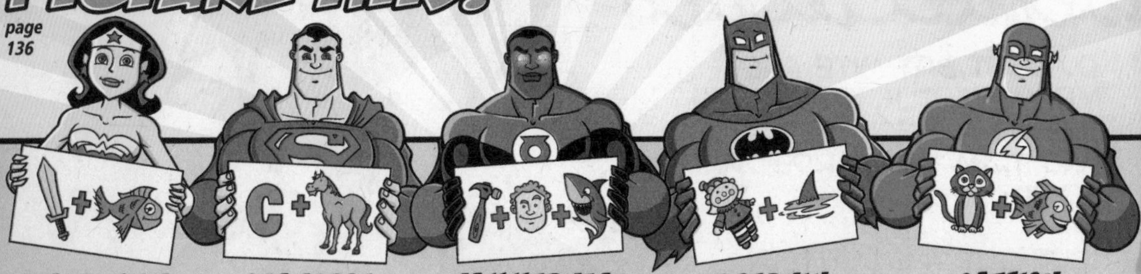

SWORDFISH SEAHORSE HAMMERHEAD SHARK DOLPHIN CATFISH

ON THE RIGHT TRACK!

page 140

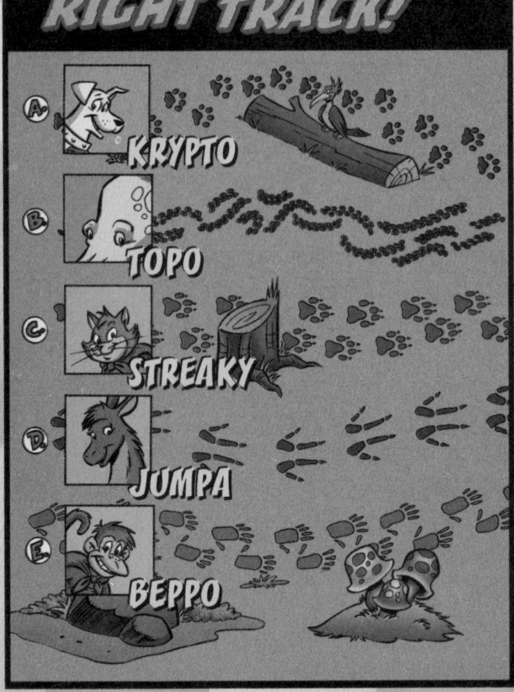

A KRYPTO
B TOPO
C STREAKY
D JUMPA
E BEPPO

MXY'S MIX-UP

page 134

THE CORRECT ORDER OF THE PANELS IS:

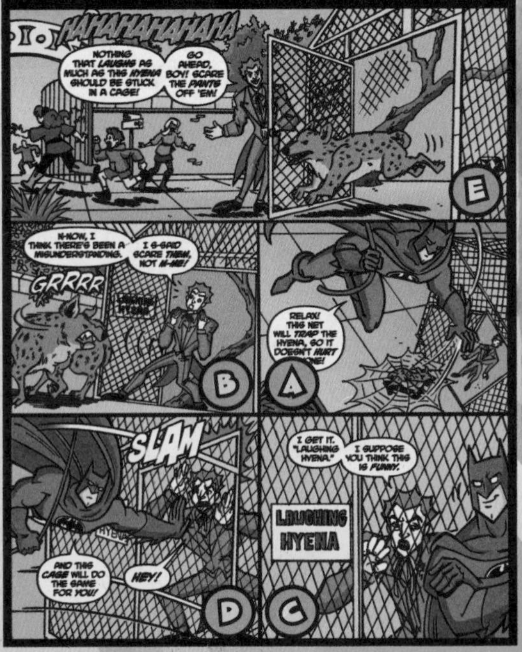

I.
HAHAHAHAHAHAHA
NOTHING THAT LAUGHS AS MUCH AS THIS HYENA SHOULD BE STUCK IN A CAGE!
GO AHEAD, BOY! SCARE THE PANTS OFF 'EM!
E
N-NOW, I THINK THERE'S BEEN A MISUNDERSTANDING.
I S-SAID SCARE THEM, NOT M-ME!
GRRRR
B
RELAX! THIS NET WILL TRAP THE HYENA, SO IT DOESN'T HURT
A
SLAM
AND THIS CAGE WILL DO THE SAME FOR YOU!
HEY!
D
I GET IT. "LAUGHING HYENA."
I SUPPOSE YOU THINK THIS IS FUNNY.
LAUGHING HYENA
C